Letters

Augustinian Heritage Institute, Inc.

THE WORKS OF SAINT AUGUSTINE
A Translation for the 21st Century

Part II – Letters
Volume 4:
Letters 211 – 270, 1* – 29*

THE WORKS OF SAINT AUGUSTINE
A Translation for the 21st Century

Letters 211 – 270, 1* – 29*
(*Epistulae*)

II/4

translation and notes by
Roland Teske, S.J.

editor
Boniface Ramsey

New City Press
Hyde Park, New York

Published in the United States by New City Press
202 Cardinal Rd., Hyde Park, New York 12538
©2005 Augustinian Heritage Institute

Library of Congress Cataloging-in-Publication Data:

Augustine, Saint, Bishop of Hippo.
    The works of Saint Augustine.
    "Augustinian Heritage Institute"
    Includes bibliographical references and indexes.
    Contents: — pt. 3, v .15. Expositions of the Psalms, 1-32
—pt. 3, v. 1. Sermons on the Old Testament, 1-19.
— pt. 3, v. 2. Sermons on the Old Testament, 20-50 — [et al.] — pt. 3,
v. 10 Sermons on various subjects, 341-400.
    1.   Theology — Early church, ca. 30-600.   I. Hill,
Edmund.   II. Rotelle, John E.   III. Augustinian
Heritage Institute.   IV. Title.
BR65.A5E53   1990   270.2   89-28878
ISBN 1-56548-055-4 (series)
ISBN 1-56548-209-3 (pt. 2, v. 4)

Printed in the United States of America

For

Dr. Dorothea Weber

a great friend and scholar

Contents

Introduction

The present volume contains ninety-four letters, the last sixty-three of the previously known letters and the thirty-one more recently discovered and edited by Johannes Divjak in the final quarter of the last century.[1] There are eighty-one letters of which Augustine is the author, including Letter 219, which was sent by Augustine and three other African bishops to two bishops in Gaul regarding Leporius, who had been accused of teaching heretical views similar to Nestorianism. There are thirteen letters from others, including Letter 27* from Jerome of Bethlehem to Aurelius of Carthage, in which Jerome congratulates Aurelius on having been made bishop of Carthage.

In his Patrologia Latina, published in the middle of the nineteenth century, J. P. Migne grouped together Letters 232 through 270 under the rubric of letters whose date of composition was unknown. To the best of our knowledge most of them can only be dated to the period after 395, in which year Augustine was ordained bishop. Since each of the letters has an introduction of its own, this general introduction will merely indicate the relation among various letters, if there is any, and the general topic of each letter.

The topic of five letters, namely, Letters 238, 239, and 242 to Pascentius, Letter 241 from Pascentius, and Letter 242 from Elpidius, is Homoian Arianism, which continued to flourish, especially in military circles. This more moderate form of Arianism held that the Son was a great God, but a lesser God than the Father.

Six letters relate to the controversy late in Augustine's life with various monks at Hadrumetum in Africa and in Provence in Gaul. Augustine wrote Letters 214, 215, and 215A to Valentine, the abbot of Hadrumetum, where some of Valentine's monks objected to Augustine's teaching on grace. In order to win over these monks to his view Augustine wrote for them *Grace and Free Choice* and *Rebuke and Grace*. Letter 216 from Valentine to Augustine describes the whole background to the dispute. Two other letters, namely, Letter 225 from Prosper of Aquitaine and Letter 226 from Hilary, a layman from Gaul, inform Augustine of the reasons that have led the monks of Provence to reject his

---

1. For the Divjak letters, see *Epistulae ex duobus codicibus nuper in lucem prolatae*, ed. Johannes Divjak. Corpus Scriptorum Ecclesiasticorum Latinorum 88 (Vienna: Hoelder-Pichler-Tempsky, 1981) and Bibliothèque Augustinienne 46B. Lettres 1*-29*, ed. J. Divjak with various commentators (Paris: Etudes Augustiniennes, 1987). The BA edition contains invaluable notes and commentary. Along with the twenty-nine letters discovered by Divjak these volumes contain one letter discovered earlier in the last century: Letter 1A*, first published by C. Lambot in *Revue Bénédictine* 51 (1939): 109-121. Letters 23* and 23A* formed a single letter in the manuscripts.

teaching on the beginning of faith, the gift of perseverance, and predestination. Augustine wrote *The Gift of Perseverance* and *The Predestination of the Saints* for them.

Four letters make up the exchange between Quodvultdeus, a deacon in the church of Carthage and later its bishop, and Augustine. In Letters 221 through 223 the deacon pleads with Augustine to write a compendium on all the heresies that have arisen since the coming of Christ. In Letter 224 Augustine finally agrees to write the work that Quodvultdeus wanted, which he produced in his final years, while he was writing his *Revisions* and the *Unfinished Work in Answer to Julian*, and which he entitled *Heresies*.

Three letters make up the exchange between Augustine and Count Darius, who had been sent to Africa to negotiate a peace with the rebellious general Boniface. Augustine sent him Letter 229, complimenting the count on his reputation and urging him to achieve peace. Darius replied in Letter 230, and Augustine in turn sent him Letter 231 along with a copy of *The Confessions*, which Darius had requested. The present volume also contains two letters to Boniface, the Count of Africa, to whom Augustine had also written Letters 185, 189, and 185A. In Letter 220 Augustine reprimands Boniface for his dissolute life, especially after his promise to live a life of continence, and urges him to conquer his love for the world. In Letter 17* Augustine tells Boniface about some people who were all but shipwrecked on the shore of Hippo and assures him of his health.

Three letters in the volume were sent to Alypius, Augustine's boyhood friend, who was now bishop of Thagaste, and a fourth letter was sent to Alypius and Peregrinus, the bishop of Thaenae. Augustine wrote Letter 9* to Alypius, who was at the time in Italy, to hear a case concerning a man who had raped a nun. He also sent Letter 10* to Alypius in Italy, asking to see him as soon as he returned and mentioning the books of Julian of Eclanum and of Caelestius that Alypius had sent him. Augustine also sent him Letter 227 about two recent converts to Christianity. Finally, he sent to Alypius and Peregrinus Letter 22*, in which he complains about the civic duties imposed upon clerics and informs them of the problems in the church of Caesarea regarding the successor of Bishop Deuterius. For the people there were demanding Honorius, whose transfer from another see would be contrary to church law. Letter 23*, which deals with the same problem and which Augustine sent to Renatus, a monk in Caesarea, along with the first book of *The Nature and Origin of the Soul*, informs Renatus that Honorius is present in Hippo and is ready to do what is needed for the peace of the Church.

Augustine sent three letters to Firmus, a Carthaginian catechumen. In Letter 1A* he explains to Firmus the division of the books of *The City of God* and warns him that he will frequently inquire about his progress in reading them. In

Letter 2* he urges Firmus to accept baptism and refutes the various reasons that he had given for postponing the reception of the sacrament. In Letter 212A he again explains the division of the books of *The City of God* which had already been sent to him.

The present volume includes two letters from Consentius, from whom Augustine had received Letter 119 and to whom he had written Letters 120 and 205. In Letter 11* Consentius informs Augustine that Patroclus, the bishop of Arles, has asked him to write a work against the Priscillianists, and he recounts in detail the encounter of a certain Fronto with various Priscillianists. In Letter 12* Consentius describes at length his aversion to learning and his love of leisure, which he loves like a mistress.

Augustine wrote two letters to Fabiola, a Roman laywoman. In Letter 267 he commends her for preferring the heavenly fatherland to our present pilgrimage on earth. In Letter 20* Augustine informs her about the background to the case of Bishop Antoninus of Fussala, who has sought Fabiola's assistance while in Rome, where he has appealed to the pope. Augustine had ordained Antoninus bishop for the people of Fussala. The young bishop proceeded to plunder the town and abuse the people, and he had to be removed from that part of his see.

Four letters, namely, Letter 252 to Felix, a Catholic layman, Letters 253 and 254 to Bishop Benenatus of Simitthus in Proconsular Africa, and Letter 255 to Rusticus, a pagan African, deal with an orphaned girl who had been left in the care of the church of Hippo and whom Rusticus wanted as his son's bride.

Augustine wrote Letter 233 to Longinianus, a pagan priest who had come to believe in one God, asking him how he believed that God should be worshiped. The priest replied with Letter 234, in which he explains the path, as he sees it, that one must follow to God, though he excuses himself from saying anything about Christ. Augustine then wrote Longinianus Letter 235, in which he tried to draw the pagan priest to the Christian faith.

Letter 250 to Auxilius, the young bishop of Nurco, states Augustine's concern over the anathematization of Classicianus, an imperial official, along with his whole family, because Classicianus had allegedly arrested some men who had taken sanctuary in a church. Letter 1* to Classicianus, of which Letter 250A is the fifth paragraph, concerns the same issue.

Letter 260 from Audax, a young Catholic rhetorician, is a plea to Augustine for the treasure of wisdom, and Letter 261 is Augustine's reply, in which he rejects the young man's flattery and suggests that he read some of the books Augustine has written.

There are also two letters to Honoratus, the bishop of Thiave. In Letter 228 Augustine replied to Honoratus, who had consulted him about how the clergy ought to behave under the threat of a barbarian attack. Augustine spells out the duties of the clergy to the people and explains under what conditions they may flee. In Letter 26* Augustine wrote to Honoratus about a certain Donantius, giving him background information on Donantius, about whom he wrote Letter 21* to the people of Suppa, and counseling him not to allow Donantius to be anything more than a lector.

Augustine wrote Letter 14* to Dorotheus, a Catholic landowner near Thagaste, about one of his employees who was accused of a crime. Augustine refuses to disclose the man's name until Dorotheus has promised not to punish the man more than is proper. In Letter 15*, which Augustine wrote to certain clerics in Thagaste, forwarding to them a memorandum from their bishop, Alypius, who was still in Italy, Augustine mentions the name and the crime of the man about whom he wrote to Dorotheus.

Letter 211 to the nuns in the monastery of Hippo contains two parts that are often treated as two works, *The Reprimand for Quarreling Nuns* and *The Rule for Nuns*.

Letter 213 has no addressee and contains the ecclesiastical proceedings in which Augustine designated Heraclius as his successor and obtained the approval of the clergy and people of Hippo.

There remain forty-one letters without any relation to one another aside from the fact that Augustine is in most cases their author. In Letter 212 Augustine commends to Bishop Quintilian of some see in Africa the care of a widow and her daughter. Letter 217 is a lengthy explanation for Vitalis, a Carthaginian layman, of the main points of the Pelagian heresy. In it Augustine states and explains twelve points of doctrine against the Pelagians. Letter 219 is an exhortation to Palatinus, a Catholic layman, to pursue Christian wisdom. Letter 232 was sent to the pagan leaders of the city of Madaura; in it he questions their addressing him as father and sending him greetings in the Lord. He goes on to explain to them, however, the elements of the Christian faith.

In Letter 237 to Bishop Ceretius, whose see was perhaps in Spain, Augustine informs the bishop that the books he had sent him were full of Priscillianist teaching, of which he explains various features. Letter 242 to Laetus, a Catholic layman who had entered a monastery, is an exhortation urging the man to persevere and to free himself from the excessive affection he has for his mother. Letter 244 to Chrisimus, another Catholic layman, urges him not to be discouraged at his temporal losses, which had brought him to the point of contemplating suicide. In Letter 245 Augustine wrote to his friend, Bishop Possidius of Calama, offering him advice about the use of jewelry and cosmetics by women and of amulets by men. Letter 246 to Lampadius, a Catholic layman, offers the man arguments against fate and astrology. Letter 247 to Romulus, an influential convert to Christianity, is a rebuke to the man for trying to collect taxes from his tenant farmers a second time because they had supposedly paid them the first time to the wrong person. Letter 248 to Sebastian, the superior of an African monastery, is a consoling message to the monk, who is saddened over the prevalence of sinners in the world. Letter 249 to Restitutus, a deacon, explains how one must tolerate sinners in the Church and advises the deacon to read Tyconius, a Donatist writer whose exegetical methods Augustine found useful. Letter 251 to Pancarius, a layman in Numidia, deals with complaints from the people about their priest, Secundinus.

In Letter 256 Augustine writes to Christinus, a layman, who had asked for a letter from Augustine, offering him an expression of his love and words of encouragement. Letter 257 to Orontius, a landowner near Hippo, announces Augustine's imminent arrival. In Letter 258 Augustine greets Martianus, an old friend from before his baptism. Augustine tells Martianus that they were not true friends then, though they are now because Martianus is not a stranger to Christ. He urges Martianus to submit his name as a candidate for baptism. Letter 259 to Cornelius, who may have been Augustine's former patron and the father of Licentius, one of Augustine's students at Cassiciacum, is a reply to the man's request for a eulogy for his recently deceased wife. Augustine rebukes Cornelius for his dissolute life and promises to write the eulogy he wants if he will pay for it by living a life of chastity.

There follows soon after a cluster of letters to Catholic women. In Letter 262 Augustine rebukes Ecdicia, who vowed continence without her husband's consent, disposed of most of her possessions and gave them to some itinerant monks without consulting her husband, and dressed as a widow though her husband was still alive. Augustine points out that her actions have led her husband to commit adultery and urges her to apologize and win her husband to repentance. In Letter 263 Augustine writes a message of consolation to the virgin Sapida on the death of her brother Timothy, a deacon. He thanks Sapida for giving him the tunic she had woven for Timothy and admonishes her not to mourn like a pagan who has no hope. In Letter 264 Augustine consoles Maxima, probably a Spanish woman, over the errors in her province, commends her for her correct faith in the incarnation, and asks her to send him any writings she can find in which the heretics defend their beliefs. In Letter 265 Augustine writes to Seleuciana, an African woman, who has encountered the supposedly Novatian teaching that Peter and the other apostles were not baptized and that Peter was a penitent. Augustine explains that the apostles were baptized even if scripture does not say so and that there are various forms of penance in the Church. In Letter 266 Augustine writes to Florentina, a young African girl, who wanted to be taught by Augustine. Augustine tells her that he is willing to be her teacher, though he emphasizes his deficiencies as a teacher, points out the dangers of pride in teaching, and reminds her that Christ is the true teacher.

Of the three remaining letters contained in Migne's Patrologia Latina, Letter 268 is addressed to the leaders of Augustine's congregation; he asks them to help him repay money he borrowed to pay off a debt of one of their congregation. In Letter 269 Augustine writes to Nobilius, an African bishop, that he was unable to attend the dedication of his new church. Finally, in Letter 270 an unknown writer expresses his sorrow at not finding Augustine when he met Bishop Severus of Milevis.

Of the remaining Divjak letters, Letter 3* is a reply to Felix, a deacon, who had consulted Augustine about a woman who had vowed that her young daughter would lead a life of virginity if she survived a grave illness, but then decided that she wanted grandchildren and tried to substitute her own consecrated widowhood for her daughter's virginity. Augustine wrote Letter 4* to Cyril, the bishop of Alexandria; in it he explains the circumstances that led to his writing *The Deeds of Pelagius*. The courier, Justus, had been told that his copy of the work had been falsified where it said that not all sinners were destined for eternal fire. Augustine tells Cyril that Justus' copy is correct and warns Cyril that Justus' accusers may be Pelagians. Letter 5* is a reply to the questions of Valentinian, the bishop of Baiana in Numidia, about why the Our Father is said by people who have just been baptized and about a passage from scripture.

In Letter 6* Augustine writes to Atticus, the bishop of Constantinople, telling Atticus of his joy at learning that he has corrected some persons holding Pelagian errors. He argues against the charge that Catholic teaching holds that marital concupiscence is the work of the devil. Letter 7* is addressed to Faustinus, a deacon in Augustine's monastery in Hippo. Augustine asks Faustinus to urge Novatus, the bishop of Sitifis, to help settle a financial issue. Augustine wrote Letter 8* to Victor, an African bishop, who had seized some property of Licentius, a Jew, because of a financial dispute. In Letter 13* Augustine offers the priest Restitutus counsel about what to do with another priest accused of misbehavior with a nun.

Letter 16* addressed to Aurelius, the bishop of Carthage and a long-standing friend of Augustine, asks Aurelius for news of their mutual friend Alypius, who was at the imperial court, and mentions the action Pope Boniface has taken against the Pelagians. In Letter 18* Augustine tells the people of an African town that he cannot give them the man they want as a priest because the man should not even have been made a deacon. He tells them to find someone else and, if they cannot, he will provide someone. In Letter 19* to Jerome of Bethlehem Augustine tells Jerome that he has heard of the positive results that Jerome's work against the Pelagians have had at the imperial court and explains how he obtained Pelagius' work, *Nature*, to which he replied in *Nature and Grace*.

In Letter 23A* Augustine writes to Possidius, the bishop of Calama, reporting what he had heard from Alypius, mentioning the arrival of the priest, Josias, listing the works he had written in the previous months, and informing him of some details of Church discipline. Augustine wrote Letter 24* to Eustochius, a Catholic layman and lawyer, asking him for advice about various cases of enslavement. Letter 25* informs a group of clerics in Carthage that Augustine has returned safely to Hippo. In Letter 28* to Novatus, the bishop of Sitifis, to whom he had also written Letter 83, Augustine thanks Novatus for his letter and offers some advice on dealing with the remnants of the Donatists. Finally, Augustine wrote Letter 29* to Paulinus, a deacon who had been secretary to Ambrose of Milan, explaining the difficulty he has in complying with Paulinus' request that Augustine write the lives of the martyrs in his own language.

Letter 211

In approximately 424 Augustine wrote this letter in which, first, he calls back to harmony some nuns in the monastery at Hippo who, in trying to change their superior, had created a state of disorder in the monastery. Then he goes on to prescribe a set of rules for their life. The first part of the letter, namely, paragraphs 1 to 4, is often treated as a separate work, *The Reprimand for Quarreling Nuns* (*Objurgatio*), while the second part is commonly called *The Rule for Nuns* (*Regularis informatio*).[1]

Augustine admonishes the nuns for having caused a disturbance (paragraph 1). He tells them that, as Saint Paul said to the Corinthians, he has not come to them so that he might spare them his anger. Rather, he has been praying for them to the Lord (paragraph 2). He tells them of his desire that they may not be corrupted but may be changed for the better (paragraph 3). He expresses his astonishment at the nuns' desire for a new superior in view of all the good the present superior has done for them (paragraph 4).

Then he begins to spell out the rules for the monastery. He first prescribes that the nuns possess all things in common as the members of the early Church did (paragraph 5). He warns them against pride, whether because of the families from which they have come or because of the community into which they have entered (paragraph 6). He adds prescriptions about set times for prayer, about fasting and abstinence, and reading at meals (paragraphs 7 and 8). He provides rules touching upon the nuns' care of the sick (paragraph 9) and the cleanliness of their clothing and the modesty of their behavior (paragraph 10). He lays down guidelines for rebuking a sister, for reporting her to the superior, and for expelling her from the monastery if she refuses to reform (paragraph 11). He establishes various norms for the common care and custody of clothing and for the reception of gifts (paragraph 12). He spells out further norms for the washing of clothes, for bathing, for caring for the sick, and for the dispensation of food, clothing, and books (paragraph 13). He warns about the evils of quarreling and the need for quickly forgiving a sister who has injured another (paragraph 14). He prescribes obedience to the superior and to the priest and describes what the superior's behavior toward her subjects should be (paragraph 15). Finally, he tells the sisters that they should use this letter, which he refers to as a book, as a mirror in which they can see how much progress they have made or have failed to make, and he asks that it be read to them weekly (paragraph 16).

1. Just as severity is ready to punish the sins that it finds, so love does not want to find any to punish. This is the reason that caused me not to come to you, though you were asking for my presence, not in order that I might enjoy your

---

1. See George Lawless, O.S.A., *Augustine of Hippo and his Monastic Rule* (Oxford: Clarendon Press, 1987), for an analysis of the various Augustinian legislative texts as well as their translations.

peace but in order that I might increase your dissension. After all, how would I overlook it and leave it unpunished if your uproar was as great in my presence as it was in my absence when it pummeled my ears with your words, though it was hidden from my eyes? For your rebelliousness might perhaps be even greater in my presence. After all, it would be necessary to refuse you those things that you asked for contrary to sound discipline, because they would set a most destructive precedent and would not be beneficial for you. And thus I might find you to be the sort of persons I do not want you to be, and you might find me to be the sort of person you did not want me to be.

2. As, therefore, the apostle writes to the Corinthians, *I call God as witness to my soul that, in order to spare you, I have not yet come to Corinth. We do not want to dominate your faith. Rather, we are working with you for your joy.* (2 Cor 1:23-24) I also say to you that I have not come to you in order to spare you. I have also spared myself, *so that I would not have sadness upon sadness* (Phil 2:27; 2 Cor 2:3), and I chose not to show my face to you but to pour out my heart to God for you,[2] and I pleaded the case that involves great peril for you, not with words in your presence but with tears in God's presence. I prayed that he would not turn into grief the joy with which I often rejoice and am at times consoled over you amid the great scandals with which this world everywhere abounds. For I am consoled when I consider your large community, your chaste love, your holy way of life, and the more abundant grace that God has given you so that you would not only renounce carnal marriage but also choose a community where you might dwell together in a house with oneness of heart in order to be one soul and one heart for God.[3]

3. Considering these goods you have, these gifts of God, my heart usually quiets down somewhat amid the many storms by which it is shaken because of other evils. *You were running well. Who has bewitched you? That idea does not come from God who has called you.* (Gal 5:7-9) *A small amount of yeast* (1 Cor 5:6)—I do not want to say what follows. After all, I desire more, and I pray and urge that the yeast may be changed for the better so that the whole lump of dough does not change for the worse, as it had almost done. If, then, you have come to your senses, *pray that you may not enter into temptation* (Mt 26:41; Mk 14:38; Lk 22:46), in order that you may not fall back *into quarrels, rivalries, anger, dissensions, backbiting, rebelliousness, and murmuring* (2 Cor 12:20).[4] For we did not plant and water the Lord's garden in your midst[5] so that we should reap these thorns from you.[6] But if your weakness is still in an uproar, pray that you

---

2. See Lam 2:19.
3. See Acts 4:32.
4. See Gal 5:20; Rom 13:13.
5. See Sir 24:42; 1 Cor 3:6-8.
6. See Jer 12:13.

may be rescued from temptation.[7] If, however, those who were disturbing you still disturb you, they will receive judgment, whoever they are, if they are not corrected.[8]

4. Think what an evil it is that, though we rejoice over the Donatists[9] in the unity of the Church,[10] we mourn over internal divisions in the monastery. Persevere in your good resolve, and you will not want to change your superior by whom you have grown both in number and in age in that monastery, which has lasted through so many years and which received you like a mother, not in her womb but in her heart. For all of you who entered there found her either serving and obeying the holy superior, my sister,[11] or found her as the superior herself who received you.[12] Under her you were trained; under her you received the veil; under her you have grown many. And you are in such an uproar in order to have her replaced, though you ought to be in a state of grief if we wanted to replace her for you. She is the one you have known; she is the one to whom you came; she is the one under whom you grew many through having her. You have only received a new priest.[13] Or if on his account you are seeking change and have rebelled against your mother out of hatred for him, why did you not rather ask that he be replaced for you? If you are horrified at this, because I know how much you reverently love him in Christ, why do you not rather love her? For the basic principles of the priest for directing you are so thrown into confusion that he himself would prefer to abandon you rather than that she suffer hateful gossip from you, namely, that it is being said that you would not have sought another superior if he had not begun to be your priest. May God make your hearts calm and composed; let not the work of the devil prevail among you, but *let the peace of Christ win out in your hearts* (1 Jn 3:8). And may you not shamefully run to your destruction with sorrow in your heart because you do not get what you want or because you are ashamed to have wanted what you ought not to have wanted. Rather, by doing penance, may you return to virtue,[14] and may you not have the repentance of Judas the betrayer but rather the tears of Peter the shepherd.[15]

5. These are the rules that you should observe when you are living in the monastery. The first reason on account of which you are gathered together is that you may dwell in the house in unity of mind and that you may have *one heart and*

---

7. See Ps 18:30; 2 Pt 2:9.
8. See Gal 5:10.
9. The CSEL edition has *de Deo natis* ("over those born for God") in place of *de Donatistis.*
10. See 1 Jn 5:1-2.18; 3:9.
11. The name of Augustine's sister is not known. At the time he wrote this letter she had already died.
12. The letter is dealing with two superiors, one of which was Augustine's own sister.
13. The priest was assigned by the bishop as chaplain and spiritual director to the nuns. From Letter 210 we know that his name was Rusticus.
14. See Mt 27:3-5.
15. See Mt 26:75; Mk 14:72; Lk 22:62.

one soul for God (Acts 4:32). And you should not call anything your own, but everything ought to be yours in common, and food and clothing should be distributed to each of you by your superior, not equally to all, because you are not all equally well, but to each one according to her need. After all, you read this in the Acts of the Apostles, *They held everything in common, and it was distributed to individuals according to need* (Act 4:32.35). Those who owned something in the world should gladly want it to be owned in common when they have entered the monastery. But those who did not own anything should not seek in the monastery what they could not have owned outside. Still, what is necessary should be provided for their infirmity, even if their poverty when they were in the world could not obtain for them what they needed. And let them not now consider themselves fortunate because they have found food and clothing of the sort that they could not find in the world.

6. Nor should they act in a haughty manner because they are in community with those whom they would not dare to approach in the world, but let them lift up their heart and not seek earthly goods, for fear that monasteries may begin to be useful for the rich, not for the poor, if the rich are humbled in them and the poor are puffed up with pride.[16] But, on the other hand, let those who considered themselves to be important in the world not show disdain for their sisters who came to that holy community from poverty. They should, however, strive to boast not over the social status of their rich relatives but over their community with their poor sisters. And let them not be filled with pride if they have contributed something to common life from their own wealth, for fear that they should be more proud over their own riches because they gave them to the monastery than if they enjoyed them in the world. Any other form of sinfulness is, of course, found in the commission of bad actions, but pride lies in ambush for good actions in order to destroy them. And what good does it do to distribute one's goods by giving them to the poor and to become poor, if a wretched soul becomes more proud when it scorns them than it was when it possessed them? All of you, then, live in unity of mind and in oneness of heart, and reverence in one another God, whose temples you have become.[17]

7. Be diligent about the prayers appointed for the various hours and seasons.[18] In the oratory let no one do anything but that for which it was built, from which it also derives its name, so that, if any wish to pray, if they are free, even apart from the appointed hours, those who wanted to do something else there may not prevent them. When you pray to God in psalms and hymns, let what you utter with your voice be weighed in your heart, and sing only what you read is to be sung. But anything that is not prescribed for singing should not be sung.

---

16. See Letter 131.
17. See 1 Cor 3:16; 2 Cor 6:16.
18. See Col 4:2.

8. As much as your health permits, subdue your flesh by fasts and abstinence from food and drink. When, however, some sister cannot fast, let her not, nonetheless, take any nourishment apart from the hour of dinner, except when she is ill. From when you approach the table until you get up from it, listen without disturbance and arguments to what is read to you according to custom, and let not only your mouths receive food but let your ears receive the word of God as well.

9. If those who are infirm as a result of their previous manner of life are treated differently in terms of food, it ought not to be troubling or seem unjust to the others, whom another manner of life has made stronger. And let them not suppose that those others are more fortunate because they eat what they themselves cannot eat. And if something in the line of food, clothing, bed, and blankets is given to those who have come to the monastery from a more delicate lifestyle, though it is not given to others who are stronger and for this reason more fortunate, those who do not receive such treatment should consider how far the others have come down from their life in the world to this present life, though they could not attain the frugality of the others who are stronger in body. Nor should they be disturbed because they see them receive more, for they are not being honored but are being tolerated. Otherwise, there might result the detestable perversity that in the monastery where, as far as possible, wealthy ladies become working women, poor women become dainty and delicate ladies. Certainly, those nuns who are ill must receive less food so that they are not made worse. And after their illness they should be treated in such a manner that they recover more quickly, even if they came from the very lowest poverty in the world, as if their rather recent illness provided for them what rich women's previous manner of living bestowed on them. But when they recover their original strength, let them return to their happier way of life, which is more fitting for the servants of God to the extent that they need less. Nor should their desire keep them, once restored to health, at a level to which necessity raised them when they were infirm. Those who are stronger in enduring scarcity ought to judge themselves richer. For it is better to need less than to have more.

10. Let your habit not stand out, and do not aim to please people by your clothing but by your way of life. Let the veils on your heads not be so fine that your hairnets are seen beneath them. Nowhere should your hair be uncovered; let neither carelessness spread it outside the veil nor meticulousness arrange it. When you go out, walk together; when you arrive where you are going, stay together. In your walk, your posture, your habit, and all your movements let there be nothing that might arouse the desire of anyone but only what might fit with your holiness. Even should your eyes fall upon someone, they should not be fixed upon anyone. For, when you go out, you are forbidden not to see men but to desire them or to want to be desired by them. A woman is desired and has desires

not only because of touches but also because of affection and glances. Do not say that you have modest minds if you do not have modest eyes, for an immodest eye is the messenger of an immodest heart. And when, even if the tongue is silent, immodest hearts send messages to each other by glances at each other and find delight in terms of concupiscence of the flesh from each other's passion, chastity itself flees from their manner of life, even if their bodies are untouched by any impure violation. Nor should the sister who fixes her eye upon a man and likes to have his eye fixed upon her think that she is not seen by others when she does this; she certainly is seen—and by those who she does not think see her. But suppose that she is concealed and is not seen by any human being. What will she do about that observer on high from whom nothing can be hidden?[19] Should we think that he does not see because he sees with more patience to the extent he sees with more wisdom? Let a holy woman, then, fear to be displeasing to him so that she does not want to be pleasing to a man in the wrong way. Let her bear in mind that God sees all things so that she does not want a man to see her in the wrong way. For fear of God was taught to us even in this matter where scripture says, *She who fixes her eye on someone is an abomination to the Lord* (Prv 27:20, LXX). When, therefore, you are together in church and wherever there are also men, mutually guard your chastity. For in this way God, who dwells in you, will guard you by means of one another.[20]

11. And if you notice this flirting with the eye, of which I am speaking, in one of yours, admonish her immediately so that she does not continue what she has begun but is corrected right away. But if you see her do this same thing again after the admonition or on any other day, let any sister who was able to discover this report her, for she is now like someone who has been wounded and is in need of being healed. But she should first be made known to a second or third sister in order that she can be accused by the lips of two or three[21] and corrected with adequate severity. And do not consider yourselves as having bad will when you report this. You are in fact more lacking in innocence if you allow your sisters, whom you can correct by reporting them, to perish by keeping silence. After all, if your sister had an ulcer in her body that she wanted to hide because she feared surgery, would you not be cruel in keeping silent about it and merciful in reporting it? Ought you not that much more to report her for fear that she may be more dangerously infected in her heart? But if, after having been admonished, she does not take care to correct herself, she ought to be reported to the superior before she is made known to others who would have to bring accusations against her if she denies it. Thus she can perhaps be privately rebuked and not made known to others. But if she denies it, then others are to be summoned for the

19. See Prv 24:12.
20. See 1 Cor 3:16; 2 Cor 6:16.
21. See Dt 19:15; Mt 18:16; 2 Cor 13:1.

sister who is lying so that, in the presence of all, she may not be accused by one witness but proven guilty by two or three. But once proven guilty, she must submit to the corrective penalty according to the judgment of the superior or the priest, and if she refuses to submit to it and if she does not go away on her own, she should be thrown out of your community. After all, this is not done out of cruelty but out of mercy, so that she may not destroy a great number with a deadly infection. And what I said about making eyes at someone should also be observed with love for the persons and a hatred for their vices in discovering, prohibiting, reporting, proving, and punishing other sins. But any sister who has gone so far in wrongdoing that she secretly receives a letter or any little gifts from a man should be forgiven if she confesses this on her own, and you should pray for her. But if she is caught and proven guilty, she should be more severely corrected according to the judgment of the superior or of the priest or even of the bishop.

12. Keep your clothing in one place under one or two custodians or however many are enough to air them out in order that they may not be damaged by moths. And just as you are fed from one storeroom, so clothe yourselves from one wardrobe. And, if possible, it should not be up to you what you will be given to wear in accord with the needs of the season, whether each sister receives the garment she had left there or another that another sister had worn, provided, nonetheless, that each is not denied what she needs. If, however, quarrels and murmuring arise among you over this, and if some sister complains that she has received something worse than she previously had, and if the one who is dressed in that way considers herself not to deserve to be dressed as the other sister was dressed, you who are quarreling about the habit of the body can learn from this how much you are lacking in that interior *holy habit* (Ti 2:3) of the heart. If, nonetheless, your weakness is tolerated so that you receive back what you left in the wardrobe, at least keep what you put away in one place under common custodians. In that way no one may make something for herself, whether to wear or to lie on or to use as a cincture or a cloak or a veil for the head. Rather, you should make everything that you make for the common good with greater zeal and greater speed than if you were making something for yourself. For the love of which scripture says that *it does not seek what is its own* (1 Cor 13:5) is understood to mean that it sets the common good before one's own good, not one's own good before the common good. And so you can know that you have made more progress the more concern you show for the common good than for your own. As a result, in all the things that passing necessity makes use of, the love that lasts should stand out.[22] Hence it follows that, if a man or woman gives clothing or any other necessity either to his or her own daughters or to any others

---

22. See Eph 3:19; 1 Cor 13:8.

in the monastery in some way related to him or her, it should not be accepted secretly. Rather, it should be in the control of the superior in order that, as something given to the community, it may be offered to one who needs it. But if a sister conceals some gift given to her, she should be judged guilty of theft.

13. Your clothing should be washed according to the judgment of the superior, either by you or by laundresses, lest an excessive desire for clean clothes soil the soul interiorly. The washing of the body and the use of the baths should not be too frequent, but it should be permitted at the usual interval of time, that is, once a month. But if the demands of some illness necessitate bathing the body, it should not be postponed too long. Let it be done without complaint at the advice of a physician so that, even if a sister is unwilling, she may do what needs to be done for her health when the superior commands. But if she wants to and it is perhaps not good for her, she should not follow her desire, for at times what causes pleasure is thought to be beneficial, even if it is harmful. Finally, if the source of a pain in the body of a servant of God is not apparent, the sister who says that she is in pain should be believed without hesitation. But if it is not certain whether something that causes pleasure is useful for healing that pain, a physician should be consulted. Nor should fewer than three go to the baths or wherever it is necessary to go. Neither should the sister who needs to go somewhere go with those with whom she wants but with those whom the superior commands. The care of the ill or of those recovering after illness or suffering under some infirmity, even without fevers, ought to be assigned to some sister in order that she may ask from the storeroom for whatever she sees is necessary for anyone. But those placed in charge of the storeroom or clothing or books should serve their sisters without complaint. Books should be asked for at a certain hour each day; those who ask for them outside that hour should not receive them. But when clothes or sandals are necessary for one who asks, the sisters under whose keeping they are should not delay giving them.

14. Either have no disputes or end them as fast as possible for fear that anger may grow into hatred and make a beam out of a piece of straw and make the soul murderous.[23] For the words of scripture are not true of men alone: *He who hates his brother is a murderer* (1 Jn 3:15). For in the male sex, which God created first, the female sex also received the commandment. Let, then, whoever offends another by insolence, cursing, or even by the accusation of a crime, remember to make reparation for her action as soon as possible, and let her who was offended forgive without discussion. But if they offend each other, they ought to forgive each other their debts on account of your prayers, which ought to be more holy the more frequently you offer them. But the sister who, though she is often tempted by anger, quickly asks the one whom she recognizes that she has

---

23. See Mt 7:3-5; Lk 6:41-42.

wronged to forgive her is better than the sister who grows angry more slowly and finds it more difficult to ask for forgiveness. If she is unwilling to forgive a sister, she should not expect to have her prayer heard, but one who is never willing to ask for forgiveness or does not ask from the heart is living in a monastery for no reason, even if she is not thrown out. Hence, keep yourselves from harsh words, and, if they have passed from your lips, do not be slow to bring forth the remedies from the same lips by which you produced the wounds. But when the need for discipline forces you to speak harsh words to your subjects in order to keep them in line, it is not required of you that you ask pardon of them even if you feel that you have exceeded the limit in their regard. Otherwise, while you show too much humility, you may diminish your authority for governing in the eyes of those who should be subordinate. But you should, nonetheless, ask pardon from the Lord of all, who knows the great good will with which you love even those whom you perhaps rebuke more than is just. The love between you ought to be spiritual, however, not carnal. For the actions of persons not mindful of modesty, even of women with one another, in shameful jokes and games, ought to be avoided not only by widows and virgin servants of Christ living in their holy profession but even by married women or young girls destined for marriage.

15. Obey the superior as a mother, giving her due honor in order that you may not offend God in her person; obey much more the priest who has care for all of you. It pertains especially to the superior, therefore, that all these points be observed and that, if something is not observed, it not be passed over in negligence but care be taken to rectify and correct it. What exceeds her limits and powers[24] he should refer to the priest who directs you. But she should not consider herself fortunate because of the power by which she rules but because of the love with which she serves. She is raised above you in honor before human beings; she is prostrate at your feet in fear before God. Let her show herself to be a model of good actions for all.[25] Let her rebuke the restless, console the fainthearted, help the weak, be patient toward all,[26] gladly have discipline, but fearfully impose it. And though both are necessary, still let her seek to be loved by you rather than to be feared, always having in mind that she will give an account to God concerning you. For this reason, by obeying, show mercy not only to yourselves but also to her, because among you a sister is in greater danger to the extent that she is in a higher position.

16. May the Lord grant that you observe all these norms with love, like lovers of spiritual beauty and persons fragrant with the good odor of Christ[27] because of your good way of life, not like serving girls under the law but like free women

24. See Dn 11:4; Gal 5:13.
25. See Ti 2:7.
26. See 1 Thes 5:14.
27. See 2 Cor 2:15.

living under grace.[28] But in order that you may see yourselves in this little book as in a mirror, have it read to you once a week lest you overlook anything through forgetfulness, and, where you find yourselves doing what has been written, give thanks to the Lord, the giver of all good gifts. But where anyone of you sees that she is lacking something, let her be sorry for the past and watch out for the future, praying that her debt may be forgiven and that she may not be led into temptation.[29]

---

28. See Rom 6:14-15.
29. See Mt 6:12-13; Lk 11:4.

Letter 212

In 424 or 425 Augustine wrote to Quintilian, an African bishop, in order to recommend to his care the widow Galla and her daughter Simpliciola, a virgin. Augustine tells Quintilian that the women are carrying relics of Saint Stephen and expresses his hope that Quintilian will reverence them as he himself has.

To his most blessed lord and rightly venerable brother and fellow bishop, Quintilian, Augustine sends greetings in the Lord.

I commend to Your Reverence in the love of Christ the honorable servants of God and precious members of Christ, Galla, a widow who has made a holy commitment, and her daughter Simpliciola, a consecrated virgin, less than her mother in age but greater than her in holiness, whom we have nurtured as best we could with the word of the Lord. By this letter, as if by my own hand, I entrust them to you to be consoled and assisted in every way that their benefit or need demands. Your Holiness would undoubtedly do this even without my commendation. For if on account of the Jerusalem above, of which we are all citizens[1] and in which they have desired to have a place of more excellent holiness, we owe them not only the love that we have for fellow citizens but also the love that we have for brothers and sisters, how much more do you owe them this love, since you share with them the homeland according to the flesh in which, for the love of Christ, these ladies hold in scorn the renown of this world? I ask that you graciously receive my dutiful greeting with the same love with which I sent it and remember us in your prayers. In fact they are carrying with them relics of the most blessed and most glorious martyr, Stephen.[2] Your Holiness knows how you ought to pay them due honor, as we also have done.

---

1. See Gal 4:26; Heb 12:22.
2. The body of Saint Stephen, the protomartyr, was discovered in 416. See *The City of God* XXII, 8, where Augustine recounts the miracles worked when the relics were brought to Africa. Also see Sermon 317, which Augustine probably preached upon the arrival of the relics in Hippo.

Letter 212A

In 426 Augustine wrote to Firmus, a Catholic layman in Carthage, sending him the twenty-two books of *The City of God* along with instructions about how the books were to be divided into either two or five volumes. This letter was published for the first time by C. Lambot in *Revue Bénédictine* 51 (1939): 109-121.

To his excellent lord and rightly honorable and venerable son, Firmus, Augustine sends greetings in the Lord.

Once they were checked, I sent, as I had promised, the books on *The City of God*, which you most eagerly demanded of me, and with God's help my son, your brother Cyprian, was truly as insistent with me that this be done as I wanted him to be insistent. The twenty-two books, which would be too much to publish as one volume, fall into sections. And if you want there to be two volumes, they should be divided so that one has ten books and the other twelve. The first ten refute the vanities of non-believers, but the rest demonstrate and defend our religion, though, where it was more opportune, the latter is also done in the earlier books, and the former in the latter ones. If you prefer that there be more than two volumes, you should make five volumes. Of these the first should contain the first five books, in which I argued against those who claim that the worship clearly not of gods but of demons contributes to the happiness of this life, and the second volume should contain the next five books against those who think that either such gods or many gods of any sort whatever should be worshiped by sacred rites and sacrifices on account of the life that will exist after death. Now the three other volumes that follow ought to have four books each. For the same part was arranged by us so that four books might show the origin of that city and another four its progress or, as we have preferred to say, its development and the last four its due ends. If you are as diligent in reading those books as you were about possessing them, you will discover from your own experience rather than from my promise how helpful they are. I ask that you graciously and willingly give to those who ask for them the books belonging to the work called *The City of God* which our brothers there in Carthage do not have, so that they may copy them. After all, you will not be giving them to many people but to one or two, and they will give them to the rest. But you yourself will know how you should share them with your friends, whether they are in the Christian people and want to be instructed or are caught up in some superstition from which you see that they can be set free, by the grace of God, through our labor. I myself will take care, if God wills, to ask you frequently about the progress you have made in reading my writings. But you, as an educated man, are well aware of how much a repetition of the reading helps for coming to know what one is reading. For there is either no difficulty or only a slight one in understanding where it is easy to read a text, and it is easier to read the more often the reading is repeated. In that way what remained unclear due to inattentiveness may become clear by repeated reading. I want you, Firmus, my excellent lord and my rightly honorable and venerable son, to be so kind as to write back about how you came upon those books entitled *Answer to the Skeptics*, which I wrote soon after our conversion, because you showed in your previous letter to me that Your Excellency was acquainted with them. The summary I sent you, however, will indicate how much the composition of the twenty-two books has included.

Letter 213

On 26 September 426 Augustine held a convocation of clergy and laity in the church of Hippo in which he designated the priest Heraclius as his successor in the episcopacy (paragraphs 1 to 4) and arranged for Heraclius to relieve him meanwhile of many of his administrative duties (paragraphs 5 and 6). The present document is a record of the ecclesiastical proceedings rather than a letter, though it was undoubtedly presented to Heraclius with a view to the day on which he would succeed to the episcopacy in Hippo.

1. Under the most glorious Theodosius, consul for the twelfth time, and Valentinian Augustus, consul for the second time, on the twenty-sixth of September, after Bishop Augustine, along with his fellow bishops Religianus and Martinianus, had sat down in the Church of Peace in Hippo Regius, with the priests Saturninus, Leporius, Barnabas, Fortunatianus, Rusticus, Lazarus, and Heraclius present, along with the clergy and a crowd of people, Bishop Augustine said:

"Without any delay I must do what I promised yesterday to Your Charity. On account of this I wanted you to gather in larger numbers, and I see that you have gathered in larger numbers. After all, if I wanted to say something else, you would listen less because you were awaiting that other topic. In this life we are all subject to death, and the last day of this life is always uncertain for every human being. Yet in infancy one looks forward to childhood, and in childhood one looks forward to adolescence, and in adolescence one looks forward to young adulthood, and in young adulthood one looks forward to maturity, and in maturity one looks forward to old age. Whether it will come is uncertain, and yet one looks forward to it. Old age, however, does not have another age that it looks forward to. It is also uncertain how long one's old age will be; it is certain, nevertheless, that no age remains that will come after old age. Because God willed it, I came to this city at a vigorous time of my life, but I was young, though, and now I have grown old.[1] I know that after the deaths of bishops cities are often upset because of those who are ambitious and quarrelsome, and I ought, as far as it is up to me, to look out for this city so that what I have often experienced and sorrowed over does not happen. As Your Charity knows, I was recently in the church of Milevis, for the brothers and especially the servants of God who are there asked me to come, because after the death of Severus, a brother of blessed memory and my fellow bishop, they feared some disturbance there. I went there and, as the Lord willed, he helped us in accord with his mercy that the people might peacefully accept the bishop whom their bishop had designated when he

---

1. See Ps 37:25.

32

was still alive. For, after they had come to know this, they willingly embraced the will of their previous bishop. But he did not do as much as he should have, and on this account some were disappointed, for Brother Severus thought that it could suffice to designate his successor in the presence of his clerics, but he did not speak to the people about this. And some of them were saddened over this. But why say more? By the will of God their sadness was dispelled; joy took its place; the bishop whom the previous bishop had designated was ordained. Hence, lest anyone complain about me, I bring to the knowledge of all of you my will, which I believe is God's will: I want Heraclius to be my successor."

The people cried out, "Thanks be to God! Christ be praised!" This was repeated twenty-three times. They cried out, "Hear us, O Christ! Long live Augustine!" This was repeated sixteen times. They cried out, "You are our father, you are our bishop!" This was repeated eight times.

2. When quiet was restored, Bishop Augustine said: "There is no need for me to say anything in praise of him. I esteem his wisdom, and I respect his modesty. It is enough that you know him. And I am saying that I want what I know you want. And if I did not know it before, I would test it today. This, then, is what I want; this I ask of the Lord our God with fervent prayers even now in the chill of old age. I exhort, admonish, and beg that you pray for this along with me, that is, that God may bring together and unite in the peace of Christ the minds of all and may confirm what he has done through us. May God who has sent him to me preserve him; may he keep him safe and sound; may he keep him without serious sin in order that the man who brings joy to me in my life may take my place when I die. The stenographers of the church, as you see, are taking down what we are saying; they are taking down what you say, and my words and your shouts of approval do not fall to the ground. To state it more plainly, we are compiling an ecclesiastical record. For I want this to be confirmed in this way to the extent that it is humanly possible."

The people cried out thirty-six times, "Thanks be to God! Christ be praised!" They said thirteen times, "Hear us, O Christ! Long live Augustine!" They said eight times, "You are our father, you are our bishop!" They said twenty times, "He is worthy and righteous!" They said five times, "He is truly deserving, he is truly worthy!" They said six times, "He is worthy and righteous!"

3. When quiet was restored, Bishop Augustine said: "Hence, as I was saying, I want my will and your will to be confirmed, insofar as it is up to human beings, by ecclesiastical records, but, insofar as it depends upon the hidden will of the Almighty, let us all pray, as I said, that God may confirm what he has done through us."

The people cried out, "We give thanks for your judgment!" This was said sixteen times. They said twelve times, "So be it, so be it!" They said six times, "You are our father, Heraclius is our bishop!"

4. When quiet was restored, Bishop Augustine said: "I know what you also know, and I do not want what happened to me to happen to him. Many of you, however, know what happened; the only ones who do not know either were not yet born at that time or were not old enough to be able to know. I was ordained bishop when my father and bishop, the old man Valerius of blessed memory, was still alive, and I occupied the episcopal chair along with him. I did not know that this had been forbidden by the Council of Nicaea, nor did he know that.[2] I do not want what was reprimanded in my case to be reprimanded in his.

The people cried out, "Thanks be to God! Christ be praised!" They said this thirteen times.

5. When quiet was restored, Bishop Augustine said: "He will remain a priest, as he is; when God wills, he will become a bishop. But now I am simply going to do with the help of Christ's mercy what I have not up to this point done. You knew some years ago what I wanted to do, and you did not permit me to do it. You and I decided that no one would bother me for five days of the week for the sake of the study of the scriptures that my brothers and fathers, my fellow bishops, chose to impose upon me at the two councils of Numidia and Carthage.[3] The proceedings were recorded; they were approved; you cried out your agreement. Your vote and shouts of approval were read out. For a short time people observed this agreement with regard to me, but since then it has been frequently violated and I am not permitted to be free for what I want. Both mornings and afternoons I am involved in people's affairs. I beseech you and by Christ I place you under obligation to allow me to transfer the burdens of my tasks to this young man, that is, to Heraclius, whom today, in the name of Christ, I designate as the bishop who will succeed me."

The people cried out, "We give thanks for your judgment!" They said this twenty-six times.

6. When quiet was restored, Bishop Augustine said: "I give thanks to you for your love and good will before the Lord our God, or rather I give thanks to God for it. And so, brothers, let what used to be brought to me be brought to him. Where he needs my counsel, I will not deny my help; heaven forbid that I should withdraw it. Let whatever used to be brought to me, nonetheless, be brought to him. Let him consult me if he perhaps does not find what he ought to do, or ask

---

2. The eighth canon of the Council of Nicaea on the admission of former Cathars to ordination concludes: "But if this does not meet with his [the former Cathar's] approval, the bishop will provide for him a place as chorepiscopus or presbyter, so as to make his ordinary clerical status evident and so prevent there being two bishops in the city" (*Decrees of the Ecumenical Councils*, ed. By Norman P. Tanner, S.J. [Washington, DC: Georgetown University Press, 1990], I, 10).
3. Augustine is perhaps referring to the Councils of Carthage and Numidia in 418, at which Pelagianism was condemned, or to the Council of Carthage in 419, after which he remained in Carthage for the summer and began his two works on the Heptateuch.

the help of me, who he knows am his father, so that you may lack nothing and so that I at long last, if God grants me a little more time in this life, may not devote my remaining days to laziness or spend them in inactivity but may exercise my mind in the holy scriptures as much as he permits and grants. This will also benefit Heraclius and through him you as well. Let no one, then, begrudge me my leisure, because my leisure will involve important work. I see that I have dealt with everything that I should have concerning this matter for the sake of which I convoked you. Finally, I ask you who are able to be so kind as to sign these records. Here I need your reply. May I have your reply? Give a sign of your agreement by your shouts."

The people cried out, "So be it, so be it!" They said this fifteen times. They said twenty-eight times, "It is right and proper!" They said fourteen times, "So be it, so be it!" They said twenty-five times, "He has long been worthy of this! He has long deserved this!" They said thirteen times, "We are grateful for your judgment!" They said eighteen times, "Hear us, O Christ! Protect Heraclius!"

7. When quiet was restored, Bishop Augustine said: "It is good that we are able to take care of God's business at the time his sacrifice is offered. At this hour of supplication I especially recommend to Your Charity that you interrupt all your concerns and tasks and pour out prayers for this church, for me, and for Heraclius."[4]

---

4. After this decision Heraclius preached while Augustine sat upon the episcopal throne. In a sermon delivered in the presence of Augustine, Heraclius said, "The cicada cries out; the swan is silent" (PL 39, 1718-1719).

Letter 214

Just before Easter in 426 or more probably in 427, Augustine wrote to Valentine, the abbot of the monastery of Hadrumetum. Florus, a monk of that monastery, had discovered Augustine's Letter 194 on the subject of grace, which had been addressed to Sixtus in Evodius' monastery in Uzalis. He had the letter copied and brought it back to his own monastery, where it created a disturbance among the monks. Some argued that, in light of Augustine's doctrine on grace, superiors should not rebuke monks for wrongdoing but should simply pray for them. Augustine wrote two works for Valentine, *Rebuke and Grace* and *Grace and Free Choice*.

Augustine tells Valentine of the arrival in Hippo of two monks, Cresconius and Felix, who reported to him the disturbance in the monastery of Hadrumetum over free choice and grace (paragraph 1). He exhorts the monks to come to an understanding in which they will maintain the existence of free choice as well as the need for grace (paragraph 2). He explains that his letter to Sixtus, which had caused the disturbance at Hadrumetum, was written against the Pelagians, who claimed that grace was given in accord with human merits so that human beings might boast in their own strength and not in the Lord (paragraph 3). On account of that heresy, Augustine explains, he wrote the letter to Sixtus in which he insisted that we have our good works, our pious prayers, and our faith only from the grace of God (paragraph 4).

Augustine tells Valentine that he wanted to send him a variety of documents on the Pelagian heresy but was not able to do so, since the monks were in a hurry to return to Hadrumetum for Easter, though they did not in fact return until after Easter, as we learn from another letter (paragraph 5). He admits that the question of grace and free choice is very difficult to understand and encourages Valentine to send him the monk who has difficulties with his work (paragraph 6). He urges Valentine to believe in the meanwhile the words of God and to pray that he may come to understand what he believes (paragraph 7).

To our brother, Valentine, our most beloved lord worthy of honor among the members of Christ, and to the brothers with you, Augustine sends greetings in the Lord.

1. Two young men, Cresconius and Felix, came to us, saying that they were from your community. They reported to us that your monastery was troubled by some disagreement because certain men among you preach grace in such a way as to deny that human beings have free choice. And what is worse, they say that on the day of judgment God will not recompense *each one in accord with his works* (Mt 16:27; Rom 2:6; Rev 22:12). Yet they also indicated that the majority of you do not hold these views but admit that free choice is helped by the grace of God in order that we may think and do what is right so that, when the Lord comes

36

to recompense *each one in accord with his works*, he may find our good works, which *God has prepared in order that we may walk in them* (Eph 2:10). Those who hold these latter views are correct.

2. *I beg you, therefore, my brothers*, as the apostle begged the Corinthians, *in the name of our Lord Jesus Christ that you all say the same thing, and let there be no divisions among you* (1 Cor 1:10). For the Lord Jesus, as is written in the gospel of John the apostle, *did not* first *come in order to judge the world, but in order that the world might be saved by him* (Jn 3:17). But afterwards, as the apostle Paul writes, *God will judge the world* (Rom 3:6) when, as the whole Church professes in the creed, "he will come to judge the living and the dead."[1] If, then, there is no grace of God, how will he save the world? And if there is no free choice, how will he judge the world? Hence, understand in accord with this faith my book or letter,[2] which those I mentioned above brought with them to you so that you may neither deny the grace of God nor defend free choice in such a way that you make it independent of the grace of God, as if without grace we could think or do anything at all as God wants. For we absolutely cannot! On this account, after all, when the Lord was speaking of the fruit of righteousness, he said to his disciples, *Without me you can do nothing* (Jn 15:5).

3. Hence you should know that the previously-mentioned letter to Sixtus of the Roman church was written in answer to the new Pelagian heretics. They say that the grace of God is given in accord with our merits so that one who boasts may boast not in the Lord but in himself, that is, in a human being, not in the Lord. The apostle forbids this when he says, *Let no one boast in a human being* (1 Cor 3:21), and in another place he says, *Let one who boasts boast in the Lord* (1 Cor 1:31; 2 Cor 10:17). But when these heretics suppose that they themselves can make themselves righteous, as if God did not give this to them but they themselves gave it to themselves, they certainly boast not in the Lord but in themselves. The apostle says to such people, *Who has set you apart?* (1 Cor 4:7) The reason he says this is that, from the mass of that perdition which Adam produced, only God sets a human being apart in order to make him into a vessel of honor, not into a vessel of dishonor.[3] But because, when a carnal and vainly proud human being hears, *Who has set you apart?* he could reply and say, whether by word or in thought, "My faith has set me apart; my prayer has set me apart; my righteousness has set me apart," the apostle immediately counters his thoughts and says, *What do you have that you have not received? But if you have received,*

---

1. These words found in 2 Tm 4:1 and 1 Pt 4:5 appear in most Christian creeds from the beginning of the third century. In his *The Faith and the Creed*, Augustine explained the creed to the bishops of Africa. For the creed used at Hippo see J. N. D. Kelly, *Early Christian Creeds*, 3rd ed. (New York: David McKay, 1972) 176.
2. Augustine refers to Letter 194 to Sixtus.
3. See Rom 9:21,

why do you boast as if you have not received? (1 Cor 4:7) For they boast in this way, as if they have not received, when they suppose that they make themselves righteous and therefore boast in themselves, not in the Lord.

4. For this reason, in this letter that reached you, I proved by the testimonies of the holy scriptures, which you can examine in them, that we could never have our good works and pious prayers and correct faith if we did not receive them from him of whom the apostle James says, *Every good gift and every perfect gift comes from above, descending from the Father of lights* (Jas 1:17). Let no one, therefore, say that he has received the grace of God because of the merits of his works or because of the merits of his prayers or because of the merits of his faith. That is utterly false. It is not that there is no merit, whether the good merit of pious people or the bad merit of sinners. Otherwise, how will he judge the world? Rather, the mercy and grace of God produces a person's conversion. Of this the psalm says, *My God, his mercy will go ahead of me* (Ps 59:11), in order that the sinner may be justified, that is, be made a righteous person from a sinner, and may begin to have the good merit which the Lord will crown when he judges the world.

5. There were many documents that I wanted to send you; by reading them you could acquaint yourself more precisely and fully with this whole issue, which has been dealt with in episcopal councils in opposition to the same Pelagian heretics. But the brothers who came to us from your number were in a hurry, and through them we have not written a reply to you but have simply written to you. For they did not bring to us any letter of Your Charity. We nonetheless welcomed them, for their simplicity made it quite clear to us that they could not have made up any such story for us. They were, however, in a hurry so that they could celebrate the feast of Easter with you.[4] By the help of the Lord, may so holy a day find you at peace rather than at odds with one another.

6. You will, however, do better—something for which I pray very much—if you do not hesitate to send me that monk by whom they say that they were disturbed.[5] For he either does not understand my book, or he himself may be misunderstood when he tries to resolve and untangle a most difficult question, which only a few can understand. For it is the question about the grace of God which caused those who did not understand to suppose that the apostle Paul said, *Let us do evil that good may come of it* (Rom 3:8). For this reason the apostle Peter says in his second Letter, *Hence, my dear brothers, while we await these things, strive that God may find you in peace without blemish and without fault, and consider the patience of our Lord as salvation, as our beloved brother, Paul, wrote to you in accord with the wisdom that was given him. For in all his letters*

---

4. From the following letter we learn that the monks did in fact remain with Augustine past Easter for further instruction on the Pelagian heresy.
5. In light of the final sentence of Letter 215 it would seem that Augustine means Florus.

he spoke of these topics. In them there are some things difficult to understand, and the unlearned and unstable distort them to their own destruction, just as they also do with the other scriptures. (2 Pt 3:14-16)

7. Be attentive, then, to the frightening words of such a great apostle, and where you think that you do not understand, believe for the time being the words of God that there exist both the free choice of a human being and the grace of God, without the help of which free choice can neither turn back to God nor make progress toward God. And pray that you may also wisely understand what you piously believe. You have free choice, after all, for this very purpose, that is, that you may wisely understand. For, if we did not have understanding and wisdom through free choice, we would not have been commanded in the words of scripture, *Have understanding, then, you among the people who are lacking in wisdom, and become wise at last, you fools* (Ps 94:8). By the very fact that we have been commanded and ordered to have understanding and wisdom, our obedience is required,[6] and that obedience cannot exist without free choice. But if we could bring it about by free choice without the help of grace that we have understanding and wisdom, we would not say to God, *Give me understanding that I may learn your commandments* (Ps 119:125). Nor would it be written in the gospel, *Then he opened their minds that they might understand the scriptures* (Lk 24:45). Nor would the apostle James say, *But if anyone among you lacks wisdom, let him ask for it from God who gives to all generously and without reproach, and it will be given to him* (Jas 1:5). The Lord, however, is powerful, and I pray that he may grant to you and to us that by the fastest means possible we may rejoice over your peace and agreement. I send you greetings not only in my own name but also in the name of the brothers with me, and I beg you to pray for us in harmony and with persistence. May the Lord be with you. Amen.

---

6. I have followed the reading of *requiritur* found in PL in place of *requirit* in the CSEL edition.

Letter 215

Shortly after Easter, most probably in 427, Augustine again wrote to Valentine, the abbot of Hadrumetum. He tells Valentine that the monks who had come to him from Hadrumetum have spent Easter with him and will be returning to Valentine better instructed concerning the errors of the Pelagians (paragraph 1). He says that he has written *Grace and Free Choice* for him and is sending with it a number of papal letters and conciliar documents (paragraph 2). He mentions that he also read Cyprian's work, *The Lord's Prayer*, with the visiting monks as well as his own letter to Sixtus (paragraph 3). He explains that he has done all he could so that the monks would neither deny free choice nor suppose that free choice could do anything good without the grace of God (paragraph 4).

Augustine then turns to a passage from the Book of Proverbs, which he uses to illustrate both the existence of free choice and the need for God's grace for any good actions (paragraphs 5 to 8).

To our brother, Valentine, our most beloved lord worthy of honor among the members of Christ, and to the brothers with you, Augustine sends greetings in the Lord.

1. May I inform Your Charity that Cresconius, Felix, and the other Felix, servants of God, who came to us from your congregation, have celebrated the feast of Easter with us. We have kept them a little longer so that they might return to you better instructed against the new Pelagian heretics. A person falls into the Pelagian error if he thinks that the grace of God, which alone sets a human being free through our Lord Jesus Christ, is given in accord with some human merits. But on the other hand a person is also and no less in error who thinks that, when the Lord comes for judgment, he will not judge human beings in accord with their works—I mean those human beings who could already by reason of their age use the free choice of the will. For only small children who do not yet have their own actions, whether good ones or bad ones, will be condemned by reason of original sin alone if the grace of the savior does not come to their aid by the bath of rebirth.[1] But all the rest who, in using free choice, have added their own personal sins to original sin, will, if they are not rescued from the power of darkness by the grace of God and transferred to the kingdom of Christ,[2] receive judgment not only in accordance with the merits of their origin but also in accordance with the merits of their own will. But good persons will also receive their reward in accordance with the merits of their good will; they have attained this good will itself, however, through the grace of God. And in that way there are fulfilled the

---

1. See Ti 3:5.
2. See Col 1:13.

words of scripture, *There will be anger and indignation, tribulation and anguish, for every human soul that does evil, the Jews first and then the Greeks, but there will be glory, honor, and peace for one whose works are good, the Jews first and then the Greeks* (Rom 2:8-10).

2. I had no need to discuss at greater length in this letter as well this most difficult question, namely, concerning the will and grace, because I had already given the monks another letter on the supposition that they were going to return earlier. And I also wrote a book for you;[3] if you read it carefully with the help of the Lord and understand it with a lively mind, I think that there will no longer be any disputes among you on this topic. The monks, however, also carry with them other writings that we believed we ought to send to you by which you may know how, by the mercy of God, the Catholic Church repelled the venom of the Pelagian heresy. These are the letters to Pope Innocent, the bishop of the city of Rome—one from the Council of the Province of Carthage, another from the Council of Numidia,[4] a more detailed letter sent to him by five bishops,[5] and his responses to these three letters.[6] There is also a letter to Pope Zosimus from an African Council[7] and his reply sent to all the bishops of the world.[8] There are also the decrees drawn up in brief statements by a later plenary council of the whole of Africa against this error,[9] and there is the previously mentioned book of mine that I have just written for you. We have also read all these documents on the present question together with the monks, and we sent them to you along with them.

3. We also read to them the book of the blessed martyr Cyprian entitled *The Lord's Prayer*,[10] and we showed how he taught that we must ask from our Father who is in heaven for everything that pertains to our moral conduct and the way we live correctly, so that we do not put our trust in free choice and fall away from God's grace. There we also demonstrated how the same most glorious martyr warned us that we ought to pray even for our enemies who have not yet believed in Christ, so that they may come to believe. This would, of course, be a pointless act if the Church did not believe that even the evil and unbelieving wills of human beings can be converted to the good by the grace of God. But since they

---

3. The book is *Grace and Free Choice*.
4. These are Letters 175 and 176.
5. This is Letter 177 from the bishops Aurelius, Alypius, Augustine, Evodius, and Possidius.
6. These are Letters 181, 182, and 183.
7. This African council met in the winter of 417-418; it probably included only the bishops of Proconsular Africa.
8. Augustine refers to the *Tractoria* of Zosimus written in the summer of 418; it is extant only in fragments.
9. This was the plenary Council of Carthage held on May 18, which drew up nine canons on original sin and grace. For a translation of the canons, see *Answer to the Pelagians* I, pp. 389-391.
10. Cyprian, *The Lord's Prayer* (*De dominica oratione*), is found in CCL 3/A, 87-113.

said that this book of Saint Cyprian was already available in the monastery, we did not send it to you. We also read with them the letter that I sent to Sixtus,[11] a priest of the church of Rome, which they brought with them to me, and we showed that it was written in opposition to those who say that the grace of God is given in accordance with our merits, that is, in opposition to the same Pelagians.

4. To the extent, then, that we were able, we worked with these brothers, both yours and ours, in order that they might persevere in the sound Catholic faith, which does not deny that there is free choice, whether for a good life or a bad one, but does not attribute to it such power that, apart from the grace of God, it is able to do something, whether it turns from bad to good, or makes progress toward the good with perseverance, or attains the everlasting good where it no longer fears that it may fall. In this letter I exhort you too, my dear brothers, as the apostle exhorts all of us, *not to be more wise that one ought to be, but to be wise in moderation, as the Lord has given to each one a measure of faith* (Rom 12:3).

5. Pay attention to the warning which the Holy Spirit gives through Solomon. He says, *Make straight paths for your feet, and direct your ways so that you do not turn aside to the right or to the left. But turn your foot away from the evil way. For the Lord knows the ways on the right, but those on the left are perverse. But he will make your paths straight and will guide your journeys in peace.* (Prv 4:26-27)[12] In these works of scripture, my brothers, consider that, if free choice did not exist, it would not say, *Make straight paths for your feet, and direct your ways so that you do not turn aside to the right or to the left.* And yet, if one could do this apart from the grace of God, it would not say later, *He will make your paths straight and will guide your journeys in peace.*

6. Do not, therefore, turn aside to the right or to the left, although the ways on the right are praised and those on the left are blamed. This, after all, is the reason he added, *But turn your foot away from the evil way*, that is, from the left. He makes this clear in the following words when he says, *For the Lord knows the ways which are on the right, but those on the left are perverse.* We ought, then, to walk in those ways which the Lord knows; of them we read in the psalm, *The Lord knows the way of the righteous, and he will destroy the way of the wicked* (Ps 1:6). For the Lord does not know this latter way, which is on the left, just as he is going to say to those placed on the left, *I do not know you* (Mt 15:12; 7:23; Lk 13:27). But why is it that he does not know them, since he certainly knows everything good or bad about human beings? What does *I do not know you* mean but "I did not make you such"? So too, what does the statement about the Lord Jesus that he *did not know sin* (2 Cor 5:21; 1 Pt 2:22) mean but that he did not commit sin? And for this reason how should we interpret the words, *The Lord*

---

11. This is the work which the monk Florus found in the monastery of Evodius at Uzalis and had transcribed and sent to Hadrumetum.
12. Augustine's Latin text is closer to the wording of the Septuagint than to that of the Vulgate.

knows the ways on the right, if not in the sense that he made the ways on the right, that is, the ways of the righteous? These are, of course, the good works that *God has prepared*, as the apostle says, *in order that we might walk in them* (Eph 2:10). But he certainly does not know the perverse ways on the left, that is, the ways of the wicked, because he did not make them for human beings, but human beings made them for themselves. For this reason he says, *But I hate the perverse ways of the evil* (Ps 119:4); these are on the left.

7. But they reply to us, "Why, then, did he say, *Do not turn aside to the right or to the left* (Prv 4:27), since it seems that he ought to have said, 'Hold to the right, and do not turn aside to the left,' if the ways on the right are good?" Why do we suppose he said this if not because the ways on the right are good such that it is nonetheless not good to turn to the right? He must be understood to turn to the right, indeed, who wants to attribute to himself and not to God the good works that pertain to the ways on the right. And so, when he said, *For the Lord knows the ways on the right, but the ways on the left are perverse*, as if someone said to him, "Why then do you not want us to turn to the right?" he continued, *But he will make your paths straight and will guide your journeys in peace* (Prv 4:27). Understand in that sense, then, the commandment given you, *Make straight paths for your feet, and direct your ways* (Prv 4:26), in order that, when you do this, you may know that the Lord God grants it to you that you do it. And you shall not turn aside to the left, though you walk in the ways on the right, not trusting in your own virtue, and he will be your virtue *who will make your paths straight and will guide your journeys in peace* (Prv 4:27).

8. Hence, dearest brothers, whoever says, "My will is sufficient for me to do good works," turns aside to the right. But , on the other hand, those turn aside to the left who think that they should give up their efforts to live well when they hear that the grace of God is preached in such a way that it is believed and understood to make human wills good from bad and also to preserve the good wills it makes. Hence they say, *Let us do evil that good may come of it* (Rom 3:8). This is the reason why I said to you, "Do not turn aside to the right or to the left," that is, neither defend free choice so that you attribute to it good works without the grace of God nor defend grace so that, as if you were safe because of it, you love evil works. God keep you from this! Posing such an objection to himself, the apostle says, *What then shall we say? Shall we remain in sin in order that grace may abound?* (Rom 6:1) And he replies, as he ought, to these words of human beings in error who do not understand the grace of God; he says, *Heaven forbid! For, if we have died to sin, how shall we continue to live in it?* (Rom 6:2) He could have said nothing briefer or better. After all, what greater benefit does the grace of God bestow in this present evil world than that we die to sin? And for this reason the person who wants to live in sin because of that by which we die to sin is found ungrateful to grace itself. But may *God who is rich in mercy* (Eph 2:4) grant that

you have sound wisdom and persevere up to the end, making progress in the good you have undertaken. Pray for this grace for yourselves; pray for it for us; pray for it for all those who love you and for those who hate you; pray for it persistently and vigilantly in brotherly peace. May you live for God.

If I have merited anything from you, let brother Florus come to me.

Letter 215A

Sometime after having written the previous letter Augustine again wrote to Valentine, thanking him for sending Florus to him for instruction and asking that he be sent back to Hippo again in order that Augustine might instruct the monk still further.

To Valentine, his most beloved lord and brother worthy to be embraced in the heart of Christ, Augustine sends greetings in the Lord.

I am indeed most grateful to Your Charity because you sent Brother Florus to me as I desired, and I am even more grateful to our God because I found him to be the sort of man I had hoped. But though he may seem to have returned to you somewhat late, he was with me less time than I wanted. In fact, when he was present, such weakness of the body held me in its grip for so many days that I could not be with him, my beloved lord and brother worthy to be embraced in the heart of Christ. Hence I ask you again that you be so good as to fulfill not merely my own desire but that of both of us, and that you send him again that he may be with us for some time. For I think that this will be beneficial both for him and for us and that his fuller instruction, which he will be able to obtain through us with the help of the Lord, will be profitable for the brothers as well. May you always be pleasing to God.

Letter 216

Soon after having received the previous letter Valentine, the abbot of Hadrumetum, wrote to Augustine. He expresses his embarrassment over the rusticity of his monks and apologizes for not having sent a letter to Augustine with the monks who went to Hippo (paragraph 1). Valentine explains how the disturbance at Hadrumetum arose as the result of Florus' finding Augustine's letter in the monastery at Uzalis (paragraph 2). He tells Augustine how he had tried to calm the dispute and how Augustine's book had finally healed the wounds of the monks involved (paragraphs 3 and 4). Valentine expresses his faith in the fact that the human will, unaided by the grace of God, is helpless (paragraph 5). Finally, he asks that Augustine pray for him and his monks (paragraph 6).

To the most blessed Bishop Augustine, my truly holy lord, who are worthy to be preferred to all else in our respect and to be honored with pious exultation, Valentine, the servant of Your Holiness, and the whole congregation, which along with me places its hopes in your prayers, send greetings in the Lord.

1. We received the venerable letters and the book of Your Holiness with a trembling heart.[1] Just as blessed Elijah veiled his face when the glory of the Lord passed by, when he was standing at the threshold of the cave,[2] so we covered our eyes before your reproaches. For we were embarrassed at the decision that we made on account of the rusticity of our brothers, and because of their disorderly departure from here we were afraid to send our greetings to Your Beatitude, for there is a time for speaking and a time for being silent.[3] After all, we did not want to write to you through men who were in doubt or were wavering about the truth for fear that we might seem to be in doubt along with them about the statements of your wisdom, which is like the wisdom of an angel of God. For it was not necessary for us to make inquiries about Your Beatitude and Your Wisdom, for by the grace of the Lord your character is well known to us. We were, after all, so quickly pleased by the book of Your Holiness[4] that, just as the apostles after the resurrection did not dare to ask who it was who was eating with them,[5] for they knew it was Jesus, neither did we wish or dare to ask whether that book was the work of Your Holiness, since the grace of a man of faith, which is so extensively

---

1. Valentine refers to Letters 214 and 215 and the book known as *Grace and Free Choice*.
2. See 1 Kgs 19:13.
3. See Eccl 3:7.
4. Valentine refers to Letter 194, the letter to Sixtus which Florus had copied and sent to Hadrumetum.
5. See Jn 21:12.

commended to us in it, testifies by such life-giving words that it is yours, my lord and holy bishop.

2. Let us, however, my lord and most blessed bishop, set forth the account of this disturbance. Our dear brother, Florus, the servant of Your Paternity, visited his native Uzalis from a motive of charity, and during his stay in his hometown he sent back to us as breads of blessing[6] for the monastery one of the writings of Your Holiness. One of the brothers, Felix, who, as you know, arrived at the monastery of Your Holiness somewhat later after the arrival of his companions, faithfully dictated the same book. He returned to the monastery with the book while our brother Florus set out for Carthage from the city of Uzalis. Without having shown the book to me, they began to read it to some brothers who had little education. It upset the hearts of certain of them who did not understand it. After all, when the Lord himself said, *He who does not eat the flesh of the Son of Man and drink his blood will not have life in himself* (Jn 6:54), those who understood him incorrectly left, not because of the fault of the Lord who said this but because of the hardness of their impious hearts.

3. The brothers I mentioned who threw everything into turmoil disturbed the souls of the innocent, while my humble self remained completely unaware of this; I was so ignorant of their grumbling meetings that if our brother Florus, on returning from Carthage and recognizing their agitation, had not reported it to me out of concern. . . . There was among them a furtive and almost servile quarrel about the truth, which they could not understand. In order to resolve these impious questions I proposed that we send someone to our holy father and lord Evodius, in order that he might write back to us something more certain regarding this holy book for the sake of the ignorant brothers. Nor were they willing to accept his reply with more patience, but they abruptly departed from here in a way we had not wanted. Brother Florus was nearly in consternation over their furor, for their anger was directed at him, since they thought that he had introduced the wounds of this book in which the weak could find no remedy. Hence we appealed to the holy priest Sabinus for greater authority, and His Holiness read us the book with clear interpretations. But their wounded soul was not cured even in that way. We therefore gave them the expenses for the trip out of our fatherly concern, for fear that we would increase their wounds, which the grace of this book could heal, for your holy presence shines forth in it. Once they had departed, all the brethren rejoiced in the Lord in peace and quiet. For by their animosity five or at most six brothers had given rise to this dispute.

4. But since in the meanwhile, my lord and bishop, our sadness has turned into joy, we are not so troubled, for we have merited to be enlightened by the

---

6. Valentine uses the term *eulogias*, which refers to the as yet unconsecrated bread offered by the faithful to the Eucharist.

gentle admonitions of Your Holiness through those ignorant and curious monks. For the doubting of the blessed apostle Thomas, who wanted to see the holes made by the nails,[7] was a source of strength for the whole Church. We have, therefore, my lord and bishop, received with gratitude the medicine of your letters, which bring healing with their piety, but we beat our breast in order that our conscience may at least in that way be healed, for grace heals it and brings it to life by our free choice, which mercy grants, but only in this time when we sing of his mercy in this delay that we face.[8]

For, when we begin to sing of judgment to the Lord, we shall receive the recompense for our work, because the Lord is merciful and just, compassionate and righteous.[9] For, as Your Holiness teaches us, *We must appear before the judgment seat of Christ so that each of us may receive recompense for what we have done in the body, whether good or evil* (2 Cor 5:10), for *the Lord will come, and his recompense with him*, because a man will stand *before him with his work* (Is 40:10). For the Lord will come like a blazing furnace to burn up the wicked like stubble, and for those who fear the name of the Lord he will rise up like the sun of justice, while the wicked will be punished by the judgment of justice.[10] The just man, of whom you, my lord and bishop, are a friend, cries out, trembles, and says in supplication, *Lord, do not enter into judgment with your servant* (Ps 143:2). If this judgment were the grace of the one who gives the recompense, the righteous person would not fear the secret courtroom of the judgment of the divine majesty.

This, my lord, is the faith of your servant Florus, not what these brothers have stated. They have heard that he said that for the present life the gift of piety is not given in accord with our merits but by the grace of the redeemer. After all, who has any doubt that grace will be far distant on that day when justice begins to show its anger. This we cry out, father; this we sing, as you teach us, not in confidence but in fear: *Lord, in your wrath do not blame me, and in your anger do not chastise me* (Ps 6:2). This we say: "Correct us, Lord, and teach us about your law that you may be gentle with us on bad days."[11] This we believe, as you teach us, venerable father, because the Lord examines the just and the unjust.[12] For to the good placed on his right and to the evil placed on his left he will credit the works of piety to be recompensed and count the stubbornness of impiety to be punished. Where will grace be when works will be checked off in accord with their quality, whether good or evil?

---

7. See Jn 20:25.
8. See Ps 101:1.
9. See Ps 12:4.
10. See Mal 4:1-3.
11. See Ps 94:12-13.
12. See Ps 10:6.

5. But why do they not fear to bring forth a subtle lie? We do not deny that free choice is healed by the grace of God, but we believe that we make progress by the daily grace of Christ and are confident that we are helped by it. And some men[13] say, "It is in my power to do good." If only they would do good! O the foolish boast of these wretches! Daily they accuse themselves of sins, and they claim for themselves in their boasting a free choice unaided by grace. They do not examine their conscience, which can only be healed by grace, so that they might say, *Have mercy on me; heal my soul for I have sinned against you* (Ps 41:5). Why do these men, who boast of their free choice, a choice that we do not deny as long as it has the help of God, act as if death were already swallowed up in victory, as if our mortal body had already put on immortality and our corruptible body had put on incorruptibility?[14] See, their wounds stink, and with pride they ask for medicine. For they do not say as the righteous man says, *If the Lord had not helped me, my soul would soon have dwelled in hell* (Ps 94:17); they do not say as the holy man says, *If the Lord does not guard the city, in vain does he who guards it keep watch* (Ps 127:1).

6. But pray, best of fathers, that we may have no other concern but to wipe away our sin by tears and to praise the grace of God. Pray, lord father, that the pit does not close its jaws over us,[15] so that we may be kept safe from those going down into the ditch,[16] so that our soul may not perish with the impious through our pride[17] but may be healed through the grace of the Lord. As, then, you, our lord and bishop, have commanded, our brother Florus, the servant of Your Holiness, has left with all speed in order that he might receive instruction to enlighten his heart, for fatigue does not slow him down but spurs him on. We humbly commend him to Your Holiness, and we ask at the same time that you commend to the Lord by your prayers these ignorant monks who need to be gently quieted down. Pray, lord and dear father, that the devil may flee from our community and that, once all the storm of strange questions has been removed, the ship to which we are committed, loaded with peaceful sailors, may, as it sails through this great and immense sea, come to a secure rest within the anchorage of the safest harbor. And, within that harbor where we shall no longer have to fear any shipwreck for our life, may it receive without any dispute the price of its wares pleasing to God. We are confident that by the help of Your Holiness we shall obtain this by the grace that is in Christ Jesus our Lord.

---

13. Valentine refers not to some of his monks but to the Pelagians in general.
14. See 1 Cor 15:54.53.
15. See Ps 69:16.
16. See Ps 30:4.
17. See Ps 26:9.

We ask that you greet all the sons of your apostolic work, our lords, the clerics and saints who serve in the community to which they are committed, so that they may all deign to pray for us along with Your Beatitude.

May the Trinity of the Lord our God, in which there is no discord, preserve for us in his Church your holy apostolic work, which he has chosen by grace, and may he in the great Church crown you who are mindful of us, as we hope, my lord. But if the servant of Your Holiness, our brother Florus, makes some request regarding the rule of our monastery, we ask, father, that you willingly listen to him and instruct us, weak as we are, in every respect.[18]

---

18. In answer to this request Augustine wrote and sent to the community at Hadrumetum *The Rule for the Servants of God* (*Regula ad servos Dei*) PL 32, 1377-1384.

Letter 217

Between 426 and 428, approximately, Augustine wrote to Vitalis, a Catholic layman in Carthage. From some source unknown to us Augustine had heard that Vitalis held that believing in God and assenting to the gospel were not a gift of God but something that we did by our own will. Augustine points out that Vitalis is consequently opposed to the prayers of the Church for non-believers (paragraph 1). He challenges Vitalis to state openly that Catholics should not pray for the conversion of non-believers but should only preach to them, contrary to the teaching of Cyprian and even contrary to the teaching of Paul (paragraphs 2 and 3).

Augustine warns that Vitalis is holding the error of the Pelagians, who say that grace consists only in free choice and in the law and doctrine (paragraph 4). The genuine grace of God precedes any human good will and does not find such good will but produces it (paragraph 5). Augustine appeals to Cyprian's interpretation of the Lord's Prayer to show that we should pray for the conversion of non-believers (paragraph 6). If we pray sincerely, it makes no sense to ask God to do what we ourselves could do by our own wills (paragraph 7).

Augustine argues that, if we want to defend free choice, we should not attack grace, by which our choice is made free to avoid evil and to do good (paragraph 8). As a result of the sin of Adam even newborn infants need to be rescued from the power of the devil by the grace of baptism (paragraph 9). The angels who fell now try to keep human beings from the faith without which it is not possible to please God (paragraph 10). Hence we need the help of the grace brought by the second Adam, not the help of the nature damaged by the first Adam (paragraph 11).

Grace does not consist in the nature of free choice or in the law and teaching, but is given for individual actions by the will of God (paragraph 12). In his providence God has arranged it so that he brings some persons to the faith through answering the prayers of others (paragraph 13). We should also pray for believers that they may persevere in the faith up to the end (paragraph 14). Why some are given the gift of final perseverance and others are not remains hidden from us (paragraph 15).

Augustine lists twelve propositions that embody the Catholic faith in opposition to the Pelagian errors concerning the relation between God's grace and the human will (paragraphs 16 and 17). Then he goes on to explain how grace precedes any good will on our part, as is evident especially in the case of infants (paragraph 18). The fact that all human beings are not saved points to the gratuity of grace (paragraph 19). The human will does not merit grace, which is given to those to whom it is given by God's gratuitous mercy (paragraph 20). Final perseverance too is a gratuitous gift of God (paragraph 21). Furthermore, God's grace and judgment do not depend upon what one would have done, had one lived longer (paragraph 22). And yet anyone who believes in God does so by his free will (paragraph 23). The fact that we thank God for the conversion of non-believers is a sign that their beginning to believe is his gift (paragraph 24).

Augustine points out that all twelve propositions together (mentioned in paragraphs 16-17) as well as each of them individually teach that God's grace anticipates the human will, and he asks Vitalis to write back to him if he disagrees with any of the statements (paragraph 25). Once again he shows how the prayer of the Church presupposes that faith is a gift of God (paragraph 26). The prayers of Saint Paul for non-believers and those making progress in the faith show that it is God who produces and preserves faith in the hearts of human beings (paragraph 27). As prayers for the conversion of non-believers show that faith is God's gift, so our thanking God once they have been converted shows that it is God who produces their faith (paragraphs 28 and 29). Finally, Augustine expresses his hope that Vitalis will agree that the prayers of Christians prove that faith is a gift of God's grace (paragraph 30).

Bishop Augustine, a servant of Christ and through him a servant of his servants, sends greetings in Christ to his brother Vitalis.

1, 1. Since the news reported to me about you was not good, I begged the Lord, and I still beg him until good news is reported to me, that you may not receive my letter with scorn but read it in a way conducive to salvation. If he hears this prayer of mine for you, he also gives me reason to offer thanksgiving for you. If I obtain this favor, you will undoubtedly not speak against this beginning of my letter. After all, my prayer for you is that you may be a man of correct faith. If, then, you are not displeased that we pray for this for our friends, if you recognize that this is a Christian prayer, if you either recall that you also make such prayers for your friends or recognize that you ought to, how do you say what I hear that you say—that the fact that we have the correct faith in God and assent to the gospel is not a gift of God, but that we have this from ourselves, that is, from our own will, which God has not produced in our heart? And when you hear, "Why is it, then, that the apostle said, *God produces in you even the will*" (Phil 2:13), you reply to this: "God causes us to will through his law, through his scriptures, which we either read or hear, but to assent or not to assent to them is up to us so that, if we will to, we do, but if we do not will to, we cause God's activity to be without effect in us. Of course," you say, "he causes us to will to the extent he can when his words become known to us. But if we refuse to go along with them, we bring it about that his activity accomplishes nothing in us. If you say this, you certainly speak in opposition to our prayers."

2. State most openly, then, that we should not pray that those to whom we preach the gospel may believe, but that we should only preach to them. Employ your arguments against the prayers of the Church, and, when you hear a priest of God at the altar exhorting the people of God to pray for non-believers that God may convert them to the faith and for catechumens that he may inspire them with the desire for rebirth and for the faithful that by his gift they may continue in what they have begun to be, sneer at such pious words, and say that you do not do

what he urges, that is, that you do not ask God on behalf of non-believers that he may make them believers, on the ground that these things are not benefits of God's mercy but tasks of the human will. And as a learned man in the church of Carthage, condemn as well the book of the most blessed Cyprian on *The Lord's Prayer*. When that teacher explained this prayer, he showed that we petition from God the Father what you say is given to a human being by a human being, that is, by oneself.

3. But if you believe that what I said about the prayers of the Church and the martyr Cyprian is not enough, be bolder; rebuke the apostle who said, *We pray to God that you may do no evil* (2 Cor 13:7). After all, you are not going to say that one who does not believe in Christ or who gives up faith in Christ does no evil. And for this reason he who says *that you may do no evil* does not want us to do these actions. And it is not enough for him to give the command, but he confesses that he asks God that we may not do these actions, knowing that God corrects and directs the will of human beings so that they do not do them. For *the steps of a man are directed by the Lord, and he will choose the Lord's way* (Ps 37:23). He did not say, "And he will learn the Lord's way," or, "He will hold onto it," or, "He will walk in it," or some such thing that you could say is indeed given by God, but to a person who already wills it, that is, so that the gift of God by which he directs the steps of a man so that he may learn, hold onto, and walk in the Lord's way are preceded by the man's will, and the man merits this gift of God by his antecedent will. Rather, he said, *The steps of a man are directed by the Lord, and he will choose the Lord's way*, in order that we might understand that the good will itself, by which we begin to will to believe (for what is God's way but the correct faith?), is a gift of him who first directs our steps in order that we may will. After all, scripture does not say, *The steps of a man are directed by the Lord* because the man chose his way, but it says that they *are directed* and that *he will choose*. They are not, then, directed because the man chose, but he will choose because they are directed.

2, 4. Here you are again perhaps going to say that the Lord does this when we read or hear his teaching, if a person assents with his will to the truth that he reads or hears. You say, "For, if God's teaching were concealed from him, God would not direct his steps in order that, once they had been directed, a man would choose God's way." And for this reason you think that the Lord directs the steps of a man to choose God's way only in the sense that without God's teaching he could not come to know the truth to which he assents by his will. You say, "If a man assents to it (something that lies within his free choice), the Lord is correctly said to direct his steps in order that he may choose the way of him whose teaching he follows because he was first persuaded and then assented, which he does by his natural freedom if he wills to, but does not do if he does not will to. And he will receive a reward or punishment in accord with what he has done."

This is the teaching of the Pelagians that is wrongly spread about and rightly condemned, and Pelagius himself, fearing that he would be condemned in the courtroom of the Eastern bishops, condemned the view by which they say that the grace of God is not given for individual actions but lies in free choice or in the law and teaching.[1] Will we be hardhearted to such a point, my brother, that we hold that Pelagian view on the grace of God, or rather against the grace of God, that Pelagius himself condemned with a false heart, but still in fear of Catholic judges?

5. And how, you will ask, shall we reply? How do you suppose we shall do so more easily or more clearly than by embracing what we said above about praying to God so that no invasion of forgetfulness, no clever argument may tear it from our mind? For scripture says, *The steps of a man are directed by the Lord, and he will choose the Lord's way* (Ps 37:23), and, *The will is prepared by the Lord* (Prv 8:35, LXX), and, *For it is the Lord who produces in you even to will* (Phil 2:13). And there are many such passages by which the true grace of God is taught, that is, the grace that is not given according to our merits, but that gives our merits themselves when it is given, because it precedes a person's good will and does not find it in anyone's heart, but produces it. If, then, God so prepares and so produces a person's will that he only proposes his law and teaching to the person's will and does not move his mind by that deep and hidden calling, so that he gives his assent to the same law and teaching, it would undoubtedly be enough to read it or to understand it through reading or even to explain and preach it, and it would not be necessary to pray that God might convert the hearts of non-believers to his faith and that, by the bounteousness of the same grace of his, he might give to those already converted growth and perseverance. If, then, you do not deny that we must ask for this from the Lord, what remains, Brother Vitalis, but that you admit that he—from whom you agree that we must ask for them—gives these things? But if you deny that we ought to ask him for them, you contradict the same teaching of his, because we also learn in it that we should ask for these things from him.

6. You know the Lord's prayer, and I do not doubt that you say to God, *Our Father, who are in heaven* (Mt 6:9), and so on. Read the most blessed Cyprian, who has explained it,[2] and pay careful attention to how he explained the words, *May your will also be done on earth as it is in heaven* (Mt 6:10), and humbly understand what he said. He will certainly teach you to pray for non-believers who are enemies of the Church, in accord with the command of the Lord who says, *Pray for your enemies* (Mt 5:44; Lk 6:28), and to pray that God's will also be done in those who, because of their unbelief, bear only the image of the

---

1. See *The Deeds of Pelagius* 14, 30.
2. See Cyprian, *The Lord's Prayer* (*De dominica oratione*) 14-17.

earthly man and for this reason are rightly called "earth," just as it is done in those who are already believers and who bear the image of the heavenly man and are for this reason called "heaven."[3] The former, of course, are the enemies for whom the Lord commanded us to pray, and the most glorious martyr explained in that sense what we say in the prayer, *May your will also be done on earth as it is in heaven* (Mt 6:10), in order that we might also ask for them the faith that believers have. Of course those enemies of the Christian faith either do not at all want to hear the law and teaching of God by which the faith of Christ is preached, or they listen to it and also read it in order to mock, despise, and blaspheme it with as much opposition as they can. Vainly and perfunctorily rather than truthfully do we pour forth prayers to God for them, so that by believing they may assent to the teaching they oppose, if it does not pertain to his grace to convert to his faith the wills of persons who are opposed to that faith. Uselessly and insincerely rather than truthfully do we thank God in exultation, when some of them come to believe, if he does not cause this in them.

7. Let us not deceive human beings, for we cannot deceive God. We surely do not pray to God, but we pretend to pray to him, if we believe that it is we ourselves, not God, who do what we pray for. We surely do not thank God, but pretend that we do, if we think that he does not do that for which we thank him. If we have deceitful lips[4] in any conversations with human beings, let us at least not have them in our prayers. Far be it from us to deny in our hearts that God does what we ask him to do with our lips and voices. And—what is worse—far be it from us to remain silent about this in our discussions in order to deceive others; and, when we want to defend free choice before human beings, to lose before God the help of prayer; and not to give true thanks, since we do not acknowledge true grace.

3, 8. If we truly want to defend free choice, we should not attack that by which it becomes free. For one who attacks the grace by which our choice is set free in order to turn away from evil and to do good wants his will to be still captive. Answer me, I beg you: How does the apostle say, *Giving thanks to the Father who makes us fit to partake of the lot of the saints in light, who has rescued us from the power of darkness and transferred us into the kingdom of his beloved Son* (Col 1:12-13), if he himself does not set our choice free but our choice sets itself free? We lie, therefore, when we give thanks to the Father as if he himself does what he does not do, and the apostle was mistaken when he said that *he makes us fit to partake of the lot of the saints in light because he has rescued us from the power of darkness and transferred us into the kingdom of his beloved Son.* Answer me: How did we have free choice in order to turn away from evil

---

3. See 1 Cor 15:47-49.
4. See Ps 12:3-4; 17:1; 31:19.

and to do good when it was under the power of darkness? If, as the apostle says, God rescued us, he certainly set our choice free from it. If he causes so great a good as this only through the proclamation of his teaching, what shall we say of those whom he has not rescued from the power of darkness? Are we only to preach God's teaching to them, or should we also pray for them that they may be rescued from the power of darkness by God's power? If you say that we should only preach to them, you contradict the command of the Lord and the prayers of the Church. But if you admit that we should pray for them, you admit that we should pray that they assent to the same teaching by their choice, which has been set free from the power of darkness. In that way it happens that they do not become believers except by free choice, and yet they become believers by the grace of him who has set free their choice from the power of darkness. Thus the grace of God is not denied but shown to be true grace without any preceding human merits, and free choice is defended in such a way that it is strengthened by humility, not hurled down by pride, so that *he who boasts may boast not in a human being,* whether someone else or himself, but *in the Lord* (1 Cor 1:31; 2 Cor 10:17).[5]

9. After all, what is the power of darkness but the power of the devil and his angels,[6] who, though they were angels of light,[7] because they did not remain standing in the truth by free choice[8] but fell from there, became darkness? I am not teaching you these things, but I am admonishing you to recall what you know. The human race, then, was made subject to this power of darkness through the fall of that first human being, who was persuaded to transgress the commandment by that power and in whom we all fell.[9] On this account even infants are rescued from this power of darkness when they are reborn in Christ. And this is not seen in their choice, which has been set free, except when they come to an age when they have the use of reason, have a will that assents to the saving doctrine in which they have been raised, and end this life with that will, if they were chosen in Christ before the creation of the world in order that they might be holy and spotless in his sight in love, predestined for adoption as his children.[10]

10. But this power of darkness, that is, the devil, who is also called the prince of the power of the air, is at work in the children of unbelief.[11] This prince, the devil, the ruler of darkness, that is, of those children of unbelief, rules them by his choice. Nor does he possess his choice as free to do good but as hardened into

---

5. See Jer 9:23-24.
6. See Mt 25:41.
7. See 2 Cor 11:14.
8. See Jn 8:44.
9. See Gn 3:1-6; 1 Tm 2:14; Rom 5:12.
10. See Eph 1:4-5.
11. See Eph 2:2.

the greatest malice as punishment for his sin.[12] From this no one of sound faith believes or says that those rebel angels are converted to their former goodness once their will has at some point been corrected. What, then, does this power produce in the children of unbelief but its own evil works and, first of all and especially, the very unbelief and infidelity by which they are enemies of the faith? For by that faith this power knows that the children of unbelief can be purified, can be healed, and can reign as perfectly free in eternity, which he intensely hates. And so he allows some of them, through whom he tries to deceive more extensively, to have some seemingly good works for which they are praised. There are found among any number of peoples, but especially in the people of Rome, those who have lived illustrious and most glorious lives. But, as scripture says, which is perfectly true, *Everything that does not come from faith is sin* (Rom 14:23), and, *Without faith it is* indeed *impossible to please God* (Heb 11:6)—not human beings. Hence this prince aims at nothing but that people not believe in God or, by believing, come to his mediator, by whom his works are destroyed.

11. But the mediator himself enters *into the house of a strong man* (Mt 12:29), that is, into the world of mortals situated under the power of the devil insofar as it belongs to him; of him scripture says, to be sure, that he has the power of death.[13] The mediator enters *into the house of a strong man*, that is, of him who has the human race under his dominion, and he first ties him up, that is, checks and restrains his power by the mightier chains of his own power. And in that way he carries off whichever of his vessels he predestined to carry off, setting free from his power their choice so that, without the devil's interference, they might believe in him by their free will. Hence this is a work of grace, not of nature. It is, I say, a work of the grace that the second Adam brought us, not of the nature that the first Adam destroyed as a whole in himself. It is a work of grace that takes away sin and gives life to the dead sinner, not a work of the law that reveals the sin but does not give life to the sinner. For that great preacher of grace says, *I knew sin only through the law* (Rom 7:7), and, *If a law were given that could give life, righteousness would certainly come from the law* (Gal 3:21). This is a work of grace by which those who receive it are made friends of that salutary teaching of holy scripture, though they were its enemies, not the work of that teaching by which those who hear it and read it without the grace of God become that much fiercer enemies of it.

4, 12. The grace of God, then, is not found in the nature of free choice and in the law and teaching, as the Pelagian error foolishly supposes. Rather, it is given for individual actions by the will of him of whom scripture says, *You will set*

---

12. See 2 Tm 2:26.
13. See Heb 2:14.

apart a voluntary rain, O God, for your heritage (Ps 68:10), because we lost free choice for loving God by the enormity of the first sin, and the law and teaching of God, though holy and righteous and good,[14] nonetheless kills if the Spirit does not give life.[15] The Spirit brings it about that we hold on to the law not by hearing it but by obeying it, not because we read it but because we love it. Hence, that we believe in God and live a pious life *does not depend upon the one who wills or the one who runs, but upon God who shows mercy* (Rom 9:16), not because we ought not to will and to run but because God produces the willing and the running in us.[16] For this reason, when the Lord Jesus himself distinguished those who believe from those who do not believe, that is, the vessels of mercy from the vessels of anger,[17] he said, *No one comes to me unless it has been given him by the Father* (Jn 6:65-66), and his disciples who afterwards did not follow him[18] were of course scandalized that he said this. Let us, therefore, not call teaching grace, but let us acknowledge the grace that makes teaching beneficial. If that grace is lacking, we see that even teaching is harmful.

13. For this reason, though God foreknew all his future actions in his predestination, he arranged them so that he would convert certain non-believers to faith in him by answering the prayers of believers for them. And in this way those who think that grace is the nature of free choice with which we are born or that grace is teaching, however useful, which is proclaimed aloud and in writing, are refuted, and, if he is merciful to them, they are corrected. After all, we do not pray for non-believers that God may cause their nature, that is, that they may be human beings, or that they may be given the teaching that they hear to their misfortune if they do not believe it—and we very often pray for those who, when they read or hear it, refuse to believe. Rather, we pray that their will may be corrected, that they may assent to the teaching, and that their nature may be healed.

14. But now believers pray even for themselves, that they may persevere in what they have begun to be. It is, of course, beneficial for all or for almost all, for the sake of a most salutary humility, that they cannot know the sort of persons they are going to be. For this reason scripture says, *Let him who seems to be standing firmly see to it that he does not fall* (1 Cor 10:12). Because of the usefulness of this fear that, after we have been reborn and begin to live a holy life, we might have proud thoughts,[19] as if we were safe, certain persons who are not going to persevere are by God's permission, provision, or disposition mingled

14. See Rom 7:11-12.
15. See 2 Cor 3:6; Jn 6:63.
16. See Phil 2:13.
17. See Rom 9:22-23.
18. See Jn 6:61-62.67.
19. See Rom 11:20; 12:8.

with those who are going to persevere in order that, terrified by their fall, we may follow the righteous road *with fear and trembling* (2 Cor 7:15; Eph 6:5; Phil 2:12) until we pass from this life, which *is a temptation upon the earth* (Job 7:1), to the other life, where pride no longer has to be suppressed and we do not have to struggle against its suggestions and temptations.

15. But concerning this issue, that is, why certain people who are not going to remain in Christian faith and holiness still receive this grace for a time and are allowed to live here until they fall away, though they could be snatched from this life *so that malice would not change their mind* (Wis 4:11), as was written in the Book of Wisdom about one who died at a tender age, let each person investigate as he can. And, if he finds another credible account apart from the one that I have given, without deviating from the rule of the correct faith, let him hold it, and I will hold it along with him if I come to know it. Let us nonetheless, if we have some other idea, continue to walk on the path to which we have come until God makes it clear to us, as we are taught in the letter of the apostle.[20] But we have come to those truths, which we most firmly know belong to the true and Catholic faith and in which, with the help and mercy of him to whom we say, *Lead me, O Lord, on your path, and I will walk in your truth* (Ps 86:11), we should walk in such a way that we never turn aside from them.

Twelve Propositions against the Pelagians[21]

5, 16. Because by the mercy of Christ we are Catholic Christians:

1. We know that those not yet born have done nothing good or bad in their own life and did not come into the miseries of this life in accord with the merits of some previous life of their own, which as individuals they could not have, but that those born in the flesh after Adam contract by their first birth the contagion of the ancient death and are not set free from the punishment of eternal death that a just condemnation carries with it, passing from the one to all,[22] unless they are reborn in Christ through grace.

2. We know that the grace of God is given neither to infants nor to adults in accord with our merits.

3. We know that it is given to adults for individual actions.

4. We know that it is not given to all human beings and that it is not only not given to those to whom it is given according to the merits of their actions but that it is also not given to those to whom it is given according to the merits of their wills, something that is seen especially in infants.

---

20. See Phil 3:16.15; 2 Jn 6.
21. The CSEL edition omits this subtitle and the numbering of the propositions.
22. See Rom 5:12.

5. We know that the mercy of God is given as gratuitous to those to whom it is given.

6. We know that by the just judgment of God it is not given to those to whom it is not given.

7. We know that *we shall all stand before the judgment seat of Christ in order that each may receive recompense in accord with what he did in the body* (Rom 14:10; 2 Cor 5:10), not in accord with what one would have done if one had lived longer.

8. We know that infants too will receive either reward or punishment in accord with what they did in the body. They did nothing by themselves, however, but by those who make the responses for them and by whom they are said to renounce the devil and to believe in God. Hence they are counted in the number of believers, included in the Lord's statement when he says, *One who believes and is baptized will be saved* (Mk 16:16). For this reason there also applies to those who do not receive this sacrament what follows: *But one who does not believe will be condemned* (Mk 16:16). Hence, if they die at that early age, they too, as I said, are certainly judged in accord with what they did in the body, that is, at the time when they were in the body, when by the hearts and lips of those presenting them they believed or did not believe, when they were or were not baptized, when they ate or did not eat the flesh of Christ, when they drank or did not drink the blood of Christ.[23] They are not judged in accord with what they were going to do if they had lived here longer.

9. We know that the dead *who die in the Lord* (Rv 14:13) are happy and that whatever they would have done if they had lived for a longer time does not pertain to them.

10. We know that those who believe in the Lord in their own heart do this by will and by free choice.

11. We know that we who already believe act in accord with the correct faith when we pray to God for those who refuse to believe so that they may will to believe.

12. We know that we correctly and truly both should and are accustomed to offer thanks to God for those who have come to believe, as for so many benefits.

17. You recognize, I think, that I did not want to mention all the truths that pertain to the Catholic faith in those that I said that we know but only those that pertain to what we are discussing regarding the grace of God, namely, whether this grace precedes or follows upon the will of a human being, that is (to speak more plainly), whether grace is given to us because we will it or, by grace, God

---

23. See Jn 6:54-55.

also makes us will it. If, then, you, my brother, also hold along with us these twelve propositions that I have said we know pertain to the correct and Catholic faith, I give thanks to God, and I would not truthfully give thanks unless the grace of God brought it about that you held them. If you hold them, there will remain no dispute at all with us on this question.

6, 18. Let me run through these twelve propositions with a brief explanation. How does grace follow upon the merit of the human will when it is given even to infants who are not yet able either to will or not to will? How are merits of the will said to come before grace even in adults if, in order to be true grace, grace is not given according to our merits? Pelagius himself was so afraid of this Catholic statement that, without any hesitation, he condemned those who say that the grace of God is given in accord with our merits, for fear that he would be condemned by Catholic judges.[24] How is grace said to be found in the nature of free choice or in the law and teaching since Pelagius also condemned this statement, confessing without any doubt that the grace of God is given for individual actions to those who of course already have use of free choice?

19. How can one say that all human beings would receive grace if those to whom it is not given would not reject it by their own will, because *God wills that all human beings be saved* (1 Tm 2:4), since it is not given to many infants? For very many die without it who do not have a will opposed to it, and at times their parents desire it and hasten to it, and the ministers are also willing and ready. But, because God does not will it, it is not given, when the infant suddenly dies before the sacrament is given to which his parents had hastened so that he might receive it. Hence it is obvious that those who resist this truth, which is so clear, do not at all understand the sense in which it was said that *God wills that all human beings be saved*, though so many are not saved not because they do not will it but because God does not will it, which is perfectly clear in the case of infants. But just as the statement, *All will be brought to life in Christ* (1 Cor 15:22), though so many are punished with eternal death, was said in the sense that all who receive eternal life receive it only in Christ, so the statement, *God wills that all human beings be saved*, though he does not will that so many be saved, was said in the sense that all who are saved are saved only by his will. And if these words of the apostle can be understood in any other way, they still cannot contradict this absolutely obvious truth by which we see that so many are not saved because God does not will this, though human beings do.

20. And how does the human will merit that God's grace be given, if it is given out of gratuitous mercy to those to whom it is given in order that it may be true grace? How are the merits of the human will weighed in this case, since by

---

24. At the Council of Diospolis Pelagius condemned those who said that grace was given according to human merits and confessed that it is given for individual actions. See *The Deeds of Pelagius* 14, 30.

the just judgment of God—for there is no injustice in God[25]—this grace is not given to those to whom it is not given, though they do not differ by any merit or any will from those to whom it is given, but are with them in one and the same condition? As a result, those to whom it is given should understand how gratuitously it is given when of course it might justly not be given, since it is justly not given to those who are in a similar condition.

21. How is not only the will to believe from the beginning but also the will to persevere up to the end[26] not due to the grace of God, since the end of this life is not in the power of a human being but in God's power, and God could certainly also bestow this benefit on someone who was not going to persevere, so that he would be taken from the body *in order that malice might not change his mind* (Wis 4:11)? For a human being will not receive either reward or punishment[27] except in accord with what he has done in this life, not in accord with what he would have done if he had lived longer.

22. How is it said that the grace of God is not given to certain infants and is given to certain others who are going to die, because he foresees their future wills, which they would have had if they had lived? For, as the apostle says, each person will receive either reward or punishment in accord with what he did in the body, not in accord with what he would have done if he had lived longer in the body.[28] How are human beings judged in accord with their future wills, which it is said that they would have had if they lived longer in the flesh, since scripture says, *Happy are the dead who die in the Lord* (Rv 14:13)? Their happiness is undoubtedly not certain and secure if God will also judge those actions that they did not do but were going to do if their life were longer, and he receives no benefit who is carried off *in order that malice might not change his mind* (Wis 4:11), because he also suffers the punishment for that malice from which he was removed when it was perhaps imminent. Nor should we rejoice over those who we know have died in the correct faith after a good life, lest they be judged in accord with some crimes that they perhaps would have committed if they had lived. Nor are they to be mourned and despised who have ended this life in unbelief and corrupt morals, because, if they had lived, they would perhaps have done penance, would have lived piously, and would have been judged in terms of this. We would have to disagree with and reject in its entirety the book *Mortality* of the most glorious martyr Cyprian,[29] in which his whole aim is that we should know that we ought to rejoice over the good faithful when they die, since they are removed from the temptations of this life and will thereafter remain in most

---

25. See Rom 9:14.
26. See Mt 24:13.
27. See 2 Cor 5:10.
28. See 2 Cor 5:10.
29. See Cyprian, *Mortality* (*De mortalitate*) 7, 20-21.

blessed security. But since this is not false and because *the dead who die in the Lord are* undoubtedly *happy* (Rv 14:13), we should mock and curse the error by which it is supposed that human beings are going to be judged according to the future dispositions of their wills, which are not going to exist in the case of those who die.

23. How are those said to deny the free choice of the will who confess that every human being who believes in God from his heart believes only with his free will? For they, rather, attack free choice who attack the grace of God by which choice becomes truly free for choosing and doing good. How does someone say that the law and teaching of God and not rather the hidden inspiration of the grace of God bring about what the same scripture says: *The will is prepared by the Lord* (Prv 8:35, LXX)? For, on behalf of those who contradict the same teaching and refuse to believe it, we beg God with the correct faith that they might desire to believe.

24. How does God wait for the wills of human beings so that those to whom he gives grace may anticipate him, though we correctly thank him for those to whom he granted mercy when they did not believe in him and were attacking his teaching with their wicked will and whom he converted to himself with his omnipotent ease, making them willing instead of unwilling? Why do we thank him for this if he himself did not do it? Why do we glorify him more to the extent that those who we rejoice have come to believe used to refuse to believe with greater obstinacy, if the human will is not changed for the better by God's grace? The apostle Paul says, *I was unknown by appearance to the churches of Judea that are in Christ. They only heard that he who once was persecuting us is now spreading the good news of the faith that he once ravaged, and they glorified God in me.* (Gal 1:22-24) Why did they glorify God if God had not converted the heart of that man to himself by the goodness of his grace, since, as he himself admits, he obtained mercy in order that he might become a believer[30] in the faith that he once ravaged? Who but God produced this great good, according to the expression that he used? After all, what does *They glorified God in me* mean but "They declared God glorious because of me"? But how did they declare God glorious if God himself had not produced that great deed of Paul's conversion? And how did he himself do it if he did not, from being unwilling, make him willing to believe?

25. It is, of course, evident from those twelve propositions, which you are not permitted to deny pertain to the Catholic faith, that not only all of them together but also each of them individually makes us confess that the grace of God precedes human wills and that they are prepared by grace rather than that grace is given on account of their merit. Or if you deny that one of those twelve is true,

---

30. See 1 Cor 7:25.

whose number I also mention so that they may more easily be committed to memory and held there more distinctly, do not hesitate to write back in order that I may know and reply with the ability that the Lord has given me. For I do not in fact believe that you are a Pelagian heretic, but I want you to be such a man that none of that error passes into you or remains in you.

7, 26. But you will perhaps find some point among those twelve which you think that you should deny or hold as doubtful and over which you would force us to argue in more detail. You surely do not, do you, forbid the Church to pray for non-believers in order that they may become believers, for those who refuse to believe in order that they may will to believe, for those who disagree with its law and teaching in order that they may agree with its law and teaching, in order that God may give them what he promised through the prophet: *a heart for knowing him and ears for hearing* (Bar 2:31)? Those of whom the Lord said, *Let those hear who have ears for hearing* (Mt 13:9; Mk 4:9; Lk 8:8), had of course received these ears. When you hear the priest of God at his altar exhorting the people to pray to God, or when you hear him praying aloud that God would compel unbelieving peoples to come to faith in him, will you not respond "Amen?" Or will you argue in opposition to the soundness of this faith? Will you cry out or whisper that the most blessed Cyprian was in error on this point, when he teaches us to pray for the enemies of the Christian faith that they too might be converted to it?

27. Finally, will you blame the apostle Paul, who made prayers of this sort for the non-believing Jews? He says of them, *The good will of my heart and my prayer to God is of course for their salvation* (Rom 10:1). He also says to the Thessalonians, *Finally, brothers, pray for us, that the word of God may spread rapidly and may be glorified, as it is also among you, and that we may be rescued from wicked and evil persons. For not all have the faith.* (2 Thes 3:1-2) How would the word of God spread rapidly and be glorified if not by the conversion to the faith of those to whom it was preached, since he says to those who already believe, *as it is also among you*? He surely knows that God, whom he wants them to ask to do this, is the one who acts in order that he may also be rescued from wicked and evil persons who were certainly not going to believe despite their prayers. For this reason he added, *For not all have the faith*, as if to say, "For the word of God will not be glorified among all despite your prayers," because they were certainly going to believe *who were destined for eternal life* (Acts 13:48), predestined *for adoption as his children through Jesus Christ and chosen in him before the creation of the world* (Eph 1:5.4). But by means of the prayers of believers God makes those who are still non-believers believe in order to show that he himself does this. For there is no one so ignorant, so carnal, so slow in mind as not to see that God does what he commands us to ask him to do.

28. These and other divine testimonies, which it would take too long to mention, show that by his grace God removes from non-believers their heart of stone[31] and that he anticipates in human beings the merits of their good wills so that he might prepare their wills by his antecedent grace, not so that grace might be given because of the antecedent merit of their wills. Thanksgiving indicates the same thing as prayer: prayer for non-believers, thanksgiving for believers. For to him to whom we must pray that he might do this we must offer thanksgiving when he has done it. For this reason the same apostle says to the Ephesians, *On this account, having heard of your faith in the Lord Jesus and of your love for all the saints, I too do not cease to offer thanks for you* (Eph 1:15-16).

29. But we are now speaking about the very beginnings, when people who were turned away from and set against God are turned back to him and begin to will what they did not will and to have the faith that they did not have. In order that this may come about, prayer is offered *for* them, even though it is not offered *by* them. After all, *how will they call upon him in whom they have not believed?* (Rom 10:14) But when what is prayed for has come about, thanksgiving is offered both for them and by them to him who did this. I do not, however, think that it is necessary to dispute with you about the prayers of those who are already believers, which they offer both for themselves and for others of the faithful in order that they may make progress in what they have begun, and about their thanksgiving because they are making progress. This dispute with the Pelagians is something that you and I have in common. They of course attribute to the free choice of the will all the things that have to do with the faithful and holy life of human beings in such a way that they think that they are to be had from ourselves, not asked for from God. But if what I hear about you is true, you do not want the beginning of faith, in which there is also found the beginning of a good, that is, of a pious will, to be a gift of God; rather, you claim that we have it from ourselves that we begin to believe. Yet you agree that through his grace God grants the other goods pertaining to a religious life to those who ask, seek, and knock with faith.[32] You do not notice that we pray to God on behalf of non-believers in order that they may believe because God also gives faith, and that we give thanks to God on behalf of those who have come to believe because he also has given faith.

30. Hence, in order to bring this letter to you to an end, if you deny that we should pray that those who refuse to believe may will to believe, if you deny that we should give thanks to God because those who refused to believe have willed to believe, we must deal with you in another way so that you may not be in such

31. See Ez 11:19; 36:26.
32. See Mt 7:7-8; Lk 11:9-10.

an error or so that, if you persist in error, you may not bring others into error. But if, as I prefer to believe of you, you hold and agree that we ought to pray to God and often do pray to God for those who are unwilling to believe in order that they may will to believe and for those who are opposed to and contradict his law and teaching in order that they may believe and follow it, if you hold and agree that we also ought to give thanks to God and often do give thanks to God for such people when they have been converted to his faith and teaching and become willing from having been unwilling, you ought undoubtedly to admit that the wills of human beings are anticipated by the grace of God and that God, whom we ask to do this and whom we know it is right and just to thank when he has done this, brings it about that human beings will the good that they did not will. May the Lord grant you understanding on all these points, my lord and brother.

Letter 218

In 427 or 428 Augustine wrote to Palatinus, a Catholic layman, to exhort him to the life of Christian wisdom that he has already undertaken (paragraph 1). He urges his correspondent, who has given up his hopes for worldly riches, not to place his trust in his own strength but in the Lord (paragraph 2). He warns Palatinus that he must watch and pray so that he may not enter into temptation, because of itself our will is not sufficient for this (paragraph 3). Finally, Augustine expresses his desire to be united with Palatinus in the one Spirit, even if they are physically separated (paragraph 4).

To his most beloved lord and dearest son Palatinus Augustine sends greetings.

1. Your manner of life, which is so courageous and fruitful for the Lord our God, has brought us great joy. For from your youth you have chosen instruction[1] in order that you may find wisdom in the grey hairs of age.[2] Hence your grey hairs are a sign of human wisdom, and your old age is a sign of a spotless life.[3] May the Lord, who knows how to give good gifts to his children, grant you this as you ask, seek, and knock.[4] For, although there are many who exhort you and you have had numerous exhortations toward the road to salvation and eternal glory, especially the grace of Christ that has spoken salutary words in your heart, out of the duty of love that we owe you we too offer you an exhortation in this response of ours to your greeting. By it we do not rouse you, as if you were lazy and asleep, but challenge and urge you on, since you are already running.

2. Because you were wise enough to make this choice, you ought to be wise enough to persevere in it. Let this be part of your wisdom: to know whose gift this is.[5] *Reveal to the Lord your way, and hope in him. And he himself will act and bring forth your righteousness like the light and your judgment like the noonday.* (Ps 37:5-6) *He will make your steps straight and guide your journeys in peace* (Prv 4:27). As you have scorned what you were hoping for in the world for fear that you would boast in the abundance of riches[6] which you had begun to desire in the manner of the children of this world, so now do not trust in your own strength for bearing the yoke of the Lord and his burden, and the former will be gentle and the latter light.[7] In the psalm those people are equally blamed *who place their trust in their own strength* and *who boast in the abundance of their*

---

1. See Sir 6:18.
2. See Wis 4:8-9.
3. See Wis 4:8-9.
4. See Mt 7:7-8.11; Lk 11:9-10.13.
5. See Wis 8:21.
6. See Ps 49:7.
7. See Mt 11:29-30.

riches (Ps 49:7). You do not now have the boast of riches, therefore, but you have most wisely held in contempt that reason for boasting that you desired to have. Watch out that trust in your own strength does not sneak up on you. After all, you are a human being, and *cursed is everyone who puts his trust in a human being* (Jer 17:5). But with your whole heart put your trust clearly in the Lord, and he will be your strength, in which you may piously and gratefully put your trust, when you humbly and faithfully say to him, *I love you, O Lord, my strength* (Ps 18:2), because *the love of God* that, when perfect, *casts out fear* (1 Jn 4:18), *is poured out in our hearts* not by our strength, that is, human strength, but, as the apostle says, *by the Holy Spirit who has been given to us* (Rom 5:5).

3. Watch, therefore, and pray that you may not enter into temptation.[8] Prayer itself reminds you that you need the help of your Lord in order not to place the hope of living well in yourself. For you are not praying now to receive the riches and honors of the present world or something pertaining to human vanity but that you might not enter into temptation, and if a human being could give that to himself by his own will, he would not ask for it by his prayers. Hence, if the will were suffi-cient for us not to enter into temptation, we *would* not pray for this, and yet, if we lacked a will, we *could* not pray either. Let the will, then, be present in order that we may will; let us pray, however, in order that we may be able to do what we will, when by his gift we think correctly. Since you have already begun to have this good, there is reason for you to give thanks. After all, *what do you have that you had not received? But if you have received, beware of boasting as if you have not received* (1 Cor 4:7), that is, as if you could have had it from yourself. But, knowing from whom you have received it, ask him who has given you this beginning to bring it to perfection. And so, *with fear and trembling* work out *your salvation. For it is God who produces* in you both *the willing and the action in accord with good will.* (Phil 2:12-13) For *the will is prepared by the Lord* (Prv 8:35, LXX). And *the steps of a man are directed* by him, *and he will choose the Lord's way* (Ps 37:23). This holy thought will protect you so that your wisdom may be piety,[9] that is, so that you may be good by God's gift and not be ungrateful for the grace of Christ.

4. Your parents long for you, rejoicing with faith over the better hope that you have begun to have in the Lord.[10] But we desire to possess you, whether absent or present in terms of the body, in the one Spirit by whom *love is poured out in our hearts* (Rom 5:5), in order that, wherever our flesh may be, our soul may in no way be separated. We have most gratefully received the goatskin coat you sent when you earlier reminded us of increasing and preserving the humility of our prayers.

---

8. See Mt 26:41; Mk 14:38; Lk 22:46.
9. See Jb 28:28.
10. See Phil 1:27; 1 Cor 12:9; Eph 2:18.

Letter 219

In 418 Aurelius, bishop of Carthage, Augustine, bishop of Hippo, Florentius, bishop of Hippo Diarrytus, and Secundus, a Numidian bishop, wrote to Proculus, bishop of Marseilles, and Cillenius, a bishop from elsewhere in the south of France.[1] The African bishops tell their Gallic counterparts that they welcomed the monk Leporius after he had been rebuked by the Gallic bishops and expelled from their country. Leporius had denied that God had become man for fear that the divinity would suffer change or corruption[2] (paragraph 1). As God chastised Leporius through the bishops of Gaul, so he has healed him through the efforts of the African bishops (paragraph 2). Leporius has written a document in which he repudiates his errors, and the African bishops have added to it their signatures. They now ask the bishops of Gaul to welcome back Leporius and to inform those he scandalized of his amendment (paragraph 3).

To Proculus and Cillenius, their most beloved and honorable brothers and fellow priests, Aurelius, Augustine, Florentius, and Secundus send greetings in the Lord.

1. After having rightly and appropriately been rebuked by Your Holiness for the arrogance of his error, our son Leporius came to us after he had been expelled from your territory, and we received him, a man who was disturbed in a salutary way, in order to correct and heal him. For, just as you obeyed the apostle in rebuking the restless, so we obey him in consoling the fainthearted and in welcoming the weak.[3] For he was like *a man caught in some sin* (Gal 6:1), and that not a small one, inasmuch as he had some incorrect ideas and held some false views concerning the only-begotten Son of God, who *in the beginning was the Word, and the Word was with God, and the Word was God* (Jn 1:1), *but, when the fullness of time came* (Gal 4:4), *the Word became flesh and dwelled among us* (Jn 1:14). He denied that the Word became man for fear, that is, that there would ensue a change or corruption[4] unworthy of the divine substance, by which he is equal to the Father.[5] Nor did he see that he was introducing a fourth person into

---

1. Older literature dates this Letter to 426; more recent literature, however, assigns the date of 418. See A. Mandouze, *Prosopographie de l'Afrique chrétienne (303-533)* (Paris: Centre national de recherche scientifique, 1982), p. 635.
2. Though Leporius taught certain views that are similar to those of Nestorius, there is no clear evidence that he was a Nestorian before Nestorius. According to Gennadius, *Illustrious Men* (*De viris illustribus*) 59, Leporius was first a monk and later a priest, who began by teaching Pelagianism and added to that various errors in christology. See also John Cassian, *The Incarnation* (*De incarnatione*) I, 2, 4-5, for his account of Leporius' errors and his public correction of them.
3. See 1 Thes 5:14.
4. See Phil 2:6.
5. See Jn 5:18.

the Trinity, something that is certainly foreign to the soundness of the creed and the Catholic truth. With the help of the Lord, we instructed him as best we could *in a spirit of gentleness* (Gal 6:1), especially since, when he gave this counsel, *God's chosen vessel* (Acts 9:15) added, *with an eye on yourself lest you be tempted* (Gal 6:1), for fear that certain persons would rejoice at having made spiritual progress to the point that they thought that they could not be tempted like human beings. And he added the statement conducive to salvation and productive of peace that we should carry one another's burdens, because in that way, most beloved and honorable brothers, we shall fulfill the law of Christ.[6] *For whoever thinks that he is important, though he is nothing, misleads himself* (Gal 6:2-3).

2. But we would perhaps have been unable to complete his correction if you had not previously condemned his errors. It is our same Lord and physician who, using his vessels and ministers, said, *I will strike, and I will heal* (Dt 32:39). Through you he struck a proud man; through us he healed a sorrowful man. The same governor and manager of his house through you tore down what was badly constructed and through us built up what needed to be constructed. The same hardworking farmer through you uprooted the barren and harmful trees on his land and through us also planted useful and fruitful ones. Let us, therefore, give glory not to ourselves but to the mercy of him who holds us and our words in his hand.[7] And just as we have humbly praised your ministry toward this son of ours whom we mentioned above, so may Your Holiness also be grateful for our ministry. With a fatherly and brotherly heart, then, welcome the man who has been corrected by us with merciful gentleness, just as we welcomed him when he was rebuked by you with merciful severity. For, though you did one thing and we did another, one love, nonetheless, did what was necessary for our brother's salvation. One God, therefore, did it, because *God is love* (1 Jn 4:8.16).

3. Hence, just as he was welcomed by us through his presence, so let him be welcomed by you through this letter. We certainly thought that we should sign this letter with our own hand, testifying to its authenticity.[8] Once admonished, he of course saw that God had become man, because *the Word was made flesh* (Jn 1:14) *and the Word was God* (Jn 1:1), and the apostle taught that he became man not by losing what he was but by assuming what he was not. For *he emptied himself* not by losing the nature of God but *by receiving the nature of man* (Phil 2:6-7). For, when he refused to admit that God was born of a virgin, that God was crucified and endured other human sufferings, he was afraid that the divinity would be believed to have been changed in the man or corrupted by uniting with

---

6. See Gal 6:2.
7. See Dt 33:3.
8. The bishops refer to *Leporius' Statement of his Correction or Satisfaction* (*Libellus emendationis sive satisfactionis Leporii*) PL 31, 1221-1232.

the man. This was a pious fear but a careless error. He piously saw that the divinity could not be changed, but he carelessly presumed that the Son of Man could be separated from the Son of God so that the one would not be the other and so that one would be Christ and the other would not be or that there would be two Christs. But after he recognized that the Word of God, that is, the only begotten Son of God, had become man in such a way that neither was changed into the other, but that, with each remaining in its own substance, God endured human sufferings in the man in such a way that he retained in himself his divinity unimpaired, without any fear he confessed Christ as God and man and he feared the addition of a fourth person in the Trinity more than that loss to the substance in the divinity. We do not doubt that Your Charity will gratefully accept this correction of his and make it known to those for whom his error was a scandal. For those who came to us along with him were also corrected and healed with him, as you find expressed by their signatures, which were signed in our presence. There remains for you who were gladdened over the salvation of a brother to be so good as to gladden us in return by the reply of Your Beatitude. We hope, most beloved and honorable brothers, that you are well in the Lord and are mindful of us.

Letter 220

Toward the end of 427 Augustine wrote to Boniface, the count of Africa, to whom he also wrote Letters 185 and 189, the fragment listed as Letter 185A, and Letter 17*. In the present letter Augustine exhorts Boniface to place little value on the things of this world and to follow the example of Christ (paragraph 1). Boniface has many who can counsel him in relation to his life in the world; Augustine wants to counsel him about his life in relation to God (paragraph 2). He asks him what could have so drastically changed his resolve. For, after the death of his wife, Boniface had wanted to live a life of continence as a servant of God, though Augustine had then argued that he was needed to fight the barbarians in order to maintain peaceful conditions for the churches of Africa (paragraph 3). Augustine tells Boniface that he was astonished at his subsequent marriage and his involvement with concubines after he had been summoned to the imperial court in Ravenna (paragraph 4). He urges Boniface to do penance. Though Augustine cannot judge the justice of Boniface's quarrel with the imperial court, he insists that Boniface's sins stem from his love of this world (paragraph 5).

Augustine warns Boniface that he is surrounded by men who are motivated mainly by worldly cravings and that he can counter such cravings only by acting vigilantly against the concupiscences of the world, which do not come from God (paragraph 6). Furthermore, the barbarians, whom Boniface had once held in check, are now running rampant in Africa (paragraph 7). Augustine tells Boniface that he cannot blame such evils on those who have done him harm and that he must repay neither evil with evil nor good with evil (paragraph 8). If Boniface were to ask Augustine's advice about his worldly problems, he would tell him not to love the world but to conquer his worldly desires (paragraph 9). And in order to do this, he must pray for God's help in his fight against interior and spiritual enemies (paragraph 10). In order to attain immortality and eternal peace, Boniface should give alms, pray, fast, and make good use of the good things of this world (paragraph 11). If Boniface had not been married, Augustine would have recommended that he live a life of continence. Instead, he asks him at least to preserve marital chastity and to love God until the time when he might be able to realize his former ideal (paragraph 12).

Augustine sends greetings to Boniface, his lord and his son, who is worthy to be protected and guided by the mercy of God, for his present and eternal well-being.

1. I could never have found a more trustworthy man and one who had easier access to your presence to carry my letter than the Lord has now offered me. I mean the servant and minister of Christ, the deacon Paul, a man most dear to both of us. For I wanted to say something to you not on behalf of the power or the position of honor you have in this evil world nor on behalf of the health of your corruptible and mortal flesh, because that is passing and uncertain however long

it lasts, but on behalf of the salvation that Christ promised us. He was disgraced and crucified here in order to teach us to contemn rather than to love the goods of this world and to love and to hope for from him what he revealed in his resurrection. For *he rose from the dead and dies no more, and death will no longer have dominion over him* (1 Cor 15:53).

2. I know that you do not lack persons who love you in accord with the life of this world and who give you counsel in accord with it that is at times useful and at other times useless. After all, they are human beings, and they are as wise as they can be for the present moment, but they do not know what may happen the next day. But it is not easy for anyone to offer you advice in accord with God, lest your soul perish, not because you lack persons who might do this but because it is difficult to find an occasion when they might be able to say these things to you. For I have always wanted to but have never found the place or the time to do with you what I ought to do with a man I love greatly in Christ. You know my condition, however, which you saw when you were so good as to come to Hippo, for I was scarcely able to speak, exhausted as I was by bodily weakness. Now then, my son, listen to me at least as I speak to you by this letter, which I could never have sent you amid the dangers you were facing, since I had in mind the danger to its bearer and wanted to avoid having my letter come into the hands of the wrong people. Hence, I ask you to pardon me if you think that I was more fearful than I ought to have been; I have, nonetheless, stated why I was afraid.

3. Listen to me, then, or rather listen to the Lord our God through the ministry of my weakness. Recall what sort of a man you were when your first wife of pious memory was still alive, how you held in horror the vanity of this world soon after her death, and how you desired to become a servant of God. We know, we are witnesses to what you said to us at Tubunae[1] about your thoughts and desires. Brother Alypius and I were alone with you. I do not think, after all, that the earthly worries with which you were filled had such power that they could wipe this completely from your memory. For example, you wanted to give up completely the public life in which you were involved and to devote yourself to holy leisure and to live the life that the servants of God, the monks, live. But what held you back from doing this except that you considered, when we pointed it out, how much what you were doing was benefitting the churches of Christ? You were acting with this intention alone, namely, that they might lead *a quiet and tranquil life*, as the apostle says, *in all piety and chastity* (1 Tm 2:2), defended from the attacks of the barbarians. But you also wanted to seek nothing from this world except what would be necessary for sustaining your life and that of your family, while you were girded with the belt of a most chaste continence and, in

---

1. Tubunae was a town in the center of Numidia.

the midst of bodily weapons, were armed more safely and more strongly with the weapons of the spirit.

4. While, then, we were rejoicing that you had this resolve, you crossed the sea and took a wife.[2] But crossing the sea was a matter of obedience that, according to the apostle, you owed to higher authorities;[3] on the other hand, you would not have taken a wife if you had not abandoned the continence you had undertaken and been conquered by concupiscence. After I found this out, I admit, I was dumbfounded in amazement. The fact that I heard that you refused to marry her unless she first became Catholic eased my sorrow to some extent, and yet the heresy of those who deny the true Son of God has been so influential in your home that your daughter was baptized by them.[4] Now, if what was reported to us is not false—though I wish it were false—namely, that even young women consecrated to God have been rebaptized by these heretics, with what great fountains of tears should we not bewail so great an evil? People also say, though they may be lying, that a wife was not enough for you but that you defiled yourself by affairs with various concubines.

5. What shall I say about these many and grave sins that are known to all and that you committed after you were married? You are a Christian; you have a heart; you fear God. Consider for yourself what I do not want to say, and you will discover the great sins for which you ought to do penance. For the sake of your penance I believe that God will spare you and set you free from all dangers in order that you may repent as you ought. But I wish that you would listen to the words of scripture: *Do not be slow to turn to the Lord, and do not postpone it from day to day* (Sir 5:10). Of course you say that you have a just case of which I am not the judge, because I cannot hear both sides.[5] But whatever your reason may be, which there is no need to investigate or to argue about now, can you deny before God that you would not have gotten into this mess if you had not loved the good things of this world, which, like the servant of God whom we had earlier known you to be, you ought to have held in contempt and considered worthless? You ought to have accepted them, when offered, in order to put them to pious use, but not to have sought them when they were denied or given to others so that on their account you would be dragged into this mess. As a result, when you love vanity, sins are committed, a few by you, but many on account of

---

2. Boniface's second wife was Placida, a wealthy Arian.

3. See Rom 13:1.

4. Augustine refers to Arianism, which in its Homoian form was still influential, especially in military circles. Homoian Arianism held that the Son was like the Father but less than the Father.

5. Boniface rebelled against the military forces loyal to the empress Gallia Placida, and on this account he was summoned to the imperial court. Augustine refers to the justice of the case that Boniface has with the imperial court.

you, and when you fear those evils that are harmful for a short time, if they really *are* harmful, evils are committed that are truly harmful for eternity.

6. Who does not see (to say just one thing about these evils) that many persons flock around you to protect your power and well-being, and that, even if they are all loyal to you and you fear no treachery from any of them, they still certainly desire to attain by means of you those goods that they too do not desire in a godly but in a worldly way? And in this manner you, who ought to have reined in and quieted your own cravings, are forced to satisfy those of others. In order to do this, you have to do many things that are displeasing to God, nor are such cravings satisfied in that way. For they are more easily curtailed in those who love God than they are ever satisfied in those who love the world. For this reason divine scripture says, *Do not love the world nor those things that are in the world. If anyone loves the world, the love of the Father is not in him. For everything that is in the world is the concupiscence of the flesh and the concupiscence of the eyes and the pride of life; these do not come from the Father but from the world. And the world passes away along with its concupiscence, but he who does the will of God remains for eternity, just as God remains for eternity.* (1 Jn 2:15-17) When, therefore, will you be able, with so many armed men whose ferocity you fear while you coddle their craving, when, I say, will you be able I do not say to satisfy the desires of those who love the world, since that is in no way possible, but to feed them to some degree so that everything is not lost to an even further extent, unless you do what God forbids, while he threatens those who do it? On this account you see that so many things are destroyed that one can scarcely find anything of any worth to steal.

7. What am I to say about the plundering of Africa that the African barbarians carry out with no opposition, while you are tied up in your difficulties and make no arrangement by which this disaster might be averted? But who would have believed, who would have feared that, with Boniface as head of the imperial bodyguards[6] and stationed in Africa as count of Africa with so great an army and such great power, who as a tribune had pacified all those peoples by battling them and terrifying them with a few allies,[7] the barbarians would now have become so venturesome, would have made such advances, would have ravaged, robbed, and devastated such large areas full of people? Who did not say, when you assumed power as count, that the barbarians of Africa would not only be subdued but would even be tributaries to the Roman state? And now you see how the hope of the people has turned in the opposite direction, nor is there need to

---

6. Boniface had attained this position in 415; he had become the count of Africa in 423 and held that rank until 427.

7. In approximately 417 Boniface had defeated various Berber tribes that had invaded the south of Numidia.

speak with you any longer about this, because you can imagine these events more easily than we can state them.

8. But you may perhaps reply to this that we should instead blame this upon those who have wronged you, who have given you not a reward comparable to your acts of service but just the opposite. I myself cannot hear and adjudicate these cases; rather look at and examine your own case, which you know that you have not with any human beings but with God, because you live as a believer in Christ and ought to fear to offend him. Now I turn my eyes instead to higher courts because human beings ought to attribute it to their own sins that Africa is suffering such great evils. I would, nonetheless, not want you to belong to the number of those by whom God scourges the evil and the unjust with the temporal punishments he chooses. For he reserves for the unjust, if they are not corrected, eternal punishments, and he makes just use of their malice to inflict temporal evils on others. But pay attention to God; consider Christ, who gave such great goods and suffered such great evils. All who desire to belong to his kingdom and to live forever happily with him and under him love even their enemies, do good to those who hate them, and pray for those from whom they suffer persecution.[8] And if they ever use a harsh severity in defense of discipline, they still do not lose their most sincere love. If, then, the Roman empire has given you good things, albeit earthly and transitory ones, because it is earthly, not heavenly, and cannot give save what it has in its control — if, then, it has conferred good things upon you, do not return evil for good. But if it has imposed evils upon you, do not repay evil with evil.[9] Which of these two it may be I do not wish to examine, nor am I able to judge. I speak to a Christian. Do not give back evil in exchange for good nor evil in exchange for evil.

9. You may perhaps say to me, "In such a mess what do you want me to do?" If you are asking me for advice in terms of this world's standards about how to save this transitory well-being of yours and how to preserve this power and wealth that you now have, or how to add even more to it, I do not know what I should reply to you.[10] These uncertain matters do not, of course, admit certain advice. If you consult me in terms of God's standards for fear that your soul may perish and if you fear the words of the Truth who says, *What does it profit anyone to gain the whole world and suffer the loss of his soul?* (Mt 16:26; Mk 8:36; Lk 9:25) I certainly have something to say. I have advice for you to listen to. But what need is there for me to say anything else than what I said above? *Do not love the world nor those things that are in the world. If anyone loves the world, the love of the Father is not in him, because everything that is in the world is the concupiscence of the flesh and the concupiscence of the eyes and the pride of life.*

---

8. See Mt 5:44; Lk 6:27-28.
9. See Rom 12:17; 1 Thes 5:15; 1 Pt 3:9.
10. See Terence, *The Eunuch* (*Eunuchus*) 57-63.

*These do not come from the Father but from the world. And the world is passing
away along with its concupiscence. But one who does the will of God remains for
eternity, as God also remains for eternity.* (1 Jn 2:15-17) There is my advice;
take it and act upon it. Here let it be seen whether you are a man of courage;
conquer the cravings by which this world is loved; do penance for past sins,
when you were conquered by these cravings and dragged through desires that
were not good. If you accept this advice, if you hold onto it and follow it, you will
both come to those certain goods and live among these uncertain goods while
saving your soul.

10. But you may perhaps ask me again how you can do this when you are
involved in such great troubles from this world. Pray courageously, and say to
God what you have in the psalm, *Rescue me from my troubles* (Ps 25:17). For
these troubles come to an end when these cravings are conquered. God has heard
your prayers and ours for you that you might be set free from so many and such
great dangers of visible and bodily wars, in which only this life, which will end at
some time, is at risk, but the soul does not perish if it is not held captive by evil
cravings. He will hear your prayers in order that you may invisibly and spiritually conquer your interior and invisible enemies, that is, those cravings, and in
that way may use this world like one who is not using it,[11] so that you may
produce good things from its goods and not become bad. For those goods are
also good, nor are they given to human beings by anyone else but him who has
power over all things in heaven and on earth. But they are given even to good
people lest they be thought to be bad, and they are also given to bad people lest
they be thought to be great goods or the highest ones. So, too, they are taken
away both from good people in order to test them and from bad people in order to
torment them.

11. After all, who does not know, who is so stupid, as not to see that the health
of this mortal body, the strength of its corruptible members, victory over human
enemies, temporal honor and power, and these other earthly goods are given to
both good people and bad people and are taken away from both good people and
bad people? But the salvation of the soul, along with the immortality of the body,
the strength of righteousness, victory over enemy desires, and glory, honor, and
peace for eternity are given only to the good. Love these; desire these; seek these
in every way. For the sake of acquiring and obtaining these, give alms; pour forth
prayers; practice fasting as much as you can without injury to the body. But do
not love those earthly goods, no matter how great an abundance of them you
have. Use them so that you may produce much good from them, but do no evil on
account of them. All such things will, of course, perish, but good works do not
perish, even when they are produced from goods that perish.

11. See 1 Cor 7:31.

12. For, if you did not have a wife, I would say to you what we also said at Tubunae, namely, that you should live in the holiness of continence. I would add what we then forbade you to do, namely, that you should withdraw yourself from these military matters to the extent that you can do so without prejudicing a peaceful society and that in the company of the saints you should be free for that life for which you then wanted to be free, that life in which the soldiers of Christ fight in silence not to kill human beings but to do battle against *the princes and powers and spirits of wickedness* (Eph 6:12), that is, against the devil and his angels.[12] For the saints conquer these enemies whom they cannot see, and yet they conquer those whom they do not see by conquering what they feel. But your wife prevents me from exhorting you toward this life, and without her permission you may not live a life of continence. For, though you ought not to have married her after those words you spoke at Tubunae, she nonetheless married you innocently and in good faith, without knowing about the commitment you made. And I wish that you could persuade her to live a life of continence in order that you might not be prevented from rendering to God what you know you owe him. But if you cannot get her to do this, at least observe marital chastity, and ask God, who will rescue you from your troubles, that you may be able at some point to do what you cannot now do. But do not love the world; in that way you will love God so that you might keep faith and seek peace even in war, if it is necessary that you be involved in it. Your wife either does not prevent you, my dearest son, or should not prevent you from performing good actions by means of the goods of the world and from not performing evil actions on account of the goods of the world.

Love commanded me to write these things to you, my most beloved son; by that love I love you by God's standards, not by those of the world. For, bearing in mind the words of scripture, *Rebuke a wise man, and he will love you; rebuke a fool, and he will go on to hate you* (Prv 9:8, LXX), I certainly ought not to have thought you a fool but a wise man.

---

12. See Mt 25:41.

Letter 221

Toward the end of 427 Quodvultdeus, a deacon in the church of Carthage and subsequently bishop of Carthage, wrote to Augustine, asking him to compose a list of all the heresies that had sprung up against the Christian faith since the time of Christ. Quodvultdeus was not a man who would take no for an answer and he eventually persuaded Augustine to write the work entitled *Heresies*, which in its first part lists and briefly describes all the heresies of the Christian era. The second part which was to discuss what makes one a heretic was never completed. Quodvultdeus tells Augustine that the benevolence of Augustine gives him confidence in making his request (paragraph 1). He then asks for a catalogue of all the heresies against the Christian religion that would include what they held and how they are to be dealt with (paragraph 2). He goes on to explain that he wants a handy manual that would serve to instruct the ignorant and be a reminder for the better educated (paragraph 3). In closing, he pleads with Augustine to produce this work for the good of the Church (paragraph 4).

The deacon Quodvultdeus sends greetings to Bishop Augustine, his rightly venerable lord and truly most blessed father.

1. I long hesitated, and several times I postponed these bold requests of mine. But the benevolence of Your Beatitude, which is so well known to all, has been, as the expression goes, my main source of confidence. As long as I bear it in mind, I am more afraid that the Lord would judge me proud for not asking, idle for not seeking, and lazy for not knocking.[1] For myself I believe that the mere desire of my will would be enough, even if I were unable to attain its reward. But I am certain that your holy mind, which Christ holds in his possession, is ready not merely to open the door of God's word[2] for all those who desire it, as heavenly grace has opened it for Your Reverence, but is also ready to persuade the reluctant so that they do not hesitate to enter. Hence I will not interrupt Your Reverence's work with a long and unnecessary plea but will briefly indicate the heart of my request.

2. From my own experience I know that some of the clergy, even in this vast city, are uneducated, and I offer for the consideration of Your Holiness the great benefit that would come to the whole of the order of clerics from what I ask. For I am confident, my rightly venerable lord and truly most blessed father, that I, though unworthy, will gain this privilege for all who have a claim upon your spiritual labors. I therefore beseech Your Goodness to deign to explain, from the time that the Christian religion received the name of the heritage promised it, what heresies have existed and now exist, what errors they have introduced and

---

1. See Mt 7:7.
2. See Col 4:3.

now introduce, what they have held and now hold in opposition to the Catholic Church concerning the faith, the Trinity, baptism, penance, Christ as man, Christ as God, the resurrection, the Old and New Testaments, and absolutely every point on which they disagree with the truth. Please explain which heresies have baptism and which do not, and after which of them the Church baptizes, though she does not rebaptize. Please explain how she receives those who come to her, and what response she makes to each of them in terms of law, authority, and reason.

3. Let Your Beatitude not suppose that I am so foolish as not to see how many large volumes would be needed to address all these questions. I am not asking you to do all this now for the first time, for I have no doubt that it has already been done many times. I ask that you briefly, succinctly, and summarily set forth the opinions of each heresy and add what the Catholic Church holds in opposition to them, in a single handbook, as it were, drawn from all of them, to the extent that that may suffice for instruction. If anyone wishes to know some objection or refutation at greater length, more fully, and more clearly, he might be referred to the extensive and magnificent volumes in which others, and especially Your Reverence, have done this, as we all know. But such an aide-mémoire will, I think, suffice for both the learned and the uneducated, for those with leisure and for those who are busy, as well as for those who have been raised from whatever background to some level of ministry in the Church. A person who has read many books will have them briefly called to mind, and an ignorant person will be instructed by this compendium. Thus they will know what to hold and what to reject, what to avoid doing and what to go ahead and do. Perhaps, if I am correct, even this small work against the evil minds and the deceitful tongues of slanderers[3] will not fail, despite your other great works, to be a jewel in your crown. Thus, those who had an open field for slander will be fenced in on all sides by the strong boundaries of the faith and herded together by all kinds of prods from the truth. They may even suddenly be struck down by this one multifaceted spear so that they no longer dare to breathe forth their deadly breath.

4. I see what a burden I am to a holy old man who has better things to think of and more important affairs to manage, while suffering the body's complaints. But I beg you by Christ the Lord, who has granted you a generous share in his wisdom, to bestow this favor on the unlearned of the Church. For you admit that you owe it both to the wise and to the foolish. After all, you will rightly and justly say, *See, I have not toiled for myself alone, but for all who seek the truth* (Sir 24:47). I could still offer many supplicant entreaties and summon the unlettered masses to my support, but I prefer to enjoy your answer rather than to keep you busy reading my letter.

---

3. See Ps 11:3-4; 16:1; 30:19.

Letter 222

Soon after having received the previous letter Augustine replied to Quodvultdeus. He first explains how difficult it would be to write the sort of book that Quodvultdeus is asking of him (paragraph 1). Furthermore, he points out that there are works by Philaster of Brescia and Epiphanius of Salamis which already correspond to Quodvultdeus's request and which Augustine offers to send to Carthage (paragraph 2). Finally, he commends to Quodvultdeus the bearer of the letter and asks the deacon to intercede on his behalf (paragraph 3).

Augustine sends greetings to his most beloved son and fellow deacon, Quodvultdeus.

1. I received the letter of Your Charity in which you asked me with a most ardent zeal to write something brief on all the heresies that have emerged against the teaching of the Lord since his coming. As soon as I found the opportunity, I wrote back through Philocalus, my son, a prominent citizen of Hippo, explaining how difficult this would be.[1] Once again I have the opportunity to write you, and I am briefly going to explain the difficulty of such a work.

2. A certain Philaster,[2] bishop of Brescia, whom I myself saw with the saintly Ambrose of Milan, wrote a book on this subject. In it he included those heresies that existed among the Jewish people before the Lord's coming, and he listed twenty-eight of them and one hundred and twenty-eight after the Lord's coming. Epiphanius,[3] bishop of Cyprus, who was highly esteemed for his teaching of the Catholic faith, also wrote on this subject in Greek. He too gathered heresies from both periods and put together eighty. Although both of them intended to do what you ask of me, you see how widely they differ on the number of the sects during these times. That, of course, would not have happened if one had not considered a heresy what the other did not. After all, we should not suppose that Epiphanius was ignorant of some heresies that Philaster knew, since Epiphanius was by far the more eminent scholar. We should rather say that Philaster had missed many, if Epiphanius had gathered more and Philaster fewer. Of course, both did not have the same view on the question under discussion, namely, what heresy is. Indeed, it is very difficult to define it, and we should therefore be cautious when

---

1. Augustine alludes to a previous letter sent to Quodvultdeus by Philocalus. That letter, as Quodvultdeus notes in Letter 223, 1, did not arrive.
2. Philaster's *Book of Diverse Heresies* (*Liber diversarum haeresion*) was a principal source for Augustine's *Heresies*.
3. Epiphanius of Salamis (c. 310 to c. 403) wrote the *Panarion*, or *Medicine Chest*, a work against heresies, which someone else summarized as *The Recapitulation* (*Anacephalaiosis*); it was Augustine's principal source for the first fifty-seven heresies he lists.

we try to count them all so that we do not omit some, though they are heresies, and include others, though they are not. Consider, then, whether I ought not to send you the book of the saintly Epiphanius; after all, I think that he spoke with more learning than Philaster. It could be more easily and suitably translated into Latin at Carthage, and thus you might instead present to us what you are asking from us.

3. I highly commend the bearer of this letter. He is a subdeacon of our diocese, but from the estate of Orontus, a respected man and a dear friend of ours. On behalf of the bearer and on behalf of his father, by whom he has been adopted, I have written to Orontus. When you have read this letter, I beg you, in your kindness as a Christian, to help them by your intercession before the man I have mentioned. I have also sent with him a man of the Church lest he have difficulty in approaching Your Holiness. For I have been quite worried about him, and the Lord will free me, I hope, from this worry by the help of Your Charity. I also ask that you do not delay in writing back concerning the status in the Catholic faith of that Theodosius who turned in some Manichees and of those persons who we thought were corrected after having been turned in by him. Also, if you have perchance heard of the passing of any holy bishops, let me know about it. God keep you.

Letter 223

Soon after receiving the previous letter Quodvultdeus again wrote to Augustine, asking once more for a catalogue of heresies against the Christian faith. He tells Augustine that such a work will be beneficial to the whole Church (paragraph 1). He worries that the works of Philaster and Epiphanius either do not include everything that he wants or are too long, and in any case they could not have included heresies that arose after their time (paragraph 2). Finally, he warns Augustine that he is going to persist in his request (paragraph 3).

The deacon Quodvultdeus sends greetings to his rightly venerable lord and truly most blessed and holy father Augustine.

1. I received one memorandum from Your Reverence, which you deigned to send me through the hands of a cleric. The letter that Your Beatitude indicated had been sent earlier through the honorable man Philocalus has not yet arrived here. Although I have always been aware of my own sins, yet I clearly recognize now that my person is an obstacle to the whole Church for acquiring the favor I have asked. But I am utterly confident, my rightly venerable lord and truly most blessed holy father, that he who has deigned to wipe out the sins of the human race by the grace of his only Son will not allow my sins to cause the destruction of all. Rather, he will make his grace superabundant where sin has abounded.[1] I did not speak before without knowledge of the difficulty of the work that I humbly asked Your Beneficence to give us for instructing the unlearned, but I counted in all honesty upon the richness of the divine source that the Lord has given you.

2. For, even if we find that the venerable bishops Philaster and Epiphanius[2] wrote something of the sort—a fact which has, among other things, indeed like everything, escaped my notice—still I do not think that they observed such care and diligence that they added responses and included the practices contrary to each and every opinion. Moreover, each of their works, such as it may be, probably does not have the brevity that I want. It is also useless to offer Greek eloquence to a man like me who am not learned in Latin. I have, after all, asked not merely for advice but also for help. But why should I remind Your Reverence about not only the difficulty but even the obscurity of translators, since you yourself can judge this better and fully? Added to this is the fact that some heresies are found to have arisen after the deaths of those men, and they could make no mention of these.

---

1. See Rom 5:20.
2. See the previous letter for the works of Philaster and Epiphanius.

3. For these reasons I take refuge in the special patronage of Your Piety, and I appeal in my own words, but with the desire of all, to your holy and pious heart, which is ready to be merciful. Having considered the text of my earlier letter, do not refuse me the bread of Africa pure of any foreign flavors. To the one who is knocking late and suffering hunger you will not deny the bread of Africa flavored also with the heavenly manna, which our province has come to regard as outstanding. For I will certainly not stop knocking until you grant it. Thus tireless persistence may win what special privilege cannot, for I have none of the latter.[3]

---

3. See Lk 11:5-8.

Letter 224

Soon after receiving the previous letter Augustine again wrote to Quodvultdeus, informing him that he would write the work on heresies that Quodvultdeus had requested.

Augustine sends greetings to his sincerely most beloved lord, brother, and fellow deacon, Quodvultdeus.

1. Since this opportunity for writing has been afforded me by a priest of Fussala, whom I commend to Your Charity, I reviewed the letter in which you ask that I write something on the heresies that have been able to arise from the time when the Lord's coming in the flesh was first preached. I did this in order to see whether I ought to begin this work now and send you a part of it so that you might see that its difficulty is greater in proportion to the brevity with which you want me to carry it out. But I was not able to do even this, since I was prevented by the sort of unexpected worries that I could not ignore, for they distracted me even from the work that I had in hand.[1]

2. I am referring to my response to the eight books of Julian, which he published after the four to which I had already responded.[2] Our brother Alypius[3] obtained them when he was in Rome, but he had not yet copied them all. He did not want to pass up the chance of sending me five books, and he promised that he would soon send me the other three. He was most insistent that I not delay in answering them. Because of his insistence I was forced to go more slowly with the work I was doing. In order not to neglect either task, I worked at one during the day and at the other at night, to the extent that I was spared from other tasks which continue to come to me from all sides. But I was engaged upon a task that was quite necessary, for I was reviewing my writings.[4] And if there was anything in them that I found offensive or that might offend others, I at times corrected them and at other times defended them, explaining how they should or could be read. I had already completed two volumes in which I reviewed all my books. I was unaware of their number and have found there are two hundred and

---

1. Augustine offers no clue as to the nature of these worries; the work he has in hand is clearly the answer to Julian of Eclanum.
2. Augustine refers to Julian of Eclanum's *To Florus* (*Ad Florum*). Death prevented Augustine from completing his *Unfinished Work in Answer to Julian*. He had already answered Julian's four books *To Turbantius* (*Ad Turbantium*) in the six books of his *Answer to Julian*.
3. Alypius was Augustine's friend from boyhood and was at this point bishop of Thagaste and also active in Rome.
4. Augustine was writing *The Revisions*, in which he reviewed and commented on each of his books.

thirty-two.[5] The letters remain, and then the sermons for the people, which the Greeks call "homilies."[6] I had already read the majority of the letters, but I still had not dictated anything on them when these books of Julian began to occupy me. I have begun to reply to the fourth of them. When I have finished it and have replied to the fifth, if the other three have not arrived, I plan, if God wills, to begin what you ask for. I will work on both of these projects at the same time, this work and the revision of my writings, devoting the night to one and the day to the other.

3. I am communicating this to Your Holiness so that you will beg the Lord's help for me with an ardor that is as great as your desire to receive what you ask of me, so that I may satisfy your desire, my lord and sincerely most beloved brother, and benefit those whom you think it will help. Again I commend to you the bearer of this letter and the business that has led him to make the journey. Since you know the person with whom he must deal, I beg you not to be slow to help. We cannot, after all, abandon such people in their troubles, for they are not only our tenants but—what is more—our brothers and come under our care in the love of Christ. May God keep you.

---

5. Augustine distinguishes books (*libri*) from works (*opera*). *The City of God*, for example, is one work but contains twenty-two books.
6. Augustine reveals that he intended that his *Revisions* include his letters and his homilies so that they would have contained more than the two books we now have.

Letter 225

In 428 or 429 Prosper of Aquitaine wrote to Augustine concerning the objections raised to Augustine's teaching on grace and predestination by the monks of Marseilles. His letter, along with Letter 226 from Hilary, a Gallic layman, led Augustine to write *The Predestination of the Saints* and *The Gift of Perseverance*. Prosper, who later became secretary to Pope Leo the Great and almost certainly wrote *The Calling of All the Nations (De vocatione omnium gentium)*,[1] appeals for help to Augustine as a stalwart defender of the faith against the teachings of heretics (paragraph 1). He explains why the monks in Marseilles hold views contrary to those of Augustine on God's calling of the elect and tells Augustine that his *Rebuke and Grace* has not resolved the problem for some of them (paragraph 2). He summarizes the position of the monks, emphasizing their opposition to Augustine's teaching on predestination and their claim that it runs counter to the teaching of earlier Fathers (paragraph 3). Some of the monks hold a position quite close to that of the Pelagians insofar as they locate grace in the free choice with which human beings are created and by which they can choose either good or evil (paragraph 4). Regarding infants who die with or without having received baptism, they hold that God chooses for eternal life those who he foreknows would have chosen to be baptized and would have lived good lives if they had lived longer (paragraph 5). They insist that Jesus Christ died for all human beings and that all human beings are offered the grace of rebirth, though many reject it (paragraph 6).

Prosper points out that, by their good lives and by the fact that some of them have been raised to the episcopacy, the monks about whom he is speaking have great authority, so that they present a serious danger for less well-educated persons who hear them (paragraph 7). He lists the points that he wants Augustine to explain fully and clearly (paragraph 8). Finally, Prosper mentions one of the monks who followed Augustine's teaching on everything except on the present issue and urges Augustine to write something to instruct the humble and to rebuke the proud (paragraph 9).

To Augustine, his lord, most blessed bishop and most excellent patron, who is ineffably admirable and worthy of incomparable honor, Prosper sends his greetings.

1. Though I am unknown to you by my appearance, I am, if you recall, known to you by my thoughts and words. For I sent you a letter and received one back from you by the hands of my holy brother, the deacon Leontius.[2] But I am venturing to write to Your Beatitude now as well not merely out of a desire to greet you, as I did then, but out of love for the faith, which is the life of the

---

1. The authorship of the work, which deals with the same controversy in retrospect, has been disputed.
2. The letter to which Prosper refers is not extant.

Church. For, since you keep watch for all the members of the body of Christ with your most vigilant efforts and fight against the plots of heretical teachings with the power of the truth, I thought that I need have absolutely no fear of being a burden or a bother to you in a matter that concerns the salvation of many persons and, for this reason, Your Piety.[3] For I would otherwise consider myself guilty if I did not report to a special protector of the faith those matters that I understand to be extremely dangerous.

2. In the writings of Your Holiness, which you produced against the Pelagian heretics, many of the servants of Christ who dwell in the city of Marseilles think that whatever you discussed concerning the calling of the elect according to God's plan is opposed to the opinion of the Fathers and to the mind of the Church. And though they preferred for some time to blame their own slowness rather than to find fault with what they did not understand, some of them wanted to ask for a clearer and simpler explanation of the writings of Your Beatitude on this point. God's mercy so arranged things that, when similar problems disturbed certain persons in Africa,[4] you published the book *Rebuke and Grace*, which is filled with divine authority. When it was brought to our attention through an unexpected opportunity, we thought that all the complaints of the opposition would be put to rest. For, on all the questions about which Your Holiness was about to be consulted, you replied there as fully and completely as if you were especially concerned to settle those issues that were stirred up among us. After examining this book of Your Beatitude, those who were previously following the holy and apostolic authority of your teaching acquired much greater understanding and instruction, but those who were handicapped by the darkness of their own point of view went off more unfavorably disposed than they had been. There is reason to fear their sharp dissent first on their own account, lest the spirit of the Pelagian impiety mislead such men, who are so renowned and so outstanding in the pursuit of all the virtues. And there is reason to fear, secondly, that certain more simple people, who have a great reverence for these men from having observed their goodness, may judge that what they hear these men maintain, whose authority they follow without question, is perfectly safe for themselves.

3. For the following is what they state and profess: Every human being certainly sinned when Adam sinned, and no one can be saved by his own works but only by rebirth through the grace of God. All human beings without exception have, nonetheless, been offered the reconciliation that is present in the mystery of the blood of Christ, so that whoever chooses to come to the faith and

---

3. See the first paragraph of *The Predestination of the Saints*, where Augustine alludes to Prosper's concern about being a bother to him.
4. Prosper refers to the monks of Hadrumetum for whom he wrote both *Grace and Free Choice* and *Rebuke and Grace*.

to baptism can be saved. God, however, foreknew prior to the creation of the world those who were going to believe or who were going to continue in that faith, which after its reception needs the help of grace, and he predestined for his kingdom those whom he foresaw would, after having been gratuitously called, be worthy of election and would leave this life by a good death. And therefore every human being is admonished by the teaching of God to believe and to act in order that no one may despair of attaining eternal life, since a reward has been prepared for a person's willing devotion.

This plan of God's calling, however, which is said to have separated those who would be chosen and those who would be rejected, either before the beginning of the world or at the creation of the human race, so that in accord with the decision of the creator some were created as vessels of honor and others as vessels of dishonor,[5] both removes from those who have fallen any concern to rise up and offers to the saints an occasion for tepidity. For in both cases toil is useless if one who has been rejected cannot enter the kingdom by any effort and if one who has been chosen cannot fall away by any negligence. For, however they may have acted, nothing else can happen in their regard than what God has determined, and, when hope is uncertain, one cannot hold to a consistent course because, if the choice of God who predestines a person is different, the intention of the person who makes an effort is meaningless. And therefore all effort is removed, and all the virtues are destroyed if God's decision comes before human willing. Under this term "predestination" a necessity founded upon fate is introduced, and God is said to be the creator of different natures, if no one can be other than he was created.[6]

In order to explain more briefly and fully what they hold, these holy men proclaim with great intensity that they accept everything that Your Holiness took from the thought of your opponents and mentioned as objections for yourself in this book or whatever Julian raised as objections on this question and you refuted with great power in the books entitled *Answer to Julian*.[7]

And when we produce in answer to them the writings of Your Beatitude, which you filled with countless and very strong testimonies from the divine scriptures, and when we ourselves construct an argument to trap them on the model of your treatises, they defend their stubbornness by invoking tradition. They also maintain that the passages from the letter of Paul the apostle addressed to the Romans, which are produced to show that grace comes before the merits of the elect, had never been interpreted by anyone in the Church in the sense in

---

5. See Rom 9:18.21.
6. See *The Gift of Perseverance* 8, 19, where Augustine answers the charge that there are different natures of human beings.
7. Prosper alludes to the six books of Augustine's *Answer to Julian*, specifically to book four, chapter 8.

which they are now being interpreted. And when we ask that they interpret them in accord with the meaning of those commentators whom they prefer, they claim that they have found nothing with which they are satisfied and insist that silence should be maintained on those matters whose depth no one can plumb. Ultimately, their whole obstinacy comes down to the point at which they declare that our belief is something opposed to the edification of those who hear it, and so, even if it is true, it should not be brought into the open. For it is dangerous to hand on teachings that should not be accepted, and it involves no danger to pass over in silence ideas that cannot be understood.

4. Certain of them, however, do not wander very far from the paths of the Pelagians. For, when they are forced to acknowledge the grace of Christ which anticipates all human merits—otherwise, if it is repayment for merits, it is called "grace" to no point at all—they want this grace to pertain to the creation of every human being. In creating them the grace of the creator has established each of them with free choice and rationality but without any prior merits, since none of them previously existed. And thus a person could direct his will through distinguishing between good and evil[8] to knowing God and to obeying his commandments and could come to that grace by which we are reborn in Christ, that is, through one's natural ability, by asking, seeking, and knocking, in order to receive, to find, and to enter.[9] For, having made good use of the good of nature, a person would have merited by the help of this initial grace to arrive at the grace of salvation.

They locate the plan of the grace of the one who calls entirely in the fact that God has determined to receive no one into his kingdom except through the sacrament of rebirth and that all human beings are universally called to this gift of salvation either by the natural law or by the written law or by the preaching of the gospel. Thus those become children of God who will to, and those are without excuse who refuse to believe. The justice of God, after all, consists in the fact that those who have not believed perish,[10] but his goodness is evident in the fact that he excludes no one from life but wills that all human beings without any distinction among them *be saved and come to the knowledge of the truth* (1 Tm 2:4).

Here they produce testimonies in which exhortation from the divine scriptures rouses to obedience the wills of human beings who with free choice either do or neglect to do what they are commanded. And they think that it follows that, because a transgressor is said not to have obeyed because he did not will to, a believer is also without a doubt said to have been devout because he willed to be. And each person has as great a power for good as he has for evil, and his mind

8. See Heb 5:14.
9. See Mt 7:7.
10. See Rom 1:20.

directs itself with equal force either to vices or to virtues. And the grace of God cherishes one who seeks the good, while just condemnation follows upon one who pursues evil.

5. Among these points there is raised against them the objection of the countless number of infants who have as yet no wills, no actions of their own. They are set apart in the judgment of God, nonetheless, only by reason of original sin because of which all human beings are likewise born under the condemnation of the first human being. And yet, of those who will be taken from the enjoyment of this life before they can distinguish between good and evil, some will be adopted through rebirth as heirs of the kingdom of heaven, while others will pass without baptism into the company of those meriting eternal death. They say that such infants are lost or saved in accord with how the divine knowledge foresees that they would have been in their later years if they were to have attained the age at which they could have acted. They do not consider that they subject the grace of God, which they want to accompany and not to precede human merits, to those wills that, according to their imaginings, they do not deny are anticipated by grace. But they subject God's election to pretended merits, whatever they might be, inasmuch as, because there are no past merits, they make up future merits which will not exist, and by their new kind of absurdity actions that will not be done are foreknown and those actions that are foreknown are not done.

Of course they think that they can more reasonably defend this foreknowledge of God regarding human merits, in accord with which the grace of God who calls us works, when they turn to the consideration of those nations that in past ages were left to follow their own ways[11] or are even now still lost in the impiety of their old ignorance, nor has any light from either the law or the gospel shone upon them. Insofar, nonetheless, as a door has been opened and a path cleared for its preachers, the people of the nations who sat in darkness and in the shadow of death have seen a great light,[12] and those who were once not a people are now the people of God, and to those to whom he once did not show mercy he has now shown mercy.[13] They say that the Lord foresaw that these people would believe and that each nation received at the proper time the services of teachers when there was going to arise the faith of those with good wills. And the statement that *God wills all human beings to be saved and come to the knowledge of the truth* (1 Tm 2:4) remains unshaken. They are in fact without excuse who could be led to the worship of the one true God by their natural intelligence and have not heard the gospel because they would not have accepted it.

6. They say, moreover, that our Lord Jesus Christ has died for the whole human race and that no one is exempt from the redemption of his blood, even if a

---

11. See Acts 14:15.
12. See Mt 4:16; Is 9:2.
13. See Hos 2:2; Rom 9:25.

person passes the whole of this life with his mind completely estranged from him, for the sacrament of divine mercy belongs to all human beings. And very many are not renewed by it because God foreknows that they do not have the will to be renewed by it. And so, insofar as it pertains to God, eternal life is prepared for all, but insofar as it pertains to the freedom of choice, eternal life is attained by those who have freely believed in God and have received the help of grace by the merit of their belief.

The principal reason which led these people, whose opposition upsets us, to preach such grace, though they previously had a better view, is this: If they admitted that grace comes before all good merits and that grace grants the possibility that good merits exist, they would necessarily have to concede that according to his plan and the counsel of his will, by his hidden judgment but evident action, God creates one vessel for an honorable purpose and another for a dishonorable purpose.[14] For no one is made righteous except by grace, and no one is born except in sin. But they refuse to admit this, and they fear to ascribe to the work of God the merits of the saints.

Nor do they accept the view that the predestined number of the elect can be neither increased nor decreased for fear that the stings of exhortations would have no place in the lives of those who do not believe or who are negligent and that the encouragement to activity or to labor would be useless for one whose striving is going to be frustrated because he is not among the elect. Finally, each person can be called to correct his life and to make progress if he knows that he can be good by his own effort and that his freedom will be assisted by the help of God if he chooses to do what God commands. And so, since in these people who have reached the age of free will there are two factors that produce human salvation, namely, the grace of God and the obedience of the human being, they want obedience to come before grace so that it must be believed that the beginning of salvation comes from the one who is saved and not from the one who saves, and that it is the will of a human being that brings forth the help of divine grace for itself, not grace that subjects to itself the human will.

7. And since we have come to know through the merciful revelation of God and the teaching of Your Beatitude that this view of theirs is most perverse, we can indeed stand firm against believing it, but we are not equal to the authority of those who hold such views. For they surpass us greatly by the merits of their life, and some of them are our superiors because they have recently attained the honor of the highest priesthood,[15] nor has anyone readily dared to oppose the arguments of such eminent persons except a few fearless lovers of perfect grace. As a result the danger has increased along with their dignity not only for the

---

14. See Rom 9:21.
15. Prosper probably refers to Hilary of Lérins, who had recently been elected bishop of Arles, and possibly to Lupus, who became bishop of Troyes in 426 or 427.

people who hear them but also for those very persons to whom the people listen, since reverence for them has either held many back in an unprofitable silence or led them on to a careless agreement. And people regard as most salutary this view that meets with reproach from almost no opponent.

Hence, if the inner life of this great virulence is nourished in these remnants of the Pelagian depravity; if the beginning of salvation is wrongly located in a human being; if the human will is impiously preferred to the will of God, so that a person is helped because he has willed to be and not so that he has such a will because he is helped; if one who is evil from his origin is wrongly believed to initiate the reception of the good not from the highest good but from himself; and if God is pleased by something other than what he himself has given—then grant us the care of Your Piety in this matter, most blessed bishop and best father, to the extent that you can with the help of the Lord. Deign to open up, by explanations that are as clear as possible, what is so obscure and difficult to grasp in these questions.

8. And, first of all, since many do not think that the Christian faith is damaged by this dissent, disclose the great danger that lies in their point of view. Then, explain how free choice is not impeded by this grace that is at work before free choice and at work along with free choice. Also, explain whether the foreknowledge of God remains in accord with God's plan so that those things that he has planned should be accepted as foreknown or whether they vary in accord with different situations and categories of persons. Thus the calls to salvation are different. In those who are saved, though they are not going to perform any action, it seems as if God's plan alone is involved, but, in people who are going to perform some good actions, God's plan can follow upon his foreknowledge. Or is the situation the same in both cases, so that foreknowledge is subject to God's plan in some order, though one cannot divide foreknowledge from God's plan by a temporal distinction? And just as there is no action of any sort whatsoever that divine knowledge does not anticipate, so there is nothing good that has not flowed down from God, its source, into our participation in it. Finally, explain how this preaching of God's plan, by which those who have been predestined for eternal life become believers, is not an obstacle for any of those who need to be exhorted, and how people have no excuse for negligence if they despair of having been predestined.

We also ask you to show us, while you patiently put up with our foolishness, how this question may be resolved, namely, that, when one examines the opinions of earlier teachers on this point,[16] one finds one and the same view in the

---

16. Prosper gives no clue as to the identity of these earlier teachers. The editors of Bibliothèque Augustinienne 24 suggest in a note some possibilities, namely, Origen and John Chrysostom among the Eastern Fathers and Hilary of Poitiers and Ambrose of Milan among the Latin

case of nearly all of them, that is, that they have accepted the plan and predestination of God as based on foreknowledge, so that God has made some persons into vessels of honor and others into vessels of dishonor[17] precisely because he foresaw the end of each person and knew in advance his future willing and action even under the help of grace.

9. When you have untangled all these questions and have also examined many others that with your more penetrating gaze you can see pertain to this issue, we believe and hope not only that our weakness will be strengthened by the support of your arguments but also that those men renowned for their merits and positions of honor, over whom the darkness of this opinion has cast its shadow, will accept the purest light of grace. For Your Beatitude should know that one of them, a man of great authority and of spiritual interests, the saintly Hilary, the bishop of Arles,[18] is an admirer and follower of your teaching in all other respects, and that on this one point where he disagrees with you he has long since wanted to present his views to Your Holiness in writing. But since it is uncertain whether he is going to do this or to what purpose he is going to do it, and since the weariness of all of us is refreshed by the vigor of your love and knowledge under the providence of the grace of God in this present age, instruct the humble and reprove the proud. It is necessary and beneficial to put into writing even what has already been written so that no one may think that a point that is not often discussed is trifling. For they suppose that what does not hurt is healthy, nor do they feel a wound that has been covered over by skin. But they should realize that a wound that has a persistent swelling will have to be lanced.

May the grace of God and the peace of our Lord Jesus Christ give you a crown for all time, and for eternity may it glorify you who progress from virtue to virtue, my lord, most blessed bishop and most excellent patron, who are ineffably admirable and worthy of incomparable honor.

Fathers. For example, in commenting on Mt 22:23, Ambrose says in *Faith* (*De fide*) V, 6, 83: CSEL 78, 246-247: "And then referring to the Father, [Jesus] added, *For whom it has been prepared*, to show that even the Father is not swayed by prayers, but by merits, for God has no favoritism regarding persons. Hence, the apostle also says, *And he also predestined those whom he foreknew*. For he did not predestine them before he had foreknowledge of them; rather, he predestined the rewards of those whose merits he foreknew."

17. See Rom 9:21.
18. There has been some recent question about whether Prosper actually referred to Hilary of Arles or to Helladius, the man to whom John Cassian dedicated his first ten *Conferences*. See the note in Bibliothèque Augustinienne 24, 808, "Sur la mention d'Hilaire, évêque d'Arles, dans la lettre de Prosper." The BA editors simply recount the arguments without accepting the conjecture of "Helladius."

Letter 226

About the same time that the previous letter was written, Hilary, a layman from Gaul, wrote to Augustine about the errors of some monks living in Marseilles and other places in southern Gaul. Hilary tells Augustine that he is going to report to him their teachings that are opposed to the truth (paragraph 1). He explains that these men find that Augustine's position regarding God's choice of the elect renders preaching useless if the human will does not retain some power of its own to respond (paragraph 2). They claim that the gospel is preached to those who God foreknew would believe, and they also appeal to some of Augustine's earlier writings, in which he held that whether or not we believe is up to us (paragraph 3). They hold that predestination amounts only to God's choosing those who he foreknows are going to believe (paragraph 4). Hence they maintain that the practice of exhortation is useless if the will does not retain the power to respond and if a person is already predestined to either reward or punishment (paragraph 5).

These monks also reject Augustine's teaching on the difference between the grace that Adam had and the grace that the saints now receive (paragraph 6). They also deny that the number of those who will be chosen and of those who will be rejected is fixed, and they insist that God wills that absolutely all human beings be saved, though some choose to reject his salvation (paragraph 7). So too, they refuse to use the situation of infants as an example for understanding that of adults, and they point to Augustine's earlier position on the fate of unbaptized infants (paragraph 8).

Hilary asks Augustine to see what measures should be taken with these monks, who follow Augustine's teaching on everything except on this one issue (paragraph 9). Finally, he asks Augustine for a copy of his *Revisions*, when it is completed, and of *Grace and Free Choice*, which he does not as yet have (paragraph 10).

To Augustine, his most blessed lord and father, worthy of being loved with all his heart and of being warmly embraced in Christ, Hilary sends his greetings.

1. When the questions of our opponents cease, we generally find pleasing the inquiries of those who desire to know in order that they may learn even those things that are, without any danger, unknown. Hence I think that you will find quite pleasing the earnestness of our report. For, when it points out certain teachings opposed to the truth according to the presentations of certain people, it aims, not so much for its own sake as for the sake of those people who are upset and who upset others, to remedy this situation through the counsel of Your Holiness, my most blessed lord and father, worthy of being loved with all my heart and of being warmly embraced in Christ.

2. These, therefore, are the ideas that are being discussed at Marseilles as well as in some other places in Gaul, namely, that there is something novel and opposed to the usefulness of preaching in saying that some people will be chosen according to God's plan in such a way that they can neither acquire this election nor hold onto it unless they have been given the will to believe. They think that all the effectiveness of preaching is excluded if one says that there is nothing left in human beings that preaching can arouse. They agree that every human being perished in Adam and that no one can be set free from this perdition by his own choice. But they claim that the following view is in conformity with the truth and suitable for preaching, namely, that, when one proclaims to people who lie prostrate and will never rise up by their own powers the chance to obtain salvation, they attain, by the merit of willing and believing that they can be healed of their disease, both an increase of this faith and, as a result, complete health. Yet they agree that no one can be sufficient by himself to begin, not to mention to complete, any good work, for they do not think that it must be ascribed to some work of their healing that every sick person wills to be healed with a frightened and suppliant will.

For they maintain that the words of scripture, *Believe, and you will be saved* (Rom 10:9), demand of us one of these and offer us the other. That is, we are thereafter given what we are offered on account of what is demanded of us, if we have done it. Hence they think that it follows that someone should offer his faith to God because the will of the creator has given this ability to that person's nature, and they think that no nature has been so corrupted or destroyed that one should not or could not will to be healed. On this account a person either is healed of his disease or, if he is unwilling, is punished along with it. And they claim that grace is not denied if such a will, which seeks so great a physician, though it is itself unable to do anything, is said to precede grace. For they want to interpret the testimonies, such as this one, *As he has given to each a measure of faith* (Rom 12:3), and others like it, in the sense that one who has begun to will is helped, but not in the sense that one's willing is also a gift and that others are excluded from this gift who are equally guilty and who could be set free in a similar way, if that will to believe, which is given to those equally unworthy, were likewise given to them. If, however, a person holds, they say, that there has remained in all human beings at least such a will by which one is able either to reject or to obey <God's call>, they think that one can essentially account for those who have been chosen and for those who have been rejected insofar as each person receives the merit of his own will.

3. But when we ask them why the gospel is preached to some people and in some places and not preached to others and in other places, and why the gospel is now preached to almost all peoples, though it previously was not, just as it is now not preached to some people, they say that it pertains to the foreknowledge of

God that the truth has been preached or is preached to those people at the time and in the place when and where he foreknew that it would be believed. And they claim to prove this not only by the testimonies of other Catholics but even by the somewhat older study of Your Holiness, in which you in fact taught the same grace with just as much truthful clarity. For example, Your Holiness said the following against Porphyry in the question "On the Time of the Christian Religion": "Christ willed to appear to human beings and willed that his teaching be preached when he knew and where he knew that there would be people who would believe in him."[1] And there is the passage from the book on the Letter to the Romans: *Therefore, you say to me, Why does he still complain? For who resists his will?* (Rom 9:19) You say, of course, that "he replied to this question in order that we might understand that men who are spiritual and do not live in accord with their earthly self can grasp the first merits of faith and of unbelief, insofar as by his foreknowledge God chooses those who will believe and condemns those who will not believe, though he does not choose the former on the basis of works and does not condemn the latter on the basis of works. Rather, he gives to the faith of the former so that they do good works and hardens the disbelief of the latter by abandoning them so that they do evil works."[2]

And again in the same work you say a little earlier: "Prior to merit all are equal, and one cannot speak of a choice in things that are completely equal. But since the Holy Spirit is given only to those who believe, God does not choose the works that he himself gives, when he gives the Holy Spirit in order that we may act out of love, but he still chooses faith, because, unless one believes and persists in the will to receive the gift of God, one does not receive that gift, that is, the Holy Spirit, through whom, once love has been poured out, he can do what is good. He does not, therefore, in his foreknowledge choose the works of anyone, which he himself is going to give, but in his foreknowledge he chooses faith so that he chooses one whom he foreknows will believe, and to him he gives the Holy Spirit in order that by doing good works he may also attain eternal life. For the apostle says, *The same God does all things in all people* (1 Cor 12:6). But scripture never says that God believes all things in all people. For the fact that we believe is up to us, while the fact that we do good works is due to him."[3] And there are in the same work other passages that they claim to accept and approve of as in conformity with the truth of the gospel.

4. But they insist that God's foreknowledge, predestination, or plan means only that God foreknew, predestined, or planned to choose those who were

---

1. Letter 102, II, 14.
2. *Commentary on Some Statements in the Letter to the Romans* [Rom 9:15-21]: 62: Pl 35, 2080, or: 54, 14: CSEL 84, 38.
3. *Commentary on Some Statements in the Letter to the Romans* [Rom 9:11-13] 60: PL 35, 2078-2079, or: 52, 12: CSEL 84, 35.

going to believe and that one cannot say with regard to this faith, *What do you have that you have not received?* (1 Cor 4:7) since the ability to believe has remained in the same nature, though damaged, which was originally given as healthy and whole. They accept the words of Your Holiness, namely, that no one perseveres unless he has received the power to persevere, with the qualification that, in those to whom this power is given, it is nonetheless ascribed to their own prior, albeit ineffective, choice, and they say that it is free only to will or not to will to accept any remedy. But they also claim that they detest and condemn it if anyone thinks that any strength has remained in someone by which he can attain healing.

But they do not want this perseverance to be preached if it means that it can neither be merited by prayer nor lost by rebellion. Nor do they want to be referred to the incertitude of God's will since, as they suppose, they clearly have the beginning of their will, however weak it may be, for gaining or losing[4] it.[5] That testimony which you also cited, namely, *He was carried off so that evil would not change his mind* (Wis 4:11), they declare should be omitted as non-canonical. Hence, they accept divine foreknowledge in the sense that persons are to be understood as foreknown on account of the faith they will have, and they hold that no one is given such perseverance that he is not permitted to abandon it, but such perseverance that he can by his will fall away and grow weak.

5. They maintain that the practice of exhortation is useless if one says that nothing is left in a human being that a rebuke can arouse, and they admit that they say that something is present in our nature such that, by the very fact that the truth is preached to someone who does not know it, this should be referred to the benefit of the present grace. For, they say, if people are predestined to each side so that no one can move from the one side to the other, what good does such great insistence upon rebukes from someone else do, if there does not arise from the person if not an integral faith then at least a sorrow over his painful infirmity, or if he is not terrified at the danger of the death he has been shown? For, if a person cannot fear the source of his terror except by the will that he receives, we should not blame him because he does not now have that will. Instead we should blame him in the one and along with the one who long ago did not will this and who merited to incur that damnation along with all his descendants, so that he never willed to desire what was right but always willed to desire what was wrong.[6] If, however, there is any sorrow that arises at the exhortation of one who gives a rebuke, they say that this is the reason why one is rejected and another is

---

4. I have followed the reading in PL of *amittendum* in place of *admittendum* which is found in CSEL.
5. That is, the gift of perseverance.
6. Hillary is referring to Adam.

accepted, and that there is no need to set up two groups to which nothing can be added or from which nothing can be subtracted.

6. Next they dislike the distinction between the grace that was given to the first man and the grace that is now given to all human beings. That is, they dislike the idea that Adam received for perseverance "not the help which made him persevere but the help without which he could not persevere by free choice. But now the saints who have been predestined to the kingdom of God by grace are not given such a help toward perseverance but a help by which they receive perseverance itself, not only so that they cannot persevere without this gift but even so that by this gift they cannot fail to persevere."[7]

They are so upset by these words of Your Holiness that they say that they give human beings grounds for despair. For, according to you, they say, Adam received a help such that he could both remain standing in righteousness and fall away from righteousness, while the saints now receive a help such that they cannot fall away from righteousness. For they either have received such perseverance in willing that they cannot will anything else, or some are abandoned to the point that they either do not attain righteousness or fall away from it if they have attained it. Hence, the usefulness of exhortation or threats, they say, was applicable to Adam's will, which possessed the free power either to remain righteous or to fall away, but not to our will, which involves the rejection of righteousness with an inevitable necessity. The only exception is those people who, though they were created along with the ones who were condemned with the entire mass, were picked to be set free by grace.

Hence these men want the nature of all human beings to differ from that of the first man only insofar as grace, without which he could not have persevered, helped him who willed with the unimpaired strength of his will, while grace not merely raises up the rest who lie prostrate with their strength lost and destroyed but also supports them as they walk, provided that they have faith. Moreover, they contend that whatever has been given to the predestined can be lost or retained by each person's own will, and this would be false if they thought it was true that certain people received that perseverance in such a way that they could not fail to persevere.

7. From this there also comes an idea that they likewise reject. That is, they do not want the number of those who will be chosen and of those who will be condemned to be fixed, and they do not accept as an explanation of this view what you set forth; rather, they hold that God wills that all human beings be saved,[8] and not just those who pertain to the number of the saints but absolutely all human beings without any exception. Nor should one worry that some are

---

7. *Rebuke and Grace* 12, 34.
8. See 1 Tm 2:4.

said to perish against his will. Rather, they say, just as he does not will that anyone sin or abandon righteousness, and yet people continually abandon it against his will and commit sins, so he wills that all human beings should be saved, and yet not all human beings are saved.

They think that the testimonies of scripture concerning Saul or David[9] that you quoted do not have to do with the question concerning exhortation, but they introduce other testimonies which they interpret as commending that grace whereby each person is helped subsequent to his will or toward that calling which is offered to those who are unworthy. They claim that they prove this from passages of your works and from those of others whom it would take a long time to mention.

8. They will not, however, permit us to introduce the situation of infants as a model for adults, and they say that even Your Holiness had touched upon this issue only to the extent that you wanted the question to be left undecided and preferred instead to remain in doubt about their punishments. You remember that you stated this in the third book of *Free Will*, thereby providing them with the occasion for this objection.[10] They do the same thing with regard to the books of others who have some authority in the Church, something which Your Holiness sees offers no small help to these attackers unless we produce stronger proofs or at least ones of equal strength. For in your most wise piety you are well aware of how many there are in the Church who hold a position or move from one position to another on the basis of the authority of certain names.

Finally, when we are all weary, their attack, or rather complaint, turns, with the agreement even of these who do not dare to disapprove of this position, to the question, "What need was there that the hearts of so many simple people be disturbed by the uncertainty of such an argument? For the Catholic faith has been defended no less effectively for so many years without this doctrine," they say, "both against other heretics and especially against the Pelagians, by so many previous books of yours and of others."

9. To confess my deepest desires, I would, my father, have preferred to present to you in person these points and an endless number of other ones or, since I have not merited this, at least to gather up over a longer period of time and send on to you all the points by which these people are upset in order that I might hear to what extent one ought to refute their objections or to tolerate them if they can no longer be refuted. But since neither of these came about in accord with my desire, I preferred to send you these points, which I have grasped as best I could, rather than to be completely silent about the great opposition of certain people.

---

9. See *Rebuke and Grace* 14, 45, where Augustine appeals to 1 Sm 10:25-27 and 1 Chr 12:18 concerning the choices of Saul and David for kingship.

10. See *Free Will* III, 23, 66-68, where Augustine seems to incline toward the view that infants who die without baptism receive neither reward nor punishment in the next life.

Some of them are persons of such rank that the laity must pay them the highest reverence in accord with the custom of the Church. We have in fact taken care to preserve this practice with the help of God in such a way that, when it was necessary, we did not pass over in silence what the few talents we possess have suggested for the statement of this question. But now, as if to alert you, I have raised these points in summary to the extent that the haste of the courier has permitted. It is up to Your Holy Prudence to see what action is needed to overcome or to control the aim of such good and important men. For this purpose I think that it will do little good at this point for you to give an explanation unless you also add the authority that their tirelessly contentious hearts cannot contradict. But I clearly ought not to pass over in silence the fact that they claim to be admirers of Your Holiness in all your words and actions with this one exception. You will have to decide how one ought to put up with their opposition on this point. Do not be surprised that I have expressed some other things otherwise in this letter and added other things than I wrote in my previous letter,[11] for this is their position at present apart from those points which I have perhaps passed over out of haste or forgetfulness.

10. When the books that you are preparing concerning all your works have been published, may we please merit to receive a copy,[12] especially in order that the authority of these books may allow us not to be afraid to keep those passages separate from the reverence due to your name, if there are any passages in your books of which you do not approve. We also do not have your book entitled *Grace and Free Choice*; it remains that we may merit to receive it because we are confident that it is useful for this question.

I do not, however, want Your Holiness to think that I am writing these things as if I am in doubt about those books that you have just published.[13] Let it suffice for me as a punishment that, exiled from the delights of your presence where I drew nourishment from your health-giving breast, I am tormented not only by your absence but also by the stubbornness of certain persons who not only reject what is evident but even find fault with what they do not understand. But I am so free of this idea that I rather consider blameworthy the weakness of mine by which I tolerate such people with too little patience.

But I leave to Your Wisdom, as I said, how you should judge that these matters be dealt with. For I believed that, in virtue of the love that I owe to Christ and to you, it was my duty not to pass over in silence those issues that come into question. Given the grace that we, both little persons as well as great, admire in

---

11. The previous letter is not extant.
12. Hilary refers to Augustine's *Revisions*, which he was writing at the same time that he wrote the works for the monks of Hadrumetum and Marseilles.
13. Hilary probably refers to *Grace and Free Choice* and to *Rebuke and Grace*.

you, we shall most gratefully welcome whatever you choose or are able to say as settled by an authority most beloved and revered by us.

Since, under pressure from the courier, I was afraid that I would either not be able to write everything or would write these things in a less worthy manner, conscious as I am of my abilities, I persuaded a man renowned for his morals, his eloquence, and his zeal to convey to you by his letter all the information he could gather, and I have taken care to send you his letter along with mine. For he is a man of such a caliber that, even apart from this necessity, he should be judged worthy of your knowledge.

The holy deacon Leontius, one of your admirers, sends you abundant greetings along with my parents. May Christ the Lord grant Your Paternity to his Church for many years, and may you be mindful of me, my lord and father.

[*And below:*] I would like Your Holiness to know that my brother, primarily because of whom we left there, has vowed perfect continence to God along with his wife, by her agreement. Hence we ask Your Holiness to be so kind as to pray that the Lord may deign to confirm and preserve this vow in them.

Letter 227

In 428 or 429 Augustine wrote to Alypius, his friend from boyhood and now the bishop of Thagaste, concerning Gabinian, who had recently been baptized, and Dioscorus, a physician who was baptized at the same time and whose conversion required a series of miracles.

Augustine sends greetings to Alypius.[1]

Our brother Paul is safe with us and brings with him the concerns for his affairs, which are going well. The Lord will grant that these concerns may also come to an end. He greets you heartily and reports the joys over Gabinian, because, having been set free from his trial by the mercy of God, he is not only a Christian but also a very good member of the faithful, for he was recently baptized at Easter and carries on his lips and in his heart the grace he received.[2] When shall I ever explain how much I long for him? But you know that I love him. Also Dioscorus, the chief physician of the court, is a Christian believer, having attained grace at the same time. Listen also to how this came about. For only a miracle would bow that neck and tame that tongue. His daughter, who was his sole consolation, was ill, and her illness led to a complete loss of hope for her temporal health; even her father gave up. This is what is being said, then, and it is true, since even before Paul's return Count Peregrinus, a praiseworthy and good Christian man, who was baptized with them at the same time, made this known to me. It is said and proven that that old man was moved to implore the mercy of Christ and bound himself by a vow that he would become a Christian if he saw his daughter in good health. This happened. He pretended ignorance about fulfilling his vow, but God's hand was still upon him.[3] For he was afflicted with a sudden blindness, and it immediately entered his mind what its cause was. He cried out, admitting it, and again vowed that he would fulfill what he had vowed if he recovered his sight. He did recover it and fulfilled his vow. And God's hand was still upon him. He did not memorize the creed, or perhaps he refused to memorize it and excused himself as unable. God will know which it was. Now after all the celebration for his reception into the Church, he became paralyzed in many and almost all his members and even his tongue. Then, having been admonished by a dream, he confessed in writing that he was told that this happened because he did not recite the creed from memory. After that confession the functions of all his members, except his tongue, were restored. He none-

---

1. The original salutation is missing; the early editions have added this one.
2. See Rom 10:8.
3. See Ex 14:8; Nm 33:3.

theless stated in writing that he had in that time of trial learned the creed and therefore held it in memory. In that way there was taken from him all that childish nonsense that, as you know, spoiled a certain natural goodness he had and made him a highly sacrilegious man who used to insult Christians. What shall I say but *Let us sing a hymn* (Jdt 16:15) to the Lord and exalt him above all forever?[4] Amen.

---

4. See Dn 3:57-58.

Letter 228

In 429, after the beginning of the Vandal invasion, Augustine wrote to Honoratus, the bishop of Thiave in Numidia, who had consulted him about how the Catholic clergy should behave under the threat of the imminent invasion. Augustine tells Honoratus that he thought that he had said everything necessary on the topic in a letter to Quodvultdeus, of which he had sent a copy to Honoratus, namely, that the clergy should not deprive the people of God of the ministry needed especially in a time of danger (paragraph 1). Augustine argues that neither the words nor the example of Christ nor the actions of Saint Paul justify the clergy's abandoning the churches of Christ (paragraph 2). The words of Saint John, in fact, urge pastors to lay down their lives for their brothers and sisters (paragraph 3). Augustine admits that pastors may flee if they are not prevented by their duties to the Church (paragraph 4). He replies to Honoratus' argument that it is useless for bishops to remain and to witness the slaughter of the people by saying that, if all the people flee, the clergy may flee as well (paragraph 5). Augustine defends the action of Athanasius, the bishop of Alexandria, who fled because he in particular was the object of Constantius' persecution, for his flight did not deprive the people of ministers (paragraph 6). He reminds Honoratus that the clergy ought to fear spiritual evils more than bodily sufferings (paragraph 7), and he spells out the spiritual evils that the people of God suffer when they are abandoned by the ministers of the Church (paragraph 8). Hence Honoratus should now see what he had written that he did not see, namely, the great good that the people of God derive in times of danger if they are not abandoned by the ministers of Christ (paragraph 9). He explains the conditions under which priests may flee, using the examples of Athanasius and King David (paragraph 10). But when clergy and laity face a common danger, the clergy may not abandon the people of God (paragraph 11). If some of the clergy should flee and some should remain with the people who cannot flee, they should be chosen by lot (paragraph 12). Furthermore, the faithful should be informed of why the clergy are not fleeing so that the people themselves do not think that they must remain (paragraph 13). Finally, Augustine advises Honoratus that amid such dangers it is best that we pray to God to show us his mercy (paragraph 14).

To his holy brother and fellow bishop Honoratus Augustine sends greetings in the Lord.

1. Having sent Your Charity a copy of the letter that I wrote for Brother Quodvultdeus, our fellow bishop,[1] I thought that I was free of this burden that you have imposed upon me by asking advice about what you ought to do in these dangers that have come upon our times. For, though I wrote that letter in only a few lines, I still do not think that I omitted anything that would be necessary for a

---

1. This letter is not extant, and the addressee cannot be Quodvultdeus of Carthage since he was raised to the episcopacy only in 437.

respondent to say and for someone posing the question to hear, since I said that those who desire to move to fortified places, if they can, should not be stopped and that the chains of our ministry, by which the love of Christ has bound us, should not be broken, so that we do not abandon the churches that we ought to serve. These are the very words that I wrote in that letter: "The upshot is, then, I say, that we—whose ministry is so necessary to the people of God who are staying where we are (however small their numbers) that they should not remain without it—should say to the Lord: 'Be our protecting God and fortified place.'"[2]

2. But this advice, as you write, is not enough for you, lest we strive to act contrary to the Lord's commandment and example, when he warns that we should flee from one city to another. For we recall his words when he said, *But when they persecute you in this city, flee to another* (Mt 10:23). Who, however, would believe that the Lord wanted us to do this in such a way that the flocks whom he purchased by his blood are deprived of that necessary ministry without which they cannot live? He himself did not do this, did he, when he fled into Egypt, carried by his parents?[3] For he had not yet gathered the churches that we might say were abandoned by him. When, in order that an enemy might not arrest him, the apostle Paul was lowered in a basket through a window and escaped his clutches,[4] the church in that place was not, was it, deprived of his needed ministry? Other brothers who were there carried out what was necessary. The apostle had done this because they wanted him to save himself for the Church, for that persecutor was seeking him in particular. Let the servants of Christ, the ministers of his word and sacrament, therefore, do what he commanded or permitted. Let them certainly flee from city to city when any one of them in particular is being sought by persecutors, provided that the church is not abandoned by others who are not being sought in this way. But let them offer nourishment to their fellow servants who they know cannot live otherwise. When, however, there is a common danger for all, that is, for bishops, clerics, and laity, those who need others should not be abandoned by those whom they need. Either let all move to fortified places, then, or let those who must remain not be left behind by those who ought to take care of their needs in the church so that they either live in the same way or suffer in the same way what the head of the household wills that they suffer.

3. But if it happens that either some suffer more and others less or all suffer equally, it is clear which of them are suffering for others, namely, those who, though they could tear themselves away from such evils by fleeing, have preferred to remain so that they would not abandon others in their need. In this way especially we prove the love that John the apostle commends when he says,

2. See Ps 31:3.
3. See Mt 2:14.
4. See 2 Cor 11:33; Acts 9:25.

As Christ laid down his life for us, so we too ought to lay down our lives for our brothers and sisters (1 Jn 3:16). For if those who flee or those who cannot flee, because they are bound by their various necessities, are caught and suffer, they of course suffer for themselves and not for their brothers and sisters. But those who suffer because they refused to abandon their brothers and sisters, who needed them for their salvation as Christians, without a doubt lay down their lives for their brothers and sisters.

4. This is why a certain bishop made the statement that we have heard: "If the Lord commanded us to flee in those persecutions in which the fruit of martyrdom is found, how much more ought we to flee useless sufferings when there is a hostile invasion of the barbarians?" This is, of course, true and acceptable—but for those whom the bonds of duty to the Church do not bind. For one who does not flee slaughter from the enemy, when it is possible to escape, so as not to abandon the ministry of Christ, without which the people cannot either become or live as Christians, finds greater fruit of love than one who, while fleeing not for the sake of the brothers and sisters but for his own sake, is caught, does not deny Christ, and accepts martyrdom.

5. What, then, does that mean which you put in your first letter? For you said, "If we must remain in the churches, I do not see what good we are going to do for ourselves or for the people if not to see men being slain, women being raped, churches being burned, and ourselves not faltering under torture when they ask of us what we do not have." God is indeed able to hear the prayers of his family and to turn aside these things that they fear, and yet on account of these events, which are uncertain, we ought not to commit the certain wrong of abandoning our duty, without which the destruction of the people is certain not in matters of this life but in those of the next life, for which we ought to care with incomparably more diligence and solicitude. For, if these evils were certain which we fear may perhaps occur where we are, all those people on whose account we ought to remain there would first flee from there and would release us from the need to remain. After all, there is no one who would say that ministers must remain where there are no longer any people to whom they must minister. In that way certain holy bishops fled from Spain after the people had in part fled, were in part killed, in part perished in sieges, and were in part scattered in captivity. But many more remained in the thick of the same dangers where the people remained on whose account they remained. And if some abandoned their people, this is what we say should not be done, nor are such ministers taught this by God's authority but misled by human error or conquered by fear.

6. After all, why do they think that they should literally obey the commandment in which they read that one should flee from city to city[5] and at the same

---

5. See Mt 10:23.

time not be horrified at the hireling who *sees the wolf coming and flees because he does not care about the sheep* (Jn 10:12-13)? Why do they not strive to understand these two statements of the Lord, that is, the one in which flight is allowed or commanded and the other in which it is rebuked or blamed, so that they may not find them inconsistent with each other, as they are not? And how do they find this out unless they pay attention to what I already discussed above, namely, that, when persecution threatens, we ministers of Christ ought then to flee from the places in which we are either when there are no people of Christ to minister to or when there are and the necessary ministry can be performed by others who do not have the same reason for fleeing. In that way the apostle fled by being lowered in a basket, as we mentioned previously, when he was personally being sought by the persecutor, while the others were not by any means in similar peril. And God forbid that they should give up the ministry there so that the church is abandoned. The holy Athanasius, the bishop of Alexandria, fled under such circumstances when Emperor Constantius wanted to arrest him in particular while the other ministers never abandoned the Catholic people who remained in Alexandria.[6] But when the people remain, the ministers flee, and the ministry is withdrawn, what will we have but that damnable flight of hirelings who do not care for the sheep? For the wolf will come, not a human being but the devil, who has often persuaded the faithful to become apostates if they lacked the daily ministry of the Lord's body. *And the weak brother for whose sake Christ died will perish* not *in your knowledge* (1 Cor 8:11) but in your ignorance.

7. But with regard to those who are not misled in this matter by error but are overcome by fear, why do they not, with the Lord's mercy and help, instead fight bravely against their fear lest incomparably greater evils, which they ought to fear even more, befall them? They do this when the love of God is ablaze, not when the desires of the world are smoldering. After all, love says, *Who is weak and I am not weak? Who is scandalized and I do not burn?* (2 Cor 11:29) But love comes from God. Let us therefore pray that he who commands it may give it. And by this love let us fear more lest the sheep of Christ be butchered by the sword of spiritual wickedness in the heart than by iron in the body. For they are going to die in the body at some time by some kind of death. Let us fear more lest the purity of their faith perish through the corruption of their interior mind than that women be violently raped in the flesh, because chastity is not violated by violence if it is preserved in the mind, since it is not even violated in the body when the will of the victim does not make shameful use of the flesh but tolerates without consent what another person does. Let us fear more lest living stones[7] be

---

6. Saint Athanasius was born in Alexandria c. 293; he became bishop of Alexandria in 328, was a stalwart defender of the divinity of Christ against Arianism, and died in 373. From 338 to 346 Athanasius took refuge in Rome from the Eastern emperor, Constantius.

7. See 1 Pt 2:5.

slain when we abandon them than that the wood and stones of earthly buildings be set afire while we are there. Let us fear more lest the members of the body of Christ[8] be killed because they are deprived of spiritual food than that the members of our body be overtaken by an enemy attack and tortured. It is not that we should not avoid these evils when we can but rather that we should endure them when we cannot avoid them without sin, unless perhaps someone contends that he who withdraws a ministry needed for piety precisely when it is needed more is not a wicked minister.

8. Or, when we come to the most extreme of these dangers and there is no opportunity of escaping, do we not consider how many people of both sexes and of every age usually rush to the church, some demanding baptism, others reconciliation, still others acts of penance, and all of them the administration and conferral of the sacraments? If ministers are lacking in that case, what a great ruin results for those who leave this world either without rebirth or without absolution! What great grief there is for their believing families who will not have them with them in the repose of eternal life! What great groaning there is from all, and what a great blasphemy from some because of the absence of ministries and ministers! See what the fear of temporal evils causes, and the great accumulation of eternal evils entailed by it. But if ministers are present, in accord with the strength that the Lord supplies, all are helped. Some are baptized; some are reconciled; none are deprived of sharing in the Lord's body; all are consoled, edified, and exhorted to pray to God who is able to turn aside everything they fear. Let them be ready for either alternative so that, if this chalice cannot pass from them, the will of him may be done[9] who cannot will anything evil.

9. Surely you now see what you had written that you did not see, namely, how much good the Christian people gain if amid the present evils they do not lack the presence of Christ's ministers. You also see how much harm their absence does when *they seek their own interests, not those of Jesus Christ* (Phil 2:21). They do not have that love of which it was said, *It does not seek what is its own* (1 Cor 13:5), and they do not imitate him who said, *Not seeking what is useful for me, but what is so for many that they may be saved* (1 Cor 10:33). The apostle also would not have fled from the ambushes of that leader who was persecuting him if he had not wanted to save himself for others who needed him.[10] On this account he said, *But I am being pulled in two directions, for I have the desire to die and be with Christ, which is by far the best, but to remain in the flesh is necessary on account of you* (Phil 1:23-24).

10. Here someone may perhaps say that the ministers of God ought to flee when such dangers are imminent in order to save themselves for the benefit of

---

8. See Eph 5:30.
9. See Mt 26:42.
10. See 2 Cor 11:32-33; Acts 9:23-25.

the Church in more peaceful times. It is right for some to do this when there are not lacking others who can furnish the ministry of the Church, lest all of them abandon the Church. We mentioned above that Athanasius did this. For the Catholic faith, which his words and his love defended against the Arian heretics, knows how necessary it was for the Church and how much good it did that that man stayed alive. But when there is a common danger and we need to fear more that someone may be believed to flee not out of a desire to help but out of a fear of dying, and that he may do more harm because of his example of fleeing than he does good because of his obligation to stay alive, he should by no means flee. Finally, holy David accepted this because his people asked it, lest he expose himself to the dangers of battles and *the light of Israel,* as it says, *be extinguished* (2 Sam 21:17), but he himself did not presume to do this. Otherwise he would have produced many imitators of cowardice if they believed that he did this not out of consideration for the good of others but out of the panic of his own fear.

11. But another question comes to mind that we ought not simply to ignore. For, if we should not neglect this benefit of having some ministers flee when some devastation is imminent in order that others might be saved to minister to the survivors whom they are able to find after the slaughter, what will happen when it seems that all are going to perish unless some flee? For what should we do if that persecution is raging to the point that only ministers of the Church are being persecuted? What should I say? Should ministers abandon the Church by fleeing in order that ministers may not abandon her more miserably by dying? But if the laity are not being sought out to be put to death, they can somehow hide their bishops and clerics, as God, who holds all things in his power, provides help, for by his miraculous power he can save even one who does not flee. And so we are seeking what we ought to do in order that we may not, when it comes to everyone, be thought to be tempting the Lord by expecting miracles. For such is not the storm in which the laity and the clergy face a common danger, as there is a common danger on a single ship for the merchants and the sailors. But far be it from us that we should place so little value on this ship of ours that the sailors and especially the helmsman abandon it when it is in danger, even if they can escape by jumping into a life raft or by swimming. After all, for those who we fear might perish by our desertion, we fear not a temporal death, which is going to occur at some point, but eternal death, which could occur if we do not avoid it and could also not occur if we do avoid it. But, in a common danger affecting this life, why do we suppose that, wherever there is an enemy attack, all the clerics and not also all the laity are going to die, so that they may end this life together, which is when clerics are needed? Or why should we not hope that, just as some of the laity will survive, so some of the clergy will survive, who can provide for the laity the ministry they need?

12. And yet how wonderful it would be if there were such a dispute among the ministers of God over which of them should remain, so that the Church might not

be abandoned by the flight of all, and over which of them should flee, so that the Church might not be abandoned by the death of all! Such a struggle will take place among them when both are aflame with love and both are pleasing to Love. If this dispute cannot be brought to an end otherwise, as far as I can see, those who should remain and those who should flee ought to be chosen by lot. For those who say that they ought rather to flee will seem either cowardly because they did not want to endure the imminent suffering or arrogant because they judged that they were to be saved as men more necessary for the Church. Then perhaps those who are better will choose to lay down their lives for their brothers, and the others, whose life is less useful, will be saved by fleeing because they have less experience in providing care and governance. Still, if they are giving pious consideration to the matter, they will speak against those who they see ought rather to live but prefer to die rather than to flee. Thus, as scripture says, *Let the drawing of lots settle disputes and bring them to an end between the powerful* (Prv 18:18). For it is better that God, rather than human beings, decide in such ambiguous cases, whether he deigns to call the better to the reward of martyrdom and spare the weak or to make the weak stronger for enduring evils and to take from this life those whose life cannot benefit the Church of God as much as the life of the first group. The situation will, of course, be less frequent if this drawing of lots is practiced. But if it is practiced, who would dare to find fault with it? Who apart from someone uneducated or hateful would not praise it with fitting commendation? But if you do not want to do something of which no example comes to mind, let no one's flight cause the Church to lack the ministry that she needs and ought to have, especially in such great dangers. Let no one make an exception for himself so that, if he seems to excel in some gift, he claims that he is more deserving of life and hence of flight. For whoever thinks that is far too satisfied with himself, but whoever says this is also displeasing to everyone.

13. There are, of course, some who think that bishops and clerics who do not flee in such dangers, but remain, mislead the people, since they do not flee when they see their pastors remaining. But it is easy to turn aside this response or bad impression by addressing the same people and saying, "Do not let the fact that we are not fleeing from this place mislead you. For we are remaining here not for our own sake but rather for your sake, in order that we might provide for you whatever ministry we know is necessary for your salvation in Christ. If, then, you choose to flee, you have also freed us from these bonds by which we are held back." I think that one should say this when it truly seems useful to move to safer places. After they have heard this, if either all or some say, "We are in the power of God. No one escapes his anger wherever he goes; one who wants to go nowhere can find his mercy wherever he is, if he is either prevented by certain difficulties or unwilling to make the effort to find uncertain places of refuge, not

in order to put an end to danger but in order to change it," these people should undoubtedly not be abandoned by Christian ministers. But if, after they heard this, they preferred to depart, the ministers who were remaining on their account need not remain there, because there are no longer present those on whose account they ought still to remain.

14. Whoever, therefore, flees in this way, so that because of his flight the Church does not lack a necessary ministry, does what the Lord commands or permits. But one who flees so that the nourishment by which Christ's flock lives its spiritual life is taken from it is that hireling who *sees the wolf coming and flees because he has no care for the sheep* (Jn 10:12-13).

Because you consulted me, my most beloved brother, I wrote this response for you with the truth and certain charity that marked my thoughts, but I have not forbidden you to follow a better opinion if you find one. We cannot find anything better to do amid these dangers, however, than to offer prayers to the Lord our God that he may have mercy on us. By the gift of God some prudent and wise men have merited both the will and the strength not to abandon the churches of God, and they were not deterred from the goal of their resolve despite the teeth of their critics.

Letter 229

In perhaps the year 428 Augustine wrote to Count Darius, a high official from the imperial court in Ravenna and a Catholic, who had been sent to Africa to negotiate with the rebellious general, Boniface. After having heard from two African bishops of the excellent character of Darius, Augustine wrote him, explaining that he has come to know Darius' heart, though he was prevented by illness from seeing his external form (paragraph 1). Augustine urges Darius to obtain peace by peaceful means and reminds him that it is a greater honor to slay wars by words than men by the sword (paragraph 2).

To his rightly illustrious and most magnificent lord, Darius, his son most dear in Christ, Augustine sends greeting in the Lord.

1. I have heard from my holy brothers and fellow bishops Urban and Novatus what a good and great man you are. One of them had the opportunity to come to know you near Carthage in the town of Hilari and soon afterward in Sicca, but the other at Sitifis. Thus it happened that I could not help knowing you as well. Nor have I failed to see you, after all, because weakness of body and the double chill, that is, of winter and of age, do not allow me to converse in your presence. For the one bishop, present with me when he was so good as to come to me, and the other bishop, by letter, revealed the form not of your body but of your heart, so that I saw you with more pleasure to the extent that I saw you more interiorly. By the mercy of God both we and you yourself also see with great joy this form of yours in the holy gospel as if in a mirror, where scripture says, as the Truth speaks, *Blessed are the peacemakers because they shall be called the children of God* (Mt 5:9).

2. Those warriors are, of course, great persons and have their own glory, not only those with great courage but also those with great faith, which is the source of a more genuine praise. By their labors and dangers, with the aid of God's protection and help, the violent enemy is conquered and peace is won as calm is restored to the state and the provinces. But it is a mark of greater glory to slay wars themselves by the word rather than human beings by the sword, and to win and obtain peace by peace, not by war. After all, even those who fight, if they are good, undoubtedly seek peace, but they still do so by means of bloodshed. But you were sent in order that no one's blood would be spilled; others, then, are under that necessity, but you have this good fortune. Hence, my rightly illustrious and most magnificent lord and my son most dear in Christ, rejoice over this great and true good of yours, and enjoy in God, from whom you have received it, the grace to be such a man as you are and to have undertaken so fine a task. May God confirm what he has done for us through you.[1] Receive this greeting from us, and be so good as to

---

1. See Ps 68:29.

send yours in return. As Brother Novatus has written to me, he has brought it about that Your Excellency has with your learning come to know me also through my writings. If, therefore, you have read what he gave you, I have also become known to your inner senses. They are not greatly displeasing, so far as I am aware, if you read them with more love than severity. It is not important but would be highly appreciated by us if in return for our writings, both this letter and those works, you would send us one letter in return. I also greet that pledge of peace,[2] which you have happily received with the help of the Lord our God, with that love I owe him.

---

2. That is, the son of Darius who was called Verimodus; see Letter 230, 6. Augustine takes the son as a sign of the peace to be established between Boniface and the empress, Galla Placida.

Letter 230

Toward the end of 429 Darius replied to the previous letter from Augustine. He expresses his deep desire to meet Augustine personally and to hear from his lips the words of God (paragraph 1). He thanks Augustine for his letter and asks him to pray to God that he may be the sort of man that Augustine said that he was (paragraph 2). He tells Augustine that, if he has not slain wars, he has at least by the help of God postponed them, and he asks for Augustine's continued prayers (paragraph 3). He tells Augustine of his joy in writing this letter and asks Augustine to send him a copy of *The Confessions* (paragraph 4). He compares his plea to Augustine with the plea of Abgar, the king of Edessa, to Christ (although he does not mention Agbar's name) (paragraph 5). Finally, Darius apologizes for his long letter, sends Augustine the greetings of his son, and tells Augustine that he is sending along some medicine for his pain and illness (paragraph 6).

To his lord Augustine Darius sends greetings.

1. I wish, my lord and holy father, that, as my name was brought to your ears, as you say, by the kind favor of your fellow bishops, Urban and Novatus, so your God, the God of all, would have presented my very self to your hands and eyes, not in order that the greater clarity of your judgment might find me a greater man or perhaps as great a man as the kind words of such great men and the recommendation of a letter has made me, but in order that I might rather receive the most genuine and immortal fruits of your heavenly wisdom from your own lips, like the sweetness of some pure water from the present and perennial flow at its source. Oh, blessed would I have been, not merely three or four times, as was said by some writer, but a thousand times and more times than any number,[1] if I had been permitted to be present to and gaze upon your truly starlike countenance and had been allowed to receive and draw in your divine words, which sing of the things of God not only with food for the mind but also with pleasure for the ears. I would surely think that I had received certain laws conducive to immortality not only from heaven but as if I were located in heaven itself, and that I had heard the words of God not at a distance from his temple but while standing near the very tribunal of God.

2. I perhaps merited that this should happen to me on account of my most ardent desire for you, but on account of my conscience I admit that I have not merited it. But, while absent, I have also begun to receive no small fruits from my good desire, and I have the highest perfection of blessings from these secondary blessings. I have, after all, been recommended to him to whom I wanted to be by the lips of two holy priests, who are distant from each other in

---

1. See Virgil, *Aeneid* 1, 94.

place and region. The kind words and firsthand testimony, so to speak, of the one, as I said, and the letter of the other, which flew to you with the same content and a similar sentiment, are in agreement. Such good and great men have woven for me a crown of sorts before your eyes, not with the stems of blooming flowers but with the testimony of words of glory, like certain imperishable gems. For this reason I pray to the sovereign God on your behalf, and I ask for your intercession, my holy father, so that, though I am aware that I have not merited such high praise, I may at some point turn out to be such a man. Now, have those bishops not overcome all those losses stemming from my absence, since you deign to address, to write to, and to greet us, and since you do not allow me, though absent, to be absent? I was in sorrow because I was not known to you, who after God the savior are my savior.[2] And yet, as you say, after all, you do not pay attention to the form of my body but to that of my heart, which is more important. And there you saw me with more pleasure to the extent that you saw me more interiorly. May God bring it about that I measure up to your judgment, my father, and that I not be guilty in my conscience, since interiorly I do not see that I am such a man as you have imagined for yourself.

3. You say in the same divine and heavenly letter, in accord with your custom and with eloquence assisting you in what you would like to praise, that I slay wars, I repeat, that I slay wars by the word. At this point, my holy father, my mind emerged as if from a certain darkness of thought, as though it recognized true praise for itself. After all, to confess the whole matter briefly and simply to Your Beatitude, if we have not terminated wars, we have certainly postponed them, and with the help of God, who is the ruler of all, the evils that had increased to a certain peak of disasters have been diminished. Yet I hope from God, from whom we ought to hope for everything that is good, that this postponement of wars, which I mentioned—and I even take your letter as a sign of so great and so certain a blessing—may bring with it and maintain a lasting and perpetual foundation for peace. For you said, and you proved by the eternal law of God, that I should rejoice, as you say, over this great and true good of mine and that I should enjoy it in God, from whom you say that I received the grace to be the sort of man I am and to undertake such activities. You then add, "May God confirm what he has done for us through you."[3] Oh, these are prayers uttered not merely for me but for the security of all! For this glory of mine cannot be separated from the security of all, and, in order that I may be able to be happy because of your prayers, all must be happy along with me. At length, father, undertake and express such prayers for the Roman empire, for the Roman state, and also for these people who strike you as worthy, and when you betake yourself much later

2. The word "savior" is in Greek in both cases.
3. Letter 229, 1-2.

into heaven,[4] entrust them to your posterity and commend them to your successors.

4. I have perhaps gone on as far as I ought to have, but I have certainly said less than I wanted. For I admit it: in writing to you, I picture your countenance like that of someone present, and though my crude speech and my impoverished tongue have long since failed me, I am still not satisfied, as I would be if I were conversing and chatting in your presence. Hence from this you can measure our desire for you. Though the unpleasant wordiness of a page of a letter has long since deserved to be brought to an end, we set aside our reserve and, while we are satisfying our desire, we come to think that to break off writing is to withdraw from your presence. I want to end it, then, but I cannot. For, if you can believe me, my father, you have so penetrated our mind and heart ever since we were not content with your reputation, which is so glorious and so great, and we have preferred to contemplate you in your writings, since this one brief letter of yours to me has stirred up such great flames and fires of love. We have in fact fully and completely repudiated all the pagan rites through reading your writings, which are like none others. For, though we learned the laws of Christ from our parents, from our grandparents down to the last generation of our family, the proud vanity of useless superstition at times entered into our minds. Hence we beg you and demand with our whole mind. I ask that you be so good as to send and give us also the books of *The Confessions*, which you wrote. After all, if others too have given us your writings with a ready heart and kind disposition, how much less ought you yourself to excuse yourself in the case of your own writings?

5. It is said that a certain prince or rather king entreated by letter our God and Lord, Christ, when he was still living in the territories of Judea and had not returned to his heaven.[5] Since the king was prevented from going and traveling to him and did not believe that he could be healed in any other way, he asked that the savior and physician of the world come to him, if he would be so gracious. And for fear of seeming to do an injury to so great a majesty, which the ignorant king had grasped with an insightful but imperfect understanding, he is said to have also praised his city in order that, enticed by the beauty of the city and the hospitality of the king, God would not scorn the prayers of the supplicant. God helped the king; he was healed. And as a gift God sent to him by letter a greater benefit than what he had asked for—not only health to the supplicant but also security to the king. He commanded, moreover, that his city last forever and be

---

4. See Horace, *Odes* (*Carmina*) I, 2, 45.

5. Darius alludes to the legendary correspondence between Christ and Abgar of Edessa found in *The History of the Church* (*Historia ecclesiastica*) I, 13, of Eusebius of Caesarea. Eusebius includes the letter of the king to Christ as well as Christ's reply with the promise to send Thaddeus, the apostle, after his ascension. A council held in Rome under Pope Gelasius in 494 declared the letter of Christ apocryphal.

always safe from enemies. What could be added to these benefits? I, a lowly servant of kings, beg of you, my lord, that you not hesitate to make intercession daily for my sins before Christ, the Lord and prince of all, to pray for me without growing weary, and to ask for whatever you choose.

6. If my long letter wearies you, put up with it out of the patience of your greatness of heart, and blame yourself, since you commanded this. We nonetheless pray and beg once again that you write back. For in that way you will make us able to believe that you were glad to receive my letter. May God grant us that Your Beatitude pray for us for many years, my lord and truly holy father. Our son Verimodus greets Your Beatitude. He was quite pleased that you were so good as to make mention of him in your letter to us. We gave some medicines or other that we obtained from the chief physician, who is present here, to the holy priest Lazarus to be brought to Your Beatitude. As the man we mentioned claims, they will help no small amount for the alleviation of your pain and the curing of your disease.

Letter 231

Soon after having received the previous letter Augustine replied to Darius. He thanks Darius for his letter and tells him that he cannot express the joy it brought him (paragraph 1). He admits that he is delighted by Darius's eloquence and by his praise for him (paragraph 2). Though all human beings desire to be praised, we should flee from the sort of vanity that derives from unfounded or mistaken praise (paragraph 3). The apostle Paul taught us that we should not act correctly in order to be praised by human beings, though we may seek human praise for the sake of human beings. Augustine rejoices to find in himself the good qualities that Darius has praised in him and longs to obtain those that he sees he still lacks (paragraph 4). He expresses his pleasure at the fact that Darius' influence allows his writings to reach pagans whom they might not otherwise reach (paragraph 5). He sends Darius a copy of *The Confessions* and asks his friend to pray for him (paragraph 6). He tells him that he has also sent another five works, which he lists, and asks Darius to send him his judgment on them (paragraph 7).

Augustine, a servant of Christ and of the members of Christ, sends greetings in Christ to Darius, his son, a member of Christ.

1. You wanted my reply to serve as a proof that I was glad to receive your letter. See, I am replying, and yet I cannot prove this by a reply, either by this one or by any others, whether I write briefly or at great length. For what cannot be proven by words cannot be proven by either few or many words. And indeed I say very little, even if I speak many words. But I would certainly not concede to anyone, however eloquent, that with a letter of whatever sort or length he might arouse the affection that your letter produced in me, which I cannot do even if he could see it in my heart as I do. It remains, then, to prove to you what you wanted to know in such a way that you perceive in my words what they do not prove. What, then, shall I say except that I was delighted by your letter, delighted very, very much? The repetition of this word is not repetition but rather like an ongoing declaration; because I could not possibly utter it forever, I have at least repeated it. For in that way perhaps I can say what cannot be said.

2. If anyone asks at this point what ultimately delighted me so much in your letter, whether it was eloquence, I will reply, "No," and he will perhaps reply, "Is it, then, the praises for you?" But I will also reply "No" as far as they are concerned. It is not that these are not found in your letter. For there is such great eloquence in it that it is clear that you were born with the finest talent and were well educated in the finest disciplines, and it is utterly filled with praises for me. Some will say, "Do these, then, not delight you?" Of course they do! For, as someone said, "After all, I do not have a heart as hard as horn,"[1] so that I would not feel them or would feel

---

1. Persius, *Satires* (*Satyrae*) 1, 47.

them without delight. These things do delight me, but what are they in comparison to that by which I said that I was especially delighted? For your eloquence delights me because it is elegantly delightful and delightfully elegant. But since I am not delighted by all praises of me nor by praises from everyone but by such praises as you thought I deserved and by praises from persons like you, that is, from those who for Christ's sake love his servants, I cannot deny that I was delighted by the praises for me in your letter.

3. Let grave and learned men figure out what they should think of the famous Themistocles, at least if I recall the right name of that man. When he refused to play the lyre at banquets, something that renowned and learned men of Greece often did, and scorned that whole kind of pleasantry, he was asked, "What, then, does it delight you to hear?" To this he is said to have replied, "Praise for me." Let them, therefore, figure out the goal and intention with which they believe that he said this or with which he did say this. For he was a truly great man in the eyes of this world. After all, when someone asked him, "What, then, do you know?" he said, "How to make a great state out of a little one."[2] I myself think that one should in part approve and in part beware of what Ennius said, "All mortals want to be praised."[3] For, as the truth, which alone is undoubtedly praiseworthy, should be sought even if it is not praised, so vanity in the praise of human beings, which can easily sneak up on one, should be fled from. This occurs, however, when those goods that are worthy of praise are not considered worth having unless a human being is praised by other human beings, or when anyone wants those goods to be highly praised in himself that instead deserve either modest praise or even blame. For this reason Horace said with more alertness than Ennius,

Are you swelling with the love of praise?
There are certain remedies that could cure you
If you read the booklet three times with sincerity.[4]

4. Thus he thought that the swelling from the love of human praise ought to be driven out, like the bite of a serpent, by healing words of magic. The good teacher, therefore, taught us through his apostle that it is not right for us to act in order that we may be praised by human beings, that is, that we should not make the goal of our correct action the praises of human beings, and yet we should seek the praises of human beings on account of human beings. After all, when good persons are praised, it does not benefit those who are being praised but those who are praising them. For it is enough for the former, as far as they are concerned, that they are good, but we should rejoice with those for whom it is

---

2. See Cicero, *In Defense of Archias* (*Pro Archia*) 9, 20.
3. Ennius, *Annals* (*Annales*), 560. This verse from Ennius is also quoted in *The Trinity* XIII, 3, 6. It is preserved only in Augustine.
4. Horace, *Letters* (*Epistulae*) I, 1, 36-37.

good to imitate good persons, when they praise good persons, because in that way they show that they are pleased by those whom they sincerely praise. The apostle also says in some passage, *If I wanted to please human beings, I would not be the servant of Christ* (Gal 1:10), and the same man says in another passage, *Please all persons in every way, as I please all in every way*, but he adds the reason, *not seeking what is beneficial for myself, but what is beneficial for the many, that they may be saved* (1 Cor 10:32-33). There you see what he was seeking in the praise of human beings where he also says, *For the rest, brothers and sisters, whatever is true, whatever is modest, whatever is chaste, whatever is holy, whatever is very precious, whatever leads to a good reputation, if there is any virtue, if there is any praise, bear these in mind; do these things that you have learned and accepted, heard and saw in me, and the God of peace will be with you* (Phil 4:8-9). He included under the term *virtue,* therefore, the other things that I mentioned above, when he said, *If there is any virtue.* The words that he added, *Whatever leads to a good reputation*, he followed up with another appropriate expression when he said, *If there is any praise.* And so, his statement, *If I pleased human beings, I would not be a servant of Christ*, should of course be interpreted as if he had said, "If I did the good actions I do in order to obtain human praise, I would be swollen with the love of praise." The apostle wanted to please all persons, therefore, and rejoiced that he pleased them, though he was not swollen in himself because of their praise, but he built up in Christ those who praised him. Why, then, should I not be delighted to be praised by you since, if I am not mistaken, you are a good man and you praise what you love and what it is beneficial and salutary to love, even if these qualities are not to be found in me? Nor is this beneficial only to you but also to me. For, if these qualities are not found in me, I am embarrassed in a salutary way, and I desire strongly that they may be found in me. And for this reason I rejoice that I have what I recognize as mine in your praise, but the things that I do not recognize as mine I desire to obtain not only in order that I may have them but also in order that those who sincerely love me may not always be mistaken in praising me.

5. See how many things I have said, and I still have not said what it is that delighted me in your letter far more than your eloquence, far more than your praise for me. But what do you think it is, good man that you are, if not that I have made you who are such a good man my friend? This is so even though I have not seen you, if I ought in fact to say that I have not seen you, since I have seen not your body but your soul in your letter, in which, when it came to you, I believed not my brothers, as I had done before, but my own self. For I had already heard who you were, but I did not yet grasp what sort of a man you would be toward me. Because of your friendship I do not doubt either that your praises for me—I have already explained sufficiently the reason why they delight me—will benefit much more richly the Church of Christ, since in that way you also regard,

read, love, and praise my labors in defense of the gospel against the remnants of the wicked worshipers of demons. The result is that, the more renowned you are, the better known I am through your praises of me. For, as an illustrious man, you cast light upon my hidden works and, as a man of renown, you make them known, and where you see that they can do good, you do not allow them to remain completely unknown. If you ask how I know this, I saw you as such a man in your letter. See from this how much that letter was able to delight me; if you think well of me, you have in mind how much the gains for Christ delight me. Now you have indicated that you yourself, who, as you write, "were able to receive the laws of Christ from your parents and from your grandparents down to the last generation of your family," were helped by my labors against the pagan rites as nowhere else. Am I, then, to value slightly how much good our writings could bring to others, when you recommend and spread them about, and to how many, to what renowned persons, and how easily and how salutarily they could bring them through those people to others for whom such writings are suitable? Or, in thinking about this, can I be flooded with the pleasure of only slight or mediocre joys?

6. Since, therefore, I could not explain in words how much delight I drew from your letter, I mentioned what caused me delight. I now leave for you to conjecture what I was unable to state well enough, namely, how much it delighted me. Receive, then, my son, receive, I repeat, the books of my *Confessions*, which you desired, my lord, who are good and Christian not superficially but with Christian love. In them contemplate me so that you do not praise me beyond what I am; in them believe not others about me but me myself. In them pay attention to me and see through me what I was in myself. And, if anything in me pleases you, praise there along with me not me but him whom I have wanted to be praised because of me. *For he made us and not we ourselves* (Ps 100:3). We destroyed ourselves, but he who made us remade us. But when you find me in them, pray for me so that I may not fail but may be made perfect. Pray, my son, pray. I see what I say; I know what I ask for. Do not think it something inappropriate and beyond your merits. You will deprive me of a great help if you do not do this. Not only you, but also all who have come to love me because of your words, pray for me; indicate to them that I have asked for this, and if you think highly of me, think that we have commanded what we ask for, and yet give to us when we ask, and obey us when we command. Pray for us; read the writings of God, and you will find that those rams of our flock, the apostles, asked for this from their children or commanded this to their followers. He who hears our prayers and who saw that I was doing this previously sees to what extent I am doing what you asked me to do on your behalf. But do so in return in this matter

of love. We are your superiors; you are God's flock.[5] Consider and see that our dangers are greater than yours, and pray for us. This, after all, is appropriate both for us and for you in order that we may give a good account concerning you to the chief pastor and head of us all[6] and may, along with you, escape the allurements of this world, which are more dangerous than its difficulties, unless his peace contributes to what the apostle admonished us to pray for, *that we may lead a quiet and tranquil life in all piety and love* (1 Tm 2:2). For, if piety and love are lacking, what is tranquility and quiet with regard to the other evils of the world but food for dissoluteness and destruction or an invitation or help toward these? Therefore, in order that we may have a quiet and tranquil life in all piety and love, pray for me, as I pray for you, wherever you are, wherever we are. For he to whom we belong is absent nowhere.

7. I also sent other books for which you did not ask, so that I have done more than you asked for: *Faith in Things Not Seen, Patience, Continence, Providence,* and one large book, *Faith, Hope, and Charity.* If you read all these while you are in Africa, give me your judgment concerning them; either send it to us or send it where it may be sent to us by our lord and primate, Aurelius,[7] although we hope that we may receive your letter from wherever you are and that you may receive ours, as long as we are able, from here. I received most gratefully what you sent. By it you graciously aided our health, though only our bodily health, because you want me to have leisure for God without the impediment of ill health. And you also helped our library so that we might have the means to prepare or to repair books. May the Lord repay you both here and in the world to come with the rewards that he has prepared for such persons as he wanted you to be.[8] I beg you to greet again, as I asked that you greet him before, the pledge of peace that has been entrusted to you and is most dear to both of us.[9]

---

5. See 1 Pt 5:2; Jer 13:17.
6. See 1 Pt 5:4.
7. That is, the bishop of Carthage and primate of Africa.
8. See 1 Cor 2:9.
9. That is, Darius' son Verimodus; see Letter 229, 2.

Letter 232

Between 399 and 407 Augustine wrote to the pagan leaders of the city of Madaura, who had written to him to ask for help for a certain Florentinus. Augustine questions the sincerity of their addressing him as father and greeting him in the Lord (paragraph 1). Their use of the name of Christ is likewise either sincere or insincere. If the latter, it is mockery; if the former, they should give up their worship of idols (paragraph 2). Augustine warns them that they will have to face the judgment of God who foretold the history of the Jewish people, the coming of Christ, and the spread of his Church (paragraph 3). Since scripture has borne witness to all these events that have already occurred, Augustine asks why these pagans still do not believe that he will come as judge, as has also been predicted (paragraph 4).

Augustine then turns to a statement of the Christian doctrine of the Trinity in terms of the principle, the Word, and the sanctifier (paragraph 5). He sketches the mystery of the incarnation of the Word, who humbled himself by dying upon the cross in order that human pride might be humbled and human humility might be defended by the imitation of its God (paragraph 6). In closing, Augustine expresses the hope that the leaders of Madaura will receive his letter, in which he has spoken about Christ to worshipers of idols, in a way that will benefit them for their salvation (paragraph 7).

To his praiseworthy lords and most beloved brothers of Madaura, whose letter I received by means of Brother Florentinus, Augustine sends greetings.

1. Perhaps if those who are Catholic Christians among you had sent me such a letter, I would only be surprised that they wrote under the title of their position in government rather than under their own name. But if all or almost all men of your position really deigned to send a letter to me, I am surprised that you wrote "Father" and "greetings in the Lord."[1] For I know quite well and with great sorrow of your superstitious worship of idols, and against those idols your temples are closed more easily than your hearts, or rather those idols are enclosed in your hearts as much as in your temples. Or are you perhaps thinking of the salvation that is to be found in the Lord, in whose name you chose to greet me? For, if this is not the case, I ask you, how have I injured, how have I offended Your Benevolence that you thought that you should mock me rather than show me honor by the salutation of your letter, my praiseworthy lords and most beloved brothers?

---

1. The Latin for "greetings" (*salus*) also means "salvation," so that the pagan leaders wished for Augustine "eternal salvation in the Lord," something that surely sounded like mockery on the lips of pagans.

2. For when I read what you wrote, "To Father Augustine eternal salvation in the Lord," I was suddenly stirred up with such great hope that I believed that you were either converted to the Lord and to eternal salvation or desired to become converts through our ministry. But when I read the rest, my heart was chilled. I asked the bearer of your letter, however, whether you either were now Christians or wanted to be. After I found out from his response that you had not changed at all, I was more deeply saddened that you believed that the name of Christ, to whom you now see the whole world is subject, should not only be rejected by you but also be mocked in us. After all, I could not think of another lord with respect to whom a bishop could be called "Father" by you except Christ the Lord, and if this created some doubt as to the interpretation of your words, it was removed by the closing of your letter, where you stated with complete openness, "We hope, O lord, in God and his Christ that you will enjoy many years in your office." After I had read through and examined all this, what else could come to my mind or can come to the mind of any human being but that these lines were written with either a truthful or a deceitful intention on the part of the authors? But if you write these things with a truthful intention, who has blocked for you the path to this truth? Who has strewn harsh brambles in your way? What enemy has set a steep cliff before you? Finally, who has closed the door to the basilica for those desiring to enter so that you do not want to share with us the same salvation in the same Lord, in whose name you greet us? But if you write this as a deception and a mockery, do you impose upon me the care of your business interests so that you dare not to exalt the name of him through whom I can have some influence with due veneration but to toss it about with fawning mockery?

3. You should know, my dearest friends, that I say these things with a fear in my heart for you that I cannot express. For I know how much more serious and more dangerous a situation you are going to face before God if I say these things to you without result. Divine scripture is not silent about everything that our fathers remembered was done in past times regarding the human race and handed down to us. We also hand on to posterity everything that we see, at least everything that pertains to seeking and holding onto the true religion. But absolutely everything takes place just as it was predicted that it would take place. You surely see that the people of the Jews have been uprooted from their homes and scattered and spread about through almost every land. And the origin of the same people, their growth, the loss of their kingdom, and their dispersion everywhere came about just as it was predicted. You certainly see that the word and law of God, which proceeded from that people, has through Christ, who was born from them in a miraculous manner, won and retained belief on the part of all the nations. We have read that all these things were foretold, as we see them. You certainly see that many have been cut off from the root of the Christian community, which is being spread through the world by the sees of the apostles and the

successions of bishops in an unfailing growth. You certainly see that, like drying branches, those groups which we call heresies and schisms boast under the Christian name of only the outward shape derived from their origin. All these things were foreseen, predicted, and written down. You certainly see the temples of idols in part fallen down in disrepair, in part overgrown, in part closed, and in part turned to other uses. You certainly see that the idols are either broken or burned or shut away or destroyed. You certainly see that the powers of this world, which were at one time persecuting the people of the Christians in defense of their idols, have been defeated and subdued by Christians—not by Christians fighting back but by Christians dying. And you certainly see that those powers have turned their attacks and laws against those same idols for which they once killed Christians and that the supreme head of the most renowned empire lays aside his diadem and offers supplication at the tomb of Peter the fisherman.

4. The divine scriptures, which have come into the hands of everyone, testified ages ago that all these events would take place. We rejoice with stronger faith that all these events are taking place the more we find that they were predicted with greater authority in the sacred writings. Are we, I beg you, are we going to suppose that only the judgment of God, which we read in those same writings will take place between believers and non-believers[2]—are we going to suppose that only the judgment of God will not take place, though all these events have occurred as they were foretold? Nor will there be any human beings of our times who will be able in that judgment to defend themselves about their lack of faith, since a righteous man invokes the name of Christ to prove his justice, a perjurer to perpetrate fraud, the emperor to maintain his empire, a soldier to win his battle, a husband to govern his house, a wife to offer obedience, a father to impose his command, a son to be obedient, a master to exercise control, a servant to offer service, a humble person to show piety, a proud person to evoke emulation, a rich man to give, a poor man to receive, a drunkard in his cups, a beggar at the door, a good person to give help, a bad one to deceive, a Christian in worship, a pagan in fawning—all invoke the name of Christ, and they will undoubtedly give an account of their intention and manner of saying it.

5. There is an invisible being, the principle and creator, from whom come all these things we see—a being supreme, eternal, unchangeable, ineffable except to himself. There is a being by which the sovereign majesty reveals and makes itself known, the Word, who is equal to him who begets and speaks him and by whom he who begets the Word is revealed. There is a certain holiness, the sanctifier of all that is holy, the inseparable and undivided union of the unchangeable Word, by whom that principle is revealed, and of that principle,

2. See Qoh 3:17.

which reveals itself by its equal Word. But who can contemplate the whole of this that I have tried to speak by not speaking and not to speak by speaking? Who can contemplate the whole of this with an utterly calm and pure mind, derive happiness from that contemplation, and somehow forget himself, fading away into that which he contemplates, while he continues on into that whose vision is invisible to us, that is, dons immortality and obtains the eternal salvation which you are so good as to wish for me in your greeting? Who could do this save one who, while confessing his own sins, has brought low all the accouterments of his pride and has prostrated himself meekly and humbly to accept God as his teacher?

6. We must, then, first be brought down from the vanity of pride to the lowliness of humility in order that, rising up from there, we may attain a height that is solid. For this reason we could not be taught in a way that is as magnificent as it is gentle to subdue our arrogance not by force but by persuasion, unless that Word, by which God the Father makes himself known to the angels, the Word, which is his power and wisdom[3] and which could not be seen by the human heart blinded by the love of visible things, deigned to present and reveal his person in a man. Thus a human being might fear more to be raised up by a human being's pride than to be brought low by the example of God. And so it is not Christ adorned with an earthly kingdom, nor Christ rich with earthly wealth, nor Christ resplendent with earthly happiness, but Christ crucified, who is preached throughout the world.[4] Proud people first laughed at this and a remnant of them still laughs at it, but first a few believed and now whole peoples believe. For then, in order to support the faith of a few and to stop the mockery of the crowds, when Christ was preached as crucified,[5] the lame walked, the mute spoke, the deaf heard, the blind saw, and the dead rose. In that way at last earthly pride noticed that nothing in earthly things is more powerful than the humility of God,[6] so that human humility, which is most conducive to salvation, might be defended against the insults of the proud by the protection of the God whom it imitates.

7. Awake at long last, my brothers and fathers of Madaura. God offered me this occasion for writing to you. To the extent I was able, I assisted and helped, as God willed, in the business of Brother Florentinus, by means of whom you sent your letter. But that business was such that it could have been easily handled even without my effort. Almost all the people of that house who are present in Hippo know Florentinus, and they grieve much over his loss. You sent me a letter, and since you provided the occasion, my letter is not impudent when it says something about Christ to the worshipers of idols. But I beg you, if you have

---

3. See 1 Cor 1:24.
4. See 1 Cor 1:23.
5. See Mt 11:5; Lk 7:22.
6. See 1 Cor 1:25.

not spoken his name in vain in that letter, that I may not have written this to you in vain. If you wanted to mock me, however, fear him whom the proud world earlier mocked after he had been brought to judgment and now, after having become subject to him, awaits as its judge. For the affection for you in my heart expressed on this page as best I could will be a witness; it will be a witness against you in the judgment of God, who will confirm in glory those who believe in him and will throw into confusion those who do not. May the one and true God set you free from all the vanity of this world and convert you to him, my praise-worthy and most beloved brothers.

Letter 233

Sometime during his episcopacy (395-430) Augustine wrote to Longinianus, a pagan who held the office of priest, a learned man who had come to a belief in the one God but knew little or nothing about Christianity, as becomes evident from his reply in Letter 234. In the present letter Augustine asks Longinianus how he believes that God is to be worshiped and what he holds regarding Christ.

Augustine to Longinianus.

It is said that one of the men of old used to say that, for those who are thoroughly convinced that they should want nothing more than to be good men, the rest is easy to learn. A far older statement of a prophet had already anticipated this statement, which, if I recall correctly, comes from Socrates. For in a few words the prophet taught human beings at one and the same time not merely that they should want nothing more than to be good but also how they might become good. He said, *You shall love the Lord your God with your whole heart and with your whole soul and with your whole mind* (Dt 6:5), and, *You shall love your neighbor as yourself* (Lv 19:18). For someone who is convinced of this I do not say that the rest is easy to learn but that this is all there is to learn, at least all that is useful and conducive to salvation. For there are many teachings that are either superfluous or harmful, if they should even be called teachings. Bearing witness to the book of the former people of God, Christ said, *Upon these two commandments the whole law and the prophets depend* (Mt 22:40). Hence, since I think that I saw as if in the mirror of your letter to me that you want nothing more than to be a good man, I am venturing to ask how you believe that one should worship God, than whom nothing is better and from whom the human heart hears how it may be good. For I already know that you believe that he is to be worshiped. I also ask what you hold regarding Christ. For I have also noticed that you do not consider him to be unimportant. But I want to know (and I think not impudently) whether you think that one can come to the happy life by that way alone which he has shown us and whether for some reason you are not neglecting to take it but are postponing this. Or do you think that there is another way or other ways to such a precious possession which is to be desired above all else, and do you believe that you are already walking on one of them? For I love you for the reason I mentioned above, and I am not rash to believe that you love me. On no other topic can two people who are well disposed toward each other offer, demand, give, or receive ideas with greater benefit than on how we may become good people and happy ones.

Letter 234

In reply to the previous letter Longinianus wrote to Augustine. He explains how he understands that God should be worshiped, alluding to a wide variety of religious beliefs and praising Augustine's religious pursuits (paragraph 1). He states his understanding of the path one must take on the journey to God, namely, that it is a life of virtue under the protection of God (paragraph 2). Finally, he admits that he has nothing to say about Christ since he claims to know nothing about him (paragraph 3).

To Augustine, his venerable lord and holy father who is truly and rightly honorable, Longinianus sends greetings.

1. I am blessed and greatly enlightened by the pure light of your brilliant virtue, for you have considered me worthy of receiving in abundance the honor of your divine address. But you impose upon me quite a heavy burden and a most difficult area in which to respond, my venerable lord, especially to your inquiries, and at the same time to discuss them in accord with the views I hold, that is, as a pagan man. The topic abounds with questions upon which we have either in part long since agreed or upon which we now more and more agree as a result of this letter. I do not mean only on the teachings of Socrates, nor only of your prophets, O truly finest man of the Romans, nor only of the few from Jerusalem, but also those of Orpheus, Tagetes, and Trismegistus,[1] who are far more ancient than the former and go back almost to the barbaric ages. These are teachings that have the gods as their authors and that were revealed to the whole world, which was divided by the gods into three parts by certain boundaries, before Europe and Asia received their names or Lybia possessed a good man of the sort that you, so help me God, both have been and will be. For within human memory, unless you accept the form of the tale composed by the imaginings of Xenophon,[2] I have still heard, read, or seen no one or at least no one after that one—and I certainly say this without fear with God as my witness—who always strives like you to acknowledge God, to be able most readily to follow him with purity of mind and with the weight of the body cast aside, and to cling to him with the hope of a perfect conscience and an unwavering faith.

---

1. Orpheus was a legendary Greek hero from whose teachings a Hellenistic mystery religion was said to have come and after whom it was named. Tagetes was a legendary Etruscan prophet; see Ovid, *Metamorphoses* 15, 554. Hermes Trismegistus was an Egyptian philosopher of the second century, after whom the hermetic writings are named.
2. Xenophon was a student of Socrates; he was a minor Greek philosopher, perhaps best known for the *Anabasis*, a record of a military expedition of Cyrus into Asia Minor.

2. But it is more reasonable that you should not be unaware of the way by which it can be achieved and that you should explain it to me, without introducing something from elsewhere, than that you should learn it from me, my honorable lord. For only then, I admit, will I set out for the abode of this good, since I am hardly capable of that good as yet, as my functions as a priest demand, and still, if I can, I gather some food for the journey. But I shall state as well as I can in a few words what I hold and observe, which has been handed down in a holy manner from antiquity. The better path to God is that by which a good man hastens by the intention of his heart and mind to go by pious, just, sincere, chaste, and true words and deeds, without any wavering caused by the changing times, a man approved and defended by an escort of the gods, and certainly one who has made himself pleasing to the powers of God. That is, he is filled with the powers of that one, universal, incomprehensible, indefatigable, ineffable creator— those powers, which, according to your view, you call angels, or something second after God or from God or with God or leading to God. This is the path, I say, on which human beings, purified by the pious commandments of the ancient rites and by most pure expiations and trimmed down by practices of abstinence, run with speed, constant in soul and body.

3. But concerning the bodily Christ and spirit God of your present faith, through whom you are confident of going to that highest, blessed, and true father of all, my lord and most honorable father, I do not dare nor can I express what I think, because I believe it is most difficult to state precisely what I do not know. But as you have been so gracious as to tell me, who have long since known it, that you love me who admire your virtues, I regard it as sufficient testimony to the good life that I lead that I do not displease you who daily present yourself and your soul to God. You will undoubtedly understand that I too love you to my delight since I accept and hold to the norm and line of conduct in accord with the judgment you formed concerning me. But above all, I beg you to pardon the very insignificant opinion and the perhaps inappropriate words that I have sent to you, for you insisted upon it, and be so good as to inform me, if I merit this, what you think of them or what you hold, by your holy writings, which, as that poet said, are now not sweeter than honey but sweeter than nectar.[3] May you, my dearest father, enjoy the paternal goodness of God, and may you please God with lasting holiness, as is necessary.

---

3. See Ovid, *Tristia* V, 4, 29-30.

Letter 235

After having received the previous letter Augustine replied to Longinianus. Augustine thanks Longinianus for his reply and explains what he wanted and still wants, namely, that their conversation may be brought to a salutary conclusion. Augustine quotes from Longinianus' letter what he had said about the path to God and the use of sacred rites (paragraph 1). Then, with a view to eliminating needless questions, he asks him what he sees as the relation between living a life of perfection and the use of the sacred rites (paragraph 2).

Augustine to Longinianius.

1. I have received the fruit of my letter, namely, the reply of Your Benevolence. From it I now see that there has arisen and sprung up between us a harvest, as it were, of important discussion on this important topic. Here is what I wanted before and what I still want now, if God will grant his help: It is that this undertaking may be brought to a close with a due and salutary conclusion. And so you thought that you ought neither to deny nor to affirm anything rashly about Christ; I would not be unwilling to accept this attitude in a pagan mind. But since you wish to be instructed even by my writings, I will never refuse nor will I cease to obey this desire of yours, which is so good and dear to me. But first it is necessary to clarify in some way your view concerning the ancient rites and to have your precise thought on them. For, when you said that the better path to God is "that by which a good man hastens by the intention of his heart and mind to go by pious, just, sincere, chaste, and true words and deeds, without any wavering caused by the changing times, a man approved and defended by an escort of the gods, and certainly one who has made himself pleasing to the powers of God. That is, he is filled with the powers of that one, universal, incomprehensible, indefatigable, ineffable creator—those powers, which, according to your view, you call angels, or something second after God or from God or with God or leading to God" (you recognize these words from your letter)—then you went on to say, "This is the path, I say, on which human beings, purified by the pious commandments of the ancient rites and by most pure expiations and trimmed down by practices of abstinence, run with speed, constant in soul and body."[1]

2. In these words I perceive, if I am not mistaken, that you do not think that it is sufficient for the path by which one journeys to God that by pious, just, sincere, chaste, and true words and deeds a good man should make himself worthy of the gods by whose escort he is protected and hastens to make his way to that highest God of all, the creator—if he is not purified by the pious

---

1. Letter 234, 2.

commandments and expiations of the ancient rites. For this reason I would like to know what you think needs to be purified by sacred rites in one who makes himself worthy of the gods and, through them, of that one God of gods, by living piously, justly, sincerely, and truthfully. For, if such a man still needs to be purified by sacred rites, he is of course not pure, and if he is not pure, he does not live piously, justly, sincerely, and chastely. After all, if someone already lives in that way, he is already pure. What need, then, is there for someone pure and sincere to be purified by sacred rites of expiation? This, then, is the core of our discussion, and once it is resolved, we shall see what follows. Should a person live well in order to be purified by the sacred rites, or should a person be purified by the sacred rites in order to live well? Or, no matter how high the level of perfection a man has attained, is he still not suited for the happy life, which is received from God, unless he adds the help of the sacred rites? Or is the reception of the sacred rites like a portion of living well, that is, so that to live well is not one thing and to live in accord with the sacred rites another, but a sacred life is included within the limits of living well? Of these four that I have proposed, I beg you, do not hesitate to disclose by letter which one you favor the most. It is certainly of the utmost importance for continuing to converse with each other on the topic we have undertaken so that, when I try to refute, as if you hold them, many unnecessary points that you perhaps do not hold, we do not consume necessary time on superfluous things. Hence I did not want to make this letter burdensome for you so that, if you reply quickly, we may continue with the rest.

Letter 236

Sometime during his episcopacy, Augustine wrote to Deuterius, the Catholic bishop of Caesarea in Mauretania Caesariensis, reporting that a subdeacon, Victorinus, who had clandestinely been teaching Manichean doctrines, had been found out and corrected (paragraph 1). Augustine describes the beliefs of the Manichees and distinguishes between the roles of the elect and of the hearers in Manicheanism (paragraph 2). He explains that, after Victorinus was exposed and had admitted to being a hearer, he asked to be instructed in Catholic doctrine, but he himself expelled him from the city. Augustine warns Deuterius that he had taken the further step of deposing Victorinus from his clerical rank and that therefore he should be avoided (paragraph 3).

To his most blessed lord and venerably most dear brother and fellow bishop, Deuterius, Augustine sends greetings in the Lord.

1. I thought that I could do nothing better than write to Your Holiness, lest the enemy, who does not cease to set ambushes to destroy souls that have been purchased at so great a price, ravage the sheepfold of our Lord Jesus Christ in your province because of our negligence. We have learned that a certain subdeacon from Malliana living here, Victorinus, is a Manichee, and in so sacrilegious an error he was hiding under the guise of a cleric. For he is already an old man in terms of age. He was, however, exposed in such a way that even he himself, when questioned by me, could not deny it, before he was found guilty by witnesses. For he knew that they were so many and such good persons to whom he had recklessly revealed himself that, if he tried to deny it, he would be seen as nothing else than I will not say utterly impudent but utterly insane. He confessed that he was a hearer, of course, and not one of the Manichean elect.

2. But those who are called hearers among them eat meat and cultivate fields and, if they wish, take wives; the elect do none of these things. But the hearers kneel before the elect in order that not only their priests or bishops or deacons but even any of the elect may impose hands on these supplicants. They also adore and pray to the sun and the moon with the elect. On the Lord's day they also fast with them, and they believe along with them all the blasphemies because of which the heresy of the Manichees should be detested. That is, they deny that Christ was born of a virgin and do not confess that his flesh was real but false. And for this reason they claim that his passion was not real and that there was no resurrection. They blaspheme against the patriarchs and prophets. They say that the law given by means of Moses, the servant of God, did not come from the true God but from the prince of darkness. They think that the souls not merely of human beings but also of animals are derived from the substance of God and are

actually parts of God. They also say that the good and true God fought with the nation of darkness and mingled a part of himself with the princes of darkness, and they claim that this part, which has been defiled and imprisoned throughout the whole world, is purified through the food of the elect and through the sun and the moon, and that what will not be able to be purified from that part of God will at the end of the world be bound with an eternal chain of punishment. In that way God is not only believed to be violable, corruptible, and subject to contamination, since a part of him can be reduced to such evils, but he cannot be entirely purified from such defilement, impurity, and evil, even at the end of the world.

3. This subdeacon, posing as a Catholic, not only believed but also taught, with all the energy he could, these intolerable blasphemies. For he was exposed as teaching them when he entrusted himself to people who posed as his students. After he confessed that he was a hearer in the Manichees, he in fact asked me to bring him back to the path of truth, which is Catholic doctrine. But, I admit, I was aghast at his pretense in the guise of a cleric, and I took measures to expel him from the city after chastising him. Nor was this enough for me unless I also informed Your Holiness of this by my letter so that all might know that he should be avoided as someone fittingly deposed from the rank of clerics by the severity of the Church. But if he seeks to be admitted to penance, he should be believed if he reveals to you others whom he knows are in that heresy not only in Malliana but in the whole province.

Letter 237

Augustine wrote to Ceretius, a Catholic bishop, possibly in Spain, most probably after 414, when he first learned from the Spanish priest Orosius what the sect known as Priscillianists held.[1] Augustine tells Ceretius that the two books he sent were filled with the Priscillianist heresy, though he has lost one of them and cannot find it (paragraph 1). He explains that the hymn that the Priscillianists attribute to Jesus is found in the apocryphal books, which other heretics also use (paragraph 2). They accept all the canonical as well as the apocryphal books and conceal their own teachings, even by swearing falsely (paragraph 3). They do not merely accept the apocryphal books but prefer them to the canonical books. They claim that the hymn which they attribute to Jesus is not contained in the canon lest its secrets be disclosed to people who are not spiritual (paragraph 4). But they also explain this same hymn by using the canonical scriptures. Hence Augustine argues that the Priscillianists must actually be concealing what they really hold under the veil of such explanations (paragraph 5). He illustrates how the Priscillianists interpret the hymn by means of the canonical scriptures and draws the paradoxical conclusion that they hold that the secret doctrine is concealed from spiritual persons in the hymn but revealed to carnal people in the canonical books (paragraph 6). He shows that the ideas contained in the hymn are more clearly expressed in the canonical writings and again concludes that the Priscillianists themselves understand the words of the hymn differently than they explain them to others (paragraphs 7 and 8). Finally, Augustine points out that the Priscillianist hymn goes so far as to have Christ claim to be always a deceiver, and he urges Ceretius to be on guard against these heretics (paragraph 9).

To his most blessed lord and rightly venerable brother and fellow bishop Ceretius Augustine sends greetings in the Lord.

1. Now that I have read what Your Holiness sent, it seems to me that Argirius[2] either fell into the Priscillianists unwittingly, so that he was utterly unaware of whether they were Priscillianists, or that he was already at that time entangled in the snares of the same heresy. For I have no doubt that those writings are the work of the Priscillianists. But since one demand or another was overwhelming me without interruption, it was scarcely possible for me to have any free time at all in order to have one whole volume of those two read to me. For I do not know how the other has wandered off, and despite our most careful searching I could not find it, my most blessed lord and rightly venerable father.

---

1. See *Heresies* 70 for the Priscillianists. See Augustine's *To Orosius in Refutation of the Priscillianists and Origenists* 1, 1, where Augustine says that he learned from Orosius what the Priscillianists held.
2. Nothing further is known about Argirius than what can be inferred from this letter.

2. The hymn which they say comes from our Lord Jesus Christ, and which especially disturbs Your Reverence, is of course often found in the apocryphal writings. These are not peculiar to the Priscillianists, but other heretics of some sects also use them because of the impiety of their error. They have views that differ from one another, to be sure, because of which each of them has followed various heresies, but they hold these writings in common despite their differences, and they who do not accept the old law and the canonical prophets especially make frequent use of them. For they say that these latter do not pertain to the good God and to Christ, his Son, just as the Manichees and the Marcionites[3] do, as well as the others who find this damnable blasphemy to their liking. They also do not accept everything in the canonical scriptures of the New Testament, that is, in the genuine gospels and letters of the apostles, but only what they want, and they choose the books they accept, while rejecting others. But even in each of the individual books they distinguish passages that they think correspond with their errors, and they regard the rest as false. For certain Manichees repudiate the book whose title is The Acts of the Apostles. For they fear the perfectly obvious truth where they see that the Holy Spirit appears as one who was sent, whom the Lord Jesus Christ promised in the truth of gospel. By that name of Spirit, in whom they have absolutely no share, they deceive the hearts of unlearned people, when they claim with an amazing blindness that the same promise of the Lord was fulfilled in Mani, the founder of their heresy. Those heretics who are called Cataphrygians also do this, saying that the Holy Spirit, whom the Lord promised that he would send,[4] came in the person of some crazy people, namely, Montanus and Priscilla.[5]

3. The Priscillianists, however, accept all the canonical and apocryphal writings together. But they twist whatever is opposed to them into harmony with their error, sometimes by a clever and astute explanation and sometimes by a ridiculous and stupid one. Nor do they do this in such a way that they believe to be true the very things that they explain to persons foreign to their sect. Otherwise, they would be Catholics or persons not far removed from the truth who find Catholic meanings in the apocryphal writings or seem to want to find them. But though they hold different ideas with their own people and teach or learn them among one another, they do not dare to reveal them, since they are truly wicked and detestable. Yet they preach the Catholic faith — which they do not hold but under which they hide — to those whom they fear. For some heretics could perhaps be found who are more impure, but none is comparable to them in deceitfulness. Others, of course, lie because of the habit and weakness of this life, for such vices are human, but these people are reported to have the

3. For the Marcionites and the Manichees, see *Heresies* 22 and 46.
4. See Jn 14:16; 26:15; 16:7.
5. For the Cataphrygians or Montanists, see *Heresies* 26.

commandment in the wicked doctrine of their heresy that, for the sake of their esoteric doctrines, they should lie even with a false oath. Those who have had experience of them and belonged to them and have been set free from them by God's mercy even quote the very words of this commandment: "Swear, perjure yourself, but do not disclose the secret."

4. Hence, in order that we may see without any difficulty how they do not hold regarding the apocryphal writings what they pretend to expound, we must consider the reason that they seem to give as to why divine authority, as it were, should be ascribed to the same writings so that—what is worse—they prefer them to the canonical writings. You have their words cited in that volume as follows: "The hymn of the Lord that he spoke secretly to the holy apostles, his disciples, since it is written in the gospel, *After having recited a hymn, he went up on the mountain* (Mt 26:30; 14:26), was not placed in the canon on account of those who think according to their own ideas and not according to the spirit and truth of God.[6] For this reason scripture says, *It is good to conceal the secret of the king, but it is honorable to reveal the works of God* (Tb 12:7)." This is their powerful reason why this hymn is not in the canon, because, like *the secret of the king*, it should be hidden from those who think according to the flesh and not according to the spirit and truth of God. Hence, the canonical scriptures do not pertain to the *secret of the king*, which they thought should be hidden, and they were written for those who think according to the flesh and not according to the spirit and truth of God. What else is this but to say that the holy and canonical scriptures do not contain wisdom according to the spirit of God and do not pertain to the truth of God? Who would listen to this? Who could put up with the horror of such a great impiety? Or, if the canonical scriptures are interpreted spiritually by those who are spiritual and carnally by those who are carnal, why is this hymn not also in the canon if those who are spiritual interpret it spiritually and those who are carnal interpret it carnally?

5. Secondly, what reason is there for them to try to explain the same hymn according to the canonical scriptures? For, if it is not in the canonical scriptures precisely because those scriptures were written for those who are carnal, while this hymn was written for those who are spiritual, how is the hymn that does not pertain to those who are carnal explained from the scriptures that pertain to carnal human beings? If, for example, in this hymn one sings and says, "I want to release and I want to be released," because, as these people explain these words, Christ the Lord releases us from a life according to the world in order that we might not again be caught up in it, we learn this, of course, in the canonical scriptures. For the Lord releases us from a life according to the world, and we ought not again to be caught up in it. For what else does *You have burst my chains* (Ps

---

6. See Rom 8:5.

116:16) mean? What else does *The Lord releases captives* (Ps 146:7) mean? After all, the apostle warns those who have already been released when he says, *Stand firm, then, and do not again be bound by the yoke of slavery* (Gal 5:1). And the apostle Peter says, *For, if having fled from the defilements of the world with the knowledge of our Lord and savior, Jesus Christ, they are again caught and defeated, their later condition has become worse than their first condition* (2 Pt 2:20). In that way he shows that, after we have been released, we should not again be taken prisoner by the world. These ideas, therefore, are obvious in the canon, whether in these testimonies that I have cited or in very many others, and are constantly read and preached. Why is it, then, that these people say that this hymn, in which (to speak as they do) the words are put most obscurely, is not included in the canon in order that they may not be revealed to those who are carnal? After all, we see that these ideas are revealed in the canon, even though they claim they are completely veiled in this hymn. For, as we should rather believe, it is certainly not these ideas but some others that they hide much more fully by such an explanation and are afraid to reveal.

6. For surely, if those words signify that the Lord releases us from a life according to the world and does so in order that we may not be caught up in it again, it would not have been said, "I want to release, and I want to be released," but, "I want to release, and I do not want those whom I release to be bound again." Or if he is speaking in the person of his members, that is, those who believe in him, then, just as he said, *I was hungry, and you gave me to eat* (Mt 25:35), he would say instead, "I want to be released, and I do not want to be bound." Or does he release and is himself released, because the head releases and his members are released, who were persecuted by the man to whom he cried out from heaven, *Saul, Saul, why are you persecuting me?* (Acts 9:4; 22:7; 26:14) The expositor of these words did not say this, of course, but even if he had said it, we would reply to him what we replied a little before. Because we read these ideas in the canonical scriptures, we understand them there, we defend them from there, and we preach them daily from there. Why is it, then, that this hymn is said to have been withheld from those who are carnal so that it was not put in the canon, since what is concealed in it is openly stated in the canon? Or are they so foolish, in fact so insane, that they dare to say that *the secret of the king* in this hymn is hidden from those who are spiritual but obvious in the canon to those who are carnal?

7. The same thing could be said about the previous words of the same hymn, where it says, "I want to save, and I want to be saved." For if, as they explain it, these words signify that we are saved by the Lord through baptism and that we save, that is, preserve, in ourselves the Spirit given us through baptism, does not the canonical scripture proclaim this idea where we read, *He saved us through the bath of rebirth* (Ti 3:5), and where it is said to us, *Do not extinguish the Spirit*

(1 Thes 5:19)? How, then, is this hymn missing from the canon precisely in order that it may not become known to those who are carnal, since what is obscure in the hymn is as clear as daylight in the canon, unless they are trying to hide what they themselves really think under this explanation of sorts, which they give to just about anyone? Still, they are so blind that they even use certain words from the canon to explain the hymn that they say is not in the canon precisely in order that *the secret of the king* might not be disclosed to those who are carnal. What, then, do those clearer expressions used in the canon do by which the obscure expressions in this hymn are revealed?

8. For suppose, as they say, that we should understand in this hymn, where it says, "I want to be born," the words in the canonical letter of Paul, *Whom I am again bringing to birth until Christ is formed in you* (Gal 4:19). Suppose that we should understand in this hymn, where it says, "I want to sing," what is written in the canonical psalm, *Sing to the Lord a new song* (Ps 96:1; 98:1; 149:1; Is 42:10). Suppose that we should understand in this hymn, where it says, "All of you, dance," what is written in the canonical gospel, *We sang for you, and you did not dance* (Lk 7:32). Suppose that we should understand by the words in this hymn, "I want to grieve; all of you, beat your breasts," what is written in the gospel song, *We mourned for you, and you did not grieve* (Mt 11:17). Suppose that "I want to adorn, and I want to be adorned" in this hymn signifies the same thing as what is written in the canon, *That Christ may dwell in your hearts through faith* (Eph 3:17) and *You are the temple of God, and the Spirit of God dwells in you* (1 Cor 3:16; 2 Cor 6:16). Suppose that the words of the hymn, "I am a lamp for you, O you who see me," signify what is written in the canonical psalm, *In your light we shall see light* (Ps 36:10). Suppose that what it says in this hymn, "Whichever of you knocks at me, I am a door for you," signifies what we read in the canonical psalm, *Open for me the gates of righteousness, and having entered them I shall confess to the Lord* (Ps 118:19), and in another psalm, *Raise up the gates, O princes among you, and be lifted up, O eternal gates, and the king of glory will enter* (Ps 24:7). Suppose that what it says in this hymn, "You who see what I do, be silent about my works," signifies what is written in the Book of Tobit, *It is good to conceal the secret of the king* (Tb 12:7). Why, then, is this hymn said not to be in the canon precisely in order that *the secret of the king* may be hidden from those who are carnal? After all, those ideas that are set forth in this hymn are also found in the canon, and they are found to be so clear in the canon that those obscure ideas are explained by them. The only reason can be that they regard these explanations as places in which to hide, while in the words of that hymn, which they pretend to explain, they have ideas that they are afraid to explain to others.

9. It would take a long time to demonstrate all of this by argument. But from the examples that we have mentioned it is very easy to consider the others and to

see that the good and honest things that they say in the explanation of this hymn are also found in the canon. Hence their claim that it is not included in the canon precisely because *the secret of the king* must be hidden from those who are carnal is not a reason but an evasion. Hence it is not unfair to believe that they want not to disclose what they read but rather to cover up what they think. Nor is this surprising, since they believed that the Lord Jesus, when speaking not through the lips of prophets or apostles or angels but through his own lips, was a deceiver rather than the teacher of the truth. Indeed, they ascribe divine authority to this hymn in which some unknown author of the same hymn pretended that Jesus said, "I have always deceived by word, and I was not deceived at all." Let those outstanding spiritual people answer, if they can, where we should go, whom we should listen to, whose words we should ever believe, in whose promise we should place our hope, if Christ has always deceived by word, if the almighty teacher has always deceived by word, if he who is the Only-Begotten, the Word of God the Father, has always deceived by word. What else should I say about those wicked speakers of vanity and seducers of the mind, first their own, then that of other people predestined for eternal destruction whom they have been able to join to themselves? I have replied to Your Reverence both much later than I had wanted and more extensively than I had planned. You do very well to beware vigilantly of the wolves. But also, with the help of the Lord of shepherds, work with a shepherd's care for healing the sheep, if these wolves have perhaps attacked some or have already wounded some.

Letter 238

In probably the first decade of the fifth century Augustine wrote to Pascentius, an Arian count from the imperial court, who had challenged Augustine to a debate in Carthage, as Possidius reports in his *Life of Augustine* 17. Since Pascentius had gone back on his earlier agreement that their words be taken down by stenographers, Augustine decided to state his faith in writing and send it to Pascentius (paragraph 1). Augustine explains the need to have what they said taken down verbatim so that neither of them could later deny what they had said (paragraph 2). Augustine gives a concrete example of how Pascentius wrote down something other than what he had said (paragraph 3). Augustine recalls Pascentius' tirade over the word ὁμοούσιον and his own attempt to explain its meaning (paragraph 4). He points out that even the Arians use expressions in speaking of God that are not found in the scriptures (paragraph 5), though Pascentius claimed to avoid ὁμοούσιον because it does injury to God (paragraph 6). Despite the variances in Pascentius' articulation of his faith, he refused to have his words taken down by stenographers (paragraph 7). In another statement of his faith Pascentius omitted the words "God the Son," and he began to insult Augustine when this was pointed out (paragraph 8). Given the present letter, Augustine claims that Pascentius cannot truthfully claim that Augustine was afraid to state his own faith, and he expresses his wonder at Pascentius' alleged fear of attack from a bishop (paragraph 9).

Augustine states his faith in the one God, the Father, the Son, and the Holy Spirit, and explains in what sense the Son is equal to the Father and in what sense he is less than the Father (paragraph 10). He explains that what is said of God is said of each of the three persons, who are the one God (paragraph 11). As body and soul are together one human being, so the Father, the Son, and the Holy Spirit are together one God (paragraph 12). Augustine appeals to the unity of the many faithful in Christ to explain how the Father, the Son, and the Holy Spirit are one God (paragraph 13). He distinguishes the relative from the non-relative predications about the persons (paragraph 14) and shows how "spirit" is used in both ways in scripture (paragraph 15). Augustine argues that, if the peace of Christ can make many believers to be one heart and one soul, we ought to believe that the Father, the Son, and the Holy Spirit are not three gods but one God (paragraph 16). He explains that Catholics maintain that the Son of God is also the Son of Man on account of the form of the servant that the Son of God assumed (paragraph 17).

Augustine asks Pascentius to turn his attention to the words of scripture that demand that we confess that the Father, the Son, and the Holy Spirit are the one Lord God and resolves difficulties arising from several texts (paragraphs 18 to 20). He cites scripture texts that show that the Holy Spirit is God and equal to the Father and to the Son (paragraph 21). He deals with a passage from which one might infer that the Son is greater than the Father (paragraph 22), and he argues against the Arian claim that the Son was visible and subject to corruption even prior to the incarnation (paragraph 23). He argues that there never was a time when the Father did not have the Son, using the image of light and its brightness (paragraph 24). He challenges Pascentius to find in scripture any passage where two things not of the same substance are said to be one without qualification (paragraph 25).

In conclusion Augustine challenges Pascentius to write out a statement of his faith and to sign it (paragraph 26). He mocks Pascentius' claim to have defeated him (paragraph 27), and he challenges him to try to defeat the words of scripture that proclaim that the Father and the Son are one (paragraph 28). For the words *are one* are never used in scripture of things of a different substance (paragraph 29).

Augustine to Pascentius.[1]

1, 1. As you may deign to remember, I had certainly wanted, when you begged and pleaded—indeed, considering the merit of your age and dignity, when you commanded us—to have a conversation, even face to face, about the Christian faith, insofar as the Lord might grant me the opportunity. But, since after dinner you did not want to do what we had in the morning agreed to do, namely, to have our words taken down by stenographers so that you might not say anymore what I hear that you are in fact saying, namely, that I did not dare to state for you my faith, accept in this letter what you can both read and hand on to whom you will. And you yourself may reply with what you want by writing in return. After all, it is unfair that anyone should want to pronounce judgment on another person and not want anyone to pronounce judgment on him.

2. And from our past agreement, which you were unwilling to implement at our afternoon meeting, it can be easily decided which of us lacked confidence in his faith—whether it was the one who was willing to state it but was afraid to have it preserved, or the one who was so unwilling to remove it from the judgment of the disputants that he wanted what was committed to writing to be entrusted as well to the memory of readers. In that way neither of us might be either confused by forgetfulness or annoyed by the disagreement and might say that something that was said was not said or that something that was not said was said. For those who desire an argument more than the truth often seek concealment for their weak defense in such places. But this could be said neither by you nor by me, neither about you nor about me, if you remained faithful to our agreement that our words be taken down and recorded, especially since you yourself changed those words in which you stated your faith as often as you repeated them, something that was not done out of deceit, I believe, but out of forgetfulness.

---

1. In the critical edition the letter lacks a salutation, perhaps because, as Augustine says in paragraph 26, he thought that Pascentius might not want his name on the letter. PL adds the salutation produced here.

3. For you first said that you believed in "God the Father, almighty, invisible, unbegotten, incomprehensible, and in Jesus Christ, his Son, God born before the ages, through whom all things were made, and in the Holy Spirit." After hearing this, when I replied that you had not yet said anything that was in conflict with my faith and hence that, if you signed it, I could also add my signature, somehow or other the matter was brought to the point that you took a piece of paper and wanted to express by your own hand in writing what you had said. And when you gave it to me to read, I noticed that you had left out "Father" when you wrote "God almighty, invisible, unbegotten, unborn." When I mentioned this, after a brief dispute you added "Father" and "incomprehensible," which you had spoken in words but omitted in writing. But I made no mention of this.

4. Then, after I had said that I was ready to add my signature to indicate that those words could be mine as well, I first asked, lest what had entered my mind slip away, whether "unbegotten Father" was found anywhere in the divine scriptures. But I did this because at the beginning of our discussion, when the names Arius and Eunomius[2] were mentioned, not by me but by my brother Alypius,[3] who was asking which of them Auxentius[4] followed, a man who was extolled by you with no small praise, you immediately demanded that we condemn ὁμοούσιον,[5] as if there were any person who was called by this name, like Arius and Eunomius. Next you vigorously demanded that we show you this word in the scriptures, and you would immediately be in communion with us. We answered that, since we spoke Latin and that term was Greek, it was first necessary to investigate what ὁμοούσιον meant and then one should demand that it be shown to be in the holy books. You, on the other hand, repeated the word frequently and uttered it with hate, recalling that it was recorded in the councils of our predecessors, and you strongly urged that we show that that very word, namely, ὁμοούσιον, is in the holy books. We recalled again and again that, since our language was not Greek, we first had to translate and explain what ὁμοούσιον meant and then look for it in the divine writings. For, even if the term were not itself found there, we might nonetheless find the idea. After all, what is more a

---

2. Arius was the fourth-century Alexandrian priest after whom the Arian heresy was named. Eunomius, also of the fourth century, taught an extreme form of Arianism, maintaining that the Son was unlike the Father. For that reason his doctrine was called Anomoeanism.

3. Alypius, Augustine's friend since his youth, was now bishop of Thagaste.

4. There were two Arian bishops named Auxentius. One was the bishop of Milan immediately prior to Saint Ambrose; he died in 374. The other was a Homoian Arian, the bishop of Durostorum, and a disciple of Ulfilas, the apostle of the Goths, who came to Milan in 383 and attempted to obtain the basilica of Saint Ambrose through the intervention of the Arian empress, Justina. See *Confessions* IX, 7, 15. It is most likely the latter whom Pascentius had praised. Homoian Arianism held that the Son was like the Father, but not that he was of the same substance as the Father.

5. The word ὁμοούσιον, taken from the Creed of Nicaea, expressed the sameness of substance of the Father and the Son.

mark of quarrelsomeness than to fight over the word when we are agreed on the idea?

5. Because, then, we had already discussed this between ourselves, after we had come to the point at which you were expressing your faith in writing, as I mentioned, although I saw nothing in those words opposed to our faith and for this reason said that I was prepared to add my signature, I asked, as I said, whether God's scripture contained the statement that "the Father is unbegotten," and, when you replied that scripture did contain this, I asked more insistently that you demonstrate this. Then one of those who were present, someone who shares your faith, as far as I can understand, said to me, "So what? Do you say that the Father is begotten?" I replied, "I am not saying so." And he said, "If, then, he is not begotten, he is certainly unbegotten." I said to him, "You see that it is possible, however, to give an account of a word that is not in God's scripture in order to show that it is right to use it. In that way, then, even if we did not find in the scriptures the word ὁμοούσιον itself, which we were being obliged to show was found in the authority of the divine books, it is possible to find that to which this word is judged to have been correctly applied."

6. After this was said, I paid attention in order to hear what you thought about this, and you said that "it was correct that 'unbegotten Father' was not used in the holy scriptures for fear that an injury might be done to him by such an expression." I said, "Injury is now done to God, therefore, and this by your own hand." When you heard this, you had already begun to say that you ought not to have said this yourself. But when I warned you that, if you thought this word was such that it might injure God, you should delete it there where you had written it, you considered, I think, that it could be correctly used and could be defended. And again you stated, "I certainly say this." Then I repeated the point that I had already made, namely, that it is possible that ὁμοούσιον is not found written in the sacred books and yet it may be defensible when uttered in the statement of the faith, just as we never read "the unbegotten Father" in those books and yet its use is defensible. Then you took from me the sheet of paper that you had given and tore it up. And we agreed that in the afternoon stenographers would be present to take down our words and that we would deal more carefully with these questions between us, to the extent we could.

7. We came at the hour agreed upon, as you know; we brought along our stenographers; when yours were also present, we were seated. You again stated your faith, and in your words I did not hear "unbegotten Father." I believe that you were thinking of what was said about this in the morning and wanted to be careful. Then you asked that I too state my faith. At this point, when I asked, recalling our agreement from the morning, that you instead be so gracious as to dictate what you had said, you shouted out that we were preparing a trap for you and, for that reason, that you wanted to have your words in writing. I do not want

to recall what I said at that point, and I wish that you would not remember it either. Yet I maintained the respect due to your office, and I did not regard as an injury what I merited to hear not from the truth but from your authority. Since, nonetheless, I repeated at least those very words while saying quietly, "Are we preparing a trap for you in this way?" I ask your pardon.

8. But, when you heard this, you again repeated your faith in a louder voice and in your words I did not hear "God the Son," something that you had never omitted as often as you had stated your faith. When I asked as calmly as I could that what we had agreed upon concerning the taking down of our words be implemented, I also pointed out its usefulness from our present experience. I said that you yourself could not remember words of yours that you used very often, since you were never able to repeat them without omitting something that was very important. How much less can those who listen to us remember our words so that, if I wanted to reconsider and discuss something in your words or you in mine, they would be able to recall clearly what was said and what was not said. In such a difficulty a reading on the part of the stenographers would be of assistance to us. Then you said angrily that it would have been better if you knew me only by reputation, because you found me to be far less than it had been boasted that I was. Then I recalled that, when we greeted you in the morning and you had praised that reputation of ours, I said that the reports about me were not true. At this point you of course agreed that I was speaking the truth. Hence, since two sources have spoken different things about me, my reputation saying one thing and I another, I certainly ought to be happy that you found me rather than my reputation truthful. But because scripture says, *God alone is truthful, but every human being is a liar* (Rom 3:4), I am afraid that you were rash also in saying this about me. After all, we are not truthful in ourselves or by ourselves when we are truthful but when he who alone is truthful speaks through his servants.

9. If you recall these actions, as I have narrated them, you see how you ought not to boast before human beings that I did not dare to state my faith for you, since you refused to keep faith with our agreement. And you, a man of such importance, who in defense of the faithfulness you owe to the state do not fear the insults of provincials, fear the attacks of bishops in defense of the faithfulness you owe Christ. Then, since you wanted men of honor to be present at our discussion, I am amazed at how, in the matter of avoiding attack, you are afraid to have your words taken down by our stenographers but are not afraid to have illustrious men hear you speaking from your own lips. Do you not realize that it is difficult for people to believe that you are so afraid of any attack from us that you refused to have your words taken down, but that, though you thought that you were bound by your own words written down in the morning, at the same time you thought that you could not destroy the stenographers' tablets as easily

as you tore up that sheet of paper? If, however, you say that those actions did not take place as I have narrated them, you are either misled by forgetfulness (for I do not want to say, "You are lying"), or I am likewise misled or am lying. You see, then, how correct I am in saying that the actions taken, especially on these matters, ought to be written down and recorded and how right it also was for you to have made this decision, except that your afternoon fear shattered your morning agreement.

2, 10. Listen, then, to my faith: Powerful is the mercy of God, which allows me to state what I believe so that I do not offend his truth or your graciousness. I declare that I believe in God the Father almighty and state that he is eternal with that eternity, that is, immortality, I mean, which God alone has, and I believe this of his only-begotten Son in the form of God and also of the Holy Spirit, who is the Spirit of God the Father and of his only-begotten Son. But because, *after the fullness of time came* (Gal 4:4), the only-begotten Son of God the Father, our Lord and God Jesus Christ, opportunely assumed the form of a servant,[6] for the day of our salvation, many things are said of him in the scriptures in accord with the form of God and many in accord with the form of the servant. As an example I mention two of these in order that one may be referred to each. In accord with the form of God he said of himself, *The Father and I are one* (Jn 10:30). In accord with the form of the servant he said, *The Father is greater than I* (Jn 14:28).

11. But the words of scripture about God, *Who alone has immortality* (1 Tm 6:16), and, *To the invisible God alone be honor and glory* (1 Tm 1:17), and other expressions of this sort, we do not understand as applying to the Father alone but to the Son as well, insofar as this refers to the form of God, and to the Holy Spirit. For the Father and the Son and the Holy Spirit are one God, and the only true God, and alone immortal in accord with their absolutely immutable substance. After all, if scripture said of the flesh, with its different sexes, *He who clings to a prostitute forms one body with her* (1 Cor 6:16), and of the spirit of a human being, which is not the same as the Lord, *But one who clings to the Lord forms one spirit with him* (1 Cor 6:17), how much more is God the Father in the Son and God the Son in the Father and God the Spirit of the Father and the Son one God, where there is no diversity of nature, since it is said of two different things that somehow cling to one another that they form either one spirit or one body.

12. And since we speak of one human being instead of a soul and a body clinging to each other, why should we not for much better reasons speak of one God when referring to the Father and the Son who cling to each other, since they cling to each other inseparably, not like the body and the soul? And since the body and the soul are one human being, although the body and the soul are not

---

6. See Phil 2:7.

one, why should the Father and the Son for much better reasons not be one God, since the Father and the Son are one according to that statement of the Truth, *The Father and I are one* (Jn 10:30)? Similarly, the interior human being and the exterior human being are not one, for the nature of the exterior is not the same as that of the interior, since the exterior along with the body that was mentioned is called a human being, but the interior is understood to be found only in the rational soul. Yet the two together are not called two human beings but one. For how much better reasons are the Father and the Son one God, since the Father and the Son are one, because they are of the same nature or substance or any other term that expresses more suitably that which God is, which is why it was said, *The Father and I are one* (Jn 10:30)? And so the one Spirit of the Lord and the one spirit of a human being are not one, and yet, when someone clings to the Lord, there are not two spirits but one spirit; and one exterior human being and one interior human being are not one, and yet on account of their connection in a natural union both together are not two but one human being. For much better reasons, then, since the Son of God says, *The Father and I are one*, God the Father is one and God the Son is one, and yet both together are not two gods but one God.

13. One faith, one hope, and one love[7] has brought it about in many holy persons, who have been called *into adoption as children* (Rom 8:17; 1 Cor 13:13) to be coheirs with Christ, that they may have *one soul and one heart* (Acts 4:32) for God. This above all forces us to understand that the nature of the divinity—if we may speak that way—of the Father and of the Son is one and the same, so that the Father and the Son, who are one and inseparably one and ever-lastingly one, are not two gods but one God. For, through the sharing and union in one and the same nature by which they were all human beings, those human beings were one, and if at times they were not one because of their diverse wills and views and the dissimilarity of their opinions and conduct, they will, however, be fully and perfectly one when they come to that end, *in order that God may be all in all* (1 Cor 15:28). God the Father, however, and his Son, his Word, God with God,[8] are always and ineffably one; hence, for even better reason they are not two gods but one God.

14. But human beings who understand less well what is said for that reason prefer to have hastily-formed views, and, without having carefully examined the scriptures, they take up the defense of any opinion whatsoever and are turned aside from it either never or only with difficulty, since they want to be considered learned and wise rather than to be such. They actually want to transfer those things that were said on account of the form of the servant to the form of God,

---

7. See Eph 1:5.
8. See Jn 1:1.

and on the other hand they want those things that were said in order to indicate the mutual relations of the persons to be names of a nature or substance. But our faith consists in believing and confessing that the Father and the Son and the Holy Spirit are one God, nor do we say that he who is the Son is the Father, nor that he who is the Father is the Son, nor that he who is the Spirit of the Father and the Son is either the Father or the Son. For these names signify their mutual relations, not the very substance by which they are one. For, when he is called Father, he is called father only of a son, and the Son is understood as a son only of a father, and the Spirit, insofar as he is related to something, is a spirit of someone that breathes him forth, and the one that breathes forth, of course, breathes forth the Spirit.

15. But of God these things are not thought in a bodily fashion, nor are they understood in the usual way. As the apostle says, *He is able to do more than we ask for and understand* (Eph 3:20). But if he can *do* more, for how much better reason can he *be* more! For in the scriptures this term "spirit," not insofar as it is relative but insofar as it signifies a nature, refers to every incorporeal nature of spirit; for this reason this term applies not only to the Father, the Son, and the Holy Spirit but to every rational creature and soul. Hence the Lord says, *God is spirit, and for this reason those who worship God should worship him in spirit and in truth* (Jn 4:24). It is also written, *He made the spirits his messengers* (Ps 104:4). It was also said of certain human beings, *For they are flesh and a spirit that goes and does not return* (Ps 78:39). And the apostle says, *No one knows what is going on in a human being but the spirit of the human being who is present there* (1 Cor 2:11). Likewise scripture says, *Who knows whether the spirit of the sons of man rises upward and the spirit of an animal goes downward?* (Eccl 3:21) "Spirit" is also used in the scriptures in accord with a certain distinction in the one soul of a human being; for this reason the apostle says, *That your whole spirit and soul and body may be preserved for the day of our Lord Jesus Christ* (1 Thes 5:23). So too in another place he says, *If I pray with the tongue, my spirit prays, but my mind remains without fruit. What, then, shall I do? I will pray with the spirit, and I will pray with the mind.* (1 Cor 14:14-15) But in a certain proper way we speak of the Holy Spirit who is related to the Father and the Son, because he is their Holy Spirit. For, because it was once said in terms of substance that *God is spirit* (Jn 4:24), the Father is spirit, and the Son, and the Holy Spirit himself, and yet they are not three spirits but one spirit, just as there are not three gods but one God.

16. Why are you surprised? Peace has such power—not just any peace as it is usually understood, nor such peace as is praised in this life in the oneness of heart and love of the faithful, but *that peace of God that*, as the apostle says, *surpasses all understanding* (Phil 4:7). What understanding but ours, that is, of every rational creature? Hence, as we consider our weakness and listen to the apostle

saying, *Brothers, I do not think that I have attained the goal* (Phil 3:13), and, *Anyone who thinks that he knows something does not yet know how he ought to know something* (1 Cor 8:2), let us converse as well as we can with the divine scriptures, at peace and without strife, not striving to outdo each other in vain and childish rivalry. In that way the peace of Christ may instead triumph in our hearts,[9] to the extent that he grants us the ability to attain it in this life. Considering what that same peace produced among the brethren from whose many souls and hearts he made one soul and one heart for God,[10] let us above all believe with due piety that in that *peace of God, which surpasses all understanding,* the Father, the Son, and the Holy Spirit are not three gods but one God in a more excellent way than those believers had *one soul and one heart,* just as *that peace, which surpasses all understanding,* is more excellent than this peace that is possessed by their one heart and one soul for God.[11]

17. We say, however, that the Son of Man is the same as the Son of God, but not on account of the form of God in which he is equal to the Father, but on account of the form of the servant by which he is less than the Father.[12] And because we say that the Son of God is the Son of Man, for this reason we also say that the Son of God was crucified, not because of the power of the divinity but because of the weakness of the humanity, not because of his remaining in his own nature but because of his taking up of our nature.

3, 18. Now consider for a while the words of scripture that compel us to confess one Lord God, whether we are asked only about the Father or only about the Son or only about the Holy Spirit, or about the Father, Son, and Holy Spirit together. Scripture certainly says, *Hear, O Israel, the Lord your God is one Lord* (Dt 6:4). Of whom do you think it was said? If only of the Father, Jesus Christ is not our Lord God, and what happens to those words of Thomas as he touched him and cried out, *My Lord and my God*? Christ did not criticize those words but approved of them when he said, *Because you saw me, you believed* (Jn 20:28-29). But if the Son is the Lord God and the Father is also the Lord God and the two of them are two lords and two gods, how will this be true: *The Lord your God is one Lord* (Dt 6:4)? Or is perhaps the Father the one Lord, but the Son is not *the* one Lord but only *a* lord, just as there are many gods and many lords, not as there is that one Lord of whom scripture says, *The Lord your God is one Lord*? What, then, shall we answer the apostle when he says, *For, even if there are many who are called gods, whether in heaven or on earth, we nonetheless have one God, the Father, from whom are all things and we are in him, and our one Lord, Jesus Christ, through whom are all things and we through him* (1 Cor

---

9. See Col 3:15.
10. See Acts 4:32.
11. See Acts 4:32.
12. See Phil 2:6-7.

8:5-6)? Now, if what is said of the one God the Father forces us to separate the Son from this, let those who dare say that the Father cannot now be understood as Lord, because Paul said, *Our one Lord, Jesus Christ*. For, if he is the one Lord, he is of the only one; and if he is the only one, how is the Father also the one Lord, unless because he and the Father are the one God and the only God, without the exclusion of the Holy Spirit? The Father, then, is the one God, and with him the Son is the one God, though the Son is not one Father with him. Likewise, Jesus Christ is the one Lord, and the Father is the one Lord with him, although the Father is not the one Jesus Christ with him, as if the Father were Jesus Christ. For Jesus Christ took this name because of the dispensation of mercy and because of the humanity he assumed.

19. Or do you perhaps, in the words of the apostle, *Our one Lord, Jesus Christ, through whom all things come*, want to join the term *one* not to *Lord* but to *through whom all things come* in order that you can understand not *the one Lord* but *the one through whom all things come*? In that way it would not be the Father through whom all things come, but the Father alone from whom all things come and the Son alone through whom all things come. If that is the case, at long last admit that our one Lord and God is the Father and the Son. *For who has known the mind of the Lord? Or who has been his counselor? Or who first gave to him and will be repaid? For from him and through him and in him are all things. To him be glory.* (Rom 11:34-36) For he did not say, "From the Father are all things, and through the Son are all things," but, *From him and through him and in him*. Who is this but the Lord of whom he said, *Who has known the mind of the Lord?* From the Lord, then, and through the Lord, and in the Lord are all things, not in that one distinct from this one, but in the one Lord, since he did not say, "To them be glory," but, *To him be glory*.

20. But if anyone says that what the apostle states, *The one Lord Jesus Christ through whom are all things* (1 Cor 8:6), is not understood as "the one Lord," nor as "the one through whom all things are" but as "the one Jesus Christ," and that the one Jesus Christ is also said to be the Lord, what is that person going to say when he hears the same apostle crying out, *One Lord, one faith, one baptism, one God and Father of all* (Eph 4:5-6)? After all, since he mentions God the Father here, when he says, *One God and Father of all*, whom did he beyond any doubt want us to understand by the previous words, *one Lord*, except Jesus Christ? If he agrees, then, let the Father cease to be Lord, because Jesus Christ is the one Lord. But if that is absurd and impious to think, let us learn to understand the unity of the Father, Son, and Holy Spirit, in order that we may not be immediately kept from understanding of the Son or of the Holy Spirit what was said of the one and only God. For the Father is certainly not the Son, and the Son is not the Father, and the Spirit of both is not the Father or the Son, and yet the Father, Son, and Holy Spirit are the one Lord God, who is the only one and the true one.

4, 21. After all, if the Holy Spirit were not God and the true God, our bodies would not be his temples. The apostle says, *Do you not know that your bodies are the temple in your midst of the Holy Spirit, whom you have from God?* (1 Cor 6:19-20) And so that no one would deny that the Holy Spirit was God, he immediately went on to say, *And you are not your own, for you were purchased at a great price. Therefore glorify and carry God in your body,* the God, that is, whose temple he had just said was our bodies. Now it is astonishing if what I hear you are saying is true—that the Holy Spirit is less than the Son, just as the Son is less than the Father. For, since our bodies are members of Christ, as the apostle says, and since our bodies are also the temple of the Holy Spirit, as the same apostle says,[13] I am deeply puzzled at how the members of the greater are the temple of the lesser. Or do you perhaps now want to say that the Holy Spirit is greater than the Lord Jesus Christ? After all, the following statement also seems to favor this idea: *For one who speaks a word against the Son of Man will be forgiven, but one who speaks against the Holy Spirit will not be forgiven, not in this world, nor in the world to come* (Mt 12:32; Lk 12:10). For one sins with greater peril against the greater than against the lesser, nor may one separate the Son of Man from the Son of God, because the Son of God himself became the Son of Man not by changing what he was but by assuming what he was not. But away with such impiety of believing that the Holy Spirit is greater than the Son! Let those expressions that seem to show that one is greater than another, then, not readily drive people into error.

22. For certain expressions are used in such a way that those who are less intelligent might think that the Son is greater than the Father. For, when asked which is greater, someone true or the truth, who would not rather reply that the truth is greater? After all, whatever things are true are true by reason of the truth. But it is not that way in God. For we certainly do not say that the Son is greater than the Father, and yet the Son is said to be the truth. He says, *I am the way, the truth, and the life* (Jn 14:6). But you want us to understand of the Father alone his words, *That they may know you, the one true God, and him whom you have sent, Jesus Christ* (Jn 17:3), where we understand that Jesus Christ is also the true God, so that this is the meaning: "That they may know you and him whom you sent, Jesus Christ, to be the one true God." Otherwise, the absurdity results that, if Jesus Christ is not the true God because he said to the Father, *You, the one true God,* the Father is not Lord because *one Lord* (1 Cor 8:6) is said of Christ. And yet, in accord with an incorrect interpretation or rather an error, God the truth is greater than the true God, because the true comes from the truth. The Son, therefore, is greater than the Father, because the former is the truth, while the latter is true. One who has learned that the Father is true God by begetting the truth, not

13. See 1 Cor 6:15; 12:27.

by participating in it, drives this perversity from his mind. For the true Father does not have another substance than the truth he begets.

23. But, although the eye of the human heart is weak for the contemplation of these realities, it is in addition also disturbed by controversy. And when will it see them? Scripture says that the Son of God, our Lord and savior, Jesus Christ, the Word of God, is both truth and wisdom, and some people say that through his own nature and substance, by which he is the Word of God and the wisdom of God, he was visible and subject to corruption before receiving the flesh that he took from the Virgin Mary, without any assumption at all of a bodily creature. For they want what they hold to be consistent, namely, that it is said of the Father alone, *To the invisible, incorruptible, only God* (1 Tm 1:17). I ask you to see that the word of a human being is not visible, nor is the Word of God. But if that wisdom is corruptible of which it is said, *It reaches everywhere on account of its purity*, and, *Nothing impure enters into it*, and, *Remaining in itself, it renews all things* (Wis 7:24-25.27), and any other things like these, which are countless, I do not know what to say except that I grieve over the pride of human beings and am astonished at the patience of God.

24. But since it is said of that wisdom, *It is the splendor of eternal light* (Wis 7:26), not even your people, I think, now say that the light of the Father—after all, what is it but his substance?—was ever without the splendor that it begot, as these things can be believed and somehow or other understood in what is divine, spiritual, incorporeal, and immutable. For I hear that you have corrected those people. Or is it perhaps false that they once said that at some time the Father was without the Son, as if the eternal light were without the splendor it begot? What, then, do we say? If the Son of God was born of the Father, the Father ceased to beget him, and if he ceased, he began. But if he began to beget him, he was at some time without the Son. But he was never without the Son because his Son is his wisdom, which is *the splendor of eternal light*. Therefore, the Father always begets the Son, and the Son is always being born. Here we should again fear that the generation be thought incomplete if we do not say that he was born but is being born. Be patient with me, I beg, in these difficulties of human thought and expression, and let us together have recourse to the Spirit of God who speaks through the prophet, *Who will explain his generation?* (Is 53:8)

25. Meanwhile I ask that you search diligently for this one thing: whether somewhere the divine scripture has said of different substances that they are one. For, if we find that it is only said of those things that are clearly of one and the same substance, what need is there for us to rebel against the true and Catholic faith? But if you find that scripture somewhere says this of different substances, then I shall be forced to search for something else by which to show that the Father and the Son were correctly said to be ὁμοούσιον. For there are some who either do not know our scriptures or do not examine them with great care and

who nonetheless say that the Son is of the same substance as and equal to the Father. Suppose that they say to those who refuse to believe this, though they believe that God the Father has an only-begotten Son: "Was God unwilling to have the Son as his equal, or was he unable? If he was unwilling, he is envious. If he was unable, he is weak. But to think either of these of God is sacrilegious." I do not know whether they can find anything to say if they do not want to say things that are most absurd and most stupid.

5, 26. There, you see, I have explained my faith to you as well as I could. And many more things, indeed, could be said and discussed with greater care. But I fear that the things that I have said may be a burden for you with all your work. Yet I not only wanted to dictate them and to have them written down, but I also took care to add my signature in my own hand, something that I had wanted to do before, if what we had agreed upon were being followed. But now I am sure that you ought not to say that I was afraid to state my faith for you, since I have not only stated it but signed the written statement of it, so that no one may say that I either said what I did not say or did not say what I said. Do this yourself as well if you are looking for judges, not ones who will reverence your person to your face but who will assert their freedom with regard to your writings. For, if you fear an attack—which I would by no means dare to say if you had not mentioned it—it is permissible for you not to sign. For I too did not want to write your name in my letter for fear that you perhaps would not have wanted this.

27. It is easy for someone to defeat Augustine; you must see whether it is by the truth or by shouting. It is not up to me to say anything but that it is easy for someone to defeat Augustine. How much more easy is it that someone should seem to have defeated me or to say that he has defeated me, even if he does not seem to have! This is easy. I do not want you to think it a great achievement; I do not want you to desire it as a great achievement. For, when on this issue people notice how much your heart is burning, many will rejoice at having found the opportunity to make a powerful man their friend with a few cries of "Good going, good going." I do not want to say that, if they do not side with you or if they express the opposite view, they could also have feared you as an enemy. They surely would do so foolishly and stupidly, but most human beings are, nonetheless, like that.

28. Do not, then, pay attention to how Augustine may be defeated, just one man of whatever sort he is. But rather pay attention to whether ὁμοούσιον can be conquered, not this Greek word, which is easy for those who do not understand it to mock, but those words of scripture, *The Father and I are one* (Jn 10:30), and, *Holy Father, preserve those whom you gave me in your name that they may be one, just as we are* (Jn 17:11). So too, a little later it says, *But I do not ask for these alone, but also for those who will believe in me through their word, that all may be one, as you, Father, are in me, and I am in you, that they too may be one in*

us in order that the world may believe that you have sent me. And I have given them the glory that you gave me in order that they may be one, just as we too are one, I in them, and you in me, in order that they may be made perfectly one. (Jn 17:20-23) See how many times he said, *That they may be one, just as we too are one.* Yet he never said, "We and they are one," but, *That they too may be one in us, just as we too are one,* because, just as they were of one and the same substance whom he wanted to make partakers of eternal life, so it was said of the Father and the Son, *We are one,* because they are of one and the same substance and are not partakers of eternal life but the very source of eternal life. And he could say in accord with the form of the servant, "They and I are one, or we are one." But he did not say this because he wanted to make known the one substance, the Father's and his own and the one substance of those human beings. But if he had said, "That you and they might be one, just as you and I are one," or, "That you and I and they might be one, just as you and I are one," none of us would deny that different substances could also be said to be one. But now you see that this is not the case, because he did not speak in that way, and by saying it often he strongly emphasized what he said.

29. You find in the scriptures, therefore, that "something one" is said of different natures, as we have shown above, but there is added or understood what that one thing is, just as we say that soul and body are or is one living being or one person or one human being. But if in the scriptures you find *They are one* said without any addition of those things that are not of one substance, you will be perfectly justified in demanding that we produce another argument to illustrate the meaning of ὁμοούσιον. For there are many other things, but for the present think of this one, when you have put aside the desire to be argumentative so that you may have God's favor. The good of a human being does not consist in defeating another human being, but it is good for a human being willingly to have the truth defeat him, because it is bad for a human being to have the truth defeat him against his will. For it is necessary that the truth win out, whether one denies it or admits it. Pardon me if I have spoken too freely, not to disparage you but to defend myself. For I have presumed upon your seriousness and wisdom, since you can imagine the great obligation you imposed upon me to respond. Or if I have not done even this correctly, please also pardon it. [Augustine has signed this document, which I dictated and reread.]

Letter 239

About 404 Augustine wrote once more to Count Pascentius. Augustine claims that Pascentius did not state his faith, namely, the Arian aspects of his faith by which he differs from the Catholic faith, but only stated aspects that Arians and Catholics believed in common (paragraph 1). He blames Pascentius for refusing to allow stenographers to take down what each of them said (paragraph 2). Finally, Augustine delineates his Catholic faith regarding the Trinity and urges Pascentius to read the longer letter that he had sent him (paragraph 3).

Augustine to Pascentius.

1. If you say that you stated your faith for me and that I refused to state my faith for you, as I hear that you are in fact saying, recall, I beg you, how both of these assertions are false. For you refused to state your faith for me, and I did not refuse to state my faith for you. But I wanted to state it so that no one could say either that I said what I did not say or that I did not say what I said. But you would state your faith for me if you stated the reasons why you disagree with us, if you said, "I believe in God the Father who made the Son as the first creature before all other creatures, and in the Son who is neither equal to, nor like the Father, nor the true God, and in the Holy Spirit, made through the Son after the Son." For these are the things that I hear you are saying. Or, if it is false that you are saying these things, I want rather to know this from you. But if it is true that you are saying these things, I want to know how you defend them from the holy scriptures. But now you have said that you believe "in God the Father who is almighty, invisible, immortal, and not born from another, and from whom all things come, and in his Son, Jesus Christ, born as God before the ages, through whom all things were made, and in the Holy Spirit." This is not your faith but the faith of both of us, just as if you added that the Virgin Mary bore that same Son of God, Jesus Christ, something that we likewise believe, and any other points that we confess in common. If, therefore, you had wanted to state your faith, you would not state what is common to both of us but rather that in which we disagree with you.

2. I would say this in your presence if, as we had agreed, our words were being taken down. But because you were unwilling to do this, saying that you feared an attack from us, and withdrew in the afternoon from the agreement you made in the morning, why should I say what you might report that I said, as you want, while I would not have the means to show what I did say or how I said it? Do not, therefore, continue to boast that you stated your faith and that I did not state mine, because there are people who consider that it is really I, who wanted it to be written down, who have confidence in my faith, but that you do not, since you

feared some sort of attack. You were, therefore, ready to deny it if an objection were raised against you that you had said something contrary to my faith. See, then, what you cause people to think of you. But if you were not going to deny the objection, why did you not want what you said to be written down, especially since you greatly wanted distinguished people to be present at our discussion? Why, then, in wanting to avoid an attack, were you afraid of the pen of the stenographers, though you did not fear the testimony of such illustrious persons?

3. But if you want me to state my faith as you say that you stated yours, I can also very briefly say that I believe in the Father and the Son and the Holy Spirit. If you want, however, to hear some particular point on which you disagree with me, I believe in the Father and the Son and the Holy Spirit, and I do not say that the Son is the Father or that the Father is the Son. Nor do I say that the Holy Spirit of both of them is either the Father or the Son. And yet I say that the Father is God, the Son is God, and the Holy Spirit is God, the only God, eternal and immortal by his own substance, just as God alone is eternal and immortal by that divinity which is before the ages. If you disagree with this and you want to hear from me how it is defended from the holy scriptures, read as well what I wrote at greater length and sent to Your Goodness. If, however, you do not have time to read it, neither do I have time to toss about useless words. But I myself can reply to what you want by either dictating or writing to the extent that the Lord gives me the ability to either dictate or write to you. [I, Augustine, have signed this letter that I dictated and reread.]

Letter 240

Around the year 404 the Arian Count Pascentius wrote Augustine an insulting letter in which he challenged Augustine to tell him which of the three persons of the Trinity was the one God. He tells Augustine that, if he were confident of his faith, he and the other Catholic bishops would sit down and confer with him on matters of theology.

Pascentius to Augustine.

I had hoped, my most beloved brother, that you had abandoned the conviction of your previous error. Now I am surprised that you still remain in it, as your letter, which you sent to me, cries out. For Your Grace is like someone thirsty and overheated who finds polluted water and drinks heavily from it. Afterward, even if he finds clear and cold water and drinks it, it cannot benefit him enough since his heart and soul are already filled with pollution. Secondly, by your leave, I say that the conviction of Your Excellency is like a bent and knotty tree that has nothing straight about it and misleads the gaze of the eyes. Your Holiness writes to me that the Father is God, the Son is God, and the Holy Spirit is God, but that there is one God. Which of the three is the one God? Or is there perhaps one person with three forms who is called by that name? If you had been willing and were confident of your profession of faith, you would sit down with me along with your fellow bishops in a pure and peaceful mind and spirit, and you would discuss these questions that pertain to God and to glory and spiritual grace. Hence what need is there to write back and forth things that do not edify us?

Letter 241

Sometime after the previous letter was written, Augustine replied to Pascentius. Augustine responds to some of Pascentius' insults and denies that he believes that the person of God has three forms, as Pascentius had suggested (paragraph 1). He challenges Pascentius to explain how, though the apostle said that someone who clings to the Lord is one spirit with the Lord, he, Pascentius, can deny that the Son, who certainly clings to the Father, is one God with the Father. Finally, Augustine invites Pascentius to reply in writing (paragraph 2).

Augustine to Pascentius.

1. Your letter could neither provoke me to return insults nor deter me from replying to your letter. The things that you wrote would certainly trouble me if they were said by the truth of God, not by the authority of a human being. You said that my "conviction is like a twisted and knotty tree that has nothing straight about it and misleads the gaze of eyes."[1] What would you say of me if I had withdrawn from the agreement that we had made between ourselves in the morning and had set twists of opposition and knots of difficulty in that very easy matter that we had rightly agreed upon? For you would not think that I had drunk heavily of polluted water but that I had drowned in the intoxication of perfidy, which is much worse, if I had not come back after dinner as the same sort of person who had left before dinner. But look: did you not write back what you wanted without fear of any attack? In the same way, then, you can write the other things as well so that there might be something for ourselves and others to consider and judge. For, as to your statement that I believe in the person of God with three forms, if you had deigned to read the other somewhat longer letter I sent and had wanted to reply to what I had written in it, you would perhaps not say this. But look, you dictated, had it written down, and sent the claim that I say that the person of God has three forms, and you were not afraid of an attack. See, you have shown that what I say is true, namely, that you did not refuse to have your words taken down, as was agreed upon when we were together, because you feared an attack, but because you were not confident about the truth. Now, since you have decided to put in writing the question of whether I believe that the person of God has three forms, I reply that I do not believe that. There is one form because there is, if I may say so, one deity and, therefore, one God, Father, Son, and Holy Spirit.

---

1. See Letter 240.

2. But I ask that you be so gracious as to answer briefly how you understand the words of the apostle, *A man who clings to a prostitute forms one body with her, but one who clings to the Lord forms one spirit with him* (1 Cor 6:16-17). After all, he said that bodies of different sex clinging to each other are one body. And although the human spirit can by no means say, "The Lord and I are one," yet, when one is clinging to the Lord, one forms one spirit with him. For how much better reason are he and the Father one God, because he most truly said, *The Father and I are one* (Jn 10:30)? For he clings inseparably to the Father—at least if this term is allowed in that divinity, so that we may say that something "clings" that never was nor will be separated by any distance. Reply to this: Do you want to say that the spirit has two forms because one who clings to the Lord is one spirit? And if you do not want to say this, neither did I say that God, Father, Son, and Holy Spirit, has three forms, but that he is one God. But if you want to converse face to face, I am of course grateful to Your Grace and Benevolence. But, as you have already been so good as to write for me something else that you wanted, then be so good as write back that we will dictate what we are going to say, and I will be ready to do what you want, to the extent that the Lord helps me. For, if our writing back and forth does not edify us, how will our spoken words to each other be edifying, when, once our words have sounded, we will not find anything we can reexamine by reading? [I, Augustine, have dictated this and have signed it after rereading it.] Let us abstain from insults so that we do not spend the time uselessly, and let us rather pay attention to the issue between us.

Letter 242

Sometime during his episcopacy Augustine wrote to Elpidius, an Arian from North Africa, who had sent him a book by an Arian bishop along with a letter in which the unnamed bishop expressed the desire to win Augustine over to the Arian faith. Augustine thanks Elpidius for the good will he has shown him, especially by even sending some of his writings overseas to two learned Arians, and hopes that Elpidius will accept in a good spirit his prayers for his conversion (paragraph 1). Then Augustine turns to a proof that the Son of God, the Word, by whom all things were made, was himself not made (paragraph 2). Hence, since nothing was made without him, he is either nothing or was not made. Since it is wrong to think that he is nothing, then one must conclude that he was not made but was born from the Father (paragraph 3). Though his generation is ineffable, he is equal to the Father. Though we now hold this in faith, we must purify our hearts so that, once they have been cleansed, we may come to see what we now believe (paragraph 4). Finally, Augustine promises to reply to the book Elpidius sent him if he finds time, and he criticizes its author for claiming to teach the bare truth, though the apostle said that we now see through a glass in an enigma (paragraph 5).

To his excellent and rightly honorable and lovable lord Elpidius Augustine sends greetings.

1. Which of us is in error over the faith or knowledge of the Trinity is another question. Though I am unknown to you by sight, I am certainly grateful that you have tried to recall me from error, because you believed that I was in error. May God reward you for your good will and bring you to know what you think you know. For, in my opinion, the matter is difficult. And I ask you not to take it as any sort of insult that I have desired the gift of such knowledge for you. For I fear that the presumption of a knowledge that you suppose you have may drive from your hearing not true teachings, which I would never claim to teach you, but at least our good wishes, which I, though unlearned, am permitted to have regarding you. For these are not to be offered in the manner of a teacher but in that of a friend. And I fear that you may become angry at me because I have prayed that you may receive the gift of wisdom rather than congratulated you for already being someone wise. But I, who carry the burden of the title of bishop, most gladly embrace Your Benevolence because you have been so good as even to send my writings overseas to Bonosus and Jason, most learned men, as you write, in order that they may reap rich fruits from discussing them. And you also took care to have a book of a certain bishop of yours that was composed with talent and vigor brought to me in order to clear away the clouds of all my error. How much fairer is it for you to accept with a good heart my prayer that the Lord God might grant you those gifts that can be given by no human talent and power.

For the apostle says, *We have not received the spirit of this world, but the Spirit who comes from God, in order that we may know what God has given us, and we speak of these things not in the learned words of human wisdom, but having been taught by the Spirit we prepare spiritual things for spiritual persons. But the natural human being does not perceive the things that pertain to the Spirit of God. For such a person, after all, they are foolishness.* (1 Cor 2:12-14)

2. I would prefer, if possible, to investigate with you to what extent a human being ought to be called "natural," in order that, if we are now beyond being such a person, we might perhaps rejoice to have attained to some extent those realities that remain immutably above the human mind and intelligence. For we should beware that it not seem foolish when we hear that the Son is equal to the Father,[1] precisely because we are still a natural human being, of whom it has been said that those things that pertain to the Spirit of God are foolishness to such a person.[2] Although that majesty which is high above all things can be thought of by a spiritual person but can be expressed in words by no one, it is still easy, I think, to see that he through whom all things were made and without whom nothing was made was himself not made. For, if he was made by himself, he existed before he was made so that he could make himself, something that is more absurdly said the more foolishly it is thought. But, if he was not made by himself, he was not made at all, because whatever was made was made by him. *For all things were made by him, and without him nothing was made* (Jn 1:3).

3. I am surprised that you have paid such little attention to what the evangelist wanted to teach so explicitly so as to allow no one to pretend ignorance. For it was not enough to say, *All things were made by him*, if he did not add, *And without him nothing was made*. But though I am slow and, since the fog has not yet been wiped away, my mind's eye is too weak to look upon the incomparable and ineffable presence of the Father and the Son, I nonetheless embrace with all my might what has been sown for us in the gospel, not so that we might comprehend from it that divinity but so that we might be admonished by it not to boast rashly of our comprehension. For, if all things were made by him, whatever was not made by him was not made. But he himself was not made by himself; hence he was not made. And we are compelled by the evangelist to believe that all things were made by him; by the same evangelist, therefore, we are compelled to believe that he was not made. Likewise, if nothing was made without him, he himself is nothing, then, since he was made without himself. If it is sacrilegious to think this, it remains for us to say that he was not made without himself or was not made. But we cannot say that he was not made without himself. For, if he made himself, he already existed before he was made. But if, in order to make

---

1. See Jn 5:18; Phil 2:6.
2. See 1 Cor 2:14.

himself, he gave help to someone else by whom he was made, he already existed, nonetheless, before he was made in order that he might be made with his own help. It remains, therefore, that he was made without himself. But whatever was made without him is nothing. Either he is nothing, therefore, or he was not made. But he is not nothing; therefore, he was not made. But, if he was not made and is still the Son, he was undoubtedly born.

4. "How," you ask, "could the Son be born equal to the Father from whom he was born?" Now I cannot explain this, and I yield to the prophet who says, *Who will explain his generation?* (Is 53:8) But if you suppose that this should be understood in terms of the human generation by which the Son was born of the Virgin, examine carefully for yourself and question your soul whether, if it has failed to explain that human generation, it should dare to explain this divine generation. You say, "Do not call him equal." Why should I not say what the apostle said? He said, *He did not consider it robbery to be equal to God* (Phil 2:6). For, though he did not explain that equality to a human mind that has not yet been purified, he stated in words what the human mind might discover in reality once it has been purified. Let us, then, work at purifying our heart in order that there may emerge from it a keenness of vision by which we may be able to see these things. He says, *Blessed are the clean of heart because they shall see God* (Mt 5:8). Thus, emerging from the cloudy images of the natural human being, we shall come to that clarity and purity by which we may be able to see what we see cannot be said.

5. For, if I have the leisure and if the opportunity is given me to reply to the individual points of the book that you were so good as to send me, I think that you will recognize that each person is less clothed in the light of the truth the more he thinks that he speaks the bare truth. For, to omit other statements and to mention for now only this one, over which I have been very greatly saddened, since the apostle Paul says, *We see now through a glass in an enigma, but then we shall see face to face* (1 Cor 13:12), who would put up with this man's saying that "he brings forth the bare truth with every veil removed"? If he said, "We see the bare truth," nothing would be more blind than this arrogant claim to see. But he did not say, "We see," but, "We bring forth," so that the truth seems not only to lie open to the gaze of the mind but also to be subject to the power of the tongue. There are many things that may be said about the ineffability of the Trinity, not in order that it may be expressed in words—otherwise it would not be ineffable—but in order that it may be understood from the words that are said that it cannot be expressed in words. But now, I think, my letter has exceeded its limit, since you advised me by yours to write briefly. Because you deigned to excuse yourself for your lack of instruction in the ancients, I shall not appear strange to you if you are willing to recall the limit of certain letters of Cicero, since you also made mention of him in your letter.

Letter 243

Sometime during his episcopacy Augustine wrote to Laetus, a Catholic layman from Africa who had entered a monastery but left after his father's death because of his attachment to his mother and his family. Augustine tells Laetus of his sorrow over the temptations Laetus has encountered in his first steps in following Christ (paragraph 1). He refers to the words of Christ about the need to hate one's father, mother, brothers and sisters, and wife and children if one is to be Christ's disciple, and also to the two parables about the man who sets out to build a house and the king who is outnumbered by an enemy army (paragraph 2). He explains that each follower of Christ must renounce everything that is temporal and that belongs to him alone in order to possess what is eternal and common to all (paragraph 3). He points out that it is Laetus' carnal love for his mother that holds him back from being a disciple of Christ (paragraph 4). Augustine explains the meaning of Christ's words about hating one's parents and one's own soul (paragraph 5). He tells Laetus that the heavenly trumpet calls him, a soldier of Christ, to battle, but that his mother holds him back (paragraph 6). He looks at the claims that Laetus' mother has on him and urges him to get rid of such carnal love (paragraph 7). Mother Church is also making claims upon him, and these are more important than those of his bodily mother (paragraph 8). Augustine points to Christ's treatment of his own mother as a model of how Laetus should treat his mother, though Christ by no means denied Mary's motherhood (paragraph 9). The carnal love of Laetus' mother comes from original sin (paragraph 10). Augustine tells Laetus that the cross that a disciple of Christ must carry is his own flesh, which torments us in this life until death is swallowed up in victory (paragraph 11). Finally, he counsels Laetus on the disposition of his inheritance and urges him to greater alacrity in following the Lord (paragraph 12).

To Laetus, his most beloved lord and most longed-for brother, Augustine sends greetings in the Lord.

1. I read the letter that you sent to the brothers, and I want to console you because your first steps in religious life are troubled by many temptations. In that letter you also indicated that you desired a letter from me. I felt sorrow with you, my brother, and I could not refrain from writing for fear that I would deny not only to your desire but also to mine what I saw that I owed to the duty of charity. If, then, you profess to be Christ's recruit, do not abandon the camp; in it you must build that tower of which the Lord speaks in the gospel.[1] When you are standing on it and soldiering under the arms of the word of God, no temptations can wound you from any direction. From it weapons hurled at the enemy come down with great force, and those you see coming are deflected by its solid bulwark. Consider too that our Lord Jesus Christ, though he is our king, has

---

1. See Lk 14:28.

nonetheless, in that society in which he has also deigned to be our brother, called kings as his soldiers and has warned that each person ought to be ready to go to war with a king who has twenty thousand soldiers when he has only ten thousand.[2]

2. Pay attention to what he said shortly before he proposed the exhortatory parables about the tower and the king: *If anyone comes to me and does not hate his father, mother, wife, children, brothers, and sisters, and even his own soul, he cannot be my disciple. And if he does not carry his cross and come after me, he cannot be my disciple.* Then he added, *Who of you, if he wants to build a tower, does not first sit down and calculate whether he has the funds to complete it for fear that, having laid the foundation, he might be unable to build the tower? And then all who pass by and see it may start to say, This man began to build, and he could not complete it. Or what king going to wage war with another king does not first sit down and consider whether with ten thousand men he can confront the one who is coming at him with twenty thousand? If not, when he is far off, he sends a delegation in order to ask for peace.* (Lk 14:26-32) He shows the point of these parables quite clearly, however, at the very conclusion. For he says, *In the same way, then, any one of you who does not renounce everything that belongs to him cannot be my disciple* (Lk 14:33).

3. And so the funds for building the tower and the capabilities of ten thousand against a king who has twenty thousand signify nothing else than that each person should renounce everything that belongs to him. The beginning of the discourse above, however, fits with the final conclusion. For, in the precept that each person should *renounce everything that belongs to him,* there is also included the precept that he should *hate his father, mother, wife, children, brothers, and sisters, even his own soul.* For all these are his personal goods, which generally tie one down and prevent one from obtaining not the personal goods that pass away in time but the common goods that last for eternity. After all, by the very fact that a certain woman is your mother, she is of course not mine. Hence this is something temporal and passing, just as you see that it already belongs to the past that she conceived you, that she bore you in her womb, that she gave birth to you, and that she nursed you with milk. But insofar as she is a sister in Christ, she belongs to you and to me and to everyone who is promised the one heritage in heaven and God as Father and Christ as brother.[3] These are eternal; these do not wear out with the passing of time; these we more firmly hope to possess to the extent that we are taught that they are to be obtained not by a private but rather by a common claim.

---

2. See Lk 14:31.
3. See Rom 8:16-17.

4. You can easily recognize this in your own mother. For why does she hold you like someone trapped in a net and, after you have been impeded, why does she turn and divert you from the course you have undertaken except because she is your own mother? For, because she is the sister of everyone whose father is God and whose mother is the Church, she holds back neither you nor me nor any of our brothers who love her not with a private love as you do in your house but with a public love in the house of God. The fact, then, that you are connected to her by a blood relationship ought to give you the chance to converse with her more familiarly and to see to it more readily that the love by which she loves you as an individual may be put to death in her, so that she does not consider it more important that she gave birth to you from her womb than that she was born along with you from the womb of the Church. But what I said about one's mother should be understood of any other relationship of the sort. This is what everyone should think concerning his own soul, so that he may hate in it a private love, which is undoubtedly temporal. But he should love the community and society of which scripture said, *They had one soul and one heart for God* (Acts 4:32). For in that way your soul belongs not just to you but to all the brothers, whose souls are also yours, or rather whose souls are not souls along with yours but are one soul, that single soul of Christ, of which we sing in the psalm that it may be rescued *from the grasp of the dog* (Ps 22:21). At that point it is very easy to attain to a contempt of death.

5. Nor should parents be angry that the Lord commanded that we hate them, since the same thing is commanded us regarding our own soul.[4] For, just as we have a command concerning the soul, that we should hate it along with our parents for the sake of Christ, so what the same Lord says in another passage concerning the soul can most appropriately be applied to our parents as well. He says, *One who loves his own soul will lose it* (Jn 12:25; Mt 10:39, 16:25; Mk 8:35; Lk 17:33). I shall also say with confidence, "One who loves his parents will lose them." For in the former passage he said *hates* in regard to the soul, but here he says *loses*. This commandment, however, by which we are commanded to lose our soul, does not mean that anyone should kill himself, which is an unforgivable crime, but what it does mean is that one should kill in oneself the soul's carnal love because of which the present life causes delight and presents an obstacle to the life to come. After all, this is what the words *hates his own soul* and *will lose it* mean. This is accomplished, however, by loving, since he most clearly mentions in the same commandment the benefit of gaining one's own soul when he says, *But one who loses it in this world will find it for eternal life.* In the same way it is perfectly correct to say about one's parents that one who loves them loses them. He does not kill them like a parricide, but by the spiritual sword

---

4. See Lk 14:26.

of the word of God he piously and confidently strikes and slays the carnal love of theirs by which they try to bind themselves and their children in the entanglements of this world, and he causes that love to live in them by which they are brothers and sisters, by which along with their children in time they acknowledge God and the Church as their parents in eternity.

6. See, the desire for the truth and for knowing and finding the will of God in the holy scriptures attracts you; the duty of preaching the gospel attracts you. The Lord gives the signal that we should keep watch in the camp, that we should build the tower from which we may be able to look down on and drive off the enemy of eternal life. The heavenly trumpet calls you, a soldier of Christ, to battle, and your mother holds you back. She is clearly not a mother of the sort that the Maccabees had, nor one like the mothers of Sparta, of whom it was recorded that they roused their sons for the conflicts of war much more persistently and much more passionately than the sounding of trumpets in order that they might shed their blood for their earthly fatherland.[5] For your mother, who does not allow you to withdraw from worldly concerns in order to learn of the true life, shows well enough how she would not allow you to repudiate this world in order to face death, if that were necessary.

7. But what does she say or what reasons does she give? Perhaps those ten months during which you weighed heavily in her womb, the pains of childbirth, and the work of raising you. Slay this; slay this with the word of salvation. Lose this love of your mother that you may find her for eternal life. Remember to hate this in her if you love her, if you are Christ's recruit, if you have laid the foundation of the tower. Otherwise the passers-by will say, *This man began to build and could not finish it* (Lk 14:30). For this is carnal affection and still smacks of the old human being.[6] Christ's militia exhorts us to put to death this carnal affection both in ourselves and in our dear ones, yet not so that anyone is ungrateful to his parents and mocks those very same benefits we mentioned, by which he was born into this life, raised, and nourished. Let him rather observe filial piety everywhere, and let these duties hold where more important ones do not call us.

8. Mother Church is also the mother of your mother. She has conceived both of you from Christ; she has been in travail for you with the blood of martyrs; she has given birth to you into everlasting light; she has fed and feeds you with the milk of faith, and, though she prepares more solid foods, she sees with horror that you want to wail like small children without teeth. This mother, spread throughout the whole world, is troubled by such varied and multiple attacks from errors that her aborted offspring now do not hesitate to war against her with

---

5. See Plutarch, *Moralia III*, *"Sayings of Spartan Women"* (*Lacaenarum apophthegmata*) 241-242.
6. See Eph 4:22; Col 3:9; Rom 6:6.

unrestrained arms. Because of the neglect and laziness of certain ones whom she holds on her lap, she grieves that her members become cold in many places and become less able to embrace the small children. From where but from other children, from other members, in whose number you are included, does she demand the help that is due her in justice? Are you going to neglect her needs and turn to the words that the flesh speaks? Does she not strike the ears with more serious complaints? Does she not have a womb that is more precious and breasts filled with heavenly food? Add to this the assumption of the flesh of that man,[7] in order that you might not cling to the things of the flesh, and everything assumed by the eternal Word, of which this mother reminds you, so that you may not become entangled in them. Add to them the insults, the scourging, *and death, even death upon the cross* (Phil 2:8)

9. Though you were conceived from such seed and were brought into new life by such a union, you languish and waste away into the old human being.[8] Did your king not have an earthly mother? And yet, when her presence was reported to him as he was doing God's work, he replied, *Who is my mother and who are my brothers?* And *stretching out his hand toward his disciples*, he said that only those who did the will of his Father belonged to his family.[9] In that number he certainly, like a loving son, included Mary herself; after all, she also did the will of the Father. In that way the best and divine teacher rejected the term "mother," which they had reported to him as something private and personal to him, because it was earthly, in comparison with the close relationship of heaven. And, in mentioning the same close relationship of heaven among his disciples, he showed the kind of society in which that virgin was again united with him along with the other saints. And, in order that this most salutary teaching, by which he taught us to place little value on carnal affection for our parents, might not lend support to the error by which some deny that he had a mother, he warned his disciples in another place not to say that they have an earthly father.[10] In that way, just as it was evident that they had fathers, so he showed that he had a mother, and yet, by taking no account of his earthly relation to her, he offered his disciples an example of how to treat such relationships as of little account.

10. Are these teachings, then, interrupted by the outcries of your mother, and does the memory of her being pregnant with you and nursing you, so that you were born as a child of Adam and Eve and fed as another Adam, find a place among them? Turn your eyes, rather; turn them to the second Adam from heaven, and bear now the image of the heavenly one as you did bear that of the

---

7. That is, the humanity assumed by the Word of God.
8. See Phil 2:8.
9. See Mt 12:47-50; Mk 3:32-35; Lk 8:20-21.
10. See Mt 23:9.

earthly one.[11] In fact, even here those gifts of your mother that are listed for you to weaken your resolve should find a place; they should certainly have a place. Do not be ungrateful; thank your mother; return spiritual gifts in exchange for carnal ones, eternal gifts in exchange for temporal ones. Does she not want to be converted for the better? Watch out that she does not twist and overturn you for the worse. What difference does it make whether it is in a wife or in a mother, provided that we nonetheless avoid Eve in any woman?[12] For this shadow of a son's love for his mother comes from the leaves of that tree with which our parents first clothed themselves in that damnable nakedness. And whatever she offers you in those words and in that suggestion supposedly as a duty of love, in order to turn you aside from the most genuine and pure love of the gospel, comes from the cunning of the serpent[13] and from the duplicity of that king who has twenty thousand men, for we are taught to overcome that duplicity by the simplicity of ten thousand, that is, the simplicity of the heart by which we seek God.

11. Keep your mind on these ideas, instead, my dearest friend, and take up your cross and follow the Lord.[14] For, when you were here, I noticed that you were held back from the love of God by family concerns, and I perceived that you were carried and dragged by your cross instead of carrying and dragging it. After all, what else does our cross, which the Lord commands us to carry in order that we may follow him with the least impediment, signify but the mortality of this flesh? For it is what torments us until death is swallowed up in victory.[15] This cross itself, then, must be crucified and pierced by the nails of the fear of God.[16] Otherwise, with our members loose and free, we might not be able to carry it if it resists us. For you absolutely cannot follow the Lord except by carrying it. After all, how can you follow him if you do not belong to him? But *those who belong to Jesus Christ*, the apostle says, *have crucified their flesh along with its passions and desires* (Gal 5:24).

12. Of course, if your share of the family property, in whose management it is neither necessary nor proper that you be involved, includes some cash, it really should be given to your mother and to the others in your family. Their needs should certainly hold first place in your eyes if, in order to be perfect, you have decided to distribute such money to the poor. *For, if anyone*, the apostle says, *does not provide for his own and especially for the members of his family, he has denied the faith and is worse than a non-believer* (1 Tm 5:8). If you have left us

---

11. See 1 Cor 15:47-49.
12. See Gn 3:7.
13. See Gn 3:1.
14. See Mt 16:24; Mk 8:34; Lk 9:23.
15. See 1 Cor 15:54.
16. See Ps 119:120.

in order to deal with these matters and in order to remove your neck from these chains and to put on wisdom, how will your mother's tears flowing for her flesh and blood harm you? How will they tear you away? Or what about the flight of a slave, the death of female servants, or the ill health of brothers? If you have a well-ordered love, you should know how to prefer more important to less important things and to be touched by mercy in order that the gospel may be preached to the poor.[17] Otherwise the bountiful harvest of the Lord may fall prey to birds through a lack of workers. And you should know how to have a heart ready to follow the will of the Lord,[18] insofar as he has decided to deal with his servants either by scourging them or by pardoning them. *Meditate on these ideas; take your stand upon them in order that your progress may be evident to all* (1 Tm 4:15). I beg you to avoid causing your brothers greater sadness by your sluggishness than you caused them joy by your alacrity. But I considered it needless to recommend you by letter to those you wanted as if someone had wanted to recommend you to me in the same way.

---

17. See Mt 11:5; Lk 7:22.
18. See Mt 13:4; Mk 4:4; Lk 8:5.

Letter 244

Sometime during his episcopacy Augustine wrote this letter to Chrisimus, an African Catholic layman, who Augustine had heard was on the point of taking his own life because of the loss of his property. Augustine reminds Chrisimus that the happiness he had from his temporal possessions should by no means be compared to the happiness of heaven (paragraph 1). He urges him to raise his mind to God and admonishes him to follow the example of Christ, his redeemer, to place little value on temporal prosperity, and to endure temporal adversity bravely for the sake of the eternal reward that no one can take away (paragraph 2).

To his truly and rightly most dear lord and praiseworthy brother, Chrisimus, Augustine sends greetings in the Lord.

1. Rumor has brought to my attention—may God not let it be true—that your heart was shaken to such a degree that I am greatly astonished that a man with your wisdom and Christian mind could not realize well enough how the condition of earthly things can in no way be set on a par with those of heaven, where we ought to place our heart and our hope. Did either all your happiness consist in these things that you seem to be losing, my wise friend, or did you ascribe such great happiness to them that, when they were taken away, your mind was darkened by excessive sadness as if its light were not God but the earth? For I have heard—as I have already said, may God let what I have heard be false—that you wanted to take your own life. It is better that I not believe that this either entered your heart or fell from your lips. But since you are nonetheless so shaken that this could be said of you, I was deeply saddened for your sake, and I thought that I should console you, my dear friend, by sending you a letter. And yet I have no doubt that the Lord our God speaks better things to you in your heart. For I know that you always listen to his word with the love of a son.

2. And so, my dearest brother in Christ, be brave; our God is neither lost by his people nor loses them. But he wants to warn us of how fragile and uncertain these things that human beings love too much really are. In that way we may unfasten from them the chains of desire by which they entangle us and drag us along, and we may accustom our whole love to run toward him in whom we fear no losses. He encourages you through our ministry; consider manfully that you are a believer in Christ and were redeemed by the blood of him who taught not only by his eternal wisdom but also by his human presence that with self-control we ought to consider of little account the prosperity of this world and with bravery to endure adversity. For he promises the reward of that happiness which no one can take from us. I have of course also written to the count, who is a praiseworthy man, and it will be left to your choice whether you want to present

the letter to him. For I have no doubt that there must be someone by whom, with the help of the Lord, it might be presented, either a bishop or a priest or anyone at all.

Letter 245

Perhaps about 401, according to the suggestion of the Maurists, Augustine wrote to Possidius, the bishop of Calama in Numidia and a close friend. Augustine counsels Possidius against coming to an overly hasty judgment in prohibiting all use by Christians of jewelry and expensive clothing, though he himself is quite opposed to the use of makeup by women. Good morals are the only real ornament for Christians (paragraph 1). He deplores the wearing of amulets and earrings by men because they are linked to the worship of demons and not worn simply as ornaments. Finally, he tells Possidius that he cannot advise him about ordaining someone baptized in the Donatist sect (paragraph 2).

To his most beloved lord and venerable brother and fellow priest Possidius, and to the brothers with you, Augustine and the brothers with me send greetings in the Lord.

1. You need to consider more what you should do with those who refuse to obey than how to show them that what they do is wrong. But now the letter of Your Holiness finds me fully occupied, and the very rapid return of the carrier has permitted me neither to omit any response to you nor to respond as I ought to the questions you asked. I do not want you to come to an overly hasty judgment in forbidding gold ornamentation or expensive clothing except for those persons who, since they are neither married nor intend to marry, should consider how to please God. But the others are thinking of the things of the world—husbands of how to please their wives, and wives of how to please their husbands.[1] But no women, even those who are married, should display their hair, for the apostle commands them even to veil their heads.[2] But to apply color with makeup in order to appear more rosy or more fair is the trickery of an adulteress, by which I have no doubt that even their husbands do not want to be deceived. And women should be permitted to adorn themselves for their husbands alone—and that by way of indulgence, not by way of command. For the true ornament, especially of Christian men and women, is neither some false shade of color nor a display of gold or fine garments, but good morals.

2. The superstitious use of amulets, however, must be deplored. These also include men's earrings, which hang from a single part of the extremities of the ears and are not used to give pleasure to human beings but to give service to demons. Who is going to find in the scriptures particular prohibitions of wicked superstitions, since the apostle speaks generally, *I do not want you to have anything to do with demons* (1 Cor 10:20), and again, *What does Christ have to*

---

1. See 1 Cor 7:32-34.
2. See 1 Cor 11:5-6.

do with Belial (2 Cor 6:15)? Or perhaps, since he named Belial and forbade having anything to do with demons in general, Christians are permitted to sacrifice to Neptune, because we do not read of anything forbidden regarding Neptune in particular! In the meanwhile let those poor wretches be warned that, if they do not want to observe the more salutary commandments, they should at least not defend their sacrileges so as not to implicate themselves in a greater sin. But what should be done with them if they fear to remove their earrings and do not fear to receive the body of Christ while wearing the sign of the devil? But concerning the ordination of someone who was baptized in the sect of Donatus I cannot be of help to you. After all, it is one thing to do so if you are forced; it is quite another to advise you to do it.[3]

---

3. Augustine apparently advises against ordaining a man baptized in the Donatist sect, but see some situations in which such an ordination may be a necessity.

Letter 246

It was perhaps in 405 that Augustine wrote to Lampadius, a Catholic layman in Italy, who had asked Augustine to compose a work for him on the question of fate and fortune. He begins by warning of the great danger involved in blaming one's sins upon fate (paragraph 1). He argues that, unless the will is the cause of sin, all laws and moral principles and practices are undermined, pointing out that even an astrologer does not allow his wife to excuse her misbehavior as due to fate (paragraph 2). He goes on to make the same point regarding the astrologer's thieving servant, rebellious son, and unjust neighbor, claiming that the astrologer cannot justly blame any of them if their actions are due to fate (paragraph 3).

Augustine to Lampadius.

1. On the question of fate and fortune I noticed that your soul was troubled no small amount when I was there, and I have now come to know this with more certainty from your letter. Hence I owe you a reply of considerable length. The Lord will help me to explain this in the way he knows is appropriate for safeguarding your faith. For it is no slight evil not only to be led by erroneous opinions to commit sin because of the allurement of pleasure but also to be turned away from the remedy of confession in order to defend one's sin.

2. You should certainly know as quickly and briefly as possible that all laws and all principles of discipline, all praise, blame, exhortations, deterrence, rewards, punishments, and all the other means by which the human race is governed and ruled are completely undermined and overthrown and that absolutely nothing of justice remains if the will is not the cause of sin. How much more right and just it is, therefore, that we blame the errors of astrologers than that we are forced to condemn and abandon the laws of God or even the care of our families, something that the astrologers themselves do not do! For, when one of them sells to monied men their silly fates, as soon as he takes his eye off the ivory tables and turns it to the governance and care of his own family, he corrects his wife not only with words but also with blows if he catches her not merely joking in a rather risqué manner but even looking out the window too long. Yet if she says to him, "Why are you beating me? Beat Venus, if you can, by whom I am forced to do this," then he does not care about how to make up foolish words to mislead strangers but how to administer a just beating to correct his own family.

3. When, therefore, anyone appeals to fate when he has begun to receive correction and does not want to be blamed since, as he says, he was forced by fate to perform the action for which he is being rebuked, let him return to himself; let him observe this in his own family; let him not punish a servant who steals; let

him not complain about a rebellious son; let him not threaten an unjust neighbor. For, if he performs any of these actions, which of them does he perform justly if all those from whom he suffers injustice are moved to act not by their own sinfulness but by fate? But if by his proper right and his care as the head of the family he exhorts whatever people he has at the time under his authority to do good, if he deters them from doing wrong, if he commands them to obey his will, if he honors those who obey his least command, punishes those who pay no attention to him, repays gratitude with gifts, and hates the ungrateful, shall I, then, waste time in arguing against fate, when I find that he speaks not so much by his words as by his actions, that he seems almost by his own hands to smash the pebbles of the astrologers over their heads?[1] If, then, your desire is not satisfied with these few ideas and you desire a book on this topic to read at greater length, you must be patient and wait for a time when we are free, and you must ask God that he may grant us the leisure and ability to satisfy your mind on this topic. But I will be quicker both if Your Charity does not hesitate to remind me often and if you inform me of what you think of this letter by writing back.

---

1. These pebbles were apparently used in calculating the astrological predictions.

Letter 247

Sometime during his episcopacy Augustine wrote to Romulus, a powerful man who had been converted to Christianity by Augustine's efforts. Augustine rebukes Romulus for being harsh and unjust in demanding that his tenant farmers pay once again the taxes that they had already paid to tax collectors whom they presumed were representing Romulus (paragraph 1). Augustine asks Romulus to have pity on his own soul and complains that he left town without seeing him, though Augustine had asked to see him (paragraph 2). He examines the arguments that Romulus might muster in his own defense and defends the views of the poor tenant farmers against them (paragraph 3). Finally, Augustine warns Romulus to fear God and tells him that he has more fear for Romulus than he does for the poor whom Romulus is treating unjustly (paragraph 4).

To his most beloved lord and son, Romulus, Augustine sends greetings in the Lord.

1. The truth is both sweet and bitter. When it is sweet, it spares, and when it is bitter, it heals. If you do not refuse to drink what I offer in this letter, you will prove correct what I said. Just as whatever insults you heap upon me do me no harm, may they do you no harm either, and may the injustice you do to the wretched and the poor cause you as much harm as it does to those to whom you do it! After all, they suffer only for a time, but see what you store up for yourself *on the day of wrath and of the revelation of the just judgment of God, who will repay each person in accord with his works* (Rom 2:5-6). I implore his mercy that he may correct you in this life, as he knows how, rather than wait until the day when there will no longer be a place for correction. May he who has given you a fear of him,[1] on account of whom I do not despair over you, open your mind in order that you may see, be horrified over, and correct what you are doing. For you consider those sins small or none at all which are so great that, when your desires subside and permit you to see them, you will water the earth with your tears in order that God may have mercy on you. Or, if I am unfair in acting in this way with you so that wretched and needy people may not pay the taxes they owe twice, since the tenant farmers paid them to their tax collector, obeying the lower official and his commands, and he cannot deny that he received them—if, then, I am unfair because I think it unjust that those people, who can hardly pay them once, are asked to pay their taxes twice, do what you want. But if you see that it is unjust, do what is right; do what God commands and I petition for.

---

1. See Jer 32:40; Bar 3:7; Mal 2:5; Sir 36:2.

2. I do not make this petition as much for their sake—he whom I fear knows this—as for your sake in order that, as scripture says, *You may take pity on your own soul and be pleasing to God* (Sir 30:24). And now I should not petition you but reprimand you. For scripture also says, *I rebuke and chastise the one I love* (Rv 3:19). But if I had to petition you for my own sake, I would perhaps not petition you, but since I should petition you for your sake, I ask you in your anger to spare yourself, to make peace with yourself in order that he whom you ask may be at peace with you. I sent you a message on Saturday, while you were still having dinner, that you should not leave without seeing me. You replied that you would do so. I arose on Sunday, and, as I heard, you came to the church, prayed, departed, and refused to see me. May God forgive you. For what else shall I say to you except that God knows that I desire this? But I know that, if you do not correct yourself, God is still just. Still, when you spare yourself, you also spare me, nor am I, after all, so distant from the heart of Christ that my heart is not struck with a very deep wound when those whom I brought to birth in the gospel[2] act in this manner.

3. You are going to say again, "I did not order them to pay the taxes to Ponticanus." The answer is given you, "But you ordered them to obey Ponticanus." The tenant farmers could not distinguish how far they were to obey him and how far they were not to obey him, especially since he asked for what they knew they owed. But they ought to have had your letter to produce for the tax collector if he was demanding payment against your will and to read to him that they ought not to pay the taxes to their collector unless they had received your letter. For, if at some point you gave a verbal command that they should not give anything to the collector, it was a lot for them to remember; it is a lot for you yourself to remember whether you really gave the command or commanded them or others or everyone, especially since you now also heard that the money was given to another collector and is safe. And you were not displeased that they gave it. But when I said, "If this man misappropriated the money, why must these people be asked to pay it again?" you again began to be displeased that the tenant farmers had given him the taxes. And after you had said to me many times that you had never made either Valerius or Aginesis your representatives, suddenly, when we were dealing with the wine (since they ought to have mentioned it if it had begun to go sour) and you were told that he was absent, you forgot, I believe, what you had said to me so many times. And you said that they ought to have shown it to Aginesis and acted according to his judgment. At that point, after I had said, "Surely you do not usually command these men to take your place," you replied, "But Aginesis had my letter," as if those upon whom you impose some task always read out your letter to the country folk so that they

---

2. See 1 Cor 4:15.

may believe that you gave the order. But since they see that those men were given orders by you, they certainly do not believe that those men were rashly venturing to do something unless you gave them authority. And for this reason, amid these uncertainties, it was not clear what you ordered, nor could they hold something for certain unless they had your letter to produce for everyone and unless they only obey your letter when they are supposed to hand over something.

4. But what need is there to argue so long with you and add the burden of these words to your busyness so that, when you become angry at my words, you may perhaps want to rage against those wretched people? It will be credited to their good merit that they have suffered your anger for the sake of your salvation, on account of which I am saying all this to you. But I do not want to say anything more serious to you for fear that you may think that I am saying something of the sort not out of fear but out of a wrongful desire. Fear God if you do not want to be deceived; him *I call upon as witness to my soul* (2 Cor 1:23) that I have more fear for you when I say these things than for those for whose sake I am seen to intercede before you. If you believe me, thanks be to God. But if you do not believe, the words of the Lord console me: *Say, Peace be to this house, and if a child of peace dwells there, your peace will come to rest upon him; but if not, it will return to you* (Mt 10:12-13). May the mercy of God protect you, my most beloved son.

Letter 248

Sometime during his episcopacy Augustine wrote to Sebastian, the superior of a monastery in Africa, who in a letter to Augustine had expressed his sorrow over sinners. Augustine mentions his joy at receiving the letter from Sebastian and tells him that he has noticed his sorrow over sinners. He assures Sebastian that it is a good sorrow if he grieves over the sins of others without being involved in them and that such sorrow is something that all good Christians must endure (paragraph 1). He also points to the many sources of consolation that Sebastian can find amid his sufferings (paragraph 2). Alypius, the bishop of Thagaste, adds a few lines at the end in order to make the letter his as well.

To Sebastian, his holy and beloved lord and brother most dear in the dignity of Christ, Augustine sends greetings in the Lord.

1. Although the sweet bond of love by no means permits that you be separated from our heart, and although we constantly recall your holy conduct and conversation, you still did well and we thank you, because you brought us great joy by sending a letter with news of your bodily well-being. I perceived in your letter, however, that a sadness caused by sinners who abandon the law of the Lord has taken hold of you.[1] For you live with that spirit of which scripture says, *I saw the mindless and wasted away* (Ps 119:158). It is a pious sorrow and, if one can say so, a blessed misery to be troubled over but not involved in the sins of others, to deplore them but not to cling to them, to be afflicted by sorrow over them but not to be drawn to them by love. This is the persecution that *all suffer who want to live pious lives in Christ* (2 Tm 3:12), according to the apostle's painful but true statement. After all, what causes sorrow in the life of good people more than the life of the wicked, not when it forces them to imitate what they find displeasing, but when it forces them to grieve over what they see? For, by living a wicked life before the eyes of a good person, a wicked man makes him feel pain, though he does not force his consent. For often and over a long time the bodies of the wicked are spared suffering from worldly authorities and even from the harassment of others, whoever they may be. But the hearts of good people are never spared suffering from the evil behavior of human beings up to the end of this world. In this way, then, there are fulfilled the words of the apostle I mentioned: *All who want to live pious lives in Christ will suffer persecution* (2 Tm 3:12), and they will suffer more intensely the more interiorly they suffer until the deluge passes in which the ark carries both the raven and the dove.[2]

---

1. See Ps 119:53.
2. See Gn 8:6-12.

2. But cling, my brother, to him from whom you have heard, *One who perseveres up to the end will be saved* (Mt 10:22; 24:13; Mk 13:13). *Be united to the Lord in order that your life may increase in the last days* (Sir 2:3). For I know that you are not lacking refreshment for your heart from good brothers. Add to this the trustworthy, great, certain, everlasting promises of God and the immutable and ineffable reward for this endurance. And see how truthfully you sing to the Lord, *In accord with the multitude of my sorrows in my heart your consolations have brought joy to my soul* (Ps 94:19). Send our letter to Brother Firmus. In return the brothers and sisters with us greet in the Lord, along with us, Your Holiness and the family of God that is governed by your ministry. [In another hand:] May you be safe and sound and pray for us, most beloved and holy brothers.

I, Alypius, most eagerly greet Your Sincerity and all those united to you in the Lord, and I ask that you consider this letter as if it were mine. For, even if I could have sent another of my own, I still preferred to add my signature to this so that one page might also bear witness to our oneness of heart.

Letter 249

Sometime between 395 and 411 Augustine wrote to Restitutus, a deacon, probably in the church of Carthage, concerning how one should tolerate bad Christians and scandals in the Church, and urged him to read Tyconius and the scriptures themselves.[1]

To Restitutus, his most beloved lord, brother, and fellow deacon who is most dear with an honorable sincerity, Augustine sends greetings in the Lord.

As someone who, as you know, is most trustworthy and shares in it, Brother Deogratias[2] has disclosed to me the turmoil that reveals the pious flame that burns in your heart. Read Tyconius, therefore, whom you know well—not, of course, in order to approve of everything. For you know what must be avoided in him. I think, nonetheless, that I have thoroughly treated and resolved this question of how, while preserving the bond of unity, we must tolerate disorders and sins in the Church, if there should be any that we cannot correct or eliminate. And yet, once we have corrected only the intention in his writings, we must return to the very sources of the divine scriptures in order that we may see in them how few testimonies to opinions or examples of actions he cited and how no one could cite all of them except someone who was willing to copy nearly all the pages of the holy books into his writings. Thus there is almost no page that does not admonish us that inside the Church, in the communion of the sacraments by which we are prepared for eternal life, we ought to be at peace with those who hate peace until our long sojourn away from home passes with our groans[3] and until, in the strength of Jerusalem, our eternal mother, we enjoy in her towers[4] a most secure peace and an abundance of true brothers and sisters, whose small number we now bemoan amid many who are false. But what is the strength of that city except its God, our God? You see, then, in whom alone peace may be obtained both for individual human beings who, without him, wage war against one another, even when no external scandal has arisen, and for all together who, although they love one another in this life and are bound by the ties of loyal friendship, are still not united in the highest and perfect manner by either bodily presence or agreement of heart. May your heart be strengthened in the Lord, and may you keep us in mind.

---

1. Tyconius was a Donatist whose work on scriptural interpretation had an important influence on Augustine.
2. Presumably the Carthaginian priest to whom Augustine wrote Letters 102, 173A, and 25*.
3. See Ps 120:7.5-6.
4. See Ps 122:6-8.

Letter 250

Between the summer of 410 and the summer of 412 Augustine wrote to Auxilius, the young Catholic bishop of Nurco in Mauretania Caesariensis, who had anathematized Classicianus, a Catholic layman and the count of Africa, along with his whole family. We have further information about this event from Letters 250A and 1*, which Augustine sent to the count at the same time. Augustine tells Auxilius that Classicianus has written him, complaining about the anathema imposed upon him and his family for allegedly having violated the sanctuary that certain men had sought in the church. Augustine explains that spiritual penalties should not be imposed upon other persons for the sin of one person (paragraph 1). He tells Auxilius that, if he can offer a reasonable explanation of his action, he should share it with Augustine, though he clearly does not believe any reasonable explanation can be given (paragraph 2). Furthermore, Augustine questions the justice of anathematization in this case, even if it were imposed upon Classicianus alone, and tells Auxilius that, if he has acted wrongly out of anger, he should ask for forgiveness and restore the peace that formerly existed between the young bishop and the count (paragraph 3).

To his most beloved lord and venerable brother and fellow priest, Auxilius, Augustine sends greetings in the Lord.

1. Our son, Classicianus, a highly respected man, complained strongly to me by letter that he had suffered the wrong of being anathematized by Your Holiness. He reported that he came to the church accompanied by an entourage of a few men befitting his position of authority and spoke with you so that you would not, contrary to his salvation, favor those persons who, by falsely swearing upon the gospels, sought in the very house of faith a means to break their faith. But he said that, reflecting on the evil they had done, they left the church of their own accord and were not removed by force, and that Your Reverence became so angry at him that a sentence of anathematization was imposed upon him along with his whole house and that a record of the ecclesiastical proceedings was compiled. After I read his letter I was deeply upset and, because my thoughts were being tossed this way and that by the great storm in my heart, I decided that I could not remain silent before Your Charity, so that, if you have a decision regarding this matter that is supported by certain arguments and testimonies from the scriptures, you might be so good as to inform us too of how a son may rightly be anathematized for the sins of his father or a wife for those of her husband or a servant for those of his master or anyone in the family, even a child not yet born, if the child is born at the same time that the whole house is under the penalty of anathema, and if in danger of death the child cannot be rescued by the sacrament of rebirth. This is not, after all, the bodily punishment by which we

read that certain men who scorned God were slain along with all the members of their families who had no share in this wickedness. At that time, to be sure, mortal bodies, which were certainly going to die at some point, were killed to strike terror into the living. But spiritual punishment, which does what scripture says, *Whatever you bind on earth will also be bound in heaven* (Mt 18:18 and 16:19), binds souls. Of souls it is said, *The soul of the father is mine, and the soul of the son is mine; the soul that sins will itself die* (Ez 18:4).

2. Maybe you have heard that some priests with a great reputation anathematized some sinner along with his family. If, however, they were questioned, we would perhaps find that they were able to give an explanation of this. But if someone were to ask me whether they acted correctly, I myself do not know what I might reply to him. Never have I dared to do this, even though I was most gravely disturbed over the crimes of certain people which they brutally perpetrated against the Church. But if the Lord has perhaps revealed to you that it is right to do this, I by no means disdain your youthful age and your first steps in the office of bishop. Look, here I am, an old man and a bishop of so many years, who is ready to learn from a young man and a bishop of less than a year how we can give a just account to God or to human beings if with a spiritual punishment we punish innocent souls for the crime of someone else from whom they do not contract original sin, as they do from Adam, *in whom all have sinned* (Rom 5:12). For, even if the son of Classicianus contracted from his father the sin of the first man, which must be wiped away in the sacred font of baptism, who has any doubt that whatever sin his father committed after he fathered him, in which he had no part, does not pertain to him? What shall I say of his wife? What shall I say of so many souls in the whole family? Hence, if because of this severity, by which this whole house was anathematized, one soul perishes by leaving the body without baptism, this loss is incomparably greater than the death of countless bodies, if innocent people are violently dragged from church and killed. If you can give a reasonable explanation of this action, then, I wish that you would give it to us when you reply in order that we can do so as well. But if you cannot, what led you, out of a thoughtless impulse of your mind, to do something for which you cannot find a correct answer if you are questioned about it?

3. I have said this, however, even if our son, Classicianus, did something that you thought it was fully just to punish by anathematization. But, if the letter that he sent me was truthful, he ought not, even alone in his family, to have been restrained by such a punishment. On this point I am doing nothing else with Your Holiness but asking that you pardon him when he seeks pardon, if he acknowledges his sin. But, if you wisely recognize that he has not committed any sin because in a house of faith he himself quite justly demanded that men ought to keep their faith lest it be broken where it is taught, do what a holy man ought to do. For, if there has happened to you in your humanity what the man of God in

fact says in the psalm, *My eye is clouded because of anger*, you should cry out to the Lord, *Have mercy on me, O Lord, because I am weak* (Ps 7:8.3). In that way he will stretch out to you his right hand, suppress your anger, and calm your mind in order that you may see and do justice. For, as scripture says, *A man's anger does not carry out the justice of God* (Jas 1:20). Do not, therefore, suppose that an unjust impulse cannot creep up on us because we are bishops, but let us rather think that we live with great peril amid the snares of temptation because we are human beings. Destroy the ecclesiastical records that you perhaps made when you were quite upset, then, and let there return between you the love that you had with him when you were still a catechumen. Remove the dispute and restore peace in order that a man who is a friend may not perish on your account and the devil, who is an enemy, may not rejoice over you. But the mercy of our God is powerful to hear me as I pray, so that my sorrow over you may not be increased but that the sorrow that has emerged may be healed, and may he rule you through his grace and bring joy to your youth because you do not hold my old age in contempt. Farewell.

Letter 250A

In this fragment of a letter to Classicianus, the count of Africa who, as mentioned in the previous letter, was excommunicated by the young bishop Auxilius, Augustine says that he wants to handle the question of anathematization in a council and, if necessary, to consult the Apostolic See in order to establish a definite policy. He also wants to know whether people who take refuge in a church in order to break faith with their creditors should be driven from the church. Finally, he tells Classicianus that the Holy Spirit, by whose power anyone is bound or loosed, does not impose an unmerited penalty.

[To Classicianus].[1]

On account of those who would place under excommunication a person's entire family, that is, many souls, because of the sin of one soul, I want, with the help of the Lord, to handle the matter in our council and to write to the Apostolic See, if necessary, so that the harmonious authority of all may determine and reaffirm what we should do in these cases, especially because someone in the family might die without baptism. I also want to know whether those who seek refuge in a church in order to break faith with their creditors should be driven from there. I would say clearly without being rash that, if anyone of the faithful had been excommunicated unjustly, it would be more harmful to the one who did this injustice than to the one who suffered it. The Holy Spirit, who dwells in the saints, by whom any person is bound or loosed,[2] does not impose a punishment upon anyone that is unmerited. Through him love is certainly poured out in our hearts,[3] and *love does not do what is wrong* (1 Cor 13:4).

---

1. This fragment of a letter, which lacks a salutation, is identical with paragraph 5 of Letter 1*.
2. See Jn 20:22-23; Mt 16:19.
3. See Rom 5:5.

Letter 251

Sometime during his episcopacy Augustine wrote to Pancarius, a Catholic layman and property owner in Numidia. Augustine expresses his surprise that the people of Germanicia have raised objections against the priest Secundinus only subsequent to Pancarius' arrival. He asks Pancarius to check whether these objections perhaps stem from heretics, since Augustine will not accept charges against a priest from heretics. He asks Pancarius for information and warns against the destruction of Secundinus' house and of the church.

To his most beloved lord and rightly honorable son, Pancarius, Augustine sends greetings in the Lord.

Since before the arrival of Your Piety the priest Secundinus was not a source of displeasure to the people of Germanicia,[1] I do not know, my most beloved lord and rightly honorable son, why it has now come about that, as you wrote, they are ready to accuse him of some crimes or other. But we can only take into consideration the objections they raise against the priest if the people who lodge these objections are Catholics. For we neither can nor ought to admit the objections of heretics against a Catholic priest. Hence Your Wisdom ought first of all to make sure that there are no heretics present where there were none present before your arrival, and we will hear the case of the priest as it ought to be heard. Because your welfare and reputation is most dear to us and because the people of Germanicia fall under our humble care, I am in fact warning you, because you are being so gracious, to deign confidently to make known what concessions you have obtained from the most glorious emperors and what actions you have taken before competent judges. In that way all may see that you are doing nothing out of order, so that in a case in which you are in a dispute over property these poor people do not suffer again and be completely ruined through more serious losses. At the same time I suggest to you that the house of the same priest not be plundered and destroyed. For with regard to his church it has been reported to us that certain people want to tear it down, but I do not think that this can in any way be permitted by Your Piety.

---

1. A village in the diocese of Hippo.

Letter 252

Sometime during his episcopacy Augustine wrote to Felix, a Catholic layman and the uncle of an orphaned girl who had been left in the care of the church of Hippo. The following three letters all deal with the proposed marriage of this girl. Augustine tells Felix that, since the girl was left in the care of the Church, he could not and ought not to give her in marriage to just anyone and that he awaits the arrival of "our respected brother" in whose presence he will decide the matter. The identity of this man is unclear. The Maurists suggested that it was the same Rusticus to whom Letter 255 was addressed, but the letter seems to say that he left the girl in the care of the church of Hippo. Hence he might have been her father or some other relative.

To Felix, his most beloved lord and rightly honorable and preferred brother, Augustine sends greetings in the Lord.

Your Piety knows very well what care the Church or the bishops ought to take regarding the protection of all human beings, especially orphans. Hence, having received your letter and a copy of the letter of our respected brother, neither could I nor ought I to have entrusted the girl to just anyone, especially since he entrusted her to the Church, my most beloved lord and rightly honorable and preferred brother. For this reason I await his arrival in order to decide in his presence what should be done, and I shall do what the Lord inspires me to do.

Letter 253

Sometime after having written the previous letter Augustine wrote to Benenatus, the bishop most probably of Simitthus in Africa Proconsularis, regarding the prospective marriage of a young girl under his protection, about whom he had spoken in the previous letter, to the son of a certain Rusticus. Letters 254 and 255 supply further information. In the present letter Augustine tells Benenatus that he should negotiate the marriage with a Catholic family so that the Church does not meet with opposition but rather receives faithful assistance.

To my most blessed, venerable, and loveable brother Benenatus, and the brothers with you, Augustine sends greetings in the Lord.

We are pleased by the faith and pious zeal for the Church on the part of the man by means of whom we send this greeting to Your Holiness. But it was his wish to appear before Your Grace, my most beloved and venerable brother, with my letter. And I heard what you are planning to do about that affair, if it is true—and I wonder if it is true. For you know how you ought to look out for the Catholic Church with the fatherliness of a bishop, so that you do not settle this matter with just anyone[1]—if, as I said, what I have heard is true—but rather with a Catholic family from which the Church may be able to have not only no opposition but even faithful assistance.

---

1. Augustine most probably refers to the marriage that Benenatus is attempting to broker between a girl left in Augustine's care and the son of Rusticus.

Letter 254

Sometime after the previous letter was written, Augustine again wrote to his fellow bishop Benenatus, who was acting as an intermediary in arranging the marriage of the son of a certain Rusticus, to whom Letter 255 is addressed. Augustine explains why he cannot promise the girl, who had been the subject of Letters 252-253, to anyone—first of all because she is too young and secondly because the rights of her relatives and especially of her mother must be taken into consideration.

To his most blessed lord and venerable and loveable brother and fellow priest, Benenatus, and the brothers with you, Augustine and the brothers with me send greetings in the Lord.

The girl about whom Your Holiness wrote to me is of the mind that, if she were now old enough, she would not enter into marriage with anyone. But she is at such an age that, even if she had the desire to marry, she still ought not to be given or promised to anyone. Added to this is the fact that God watches over her in the Church in order to protect her against the wicked, not so that she could be given to whomever I chose, but so that she might not be able to be seized by the wrong person, my most beloved lord and venerable brother Benenatus. The condition that you were so good as to convey, therefore, is not displeasing to me if she is going to marry. But now we still do not know whether she is going to marry, even though we desire more what she is speaking of, for she is at an age when the fact that she says that she wants to be a nun is more the pleasantry of a talkative girl than the promise of one intending to take vows. Besides, she has a maternal aunt, whose husband is our honorable brother Felix. When I discussed this matter with him, for I neither could nor ought to have done anything else, he was not unwilling to accept this, but was, on the contrary, highly pleased. Yet on the basis of friendship he was not inappropriately saddened that they had nothing in writing about this. For perhaps the mother who is not now present will turn up, and I believe that by nature her will in giving her daughter in marriage takes precedence over all others, unless the same daughter has already attained such an age that she may choose for herself what she wants by right of her greater freedom. Your Sincerity ought also to consider this: if I were given the full and complete authority over the marriage and she were also of age and wanted to marry and entrusted herself to me, with God as my judge, to give her over to whomever I might choose, I say, and I say truly, that I would be pleased with this condition, but not so that I could, for the sake of God, my judge, reject a better one. It is, of course, uncertain whether a better one will turn up. Hence Your Charity sees how important factors that need to be considered come together so that at present I cannot at all promise the girl to anyone.

Letter 255

After having written the previous letter, Augustine wrote to Rusticus, a pagan African. He explains that he cannot offer to him the girl whom Rusticus wants to be his son's wife, who is the subject of Letters 252-254, both because she is a Catholic and Rusticus' son is not and because of the reasons mentioned in a letter of Bishop Benenatus that has not survived.

To his most beloved lord and rightly praiseworthy and respected son, Rusticus, Augustine sends greetings in the Lord.

Although I wish for you and your whole family all the good things that pertain not merely to the happiness of the present world but also to the everlasting life to come, in which you have not yet been persuaded to believe, I, my most beloved lord and venerable son, still wrote back to my holy brother and fellow bishop Benenatus the reasons that move me, to the extent I thought sufficient, as to why I do not as yet dare to promise anything regarding the girl for whom you ask. For you most certainly know that, even if it lay within our exclusive authority to give any girl in marriage, we could give a Christian girl only to a Christian man, and yet you did not want to promise me anything of the sort regarding your son, who I hear is still a pagan. How much less ought I to promise anything concerning the marriage of that girl for the reasons that you can read in the letter of my brother, whom I mentioned, even if I regarded what I said about your son as something not merely promised but even over which I might now rejoice as a fact!

Letter 256

Sometime during his episcopacy Augustine wrote to Christinus, a Catholic layman, probably an African, who had asked Augustine for a personal letter. He tells Christinus, who had wanted Augustine to seek him out by letter, that he seeks him out by love, which is better than any letter. He closes with words of encouragement for making spiritual progress.

To his rightly praiseworthy lord and sincerely most dear and loveable brother, Christinus, Augustine sends greetings in the Lord.

Your letter told me that you desired to receive a letter from me. But Brother James arrived as a more authoritative witness of that desire of yours in our regard, for he told me more charming things about you that he had personally experienced than that small page could. For this reason I congratulate Your Grace, and I give thanks for your Christian heart to the Lord our God, whose gifts these are, my rightly praiseworthy and most sincerely dear and loveable brother. But, regarding your request that I seek you out by letter, I am in fact seeking you out by a love that surpasses every letter, and I know that you understand quite well where I am seeking you. But as for your reading me, I fear that in your hands my longwindedness may be criticized rather than my words sought after. I could express a truth in a few words, and if you ponder it and think about it at length, you will find what it means. When on God's pathway we flee from easier and more fruitful things out of a cowardly fear, we endure on the pathway of the world harder and fruitless things with painful labor. May you be safe and sound, thrive, and make progress in Christ, my rightly praiseworthy and sincerely most dear and loveable brother.

Letter 257

Sometime during his episcopacy Augustine wrote to Orontius, a Catholic layman and property owner near Hippo. Augustine greets Orontius in response to the announcement of his imminent arrival.

To his excellent and rightly honorable lord and loveable son, Orontius, Augustine sends greetings.

I give thanks that you have graciously announced beforehand by letter the arrival of Your Excellency and have sent this message ahead so that we might enjoy hearing from you before seeing you. Thus, having a kind of foretaste of the knowledge we have long desired from the consolation of a letter, we might await more eagerly and ardently your visit in order to welcome it with greater joy and pleasure, my excellent and rightly honorable lord and loveable son. Hence I pay in advance to your merits and greetings the due homage of returning your greeting, rejoicing over the good health that you have reported and hoping for its continuance. And because, in asking for a reply from my lowly self by the right of the good will you have already shown, you added, "At least if we can merit this from such holiness as yours," I in no way dare to give up hope that Your Wisdom will choose not only to praise the very source of the same holiness, since by drawing from it according to our capacity we amount to something, but also to share in it with us. In that way God, who is incomparably and immutably good, who by his power is the creator of your good mind, may by his grace be its restorer. May almighty God keep you safe and sound and make you even happier, my excellent and rightly honorable lord and loveable son.

Letter 258

Sometime during his episcopacy Augustine wrote to Martianus, an old friend from the days before his baptism. Augustine tells Martianus that he has interrupted his other work in order to tell him of his joy that they are at last true friends according to Cicero's definition (paragraph 1). For to their previous agreement about things human there has been added agreement about things divine (paragraph 2). In fact, their earlier friendship was not true friendship when Martianus was a stranger to Christ (paragraph 3). Now they have in the two commandments to love God and neighbor agreement in things human and divine (paragraph 4). Finally, Augustine urges Martianus to submit his name as a candidate for baptism (paragraph 5).

To Martianus, his rightly loveable lord and brother who is most beloved and worthy of affection in Christ, Augustine sends greetings in the Lord.

1. I have snatched or rather torn and in a sense stolen myself from the many tasks that occupy me so that I might write to you, my friend of long standing, whom I did not have as long as I did not possess you in Christ. You know, of course, how "Tully, the greatest author of the Roman language,"[1] as someone said, defined friendship. For he said, and he said most correctly, "Friendship is an agreement on things human and divine along with good will and love."[2] But you, my dearest friend, at one time agreed with me on things human, when I desired to enjoy them in the manner of the crowd, and you set your course to aid me to obtain those things, over which I now repent. In fact, by the favor you showed me you were among the first of all my friends back then to fill the sails of my desires with the wind of praise. But in things divine (which is to be sure the more important part of that definition), of which the truth at that time had not shone forth for me, our friendship limped along. For it was an agreement only on things human, not also on things divine, though it was an agreement with good will and love.

2. And, after I ceased to desire those things, with your continuing good will you certainly desired that I be secure in terms of mortal well-being and happy with that prosperity of possessions that the world usually wants. And in that way you and I had to some extent a benevolent and loving agreement on things human. But now how shall I explain in words how much I rejoice over you when I presently have as a true friend the man whom I long had as a friend in some way? For there has also been added the agreement on things divine, because you

---

1. Lucan, *Pharsalia* 7, 62-63.
2. Cicero, *Laelius* 6, 20.

who once led with me a temporal life with a most pleasing good will have now begun to live with me in the hope of eternal life. But there is no longer any disagreement about things human between us, since we weigh them by the knowledge of things divine in order that we may not give them more weight than, with strict justice, their limitations demand. Nor by casting them aside with an unjust contempt do we do injury to their creator, the Lord of heavenly and earthly things. Thus it turns out that between friends who do not agree on things divine there cannot be a full and true agreement on things human either. For one who holds things divine in contempt necessarily evaluates things human other- wise than he should, nor can anyone correctly love a human being who does not love the maker of that human being. Hence I do not say that you who had been partly my friend are now more fully my friend. Rather, as reason shows, you were not even partly my friend, since even with respect to things human you did not possess a true friendship with me. You were certainly not a companion of mine in things divine, by which things human are correctly weighed, either when I myself was not concerned with them or after I began to have some wisdom regarding them, though you pulled back far from them.

3. I do not, however, want you to become angry or think it absurd that at that time, when I was passionately seeking the vanities of this world, you were not yet my friend, though you seemed to love me a great deal. For I was not then even a friend to myself, but rather an enemy. Indeed, I loved iniquity, and it is a true statement, because a divine one, by which the holy books say, *But one who loves iniquity hates his own soul* (Ps 11:6). When, therefore, I hated my own soul, how could I have a true friend who wanted for me those things in which I endured myself as an enemy? But when the goodness and grace of our savior shed its light upon me, not in accord with my merits, but in accord with his mercy,[3] how could you be my friend when you had no part in this, since you were completely igno- rant of the reason why I was able to be happy, and you did not love me in him in whom I myself had somehow become a friend to myself?

4. Thanks be to God, then, that he has finally been so gracious as to make you my friend. "For now we have an agreement on things human and divine along with good will and love"[4] in Christ Jesus, our Lord, our truest peace. He summed up all the divine teachings in two commandments when he said, *Love the Lord your God from your whole heart and your whole soul and your whole mind*, and, *Love your neighbor as yourself. The whole law and the prophets depend on these two commandments* (Mt 22:39-40; Mk 12:30-31; Lk 10:27; Dt 6:5; Lv 19:18). In the first there is agreement on things divine along with good will and love; in the second there is such agreement on things human. If you hold on to these two

3. See Ti 3:4-5.
4. Cicero, *Laelius* 6, 20.

most firmly along with me, our friendship will be true and everlasting, and it will unite us not only to each other but also to the Lord.

5. In order that this may come about, I urge Your Honor and Your Wisdom also to receive now the sacraments of the faithful, for that is appropriate for your age and is in conformity, I believe, with your moral conduct. Remember what you said to me as I was about to leave, when you recalled the comic but still most fitting and useful verse from Terence:

Now this day brings new life and requires other conduct.[5]

If you said this truthfully, as I ought not to doubt regarding you, you are already living in such a way that you are worthy to receive the forgiveness of past sins by baptism, which brings salvation. For there is absolutely no one else besides Christ the Lord to whom the human race says:

With you as our leader, if any traces of our sin remain,

They will be canceled and free the earth of endless fear.[6]

Virgil admitted that he copied this from the Cumaean, that is, the Sibylline, ode. Perhaps that prophetess had heard something in the spirit about the one and only savior, which she had to confess. I have written these ideas to you, my rightly loveable brother, whether they are few or perhaps many, while loaded down on all sides with things to do. I desire to receive your reply and also to know finally that you have submitted or will submit your name to be listed among the candidates for baptism. May the Lord our God in whom you have come to believe keep you both in this life and in the world to come, my rightly loveable lord and brother who are most beloved and worthy of affection in Christ.

---

5. Terence, *Andreas* 1, 2.
6. Virgil, *Bucolics* 4. 13-14.

Letter 259

Augustine wrote the following letter to Cornelius, who had asked Augustine to write a eulogy for his deceased wife, Cypriana, for him. It is clear from the letter that Cornelius is someone who has been a friend of Augustine for a long time and had once been a Manichee along with him. It is very likely that Cornelius is Romanianus, Augustine's patron from the days of his youth and the father of Licentius; if so, the letter was most probably written earlier than 429 or 430, the date traditionally given, since Romanianus was somewhat older than Augustine.[1]

Augustine asks Cornelius why, if he is truly grieved at the loss of his wife and wants to be consoled by her praises, he has sought consolation with so many other women (paragraph 1). Though Cornelius may complain of Augustine's harshness, he insists that, as Cicero was with Catiline, he wants to be merciful but not remiss with him (paragraph 2). Augustine admonishes Cornelius for the dissolute life he is leading and urges him to think of God and Christ (paragraph 3). He offers Cornelius a deal: he will sell Cornelius the eulogy of his wife in return for Cornelius' chastity (paragraph 4). He urges his friend to live chastely in order that he may live forever with his chaste wife (paragraph 5).

Augustine to his most beloved lord and honorable brother Cornelius.

1. You wrote to me, as you recalled that the holy Paulinus did to Macarius, in order that I might give you a long letter of consolation, because you were deeply upset over the death of your wonderful wife. Of course that soul, having been welcomed into the company of the faithful and chaste, neither cares about nor seeks human praise, but since these eulogies are produced for the sake of the living, it is first of all necessary that you, who want to be consoled by praise for her, live so that you merit to be where she is. For I do not doubt that you believe that she is where those women are who have neither sullied the marriage bed with adultery nor indulged in fornication while not in the bonds of any marriage. Hence, to want to drive away your sadness by praise of her is—for a husband who is so very unlike her—flattery, not consolation. For, if you love her as she loved you, you would have preserved for her what she preserved for you. And since, if you had died first, we should by no means think that she would have married anyone, if you were truly in need of being consoled over her loss by

---

1. On the identification of Cornelius with Romanianus, see A. Gabillan, "Romanian alias Cornelius," *Revue des études augustiniennes* 24 (1978): 58-70. At the end of the nineteenth century a stone was found in Souk Ahras–the ancient Thagaste–with the inscription "<Cor>nelius Romanianus." Since the cognomen Romanianus is rare, the probability is high that it referred to the patron of Augustine.

praises for her, would you be seeking even one lawful companion after that wife?

2. Here you are going to say, "Why do you treat me harshly? Why do you reprimand me sternly?" Look, have we not grown older during the course of this discussion while life goes on, which will be ended before it is corrected? You want me to pardon your deadly lack of concern. How much better you would do to pardon my concern, which, if it is not as attractive, is certainly more merciful! Tully certainly used to inveigh with a hostile attitude, though the aim of one governing an earthly republic is far different, and yet he said, "I desire, conscript fathers, to be merciful, but I desire in such great perils of the state not to seem remiss."[2] How much more just it is that I, having become a minister of the divine word and sacrament in the service of the eternal city, say, since you yourself know what a friendly attitude I have toward you, "I desire, Cornelius, my brother, to be merciful, but I desire in such great perils for you and for me not to seem remiss"!

3. A crowd of women keeps vigil at your side; the number of prostitutes increases every day. But are we bishops to listen patiently to the master of that multitude, or rather their slave, who is carried off by insatiable lust through so many prostitutes, while on the grounds of friendship he demands of us a eulogy for his wife, as if to assuage his sorrow? When you were I shall not say a catechumen but a youth a little older than us, situated with us in a most destructive error,[3] you corrected yourself from that vice by a will full of self-control. After a long time you fell back into it in a more sordid fashion, and then, after you were baptized in extreme danger of your life, you still did not correct yourself, when, though I will not call you a believer, I am certainly an old man and a bishop. You want to be consoled by us over the death of your good wife. Who is there to console us over *your* death, which is more real? Or, since we cannot forget the great services you did for us, are we still to be tormented by your conduct, held in contempt, and valued as worthless for this reason, when we pour out our groans over you to you? But we admit that we are of no account in correcting and healing you. Turn your mind toward God; think of Christ. Listen to the apostle as he says, *Shall I take the members of Christ and make them members of a prostitute?* (1 Cor 6:15) If you reject in your heart the words of an old bishop, your friend, whoever he may be, think of the body of your Lord in your body. Finally, are you going to sin by putting your conversion off from day to day, though you do not know your last day?

4. Now I will test how much you desire the praises of Cypriana from our lips. Surely, if I were still selling words to students in a school of rhetoric, I would

---

2. Cicero, *First Oration against Catiline* 2, 4.
3. That is, Manicheism.

first take my fee from them. I want to sell you a eulogy of your most chaste spouse; first pay me the fee: your chastity. Give it, I repeat, and receive the eulogy in return. *I speak in human terms on account of your weakness* (Rom 6:19). I think that Cypriana does not deserve from you that you prefer the love of your concubines to her praises. But this is what you will do if you would rather remain in that love than come to those praises. Why do you want to force those praises from me by your demands, though you see that what I ask is to your advantage? Why do you beg me like someone in subjection to do what you could order me to do if you corrected yourself? Let us send gifts to the spirit of your wife. You send her your imitation of her; I will send her praises of her. Although, as I said before, she does not now seek praise from human beings, yet even in death she seeks your imitation of her as much as she loved you in life, though you were also unlike her. I shall do regarding her what you want when you do what she and I want.

5. For that proud and wicked rich man, as the Lord says in the gospel, was clothed in linen and purple and feasted splendidly every day. When he was paying the penalty for his evil actions in hell and could not obtain a drop of water from the finger of the poor man whom he had held in contempt before his door, he remembered his five brothers and asked that the same poor man, whose repose in the bosom of Abraham he saw from afar, be sent to them so that they would not come to that place of torments.[4] How much more does your wife remember you? How much more does that chaste woman want you not to meet with the punishment of the adulterers, if that proud man did not want his own brothers to meet with the punishment of the proud? And since that brother did not want his brothers to be joined with him in punishment, how much less does your wife, who is now enjoying happiness, want to have her husband separated from her in punishment? Read the passage in the gospel. "These are Christ's loving words. Believe God."[5] Of course you mourn your dead wife, and you suppose that, if I praise her, you will be consoled by my words. Learn that you will grieve if you will not be with her. Or should you grieve more because she is not yet praised by me than I should grieve because you do not love her? After all, if you loved her, you would surely desire to be with her after death, where you will certainly not be if you are going be the sort of man you are. Love her whose praises you demand, therefore, so that I do not justly refuse what you insincerely ask for. [In another hand:] May the Lord grant that we rejoice over your salvation, most beloved lord and honorable brother.

---

4. See Lk 16:19-28.
5. See Letter 32, 5, from the Ode of Paulinus for Licentius.

Letter 260

Sometime during Augustine's episcopacy, Audax, a young Catholic rhetorician who probably lived in Africa, wrote this letter to Augustine, asking to receive the treasure of wisdom from him and pleading for a longer letter in reply. Audax appends to his letter five verses of a poem that equals the rest of the letter in its poor taste.

To Augustine, his truly praiseworthy and very loveable lord, and his father worthy of receiving every sort of praise, Audax sends greetings in the Lord.

I am grateful to Your Beatitude that you willingly accept my attempts at writing. For sons of good faith are given confidence when it is watered by the rains from fatherly springs. And so I have challenged you, my dear bishop, not that I may receive a little offering from your generous heart, but that I may abundantly draw in the vast river of your richness. I desired the treasure of wisdom, but I received less than I wanted, though I should not refer to as "less" (*minus*) but as a gift (*munus*) what Augustine, an oracle of the law, a priest of righteousness, a restorer of spiritual glory, a dispenser of eternal salvations, has bestowed. For you both know and censure the orb of the earth, and it both knows and approves you. I long, therefore, to be fed with the flowers of wisdom and watered with drafts from the living spring. Grant to my desire what may profit us both. For the native mantle of an oak with half its leaves fallen can become green again if it merits to be increased little by little from your streams. And so, I promise the presence of my lowly self not so much by pen as by heart, if I read another letter of Your Reverence instead of seeing you. May God's mercy protect you for countless years, my venerable lord.

Why has the world's spring watered me with so few words?
Or has he spurned[1] hearts less apt for his streams? Since every mind lies open
    for water and looks for words
As a help to religion, grant to our mind the pleasing rains
That full faith dependent upon Christ's tree expects.

---

1. I have conjectured "spurned" (*spernavit*) in place of "hoped for" (*speravit*).

Letter 261

Sometime after having received the previous letter, Augustine wrote Audax a reply. He explains that he is very busy and that even in a long letter he could not give Audax the treasure of wisdom for which he is asking (paragraph 1). He rejects some of the flattery used by Audax, though he admits to being a dispenser of salvation along with many others, some of whom are good, others bad (paragraph 2). Augustine tells Audax that he should read his writings or come to visit him (paragraph 3). He points out that the fifth verse of the poem written by Audax, which he had placed at the end of Letter 260, has an extra foot (paragraph 4), and he explains that he does not have Jerome's translation of the psalter, but has been correcting the Latin version from the Greek manuscripts (paragraph 5).

To Audax, his most beloved lord who is worthy of praise in Christ and brother who is very much longed for, Augustine sends greetings in the Lord.

1. I was not unwilling but rather even glad to receive your short letter, though it was one that clearly demanded a long letter from me, not because I could easily satisfy your desire but because I would rejoice over Your Charity. For, even if you do not seek it from an appropriate person, what you seek is still good. And I lack the leisure rather than the ability to write a long letter since I am completely occupied, that is, with tasks pertaining to the Church. From these a few drops of time scarcely relieve me, as I either ponder something or dictate those writings that are urgent and that I think will benefit more people or as I restore the strength of body necessary for our services. For I am not lacking the words with which I could fill much paper, but I reply that I am not able to do what you desire from us in the same length of discourse. After all, you said that you desired the treasure of wisdom, but that you received something less than you wanted, since I myself ask for my daily ration from that storehouse with the plea of a beggar and scarcely obtain it.

2. But how am I "an oracle of the law," since I am ignorant of far more things than I know in its wide and hidden chambers, cannot approach and penetrate its many turns and dark recesses as I want, and recognize that I am nothing but unworthy? How can I be "a priest of righteousness," when it is very difficult for me to be dedicated to it? But when you call me "a restorer of spiritual glory," pardon me, but you are quite ignorant of whom you are speaking to. I myself am in fact still being restored in this glory in such a way that I confess that I do not know from day to day not only how much I am advancing but whether I am advancing at all. Clearly I am "a dispenser of eternal salvation" along with countless other of my fellow servants. *And if I do this willingly, I have a reward, but if I do it unwillingly, I have only its dispensation entrusted to me* (1 Cor 9:17).

201

For to be a dispenser of salvation by means of the word and sacrament is not already to have a share in it. After all, if salvation were not dispensed by good men, the apostle would not be correct in saying, *Be imitators of me, as I am also of Christ* (1 Cor 11:1; 4:16). On the other hand, if salvation were not dispensed by bad men, the Lord would not say of certain ones, *Do what they say, but do not do what they do* (Mt 23:3). There are, then, many who dispense salvation, by whose ministry people come to eternal life, *but it is required of a minister that he be found faithful* (1 Cor 4:2), and among the faithful, in whose number God, who cannot be deceived, counts me, *one is this way, another that* (1 Cor 7:7), *as God gives to each one a measure of faith* (Rom 12:3).

3. And so, my dearest and most delightful brother, may the Lord rather feed you with the flowers of wisdom and water you with drafts from the living spring. But if you suppose that your desire, which is most religious, can attain anything through my slight efforts, since I understand that you have the ability and perceive that you are eager, you should turn your mind to our other works, which are contained in many volumes, rather than hope by means of a letter for something that might be able to satisfy your desire. Or at least, when present here, take what I can offer, though I suspect that you are not presenting yourself to us because you do not want to. For why would it be difficult with the Lord's help for a person free from the duties of any position to come to us, whether to be with us for a long time or to return after at least a brief time?

4. See, we have almost brought about what you mentioned in the third of your five verses, namely, that you have a long-winded rather than an eloquent letter from me. But since in the fifth and last verse there are seven feet, I do not know whether their number escaped your hearing or you wanted to find out whether I still remembered how to measure such things that those who once studied them and afterwards made much progress in the writings of the Church have perhaps now forgotten.

5. I do not have the psalter that Jerome translated from the Hebrew. We have not translated it ourselves, however, but have corrected some mistakes of the Latin manuscripts from Greek copies. Hence we have perhaps made it better than it was, but not as good as it ought to be. For even now, by comparing the manuscripts, we correct points that escaped us then, if they disturb the readers. In that way we are also, along with you, still seeking the perfect translation.[1]

---

1. Augustine's unexpected mention of his work on the Psalter perhaps reflects his strongly felt concern to have a translation better than the Old Latin version.

Letter 262

Sometime during his episcopacy Augustine wrote to Ecdicia, a Catholic laywoman, who probably lived in Africa. She had got herself into an awkward situation by having vowed continence without the consent of her husband, though he later agreed to this, and by having given away most of her possessions to two wandering monks without consulting her husband. Augustine informs her that her disobedience to her husband has made her responsible for his adultery (paragraph 1). Since her husband had consented to their life of continence, the issue is not the payment of the marital debt (paragraphs 2 and 3). What is at issue is Ecdicia's disobedience with regard to her money and her attire (paragraph 4). As a result of her actions her husband has abandoned continence, committed adultery, and spoken ill of the monks to whom she had given her money (paragraph 5). The monks were supposed to give the money to the poor, but she had acted apart from her husband, whose spiritual well-being was more important than the temporal well-being of the poor (paragraph 6). Augustine appeals to Saint Paul to show that wives should be subject to their husbands (paragraph 7). Furthermore, in giving alms to the poor one should first provide for one's children (paragraph 8). Wives should obey their husbands regarding their manner of dress, and Ecdicia should not have dressed like a widow while her husband was still living (paragraph 9). A woman can still have a humble heart even if she dresses splendidly, as the example of Esther shows (paragraph 10). Hence Augustine urges Ecdicia to apologize to her husband for her behavior and to try to win him to repentance for having given up the life of continence to which he had agreed (paragraph 11).

To his lady and most pious daughter, Ecdicia, Augustine sends greetings in the Lord.

1. After reading the letter of Your Reverence and having asked the bearer of it about the points that remained to be asked, I was deeply saddened that you chose to act with your husband in such a way that the edifice of continence that had already begun to be built in him fell wretchedly into the ruin of adultery once he lost his perseverance. For, since we ought to have grieved over him if, after vowing continence to God and having already undertaken this in his action and conduct, he returned to the flesh of his wife, how much more ought we to grieve over him now that he has plunged into a deeper destruction and commits fornication in so sudden a collapse, angry at you, dangerous to himself, as if he would rage at you all the more bitterly if he himself should perish! But this great evil has occurred because you have not treated his heart with the prudence that you ought to have. For, even if by agreement with each other you were not having sexual intercourse, as a wife you still ought to have been mindful of your husband in other matters out of marital obedience, especially since you were both members

of the body of Christ.[1] And if you had had a husband who was not a believer,[2] even then you ought to have acted submissively toward him in order to win him for Christ, as the apostles directed.

2. I omit the fact that I know that you took up a life of continence not in accord with sound teaching when he was not yet willing. For he should not have been deprived of the debt of your body that you owed him before his desire had also joined yours for that good which surpasses marital chastity. Or had you perhaps not read or heard or paid attention to the apostle saying, *It is good for a man not to touch a woman, but on account of fornication let each man have his own wife and each woman her own husband. Let the husband pay to his wife the debt he owes her; likewise, let the wife pay to her husband the debt she owes him. A wife does not have authority over her body, but her husband does; likewise, a husband does not have authority over his body, but his wife does. Do not deprive each other except by agreement for a time in order that you may be free for prayer. And return to it again for fear that Satan may tempt you on account of your lack of self-control* (1 Cor 7:1-5)? According to these words of the apostle, even if he were willing to practice continence and you were unwilling, he would be required to pay the debt he owes you, and God would credit him with continence if, yielding not to his own but to your weakness, he did not refuse to have intercourse with you, for fear that you would fall into the damnable crime of adultery. How much more ought you, who should have been more submissive, to have obeyed his will with regard to paying such a debt lest he also be carried off by a diabolical temptation to adultery? For God would have been pleased by your desire to live in continence, since you would have foregone it lest your husband perish.

3. But, as I said, I omit this, because afterwards, when you refused to agree to render him the marital debt, your husband consented to the same pact of continence, lived for a long time in complete continence with you, and by his consent absolved you from that sin by which you denied him the debt of your body. Hence, in this case of yours the question does not center on whether you ought to resume relations with your husband. After all, what you both vowed to God by the same consent you both ought to have offered to God with perseverance up to the end. If he has fallen away from his promise, at least continue yourself with full constancy. I would not exhort you to this, except that he had agreed with you to do it. For, if you never had his consent, no number of years would have defended you, but, after however much time you had consulted me, I would have given you no other answer than what the apostle says, *A wife does not have authority over her own body, but her husband does* (1 Cor 7:4). On the basis of

---

1. See Eph 5:30; 1 Cor 6:15.
2. See 1 Cor 7:13.

that authority he had already promised you that he would undertake a life of continence with you.

4. But this is what I am sorry that you have observed to a lesser degree. For the more religiously he granted you something so great by imitating you, the more humbly and obediently you ought to have yielded to him in your domestic life. After all, he did not cease to be your husband because you agreed together to refrain from carnal intercourse; quite the contrary, you remained married to each other in a holier way to the extent that you harmoniously observed holier promises. You ought, therefore, to have done nothing with your dress, nothing with your gold or silver or any money or with any earthly possessions of yours without his consent, so that you might not scandalize the man who had offered greater vows to God along with you and who had in continence abstained from what, with licit authority, he could have demanded concerning your body.

5. Finally, it came about that, when he was held in contempt, he broke the bond of continence by which he had bound himself when he was loved, and in his anger at you he did not spare himself. For, as the bearer of your letter reported to me, your husband learned that you gave everything or nearly everything that you possessed to two wandering monks, whoever they were, on the supposition that it was to be given to the poor. Then he despised them as well as you, considering them not servants of God but men who broke into another man's house, held you captive, and robbed the house. In anger he cast aside the holy burden that he had taken up along with you. After all, he was weak, and for this reason you, who seemed be the stronger in your common commitment, ought not to have upset him by your presumption but to have supported him by your love. For, even if he was perhaps moving rather sluggishly toward distributing alms more generously, he could have learned to do this as well, if he had not been stung by your unexpected outlays but had been coaxed to do so by the docility expected of you. In that way the two of you would have done in harmonious love much more wisely and much more orderly and decently what you thoughtlessly did alone. Nor would the servants of God be spoken of irreverently (if those men really *were* servants of God) who, when your husband was absent and without his knowledge, took so much from a woman they did not know and from another man's wife. And God would be praised in your works since you would have so faithful a union that you would hold in common not only perfect chastity but also glorious poverty.

6. But now see what you have done by your thoughtless haste. For I would like to think well of those monks by whom, according to your husband's complaints, you were not built up but plundered, and I would not want readily to agree with someone who had his vision blurred by anger at men who are perhaps servants of God. But was your action of refreshing the bodies of the poor by more generous alms as great a good as the harm you caused by tearing the mind

of your husband away from so good a commitment? Or should anyone's temporal well-being have been more precious to you than his eternal well-being? If, while thinking of more ample works of mercy, you postponed giving your possessions to the poor in order that your husband might not be scandalized and be lost to God, would God not credit you with giving more abundant alms? Hence, if you recall what you had acquired when you had won over your husband to serve Christ along with you in a holier form of chastity, realize how much greater are the losses that you suffered on account of those alms by which his heart was turned upside down than are those gains that you thought were from heaven. For, if bread shared with a poor person has great weight in heaven,[3] how much weight ought we to think mercy has there, by which a human being is snatched from the devil, who is like a roaring lion seeking someone to devour.[4]

7. Nor do we say this in the sense that, if anyone is scandalized by our good works, we ought to think that we should cease from them. But the relation of strangers is not the same as that of persons bound together in a society. A relation with a believer is not the same as that with a non-believer. The relation of parents to their children is not the same as that of children to their parents. Finally, still other is the relation of husband and wife, which we should especially bear in mind in these matters where a married woman may not say, "I do what I want with what is mine," since she does not belong to herself but to her head, that is, to her husband.[5] *For in that way*, as the apostle Peter mentions, *certain holy women who hoped in God adorned themselves, subject to their husbands, as Sarah was subject to Abraham, calling him lord,[6] and you are her daughters* (1 Pt 3:5-6). For he was speaking to Christian and not to Jewish women.

8. But why is it surprising if a father did not want their common son to be deprived by his mother of the means of support for this life, since he did not know what vocation he would pursue when he began to be a little older, whether it would be the profession of a monk or an ecclesiastical ministry or the bond of marital obligation? For, although the children of holy people ought to be encouraged and trained for better pursuits, *each one*, nonetheless, *has his own gift from God, one this gift, another that* (1 Cor 7:7). Or should a father who foresees such things and takes precautions be criticized, though the blessed apostle says, *But anyone who does not provide for his own and especially the members of his family denies the faith and is worse than a non-believer* (1 Tm 5:8)? But when he spoke about giving alms he said, *Not so that others are fed, while you are suffering* (2 Cor 8:13). Both of you, then, should have made a plan together about every undertaking; both of you should have regulated together what you should

---

3. See Is 58:7.
4. See 1 Pt 5:8.
5. See Eph 5:23.
6. See Gn 18:9-15.

store up in heaven and what you should leave for the needs of this life for your-selves and your son, so that others are not fed while you are suffering. And if anything strikes you as better in arranging and doing these actions, you should have respectfully suggested it to your husband and obediently followed the authority of him who is, as it were, your head. In that way all people with sound ideas to whom rumor might report this gift of yours would rejoice over the fruit and peace of your house, and an enemy would go away without having anything bad to say of you.

9. Now if, concerning the giving of alms and the distribution of your posses-sions to the poor (a good and important work about which the directives of the Lord are quite clear), you ought to have shared your plan with your husband and not to have rejected his will, for he was a believer and observed with you the holy pact to live in continence, how much more ought you not, without his permis-sion, to have changed or adopted anything concerning your clothing or dress, about which we do not read that God commanded anything? Scripture does of course say that women ought to dress with decorum, and gold jewelry, hair-dos, and other such things, which are often used for proud vanity or as a seductive snare, are rightly censured.[7] But in accord with the means of the person there is a certain mode of attire for a married woman distinct from the clothing of a widow, and it can also be appropriate for believing wives, provided God's law is observed. If your husband did not want you to put this aside so that you would not behave like a widow while he was still alive, I think that in this matter you should not have brought him to the scandal of discord—more by the evil of disobedience than by the good of any abstinence. After all, what is more absurd than that a woman should be arrogant toward her husband over her humble attire, when it would be better that you obey him with resplendent behavior than resist him with somber attire? For, even if the garb of a nun delighted you, you could have taken up even this more graciously after having consulted and asked your husband rather than presumed it without having consulted him and while holding him in contempt. If he would not allow this at all, what would be lost to your desire? Heaven forbid that you would have displeased God because you did not dress like Anna, since your husband was not yet dead, but like Susanna.

10. Even if he, who had already begun to observe the great good of continence along with you, had wanted you to wear the attire of a married woman and not that of a widow, he would not, after all, have forced you into an indecent manner of dressing. And even if you were forced to this for some serious reason, you could have had a humble heart in your proud attire. Among the men of old, the famous Queen Esther feared God, worshiped God, and was subject to God, and yet she was subject to and obeyed her husband, a king, a foreigner, who did not

---

7. See 1 Tm 2:9.

worship the same God with her. In a time of extreme danger not for herself alone, but also for her people, who were then the people of God, she prostrated herself in prayer to God and said in her prayer that she regarded her royal raiment like a rag defiled with menstrual blood,[8] and God, who as the searcher of hearts[9] knew that she spoke the truth, quickly heard her as she prayed in that way. And she of course had a husband married to many wives, a man who worshiped many alien false gods. But if your husband had continued in the commitment that he had undertaken with you and had not fallen into sin after being offended by you, you would have not only a believing husband and one worshiping the true God along with you but also one living in continence. He was undoubtedly not unmindful of your commitment, and, even if he forced you to dress like a married woman, he would still not have forced you to dress like a proud woman.

11. Because you thought that you should consult me, I have written these things to you not in order that I might break your holy commitment by my words but because I was in sorrow over what your husband did on account of your disorderly and thoughtless action. You ought to think most seriously about how to undo the damage to him, if you truly want to belong to Christ. Put on humility of mind, therefore, and do not scorn your husband who is perishing in order that God may preserve you who are persevering. Pour out for him pious and constant prayers; offer sacrifices of tears like the blood of a wounded heart. And write to him a letter of apology, asking pardon for having sinned against him because you did what you thought you should do concerning your property without his advice and consent. You need not repent over having given your property to the poor but over not having wanted to have him as a partner and guide in your good work. Promise, moreover, with the help of the Lord that, if he repents of his shameful conduct and returns to the continence he abandoned, you will obey him, as is proper, in all things, *if perhaps*, as the apostle says, *God grants* him *repentance* and he frees himself *from the snares of the devil by whom* he is held captive *in accord with his own will* (2 Tm 2:25-26). Who can fail to know, however, that your son, since you have received him from a lawful and moral marriage, falls more under his father's authority than under yours? And for this reason your son cannot be denied to your husband wherever your husband may know him to be and may rightfully ask for him. And in order that he may be nourished and raised in God's wisdom in accord with your will, your son needs oneness of heart between you and your husband.

---

8. See Est 14:16.
9. See Prv 24:12.

Letter 263

Sometime during his episcopacy Augustine wrote the following letter to the virgin Sapida. In it he consoles her over the death of her brother Timothy, who was a deacon. Augustine tells Sapida that he has accepted and has begun to wear the tunic that she wove for her brother, though he died before he could wear it (paragraph 1). Augustine sympathizes with her pain at the loss of her brother but assures her that Timothy's love for her has not perished but remains, hidden with Christ in the Lord (paragraph 2). Christians may mourn the deaths of their dear ones, but they should not mourn them like the pagans who have no hope (paragraph 3). Augustine reminds Sapida that her brother lives even now and that his body will rise again for eternal life, in which Christians should find consolation (paragraph 4).

To his most devout lady and holy daughter, Sapida, Augustine sends greetings in the Lord.

1. I accepted what you wanted me to accept from the just and pious labors of your hands so that I might not sadden you more deeply, when I saw that you needed rather to be consoled, especially since you thought that it would be no small consolation for you if I would wear the tunic that you made for your brother, a holy servant of God. After all, he has no need of perishable things now that he has left this land of the dying. I have done what you desired, therefore, and I did not deny to your love for your brother this consolation of whatever value or importance you judge it to be. I have accepted the tunic you sent, and, when I wrote this, I had already begun to wear it. Be encouraged, but find much better and much greater consolations so that the cloud over your heart that has been made dense by human weakness may be dissipated by God's authority. And live with perseverance so that you may live with your brother, for it was thus that your brother died — that he might live.

2. It is of course reason for tears that you no longer see, as you once did, your loving brother, a deacon of the church of Carthage, coming and going, busy with the work of his ministry in the Church, and revering you greatly for your life and profession of sacred virginity. And you do not hear from him the words of respect that he paid to the holiness of his sister with indulgent, pious, and dutiful affection. When one thinks of these things, one must do violence to one's feelings, one's heart is pierced, and the tears of one's heart flow like blood. But let your heart be lifted up and your eyes will be dry. For the love by which Timothy loved and loves Sapida has not perished because those things, which you mourn as having been removed from you, have passed away over time. That love remains, preserved in its repository, and *is hidden with Christ in the Lord* (Col

209

3:3). Do those who love gold lose it when they hide it away? Are they not then more confident about it, to the extent this is possible, when they keep it in safer chests removed from their own eyes? Earthly love thinks that it possesses with more safety what it loves if it does not see it. Does heavenly love, then, grieve as if it has lost what it has sent on ahead into the storehouses of heaven? Turn your attention to your own name, Sapida,[1] and savor *the things that are above where Christ is seated at the right hand of God* (Col 3:1). He was willing to die for us so that we might live, even though we have died, so that human beings would not fear death as if it were going to destroy them, and so that none of the dead for whom life itself died would grieve as if they had lost life. Let these and other such consolations from God be yours in order that human sadness might blush and yield to them.

3. We should not, of course, become incensed at the grief of mortals over their dear ones who have died, but the sorrow of believers ought not to be prolonged. If, then, you were saddened, let it be enough now, and do not be sad *like the pagans who do not have hope* (1 Thes 4:13). After all, the apostle Paul did not forbid us to be sad when he said this, but he forbade us to be sad *like the pagans who do not have hope*. For Martha and Mary, pious and believing sisters, wept over their brother Lazarus, who was going to rise,[2] though they did not know then that he was going to return to this life. And the Lord himself wept over this same Lazarus, whom he was going to raise up.[3] Even though he did not order us by a command, he certainly permitted us by his example to weep over the dead who we believe will rise up to true life. Nor does scripture, in the Book of Ecclesiasticus, say in vain, *Shed tears over one who has died, and begin to lament, as if you have suffered grievously* (Sir 38:16), but a little later it says: *And be consoled in your sadness, for from sadness comes death, and sadness of heart diminishes strength* (Sir 38:17.19).

4. Your brother is alive in his mind, my daughter, but is asleep in his body. *Will he who is asleep rise no more?* (Ps 41:9) God who received his spirit will restore to him his body, which he did not take away to destroy but set aside to restore. There is, therefore, no reason for prolonged sadness. There is better reason for everlasting joy. For even that mortal part of your brother that was buried in the earth will not be lost to you. In that part he was present to you; through that part he addressed and conversed with you. Just as he presented his face to your eyes, he produced by that mortal part of his that voice so familiar to your ears that, wherever you heard his voice, you recognized him even if you did not see him. For these things are taken away from the senses of human beings

---

1. The name Sapida means "tasty" or "savory" and is related to the verb *sapere*, which has a range of meanings from "to have good taste" to "to be intelligent" and "to be wise."
2. See Jn 11:19.33.
3. See Jn 11:35.

with the result that the absence of those who have died causes sorrow. But even our bodies will not perish for eternity, just as *not even a hair of your head will perish* (Lk 21:18), but, after having been laid aside for a time, they will be received back so that they will never again be laid aside, but they will be changed for the better and made strong. There is certainly a greater reason for rejoicing in the hope of an eternity beyond all calculation than there is reason for grief over something of only the very shortest duration. The pagans do not have this hope, *since they know neither the scriptures nor the power of God* (Mt 22:29; Mk 12:24), who can restore what has been lost, bring to life what has died, repair what has been corrupted, and keep thereafter without end what has come to an end. He who has brought us to faith by the promises that he has already fulfilled will do the things that he has promised. Your faith speaks to you of these things, because your hope will not be stolen from you even if your love is now postponed for a time. Meditate on these things; console yourself with them more richly and more truly. For, if the fact that I am clothed—because he could not be—with the garment which you had woven for your brother offers you some consolation, how much more amply and certainly ought you to be consoled because he for whom it was prepared will then need no incorruptible garb but will be clothed with incorruptibility and immortality.

Letter 264

Sometime during his episcopacy Augustine wrote to Maxima, a pious woman who had written to him because she was troubled by some harmful and destructive errors that had emerged in her province, which was probably Spain, if the errors are those of Priscillian, as is generally supposed. Augustine tells Maxima that these evils were predicted and that God knows how to make good use of evil persons for the benefit of his elect (paragraph 1). He advises Maxima to pray for those in error and explains that the correction of some of them is the cause of the greatest joy one can have in this life (paragraph 2). Finally, he commends Maxima's correct faith in the incarnation and asks her to send him any writings that she can obtain in which the heretics have defended their beliefs (paragraph 3).

To Maxima, an honorable and excellent servant of God worthy of praise among the members of Christ, Augustine sends greetings in the Lord.

1. As much as your holy zeal causes us joy, we are saddened over your informing us that your province is gravely endangered by harmful and most destructive errors. But since it has been predicted that these things would happen, we should not be surprised that they arise but should be on guard in order that they may do no harm. God, our deliverer, would not permit them to arise, however, if it were not good for his holy men and women to be taught even by trials of this sort. If they lack docility because of their arrogance and neglect to correct and straighten themselves out in the present life, those heretics, by their perverse will, gain for themselves the recompense of blindness at present and eternal punishment in the future. But they make bad use of the gifts of God, *who makes his sun rise over the good and the bad and makes it rain upon the just and the unjust* (Mt 5:45) and who by his patience calls them to repentance while they store up for themselves wrath for the day of wrath and of the revelation of the just judgment of God.[1] Just as they make bad use, then, of God's kindness and patience, that is, the gifts of God, when they are not corrected, so, in turn, God makes good use even of evil persons not only for his justice, which will pay them what they deserve in the end, but also for the training and progress of his holy people, so that the good may make progress, be tested, and be revealed even by the perversity of the evil. As the apostle says, *It is necessary that there be heresies in order that those who have been tested may be revealed in your midst* (1 Cor 11:19).

2. For if God, who brought us such a great good from the sin of Judas that we were redeemed by the blood of Christ, did not make good use even of evil

---

1. See Rom 2:4-5.

persons for the benefit of his elect, he either could have not permitted those whom he foreknew would be evil to be born or he could have destroyed them at the very beginning of their wickedness. But he only permits them to exist to the extent that he knows that they help and are necessary to warn and train his holy family. He consoles our sadness over them because even the sadness that we have for them raises us up, but it weighs them down if they persevere in their wickedness. The joy that we feel when some of them are straightened out, changed for the better, and united to the company of the saints, cannot be compared to any joy in this life. For this reason scripture says, *My son, if you will be wise, you will be wise for yourself and your neighbors. But if you turn out bad, you alone will suffer evils.* (Prv 9:12 LXX) For when we rejoice over the faithful and the just, their goodness benefits both them and us, but when we are saddened over the unbelieving and wicked, their malice and our sadness harms them alone. But it helps us very much before God that we are mercifully saddened over them and that, in accord with our sadness, we groan and pray. For this reason, my honorable servant of God worthy of praise in Christ, I highly approve and praise your sorrow over such people and your watchfulness and caution in their regard, which you expressed in your letter. And because you ask this, I exhort you, as much as my strength allows, to walk on this path with perseverance, and I advise you to have pity on them with the simplicity of a dove but to beware of them with the cunning of a serpent.[2] Work as much as you can so that those who are close to you may remain with you in the correct faith or may be corrected in accord with the correct faith if some have fallen into error.

3. Concerning the man whom *the Word of God* assumed when he *became flesh and dwelled among us* (Jn 1:14), if I found anything false or incorrect in what you believe, I would correct it. Believe, then, what you believe, namely, that the Son of God assumed in that man our whole nature, that is, a rational soul and mortal flesh without sin. For he became a sharer in our weakness, not in our sinfulness, in order that through our common weakness he might destroy our sinfulness and bring us to his righteousness, drinking in death from what is ours and offering us life from what is his. But if you have any document of theirs in which they maintain what is contrary to the faith, be so good as to send it in order that we may not only state our faith but also refute their errors to the best of our abilities. For they undoubtedly try to defend what they wrongly and impiously hold by some testimonies from the scriptures of God. In those scriptures we must show them how they do not correctly understand the sacred writings composed for the salvation of believers. It is just as if someone were deeply troubled over surgical instruments, which were, of course, not invented to wound but to heal. We have, however, labored much, and we still labor, as much as the Lord allows,

2. See Mt 10:16.

in opposition to various errors that need to be refuted. But if you perhaps desire to have the small works produced by our labors, send someone who can copy them. For God, who gave you the means to do this, willed that you could do it most easily.

Letter 265

Sometime during his episcopacy Augustine wrote to Seleuciana, a Catholic laywoman in Africa, who had appealed to Augustine for help with certain supposedly Novatianist ideas that she had encountered. Augustine begins by expressing his surprise that a Novatianist would say that the apostle Peter was not baptized (paragraph 1). He warns that one should avoid thinking that Peter did penance as if he were one of those who are properly called penitents in the Church (paragraph 2). When Peter denied Christ, he had been baptized by water, but had not yet been baptized by the Holy Spirit (paragraph 3). As the righteous before the time of Abraham did not need circumcision, so the apostles did not need to be baptized by the Holy Spirit before Christ gave them the Holy Spirit. But we should not expect to find a passage in scripture where it says that all the apostles were baptized as we find one where it says that Paul was baptized (paragraph 4). Augustine explains the sense in which Christ baptized, though he himself did not baptize anyone (paragraph 5). He expresses his bewilderment at the unnamed Novatianist's claim that the apostles imposed penance in place of baptism (paragraph 6). He explains how persons do penance before baptism and after baptism (paragraph 7). Furthermore, there is also the daily penance that good and faithful Christians perform for the minor sins that they commit daily (paragraph 8).

To Seleuciana, a most devout servant of God, worthy of honor in the love of Christ, Bishop Augustine sends greetings in the Lord.

1. I read your letter and was gladdened at your well-being, and I have not delayed in replying to the questions you wrote. And first of all I am surprised that this Novatianist[1] says that Peter had not been baptized, since a little before you had written that he said that the apostles were baptized. I do not know why he thinks that among the baptized apostles Peter had not been baptized, and for this reason I sent you a copy of your letter in case you do not have one, so that you may consider in it more carefully how I reply to what I found in your letter. For, unless a stenographer copied or wrote it incorrectly, I do not know what sort of judgment he has who says that the apostles were baptized and denies that Peter was baptized.

2. But when he says that Peter did penance, one should avoid supposing that he did this in the way that those who are properly called penitents in the Church do it. And who would tolerate the idea that the first of the apostles should be counted among such penitents? After all, he repented over denying Christ, as his tears show. For scripture says that *he wept bitterly* (Mt 26:75; Lk 22:62). For

---

1. For the teaching of Novatian see *Heresies* 38. In the first half of the third century Novatian broke away from the Church of Rome because of his rigorist position regarding those who had fallen away in the persecutions.

they had not yet been strengthened by the resurrection of the Lord and by the coming of the Holy Spirit, who appeared on the day of Pentecost, or by the conferral of the Spirit that the Lord made known after he rose from the dead, when he breathed into their face and said, *Receive the Holy Spirit* (Jn 20:22).

3. Hence it can correctly be said that, when Peter denied the Lord, the apostles were not yet baptized; they were baptized with water but not with the Holy Spirit. For he said this to them after he rose and was living with them: *John in fact baptized with water, but you will be baptized with the Holy Spirit, whom you will receive after a few days on Pentecost* (Acts 1:5). But some manuscripts have: *But you will begin to be baptized with the Holy Spirit.* Yet whether it says, *You will be baptized,* or it says, *You will begin to be baptized,* makes no difference. For certain manuscripts in which we find *You will baptize* or *You will begin to baptized* are defective, and they are easily shown to be defective from the Greek manuscripts. But if we say that they were not baptized with water, we ought to be afraid that we may err gravely regarding them and give people grounds for placing little or no value on baptism. For the apostolic teaching shows that we should value baptism highly insofar as the centurion Cornelius and those who were with him were baptized even after they had received the Holy Spirit.[2]

4. If the righteous of old were not circumcised, they did not commit a sin, but after God commanded that Abraham and his descendants be circumcised,[3] it was a serious sin if this was not done. In the same way, before Christ the Lord gave baptism in his Church as the sacrament of the New Testament in place of the circumcision of the flesh and most clearly stated, *If one is not reborn of water and the Spirit, he will not enter into the kingdom of heaven* (Jn 3:5), we ought not to look for when anyone was baptized. But wherever we read that any persons belong to the kingdom of heaven in the body of Christ, *which is the Church* (Col 1:24), we ought to understand only those who have been baptized, except perhaps for those who met with the sufferings of martyrdom and, because they refused to deny Christ, were killed before they were baptized. For such persons martyrdom was counted as baptism. But can we say this of the apostles, who had such a long time in which to be baptized that they baptized others? Yet we do not find that everything that was done is also recorded in scripture, but from other testimonies it is proven that such things were done. Scripture tells us when the apostle Paul was baptized,[4] but it does not tell us when the other apostles were baptized. We ought, nonetheless, to understand that they were also baptized, just as scripture tells us when the peoples of the churches of Jerusalem and Samaria were baptized[5] but does not, to be sure, tell us when the other peoples of the gentiles to whom the apostles sent

---

2. See Acts 10:47-48.
3. See Gn 17:10-14.
4. See Acts 9:18.
5. See Acts 2:41; 8:12.

letters were baptized. Yet, on account of the Lord's statement, *Unless one is reborn of water and the Holy Spirit, he will not enter the kingdom of heaven* (Jn 3:5), we should certainly have no doubt that they were baptized.

5. Scripture, however, makes both of these statements about the Lord, that *he baptized more people than John* and that *he himself did not baptize, but his disciples did* (Jn 4:1-2), in order that we might understand that he baptized by the presence of his majesty but did not baptize by his own hands. For the sacrament of baptism is his, but the ministry of baptizing belonged to his disciples. At one point, then, John the evangelist said in his gospel, *After this Jesus and his disciples went into the land of Judea, and he stayed there with them and baptized* (Jn 3:22). Then he said a little later, when speaking of him, *Therefore, when Jesus learned that the Pharisees heard that Jesus was making more disciples and baptizing more people than John, although Jesus himself did not baptize, but his disciple did, he left Judea and went back again to Galilee* (Jn 4:1-3). Hence, when he left Jerusalem with his disciples and went into the land of Judea and stayed there with them, he did not baptize by himself but by his disciples, who we understand were already baptized either by the baptism of John, as some people think, or by the baptism of Christ, which is more worthy of belief. For he would not have shunned the ministry of baptism in order to have baptized servants through whom he might baptize others, since he did not shun the ministry of that memorable humility when he washed their feet. And, when Peter asked him to wash not only his feet but his hands and head as well, he answered, *One who has bathed only needs to wash his feet, but he is entirely clean* (Jn 13:10), and there we understand that Peter had been baptized.

6. But the sense in which this man said what you cited in your letter, namely, that the apostles imposed a penance in place of baptism, is not clearly expressed. For, if he says "in place of baptism" because sins are forgiven through penance, what he says has some reason to it. Penance of that sort can be beneficial after baptism, if anyone commits sin. But since this fellow denies that there is a place for penance after baptism when he says, as you wrote, that there is penance only before baptism, we are given to understand that he said that the apostles imposed a penance in place of baptism in the sense that they imposed it before baptism, so that those upon whom it was imposed were not afterwards baptized, since for them that penance took the place of baptism, which I have never heard that the Novatianists say. Hence, investigate carefully lest perhaps he belong to some other error and is pretending or thinks that he is a Novatianist. Or if the Novatianists do say this, I do not know it. I do know, however, that anyone who says this is a stranger to the rule of the Catholic faith and to the teaching of Christ and the apostles as well.

7. After all, people do penance before baptism for their previous sins, but in such a way that they are also baptized, as it is written in the Acts of the Apostles,

where Peter is speaking to the Jews and says, *Do penance, and let each of you be baptized in the name of the Lord Jesus Christ, and your sins will be forgiven* (Acts 2:38). People also do penance after baptism if they have sinned in such a way as to deserve to be excommunicated, and they later merit to receive reconciliation, as those persons who are called penitents in the proper sense do in all the churches. Paul the apostle spoke of this sort of penance when he said, *I fear that God may humble me before you when I come and that I may grieve over many of those who sinned before and have not done penance for the impurity, dissoluteness, and fornication that they committed* (2 Cor 12:21). For he wrote this only to those who were already baptized. In the Acts of the Apostles we find that Simon, who was already baptized, was admonished by Peter to do penance for his serious sin, when he wanted to buy with money the conferral of the Holy Spirit through the imposition of hands.[6]

8. There is also the nearly daily penance on the part of good and humble believers, when we beat our breasts and say, *Forgive us our debts as we also forgive our debtors* (Mt 6:12; Lk 11:4). For we do not want those sins to be forgiven us that we have no doubt were forgiven in baptism, but those sins that frequently creep up on human frailty, although they are, to be sure, small ones. If they were piled up against us, they would weigh us down and oppress us like a single huge sin. After all, what difference does it make to a shipwreck whether the ship is covered and overwhelmed by one huge wave or by water which gradually seeps into the hull and is left and ignored through negligence and then fills the ship and sinks it? Fasting, almsgiving, and prayer are on the watch for these sins, and when we are in them and we say, *Forgive us our debts as we also forgive*, we show that we have something to be forgiven us, and, in humbling our souls with those words, we do not cease to perform a daily penance, so to speak. I think that I have briefly but adequately replied to what you wrote. There remains to say that the man should not be quarrelsome on account of whose conversion you thought that you ought to send me such a letter.

---

6. See Acts 8:18-23.

Letter 266

Sometime during his episcopacy Augustine wrote to Florentina, a Catholic girl in Africa who was desirous of wisdom and holiness, whose parents had asked Augustine to write to her and to offer to teach her. Augustine offers to be her teacher, but asks her to pose questions for him, which he will answer for her as well as he is able (paragraph 1). He explains that he himself has not attained perfection as a teacher but still needs to learn. He warns that it is difficult to be a teacher and to maintain humility (paragraph 2). He cites various texts from scripture to emphasize the dangers of pride involved in teaching (paragraph 3), and he reminds Florentina that, even if he does provide her with some knowledge, it is Christ, the interior teacher, who will make her see that it is true (paragraph 4).

To his excellent lady and rightly honorable daughter Florentina, who is worthy of being embraced in Christ, Bishop Augustine sends greetings in the Lord.

1. Your holy undertaking and *the chaste fear of God that remains for age upon age* (Ps 19:10), which is deeply imbedded in your heart, stirs up in no small way our concern for you not only in our prayers before God but also in our admonitions for you yourself. I have done this more than once in my letters, which I sent to the mother of Your Reverence, whom I should mention with due honor. But because she graciously wrote back to me that you were willing to receive a letter from me first and that after that you would not keep silence but, by writing back, would inform me if you had some need of my ministry, which I know that in an unforced obligation I owe, as much as I can, to the venerable desire of you and of all those like you. See, I have done what I learned that you wanted, though not through you, for fear that I might seem to close the door of faith[1] inhospitably in your face. It remains for you to formulate the question if you think you should ask me anything. For I either know the answer and will not refuse it to you, or I do not know it in such a way that my ignorance of it is not detrimental to faith and salvation, and I will also assure you of this, if I can, by giving you a reason. Or if I do not know it and it is still something that one should know, I will certainly beg for it from the Lord so that I do not fail you. For often the act of asking for something is what merits obtaining it. Or I will reply to you in such a way that you know at whose door we ought to knock[2] about that matter that together we do not know.

2. I have said these things in a prefatory way so that you may not hope that you will with certainty hear whatever you ask of me and so that, when this does not

---

1. See Acts 14:27.
2. See Mt 7:7-8; Lk 11:9-10.

happen, you may not think that I acted with more audacity than prudence in giving you the opportunity to ask a question if you wanted. For I did this not as a perfect teacher but as one growing in perfection along with those he teaches, my excellent lady and rightly honorable daughter, who are worthy of being embraced in Christ. In fact, even in those matters that I know to some extent, I desire that you yourself have knowledge rather than that you have need of our knowledge. For we ought not to wish for the ignorance of others in order that we might teach what we know; after all, it is much better that all of us be taught by God.[3] This will of course be fully realized in that fatherland above when what has been promised will be brought to fulfillment in us, so that no one need say to his neighbor, *Know the Lord. For all will know him*, as scripture says, *from the youngest to the oldest of them*. (Jer 31:34) And, in teaching, we must most earnestly avoid the vice of pride that is not present in the same way in learning. For this reason holy scripture also admonishes us when it says, *Let everyone be quick to listen, but slow to speak* (Jas 1:19), and the psalmist says in the psalm, *You will give exultation and joy to my hearing*, and he immediately adds, *and my bones that have been humbled will exult* (Ps 51:10). For he saw that in listening one easily preserves humility, which is difficult to preserve in teaching, since it is necessary that a teacher have a higher position, where it takes more effort to keep pride from sneaking up on one.

3. Do you see how we are imperiled by those who expect that we should not only be teachers but also teach about God, though we are human beings? But it is a singular consolation for our labors and perils when you make such progress that you come to the point where you need no human teacher. But it is not only we who are imperiled by this danger—for what are we in comparison to that man about whom I am going to speak? It is not only we, then; the teacher of the nations himself testifies that he was also imperiled by this danger when he says, *In order that I might not be filled with pride over the greatness of the revelations I received, I was given a thorn in my flesh* (2 Cor 12:7), and so on. For this reason even the Lord himself, the wonderful healer of this swelling, says, *Do not be called Rabbi by human beings, for one alone is your teacher, Christ* (Mt 23:8.10). Maintaining this, the same teacher of the nations himself says, *Neither one who plants nor one who waters is important, but only God who gives the increase* (1 Cor 3:7). And he remembered this who humbled himself in all things[4] to the extent that he was great among those born of women,[5] saying that he was unworthy to carry the sandals of Christ.[6] For what else did he show when he said, *He who has the bride is the bridegroom, but the friend of the bridegroom*

---

3. See Jn 6:45; Is 54:13.
4. See Sir 3:20.
5. See Mt 11:11; Lk 7:28.
6. See Mt 3:11; Mk 1:7; Lk 3:16; Jn 1:27.

stands and hears him and rejoices greatly over the voice of the bridegroom (Jn 3:29)? This is that hearing that I mentioned a little before was spoken of in the psalm, *You will give exultation and joy to my hearing, and the bones that have been humbled will exult* (Ps 51:10).

4. Hence you should know that I rejoice over your faith, hope, and love more certainly, more solidly, and more soundly the less you need to learn not only from me but from any other human being. But when I was there, at a time when you were bashful because of your age, your good parents, who are most approving of your good desires, graciously indicated to me how ardently you were ablaze for piety and true wisdom and begged me with the greatest good will not to deny you my small effort on behalf of your instruction where there might be need. Hence I believed that I ought to admonish you by this letter so that, in accord with their wishes that I mentioned above, you might ask what you want lest I be useless if I try to teach you what you know. But in any case, you must hold most firmly what he who is the interior teacher of the interior human being will teach you. For, even if through me you can come to know something conducive to salvation, he shows you in your heart that what is said is true, because *neither he who plants nor he who waters is important, but God who gives the increase* (1 Cor 3:7).

Letter 267

Sometime during his episcopacy Augustine wrote to Fabiola, a laywoman in Rome, who also received from him Letter 20* concerning Antonius of Fussala. He replies to a no longer extant letter from Fabiola and commends her for preferring the heavenly fatherland to our pilgrimage on earth. He also explains that it is not bodily presence that makes one person truly present to another but the sharing of thoughts, which can be done even though two persons are physically separated.

To Fabiola, his most devout and most excellent lady and daughter praiseworthy in the love of Christ, Augustine sends greetings in the Lord.

Although you were sending a reply, I still read the letter of Your Holiness in such a way that I thought it a duty to respond to it. For you lamented the pilgrimage on which it falls to our lot always to rejoice with the saints, and you correctly preferred the desire for the heavenly fatherland where we will not be separated by earthly expanses but will always be happy at the contemplation of the One. You are happy because you ponder such things in faith, and more happy because you love them, and so you will be most happy when you have attained them. But even now notice more carefully the reason why we are said to be distant. Is it because we do not see each other's bodies or because we do not give and receive indications of our minds, that is, converse with one another? For I think that, though separated in body in distant regions, if we could know each other's thoughts, we would be together to a greater degree than if we sat silent in one place, looking at each other but not bringing forth in words any signs of our interior thoughts and revealing our minds by no gestures of the body. Hence you understand that each person is more present to himself than one person is to another. For each person is better known to himself than to another—not by gazing upon his own face, which he carries about although it is concealed from him, unless a mirror is present, but by gazing upon his consciousness, which he sees even with eyes closed. How great, then, is our life itself, which we so highly value?

Letter 268

Sometime during his episcopacy Augustine wrote to the leaders of the church of Hippo. He explains that a certain Fascius, a Catholic of Hippo, had incurred a debt, which he, Augustine, had paid off by means of a loan from a certain Macedonius after Fascius had taken refuge in the church (paragraph 1). Since Fascius had not repaid Augustine, who must now repay Macedonius, Augustine asks the men of Hippo to take up a collection in order that he can repay Macedonius, as he promised (paragraph 2). He mentions that he has also written to the priests of Hippo, asking them to use the church's treasury to make up any shortfall in what the laymen of Hippo collect. Again, he asks them to make him happy by their generosity (paragraph 3).

To the most beloved and dearest lords of the holy people whom I serve, who are members of Christ, Augustine sends greetings in the Lord.

1. The devotion of Your Holiness, which is very well known to me and very well proven, has given me confidence in our Lord Jesus Christ that, even when absent, I may presume upon that over which, when present, I have grown accustomed to rejoice. This is not only because the grace of our Lord Jesus Christ does not cease to be ablaze with such great sweetness but also because you do not permit me, who am your servant in the gospel, to suffer any difficulty. For, when his creditors were pressing our brother Fascius to pay back a debt of seventeen pieces of gold, and when he did not at the moment find the means to extricate himself, he had recourse to the help of the Church lest he suffer bodily injury. Since his creditors were also forced to leave and could not grant him a delay, they bothered me with the gravest of complaints so that I would hand him over to them or would provide the means by which they would receive what they proved was owed to them. When I offered to Fascius to speak to Your Holiness about his needs, he begged that I not do so, since he was deterred by a sense of shame. In that way, constrained by a crisis that was quite serious, I accepted seventeen pieces of gold from Macedonius, and I immediately applied them to the situation of Fascius, since he promised that he could meet the payment of the debt by a certain day and agreed that, if he could not, I would appeal on his behalf to your brotherly mercy, which you are accustomed to show to your brothers.

2. Now then, since he is absent, it remains for you to come to the rescue not of him, whom no one may compel while he is absent, but of my promise, for my reputation is always present to you. For the day by which he promised to meet the debt has already passed, and I do not find any answer to give to him who entrusted his money to me on the basis of my promise except to do what I promised I would do. But because I was not reminded of this matter so that I might

223

speak to you on the holy day of Pentecost, when you were gathered in larger numbers, I ask that you be so good as to regard this letter as my spoken words in your presence admonishing you and exhorting you in your hearts, which fear and honor our Lord and God, whom you have believed and who never departs from us. In him we also are always united to you, though we seem to have departed from you in terms of the body. He promises you the harvest of eternal life from the seed of good works, for the apostle says, *But let us not give up in doing good; for, if we do not grow weary, we shall reap the harvest at the proper time. And so, while we have time, let us do good to all, especially to those who belong to the household of the faith.* (Gal 6:9-10) Since, then, he is a member of the household of faith, a faithful Christian, our Catholic brother, I ask that you do what the Lord commands for taking care of his need, and that you do it without sadness, without murmuring, and with joy and gladness. After all, you have believed God, not a human being, because he promises that you will not lose anything that you do out of mercy but that you will receive it back on that day with immortal interest.[1] And since the apostle says, *One who sows sparingly will also reap sparingly* (2 Cor 9:6), you ought to understand that it is time for us to procure with haste and joy the gift of eternal life while we are still in this life. For, when the end of the world comes, it will be given only to those who purchased it for themselves through faith before they were able to see it.

3. I have also written to the priests that, if there is anything lacking after the collection made by Your Holiness, they should make it up from what the Church has, provided, nonetheless, that you cheerfully offer what seems good to you. For, whether it is given from your resources or from those of the Church, they all belong to God, and your devotion will be more pleasing to me than the treasures of the Church. For the apostle says, *It is not that I seek the gift, but I ask for the fruit* (Phil 4:17). Bring joy, therefore, to my heart because I desire to rejoice over your fruit. You are, after all, the trees of God that he graciously waters by frequent showers even through our ministry. May the Lord protect you from every evil both here and in the world to come, my most beloved and dearest brothers.

---

1. See Mt 25:34-40.

Letter 269

In perhaps the winter of 429/430 Augustine wrote to Nobilius, a bishop of North Africa, explaining that he was unable to come to the dedication of what was probably a new church. Nothing further is known regarding the identity of Nobilius, and the dating of the letter is uncertain.

Augustine to his most blessed and venerable brother and fellow priest, Nobilius.

So great is the solemnity to which your brotherly love invites me that my will would drag my frail body to you if its weakness did not hold it back. I could come if it were not winter; I could ignore the winter if I were young. For either the warmth of youth would bear up under the rigor of the season or the warmth of summer would mitigate the cold of old age. Now I cannot tolerate so long a trip in winter with the chill of old age that I carry about with me, my most blessed lord and venerable brother and fellow priest. I send you the salutation owed to your merits, but I commend my salvation to your prayers, as I myself ask of the Lord that the prosperity of peace may follow upon the dedication of so great a building.[1]

---

1. Augustine plays upon the words "salutation" (*salutationem*) and "salvation" (*salutem*).

Letter 270

Between 401 and 426, after Letter 110 was written, an unknown person wrote this letter to Augustine. He expresses his sorrow at not finding the whole of Augustine at the city of Leges, where he found Bishop Severus, whom Augustine had called part of his soul. He says that he desires to see Augustine and asks for Augustine's prayers for him.

When I traveled some time ago to the city of Leges,[1] I was terribly disappointed that I could not find the whole of you there. For I found a half of you and, so to speak, a part of your soul,[2] your dearest friend, Severus, over whom I rejoiced in part. For I would have rejoiced completely if I had the whole of you. I was happy because of the part of you that I found, and on account of the part of you that I did not see at all I was saddened in every way. Therefore I said to my soul, *"Why are you sad, and why do you upset me? Hope in God* (Ps 42:5), and he will cause the friend whom you love to be present." Hence I have confidence in the Lord and hope that he will make me happy at the sight of you. Oh, if love could be seen with the eyes, you would immediately see how great our love is for you! For either it would bring you great joy if it were equal to your love for me or, if it were greater, it would bring you a great desire to imitate it. Since, then, I love you in the Lord, love me who love you. And, with the authority of the Church, exhort others to love me along with you. For in your letters you ask that I pray for you, and I would certainly do so if I myself were free from sins so that I might be permitted to pray for others. And for this reason I advise you to send forth constant prayers from your heart to the Lord on my behalf, and, mindful of your religious profession, to place before your eyes that day on which *the righteous will have no fear of bad news* (Ps 112:7). And the righteous will have no fear because they will not hear, *Enter into eternal fire* (Mt 25:34), but, *Come, blessed of my Father, receive the kingdom* (Mt 25:34). May he who lives and reigns forever and ever bring us there! Amen.

---

1. A city probably in Numidia near Milevis.
2. See Letter 110, 4, where Augustine used the same expression in reference to Severus. The expression is taken from Horace, *Odes* I, 3, 8.

Letter 1*

Most probably during the last three years of his life Augustine wrote to Classicianus, a man who held a lofty position in the imperial government, though it is not clear what rank he held. Letter 250 to Auxilius, who placed Classicianus under anathema, deals with the same issue. Augustine tells Classicianus that he is deeply saddened by a letter that he has received from him, in which he apparently refers to the anathematization of himself and his family. Though he has no definite advice to offer, Augustine states his own view in opposition to collective anathematization, which he finds especially troublesome because it could mean that some innocent person in an anathematized family might die without baptism (paragraph 1). Augustine admits that he knows that some bishops have anathematized persons in loftier positions than Classicianus, along with their whole families, though he himself has never done anything of the sort (paragraph 2). He tells Classicianus that, if he has reported what happened truthfully, he has committed no sin at all (paragraph 3). But he asks Classicianus' pardon for not believing him against the bishop and suggests that he would lose nothing by asking forgiveness if he said something he should not have (paragraph 4). Finally, he states his intention to submit the questions raised by this incident to the next council as well as to write to the Apostolic See about them (paragraph 5).

To Classicianus, his distinguished, most excellent, and most beloved son, Augustine sends greetings in the Lord.

1. The letter of Your Charity has gravely saddened me, and, while I wavered back and forth over what I should say in reply, I lacked, I admit it, any advice, and those words of scripture came to mind: *If you have some advice, reply to your neighbor, but if you have none, keep your hand over your lips* (Sir 5:14). And I wish that at the occasion of your case the bishops would decide upon some policy that we should follow from then on in such cases. But at present there are no conciliar decrees, or, if perhaps there are, I do not know of them. But there are examples of men who were anathematized—not only those individuals themselves who seemed to deserve such correction but their entire family along with them, though their people had done no such wrong. Nor has any bishop who did this been accused or forced to present his grounds for such an action since, in the flock of Christ, he did what he judged beneficial for the sheep entrusted to his governance. With regard to the holy scriptures, however, we find that sinners underwent the punishment of the same sin along with all their people who did not sin, but only in the period of the Old Testament, when that punishment was bodily, not spiritual. For, even if some criminal was put to death in the flesh along with his own family, which had not taken part in the crime, it was bodies that died, which were destined to die eventually as far as all of them were concerned, in order to inspire a great fear in the others that they would die in such

227

a way that no descendant of theirs would be left. The punishment of the soul, however, always pertained only to the person who sinned, in accord with the statement of the Lord, who spoke through the prophet: *The soul of the father is mine, and the soul of the son is mine. The soul that sins will itself die.* (Ez 18:4) And so in the period of the New Testament, when a spiritual penalty has been established in the Church, in accord with the words of Christ, *What you loose on earth will be loosed in heaven, and what you bind on earth will be bound in heaven* (Mt 18:18), I do not know how it could be right to bind both the father and the son when the father has sinned and the son has not. With much less reason would it be right in the case of a wife, a male slave, a maidservant, a boy, a girl, and the whole family together. If in that family a child should be born who was not yet born when the family was anathematized, it would not be enough for him to contract original sin, insofar as all have sinned in the one Adam, but he would contract new guilt through the sin of another, which was committed before he saw the light of day, and—what is even more cruel—if he should fall into danger of death, he would not receive help through the sacrament of baptism.

2. Since these considerations trouble me deeply, I myself have never done anything like this at all, and I know that very many colleagues and brothers of mine, whether older than I in the episcopacy or my contemporaries or men younger than I, share this view of mine. But we know that certain men, and ones situated at a level of worldly power higher than you, have been anathematized by bishops along with their whole family. And they did not question them about this action, nor did they go to other bishops with complaints but rather to those by whom they were bound, in order to be set loose after they had received forgiveness and made amends. I have said this, my distinguished, most excellent and most beloved son, <in order to show>[1] why I do not have some definite advice to offer to Your Excellency in reply to what you wrote about how, even if it was you who sinned, you yourself were not the only one anathematized by the bishop, but your whole family along with you.

3. But now, when I consider the case that you presented to me by your letter, on account of which you asked whether even you yourself deserved such a punishment, I do not find any guilt on your part, if you have reported the facts truthfully. For, if those people—who deceived you by perjury and deceived their creditor by contempt for the sacraments of Christ, and who took refuge in the house of faith in order to break with impunity the oath they made—corrected this sacrilege, this crime, this impiety, not by being violently dragged from the church, but by freely leaving it, you did not sin at all. This is true even though you had come to the church escorted by soldiers, whom you needed for the exercise of your power, and even though that sorry situation obliged you to say what you said to the bishop. For you did not want him to side with those perjurers against

---

1. The Bibliothèque Augustinienne text adds the words enclosed in brackets.

their creditor, and you did not want those who swore falsely contrary to the gospel to be defended against the man who believes their oaths upon the gospel in that place where the gospel is read with the greatest authority and veneration so that people may have and preserve faith.

4. But I ask your pardon if I lend an utterly unbiased ear to the other party and do not readily believe Your Highness over against the holiness of the bishop. You certainly lose nothing; in fact, you gain very much by the merit of pious humility by asking for forgiveness from the bishop if, in the altercation that you indicated that you had with him, you perhaps said something that you should not have said and he should not have heard.

5. On account of those who would place under anathema a person's entire family, that is, many souls, because of the sin of one soul, I want, with the help of the Lord, to handle the matter in our council and to write to the Apostolic See, if necessary, so that the harmonious authority of all may determine and reaffirm what we should do in these cases, especially because someone in the family might die without baptism I also want to know whether those who seek refuge in a church in order to break faith with their creditors should be driven from there. I would say clearly without being rash that, if anyone of the faithful had been anathematized unjustly, it would be more harmful to the one who did this injustice rather than to the one who suffered it. The Holy Spirit, who dwells in the saints, by whom any person is bound or loosed,[2] does not impose a punishment upon anyone that was unmerited. Through that Spirit love is certainly poured out in our hearts,[3] and *love does not do what is wrong* (1 Cor 13:4).[4]

6. I have, however, written to the same brother, my fellow bishop and your bishop, as I thought that I should write, after I was occupied for a long time by the great difficulties of this deliberation as to whether I ought to do this. If this is not sufficient for Your Charity, forgive me. For I thought that I was obliged to do no more.

---

2. See Jn 20:22-23; Mt 16:19.
3. See Rom 5:5.
4. This section of the letter is the same as the fragment that is Letter 250A.

Letter 1A*

In 426 or 427, soon after finishing *The City of God*, Augustine wrote to Firmus, a Carthaginian interested in Christianity but not yet a Christian, to whom he also wrote Letter 2*. The present letter was found by Dom Cyrille Lambot in a manuscript of the Bibliothèque Municipale of Reims and in a manuscript of the Bibliothèque Sainte-Geneviève of Paris. In both manuscripts it served as a prologue to *The City of God*. Augustine explains to Firmus how that work must be divided, in accord with its contents, into either two or five volumes (paragraph 1). He asks Firmus to give the work's twenty-two books to the brothers in Carthage who ask for them to copy and leaves it up to Firmus' judgment how he might give them to his friends (paragraph 2). Augustine tells Firmus that he will frequently ask him about his progress in reading the books and counsels him about the value of repeating a reading (paragraph 3).

To his excellent and rightly honorable lord and loveable son, Firmus, Augustine sends greetings in the Lord.

1. After I had reread them, I sent, as I promised, the books on *The City of God*, which you asked me for with great desire. My son and your brother Cyprian was truly insistent with me that I do this, with the help of God, as I wanted him to be insistent with me. There are twenty-two books, which are too many to put together in one volume. If you want to make two volumes, they should be divided so that one volume has ten books and the other twelve. Those ten, of course, refute the vanities of non-believers, but the rest present and defend our religion, although, where it was more opportune, I defended our religion in the first ten and refuted their vanities in the last twelve. If you want more than two volumes, you must make five. The first of them should contain the first five books, in which I argued against those who maintain that the worship clearly not of gods but of demons contributes to the happiness of this life, while the second volume should contain the five that follow against those who think that many gods, whether such gods or any whatsoever, should be worshiped through sacred rites and sacrifices on account of the life that will be after death. Now the three other volumes that follow should have four books each. For we divided that part so that four books would explain the origin of that city, the next four its progress or, as we prefer to say, its development, and the final four the ends due to those cities.

2. If you are as eager in reading these books as you were about possessing them, you will come to know from your own experience rather than from my promise how much help they offer. As for the books belonging to this work, namely, *The City of God*, which our brothers there in Carthage do not have, I ask that you graciously and willingly give them to those who ask for them in order

that they may copy them. After all, you will not have to give them to many persons but scarcely to one or two, and they will give them to the others. But you yourself must see how you might give them to your friends, whether they want to be instructed about the Christian people or they are trapped in some superstition from which it might seem possible that they can be set free by the grace of God through our effort.

3. By my letters I shall frequently take care, if the Lord wills, to ask how much progress you have made in reading them. As an educated man, however, you do not fail to recognize how much repeated reading helps one to know what one is reading. For, my excellent lord and rightly honorable and loveable son, there is either no difficulty or only a slight one in understanding if one has a facility in reading, and this facility increases with repetition, so that perseverance [brings to full understanding what inattention][1] had left only partially grasped. I ask that you write back to me about how you came to have those books, which I wrote soon after my conversion, concerning the Academics,[2] since you indicated to me by your previous letter that Your Excellency was familiar with them. But the enclosed summary will indicate how much material I collected in writing the twenty-two books.

---

1. There is a lacuna in the text. I have followed the conjecture in the Bibliothéque Augustinienne edition, which is taken from Dom Lambot in *Revue Bénédictine* 51 (1939): 111.
2. That is, *Answer to the Skeptics*, which Augustine wrote while at Cassiciacum.

Letter 2*

Probably in 428 Augustine again wrote to Firmus in reply to three letters from him, which are no longer extant. Augustine apologizes for the delay in responding to them (paragraph 1). In his first letter Firmus had thanked Augustine for sending him the last twelve books of *The City of God*, and Augustine asks him whether he has read them by now (paragraph 2). Augustine warns Firmus that he is missing the whole benefit of these books if he does not enter the city of God by receiving the bath of rebirth, which he had said in his second letter that he wanted to postpone (paragraph 3). Firmus's first excuse was that the burden would be too heavy for his weak shoulders. Augustine points to the many Christian women, including Firmus' wife, who are strong enough to carry the burden Firmus finds too heavy (paragraph 4). Augustine warns Firmus that his knowledge, even of the highest good, will be of no value to him unless he receives the bath of rebirth and becomes a member of Christ (paragraph 5).

Firmus' second reason for delaying baptism was that his slowness would demonstrate greater reverence for the mysteries. Augustine warns him in the sternest terms that baptism is necessary for salvation and that he is like the scribes and Pharisees who knew what to do but did not do it (paragraph 6). The third excuse that Firmus offered was that one must await the will of God, by whom we are moved to all our good desires, for we can do nothing without God. Augustine tells him that he should not be afraid to anticipate God's will since, if Firmus does will it, God's grace will be operative there as well (paragraph 7). Then Augustine turns to the distinction between what God does and what God does not do but only permits, since Firmus had correctly claimed that nothing is done without God's will (paragraph 8). As long as Firmus distinguishes between what God does and what he permits, Augustine has no problem in accepting the truth of his claim (paragraph 9). There remains in the baptized the concupiscence that is the result of Adam's sin and that inclines each person to sin. From that evil we will be completely free only in the next life. Augustine argues that human nature, which God made so that it could avoid sin if it had willed to, is better than if he had made it so that it could not sin (paragraph 10). Again Augustine urges Firmus to receive baptism (paragraph 11).

Finally Augustine turns to the question of Firmus' young son, for Firmus's third letter had contained a sample of his son's oratory. Augustine expresses his joy over the natural talent and fine education of the unnamed young man, whom he affectionately refers to as "our Greek," but he warns that the use to which one puts such gifts is what is important (paragraph 12). He points out that Firmus' son must aim to please with his oratory not just the most people but the best. He also asks Firmus about the books his son has been reading (paragraph 13).

To Firmus, his rightly illustrious lord and son worthy of being highly honored by me with the affection of sincere love, Augustine sends greetings in the Lord.

1. The care for my own pressing duties, not a disregard for your pious desire, has brought it about that I am replying to your letter rather late. Nor has this hindrance come to an end so that at last I have the leisure to reply; rather, it has been interrupted so that, in the midst of most troublesome problems, I can very gladly take up a pressing matter, lest I postpone too long the payment of this debt, which I have come to owe because of my own desire. But I have not undertaken to pay this debt without first studying your letters—one that you sent me in gratitude after I sent you the books of *The City of God*; another that the priest Lazarus brought, in which you put off sending the speech of our son, which I had asked for; and the third that you sent along with that same speech.

2. I have set out to speak with you about your three letters in this one of mine. In the letter of yours that I first mentioned you said that you had read the first ten of those twenty-two books, and you wrote in reply about them in such a way that it was evident that you read them well. I know that you had not yet then read the twelve that follow, but I do not know whether you have read them now. For it was possible that you were moved by good will and gave them all to friends for copying before you finished reading them all and have not received back those you gave out, or that you thought that you ought to say nothing to me about those you received and read, thinking that it was enough that you did not write back in a cursory fashion about those ten but discussed them in some sense with great care. You could also have wanted to find out whether I would be alert to demand the part of your debt which I perceived that you had not yet paid or whether I cared either to notice or to demand its complete payment. Here you have it then: I both know and demand what you have not completely done. Pay what you owe concerning the last twelve books!

3. Among these is the eighteenth book of this work, which you listened to attentively along with us when it was read on three consecutive afternoons. And because of that you were set afire with a blazing desire to have all the books, and you did not cease to insist until you obtained them. Please, I do not want to be a demanding gatherer of the harvest after having sowed seed in abundance. For, in excusing yourself in your second letter from receiving the sacrament of rebirth, you are rejecting the whole fruit of so many books that you love. For their fruit does not consist in delighting the reader or in making someone know many facts that he does not know but in persuading a person either to enter the city of God without hesitation or to remain there with perseverance. The first of these is obtained by rebirth, the second by a love for righteousness. If these books do not produce this in those who read and praise them, what do they accomplish? Insofar as it concerns you personally, since they were unable to produce in you the first of these, they have as yet accomplished nothing, no matter how much you praise them.

4. "But the burden of so great a weight, after all, cannot be supported by shoulders that are still weak and have not been strengthened." This, then, is the first reason for your excusing yourself, nor do you notice, you men whoever you are who fear this burden, that you are most easily outdone by women in bearing it, for the Church is made fruitful by a devout multitude of faithful and chaste women. For, if you did notice, you would drive out this needless fear with an inevitable sense of shame. Your wife is one of them, for I certainly ought to believe that she is the sort of woman over whom I already rejoice. After all, I do not fear to offend you when I exhort you by the example of a woman to enter the city of God. For, if it is something difficult, the weaker sex is already there, but if it is something easy, there is no reason that the stronger sex should not be there. A man should not be ashamed to follow a woman, then, as she enters into that which demands strength of mind, but instead you should be ashamed that you do not at least follow her when she enters and that you, who are more capable of strength, delay outside after she has entered and is located within, where one receives the strength of true salvation and piety. And surely, when you enter there, you will not follow her there but she will follow you. For you will precede in virtue your wife whom you will follow in time. I believe, after all, that you, even as a catechumen, may still teach her, although she is a believer, some things pertaining to religion that you have read and she has not. But those things that she knows and you do not as yet know she cannot disclose to you. Only those who receive them come to know in a correct and orderly way the mysteries of rebirth; hence, though you are found to be better instructed in knowledge, she is safer because of the sacrament.

5. What good does knowledge even of the highest good do if one does not receive the sole means by which one escapes everything evil? But it is obviously difficult to sustain the burden of new virtues, and it is easy to be weighed down by the burden of sins. These latter, rather, are the burdens we should fear; they are fastened onto human beings to crush them and drown them for eternity, and they are removed only by rebirth in Christ, when a human being becomes a member of the head, the mediator, who, though he was distinguished from us by his divine majesty, deigned to draw near to us by his human weakness.

6. "And religion," you say, "benefits from this slowness. For a man promises a greater reverence for the faith if, in coming to the awesome secrets of the sacred mystery, he approaches its greater depths with hesitation." For you said that this is the second reason for your delay. But in religion it is only safe to make progress interiorly when, on account of eternal life, there is no fear of the uncertainties of this life. For no one should ask out of that vain and damnable curiosity when someone will die or whether this body will be broken down by disease or the soul will be taken from it by the attack of some sudden and unexpected violence. Hence, just as we keep in mind that divine statement that is written in the gospel, *Unless one is reborn of water and the Spirit, he will not enter the*

kingdom of God (Jn 3:5), so, in order that we may live righteously once we have been reborn, we ought to keep in mind that other statement, because it too came from the lips of Christ, *Unless your righteousness is more abundant than that of the scribes and Pharisees, you will not enter into the kingdom of heaven* (Mt 5:20). In another passage, however, he points out that what the scribes and Pharisees teach is often good but that they do not do the good deeds of which they speak.[1] And for this reason the righteousness of those who speak of good deeds because of the truth of their teaching, and who do good deeds because of their love for righteousness, is more abundant than that of the scribes and the Pharisees. In accord with this the apostle James says, *Faith without works is in itself dead* (Jas 2:17), because *the demons also believe and tremble* (Jas 2:19), as he also said. Yet they will certainly not be saved, because they always do evil deeds. On this account the apostle Paul defined the faith of the members of Christ as that *which works through love* (Gal 5:6). In this faith, then, one must make progress interiorly; the covetousness of this world, with its evil suggestions, is certainly diminished as the love of God increases, and it is completely destroyed when that love is made perfect. In that way grace makes up for whatever one who is making progress interiorly lacks in perfect righteousness, no matter by what manner of death the last day of this life, which vanishes like mist,[2] overtakes him. But for the sake of those who think that they should put off what they do not deny is good, these words of the divine scriptures boomed forth in a terrifying way: *Do not be slow to turn to the Lord, and do not put it off from day to day! For his wrath will come suddenly, and in the time of his vengeance he will destroy you.* (Sir 5:8-9) I beg you, let this not be the case with you. "Break off all delays, and seize for yourself the armed camp,"[3] not to take it by storm but to be safe there in order to fight courageously against the enemy. Once by attacking the Christian religion and now also by praising it deceitfully, he frightens you off from accepting it. For he once suggested to human minds that so great a good was evil, <but now he suggests that it is so great a good>[4] that it is very difficult to bring it to perfection once it is begun. Such praise is insidious. Beware of the wolf clothed in a lamb's skin![5] In order to undertake the tasks that you fear as arduous, let your hope be in God, and they will become easy.

7. Now, as the third point of your excuse, you said that, "especially in these matters, one must await the will of him by whose will we are all driven to all our desires," and you added there that we need not give an account to human beings of those matters that God inclines us to will, since all the learned and unlearned

---

1. See Mt 23:2-3.
2. See Jas 4:14.
3. Virgil, *Aeneid* IX, 13.
4. There is a lacuna here; I have followed the conjecture in the Bibliothéque Augustinienne edition.
5. See Mt 7:15.

agree that without him nothing has either been done or can be done. You ought not to think of all of this, then, in such a way as to suppose that you are doing the will of God when you do not want to keep his commandments. One of them is this, which I just mentioned: *Do not be slow to turn to the Lord, and do not put it off from day to day* (Sir 5:8). Pay heed, rather, that you do not trust in your own strength so that you will do what he commanded for your everlasting salvation, but trust that you will do it by his help. And to change your life for the better and to receive the grace of rebirth, entrust yourself without delay not to yourself, the weak Firmus,[6] but to that powerful one who is able to do all things. Do not wait until he wills it, as if you were going to offend him if you willed it first. For, whenever you have willed it, you will be willing it with his help and by his working. His mercy, of course, anticipates you so that you may will it, but when you will it, you yourself certainly will it. For, if we do not will when we will, then he does not give us anything when he makes us will. What else, indeed, am I aiming at when I say these things to you but to get you to will it? But I do this in one way, God does it in another; I do it from the outside, he does it within; I do it when you hear or read, he does it when you think and in order that you may think; I do it by words, he does it wordlessly; I do it only by his gift, he does it by himself; I act as his minister and as having this ministry from him, he acts as one who does not need a minister, who creates ministers, and who uses his faithful as ministers so that he may also give them the gift of this work; finally, I act as a human being who am often unable to persuade someone, he acts as God who has the power to persuade someone whenever he wills.

8. For this is what the sacred writings and a mind imbued with even the slightest piety say of him. Who but someone turned aside from the truth, after all, would dare to think or believe that God wants to persuade us of something and cannot? He will persuade you when he wants to, then, either through our ministry or in some other way that he wants. I ought to pray that he may do this while I also do not cease to exhort you. For, if you obey his commandments, which are true and lead to salvation, it is due to his grace; if you do not obey them, it is due to your own sin. Whomever he sets free from this sin he sets free by his mercy—and I want you to be counted among them, and I urge you and beg him that you may want this. But it is by his judgment that he does not set free those whom he does not set free. We do not know his many hidden judgments, but we do know that not one of them can be unjust. He wanted the fact that he made the day of death uncertain to be of great benefit to those of his people with understanding so that they would not postpone the day of their rebirth. "By his will we are driven to all our desires," as you say. I certainly understand all the desires for those things of which you were speaking when you said this. For you said that, especially in these matters toward which I was indeed urging you and which you think should be postponed, we must await

6. Augustine puns on Firmus' name: *infirmus Firmus*: "the infirm firm one."

the will of him by whose will "we are driven to all our desires." And you added, "For we need not give an account to human beings of these things that God inclines us to will." If, then, you understand there the desires for those things, it is true. After all, it is not true that we are driven to all desires, even bad ones, by his will. Or, if you think this because it seems not unreasonable to say that what is done only if he permits it is done by his will, the opinion need not be rejected. For of course nothing happens unless he himself does it or permits that it be done, and since he willingly does it and willingly permits it, absolutely nothing happens if he does not will it. Yet it is true to say that whatever is displeasing to him is done contrary to his will. Still, he permits evils to happen because he is powerful enough to produce good, which is his, out of evils, which are not his. Everything that is just is good, to be sure, and it is just to punish sins. It is good, therefore, to punish sins. It is also good to pardon sins. It is good to produce things useful for setting human beings free; it is good to stop sins so that they do not go too far; it is good to set people free from sins and the punishments of sins, both their own sins and those of others. Therefore, by punishing some sins, by forgiving others, and by turning still others to the benefit and help of the faithful, he who permits evils to come about produces good from all these evils. Nor would God, the cause of every good, be seen as all-powerful if he did not permit evils to exist, even if I am unable to find any good that he might make out of them. He has nonetheless removed them by a huge distance from the kingdom of the blessed, and for this reason, even in the evils that he has permitted to happen, he has not given up all activity and has, where he wanted, caused there to be no evils. If he had done this everywhere, not all goods would exist in things, since there would certainly not be the goods that he could have made out of evils. And yet we do not benefit God by our sins, which come from the will of someone evil, either an angel or a human being, as if we were adding to his good works. After all, how do we benefit him even when we are good? It would have benefited us if we had never been evil, therefore, not God, who knows how to produce good even from evils. In fact, even if our goodness had always existed, it would in no way have benefited God. How much less does our sinfulness benefit him, though he can produce good things from it by the omnipotence of his goodness. And these good things would not have existed if our sins had not preceded them. But even if they did not exist, it would not be either better or worse for him, since no evil can happen to him nor can any good be added to him, because his happiness cannot be lessened by any evil or increased by any good. Hence we should say that all things happen by his will, so that we may distinguish God's permitting something from his doing something, because we cannot deny that he is our judge. But, when judging and repaying each person in accord with his works,[7] did he condemn anyone on account of those works that he himself produced in him? God forbid! Yet he has condemned some people on account of

---

7. See 2 Tm 4:14.

those works that he permitted them to do. For those things that he could not fail to know would certainly not be done without the Almighty.

9. Where you said, therefore, that all the learned and unlearned agree that nothing has been done or can be done without him, there is no need to stir up a controversy concerning the agreement of all the unlearned. Otherwise it might introduce a delay in the discussion between us. For, whether they all agree or some disagree, I still grant that you spoke the truth, as long as you distinguish, as I advised you, between God's doing something and his permitting it. For it is perfectly true to say that nothing has been done or can be done without almighty God's either permitting it or doing it. Hence he permits the commission of sins; he does not commit them. Of course, for the punishment of some sinners he hands over some of them to the desires of their hearts,[8] in order that they may do what they ought not to do, when he either abandons them or even sends or permits his bad angels to mislead them. Every sin, however, even of that sort, belongs to those who merited to be handed over by the just judgment of God so that they might sin in that way. But to God in this case there belongs only the punishment of sin, which is just.

10. Whoever is driven to forbidden desires, therefore, is drawn and enticed by his own concupiscence.[9] When God sets someone free from this, he shows mercy; when he does not set someone free, he exercises judgment. To him the Church sings of *mercy and judgment* (Ps 101:1). But as for when he does the former and when he does the latter, the decision and plan lies with him. It also pertains to his plan that we do not know these things, and I in fact think that we shall never know them. But whoever says that God ought not to have permitted man to sin does not pay sufficient attention to the fact that the nature that ought not to sin and yet can sin is undoubtedly better if it does not sin, though it was permitted to sin, than if it does not sin because it was not permitted. Hence the good and just God made human nature such from the beginning so that it would not sin, though permitted, if it had willed not to sin, and he punished it when it sinned. As a result, in obeying the sins that dominate it, it is also subject to the bad angels, because it refused to obey the justice of its Lord, though it was destined to be made equal to the angels.[10] From this there come these errors that we see and the sufferings of mortals with which this life is full. In it a false happiness more grievously harms its lovers, who in their desire to enjoy it heap sins upon sins, than the dire and harsh misery that no one wants to endure and no one knows how to endure. For no one is without such misery except after death, if one has lived this life well, because, as the words of God state, *there is a heavy yoke upon the children of Adam from the day they leave the womb of their mother*

---

8. See Rom 1:24.
9. See Jas 1:14.
10. See Lk 20:36.

until the day of their burial in the mother of all (Sir 40:1). This is so true that not even baptized infants are found to be exempt from this sentence, though their only sin, which they contracted from their condemned root, has been washed away and removed by the bath of rebirth. For what human beings receive through the grace of Christ is not this world's gift but a pledge of the world to come. Since Adam this generation as a whole has been condemned; rebirth was instituted in order that we might escape this condemnation. But with regard to the miseries of this world no one, even among the faithful, escapes this condemnation except after death, but the woes of the wicked are even increased after the dissolution of this body and their receiving it back, when those good things of which they made a bad use here are taken away. Why this rebirth is given to some and not given to others, not only in the case of adults but also in that of infants, falls under the inscrutable judgments of God,[11] but in them there is nothing hidden that is not just.

11. I urge you to receive this rebirth; do not wait for God to will it, but do what he commands. And realize that he willed if from the fact that you could not have done it unless he had willed it. For the love by which you will do it comes from God,[12] but the concupiscence by which you are held back from doing it does not come from God.[13] Hence, as long as you do not do it, because you are either unknowingly deceived by your vice or knowingly conquered by it, attribute this not to God but to yourself. But when you do it, believe that God helped you, as is absolutely true, and do not wait for this divine help by postponing it, but rather experience it by doing this!

12. Now let me say to Your Excellency concerning our Greek,[14] about whom you wrote the whole of your last letter, what I see that I ought to say. His great gifts, which are outstanding because of his great natural talent and highly developed through a liberal education, have filled me with great joy. But you know very well that the end to which these goods are applied is of great importance. If this were apparent in the sort of rhetorical exercises with which he is now occupied out of the need for practice, you would not have wanted me to become a judge of his mind rather than of his heart and, leaving aside the reasons that the demands of the subject claim for themselves, I would pass judgment on his speaking ability alone. By your request you yourself have decided that you did not want me to act as a judge now. But the more delighted I am by his natural talent and outstanding ability in speaking, the more concerned I am, since I love him more deeply, to know with what sort of disposition he applies these great gifts of his, for, as you know, human beings can make both good and bad use of

---

11. See Rom 11:33.
12. See Rom 5:5.
13. See 1 Jn 2:16.
14. That is, Firmus' young son.

them.[15] I neither agree nor desire that he should want to meet with approval not from the best people but from most people,[16] which you said was a condition of the art of oratory. For this opinion stems from a longstanding but incorrect practice of the human race, not from the fountain of truth. If you yourself did not know this, you would not say, "This seems to be a condition of this very art," but you would say, "This *is* a condition of this very art." It seems to be, therefore, and it is not, and it seems this way to those who either do not read or do not understand well or do not, after reading and understanding them, believe the better authors on the same art. For what the most prolific and most elegant teacher of this skill said is absolutely true: "Eloquence along with wisdom is most beneficial to cities, but eloquence without wisdom generally does much harm but is never beneficial."[17] Hence the ancients thought that they should define not the man of eloquence—for eloquence can exist without wisdom—but an orator in such a way as to say that he was "a good man skilled in speaking."[18] If we remove from that definition what is put in the first place, what we are left with does much harm. On this account they thought and said that, when the principles of speaking are taught to fools, they are not made into orators, but weapons are put into the hands of madmen.[19]

13. As for our Greek, then, where there is no loss of moral goodness, I desire, I hope, I urge that he may strive to please both good people and most people, but that, where he cannot do both because of the wrongheadedness of the majority, he may choose to please good people rather than most people and do this not only in his words and speeches but also in his life and actions. Hence I desire to know most of all about his moral character, about which you are pleased, in order that you may also make me share in your joys. For I have no doubt that you would want him to be better than you in every respect. Not out of curiosity, but having a concern for him that is, I think, not improper, I desire to know from your response the number of years he has attained, the works in both languages that he has read under his teachers or read under you or with you or perhaps by himself, and those to which he is now devoting the effort of his studious mind.

---

15. See Quintilian, *Instruction in Speaking* (*Institutiones oratoriae*) I, 13.
16. See Cicero, *Brutus* 183-184.
17. Cicero, *Invention* (*De inventione*) 1, 1.
18. Cato, *To his Son* (*Ad filium*), fragment 14.
19. See Cicero, *The Orator* (*De oratore*) 3, 55.

Letter 3*

Sometime during his episcopacy Augustine wrote this letter in reply to Felix, a deacon. Felix had consulted Augustine about an unnamed woman who had vowed her infant daughter to a life of virginity if she were saved from an illness but later decided to withdraw that vow and replace it with her own consecrated widowhood so that she could have grandchildren. Augustine complains about the injustice of the substitution of the woman's widowhood for her daughter's virginity and wishes that she would bear in mind the things of heaven rather than those of earth (paragraph 1). He refuses to allow the woman to make this substitution and urges instead that the woman add her widowhood to her daughter's virginity (paragraph 2). He encourages her to consecrate her widowhood to the Lord, something she has shown that she can do, but not to violate the vow she made concerning her daughter, though her daughter may later decide to marry (paragraph 3). Augustine tells Felix that he must see to it that the woman wants to live as a consecrated widow for the right reasons lest she abandon her commitment if her daughter does not bear children (paragraph 4). Finally, Augustine asks about the children of a certain Innocentia who he recently learned had died (paragraph 5).

To Felix, his sincerely most beloved lord, son, and fellow deacon, Augustine sends greetings in the Lord.

1. As I consider more and more the matter on which you consulted me, I am compelled to cry out, *O sons of men, to what point are you heavy of heart? Why do you love vanity and seek after a lie?* (Ps 4:3) For what is so vain as, out of a desire for and a delight in earthly descendants, to begrudge to one's daughter the heavenly rewards that are being prepared for consecrated virgins? What is so vain as to bewail so many losses of one's children and to want to receive from God himself—by one's only remaining daughter, whose temporal well-being is, like that of all human beings, uncertain—mortal children, who are subject to all the woes of mortal beings, by a fraudulent denial directed not against a human being but against God? And what is a greater lie than to vow to God the virginity of an imperiled baby daughter so that she might be revived, after almost having died, and to slay the vow itself because she came back to life, and to offer to God, as if he does not know which is better and cannot distinguish the two, her own widowhood as a substitute for the virginity of her daughter that she has taken back? This way of thinking smacks strongly of the earth. Let your heart be lifted up, and let it look down upon what is below for the sake of happiness on high.[1] *If you have risen with Christ*, the apostle says, *seek after the things that are above,*

---

1. See Col 3:2; Phil 3:19.

where Christ is seated at the right hand of God; be wise about the things that are above, not about those that are on earth (Col 3:1-2).

2. Hence, *if* this daughter of ours *cannot practice continence, she should marry* (1 Tm 5:14) and should be counted among those of whom the same teacher said, *I want the younger ones to marry, to bear children, and to manage their homes,* because the words that follow, *to offer no occasion to the enemy to speak ill* (1 Tm 5:14), mean being wise about the things that are above.[2] But if the daughter can practice continence so that the mother becomes inferior to her daughter, with what better reason is it possible that the holy widow herself would become better, though not equal to her daughter if the daughter is a holy virgin. Let the widow, then, be added to the virgin, not substituted for her. Let her not offer her own gift in such a way that she takes away the better gift of another. But in her own regard she has control over what to choose. For she is said not to have vowed her widowhood since, in setting forth the condition, she is still seeking whether she may compensate by her living as a widow for her daughter's not living as a virgin. But because the widowhood is hers, while the virginity is another's, she certainly ought not to seek another's loss by her own gain. Finally, if what is impossible were possible, namely, that she restore her virginity through continence, she should not seek even such an exchange. She should certainly have added herself to rather than removed someone else from such a great good, nor ought the mother to have ascended into that higher position in order to bring her daughter down from there.

3. She has herself in her own power, then, as they say, because she has not yet taken a vow, and she is still asking whether she ought to take a vow for such an affair. But what she has already vowed she ought to fulfill, and she should not ask whether she ought to fulfill it. And yet, if she asked me whether she should take a vow about her widowhood, I would more truthfully and more correctly reply: "You ought to, but you ought not to do it in order to take away the virginity of your daughter." But pay attention for a while to why I said, "You ought to, but you ought not to do it for the reason you have in mind." When the Lord Jesus pointed out the hard case of married people with regard to not dismissing a wife, his disciples answered him, *If such is the case with a wife, it is not wise to marry* (Mt 19:10), and the Lord said to that, *Not all accept this counsel, but only those to whom it is given* (Mt 19:11), and a little later, *Let him who can accept this accept it* (Mt 19:12). Accept this counsel, then, because, when you were prepared to remain a widow in place of your daughter, in fact in opposition to your daughter so that she would not be a virgin, you were shown to be capable of this. Nor is there any way to excuse yourself before him who said, *Let him who can accept this accept it.* Accept it because you can, but pay attention to those

---

2. See Col 3:2.

eunuchs who were praised because they made themselves eunuchs for the sake of the kingdom of heaven, not for the sake of an earthly benefit and consolation. Accept this counsel in order that you may increase, not in order that your daughter may decrease. Accept this in order that you also may have something to vow, not in order to take from your daughter what she vowed. Accept this for the sake of having more and richer virtues, not for the sake of having children, regarding whom you might fear the sort of losses that you have already experienced. But, concerning your daughter, fulfill your vow as much as it is up to you. *For it is better not to make a vow*, as scripture says, *than to make a vow and not fulfill it* (Eccl 5:4). And the apostle said, *Being condemned because they canceled their first commitment* (1 Tm 5:12). But I said, "Fulfill your vow as much as it is up to you," because what the child might choose if she grows up is not in your power when she comes to the age at which she must choose, but the hope with which you raise the girl whom you have vowed does pertain to you. But, if she prefers, she will choose marriage over the profession of virginity without sin not merely on your part but also on hers, and she will lose only what she would have attained if she had assented to your vow and remained a virgin. For, if someone baptized as a child comes to the age at which he can use reason and disapproves and rejects what was conferred upon him by the will of his parents, he loses what he would have attained if he had remained in the same grace, that is, to be with Christ in eternal life, and as a result of this he will remain with the devil in eternal punishment. In the same way, when an adult virgin who was raised by her parents with the hope of consecrated virginity in the future has become an adult, if she chooses to marry before she makes profession of the same holy state, she will suffer the loss—not like that man's loss of the kingdom of God but of a greater honor in the kingdom of God. For the words of scripture say, *If anyone is not reborn of water and the Spirit, he will not enter the kingdom of God* (Jn 3:5), but scripture did not also say in the same way, "Anyone who does not choose sacred virginity will not enter the kingdom of God." Certainly, if after her profession she falls away from her promise, she will be condemned because *she has canceled her first commitment* (1 Tm 5:12). What she ought to avoid after she has made her profession, therefore, you ought to avoid in the vow you made concerning her virginity. And on account of the incertitude of her will you ought rather to add your widowhood to that vow in her regard so that, if she agrees to your vow, you may remain with her in holy widowhood, for you can no longer remain in holy virginity. But if she perhaps chooses something else, remain for her sake where you can. God, however, is powerful, who can make both of you remain in his gifts. This *is* what I would say to a Christian women regarding that matter about which you thought that you should consult me.

4. But I say to you, deal with her in the way in which you see that she loves what is good for the sake of the kingdom of God. For you must watch out that, if

she perhaps desires widowhood for another reason than that for which it should be desired, she may not be able to withstand the onslaught of age, especially in view of human situations, which are always uncertain. After all, it is not in her power that her daughter should marry and bear children, and we would have to fear that, should something else happen (may that not be the case!), she might think that she was cheated and had lost, so to speak, the reward of her promise and might with this carnal idea give up. But may our God, who said, *Not all accept this counsel, but only those to whom it has been given* (Mt 19:11), hold her heart and lift it up so that she may love the heavenly things God has promised and hold in scorn the earthly things she has experienced. But, as far as her daughter is concerned, she ought to aim at and ask for nothing else than the accomplishment of what she vowed; may he *whose hand holds both us and our words* (Wis 7:16) grant her this.

5. You do not know, or rather you do know, how much I desire to rejoice over the children of the pious Innocentia, who I learned only by your more recent letter has left the body. But I ask that you not delay to reply on the first occasion that arises about the situation in the faith of Christ of all those whom she left here as the fruit of her womb.

Letter 4*

In the fall of 417 Augustine wrote to Cyril, the bishop of Alexandria, who was to lead the opposition to Nestorius at the Council of Ephesus in 431. Augustine commends himself to Cyril's prayers and expresses his pleasure at the opportunity that the servant of God Justus has provided for him to write to Cyril (paragraph 1). He recalls the circumstances that led to his composing *The Deeds of Pelagius*, in which he showed that Pelagius was acquitted at the Council of Diospolis in Palestine only because he condemned parts of his own teaching (paragraph 2). Augustine explains that Justus is returning to Cyril after having come to Hippo in order to check his copy of *The Deeds of Pelagius* against better exemplars, for he had been accused of falsifying his copy of Augustine's work where it said that not all sinners were destined for eternal fire (paragraph 3). Augustine warns Cyril that those who found this idea objectionable might very well be proponents of the Pelagian heresy (paragraph 4). Finally, he asks Cyril to investigate the matter and to defend Justus against those who slander him (paragraph 5).

To his most blessed lord and brother and fellow priest, Cyril, who deserves honor and reverence with the due signs of love, Augustine sends greetings in the Lord.

1. I commend myself greatly to your holy prayers as I pay Your Reverence the duty of greeting you by the intermediary of the servant of God, Justus by name, whom I have very recently come to know as a good brother. Since he had come to us from you and was returning to you from us, he offered us a very attractive opportunity to carry out these duties to Your Beatitude. Nor do I think that I should pass over in silence the reason that forced him to make the journey to us. I know of it, of course, because he told me.

2. Your Sincerity, I think, recalls that you sent us the ecclesiastical proceedings held in the province of Palestine where Pelagius was acquitted because he was thought to be Catholic. For he had concealed his true self in the shrewd hiding places provided by words and deceived our brothers who then sat in judgment, since no opponent from the other side argued against him.[1] After I had considered and examined those proceedings as carefully as I could, I wrote a book on them for our venerable brother and fellow priest, Aurelius, the bishop of Carthage.[2] In it I showed, to the extent that the Lord granted me, what guided the Catholic judges in the replies of Pelagius, so that they acquitted him as being

---

1. Augustine refers to the Council of Diospolis held in December of 415.
2. After Augustine received the proceedings from the Council of Diospolis he wrote *The Deeds of Pelagius*. Aurelius was the bishop of Carthage and hence the primate of Africa as well as Augustine's friend for many years.

Catholic. Of course many people caught up in his error were boasting that, since he was acquitted, his heretical teachings were confirmed as Catholic by the judgment of the Catholic bishops, and, since they were spreading these ideas everywhere, very many people who were ignorant of what had occurred believed that such was the case, to the great scandal of the churches.

3. In order to destroy this opinion, then, I produced the book I mentioned in which I showed, as well as I could, that, even though Pelagius was acquitted—not before God, whom no one deceives, but before human beings, whom Pelagius was able to deceive—those deadly teachings were nonetheless absolutely condemned, since he himself declared them anathema. The servant of God, Justus, who is the bearer of this letter to Your Reverence, had this book of mine. It shocked certain people because it argued that not all sinners are punished by eternal fire, and they said, as he reported to me, that I had not written that passage in that way but that he himself had falsified it. Hence he was upset and sailed to us with the same book in case he perhaps had a defective copy, though he was fully conscious that he had falsified nothing in it. And so, by comparing that copy with our volumes, and with my own full awareness of the matter, he found that he had a copy free from defects.

4. Then the suspicion struck us—may God keep all malice from it and make it rather full of love, though it should not in any case be disregarded—that the statement we made, that not all sinners but only certain ones are condemned to endless punishment, displeases those who say that even in this mortal life there are holy persons without sin. As a result they say that they do not need the Lord's Prayer, in which the whole Church cries out, *Forgive us our debts* (Mt 6:12), for the forgiveness of their own sins, because they have no sins. Your Holiness undoubtedly sees that these people must be corrected from the wickedness of their error. For it is certain that these ideas stem from that unhealthy Pelagian teaching that claimed that all sinners are punished by eternal fire such that no hope of pardon would be left for those who truthfully admit that they are not without sin. In that way they either swell up with pride, supposing that this life of theirs has no sin, or they waste away in despair, as if they were already destined for everlasting punishment. To be sure, the blessed apostle says, *Fire will test the quality of each person's work. If the work of anyone that he built on the foundation survives, he will receive a reward. If the work of anyone is consumed by fire, he will suffer a loss, but he himself with be saved, but as by fire.* (1 Cor 3:13-15) But these words of the apostle should be interpreted so that we may understand what was said in terms not of the fire of the last judgment but of a fire before that judgment, either in this life or after death. In any case, that error is certainly to be avoided by which all sinners are thought to be destined for the punishment of everlasting fire if they do not live a life here that is utterly without sin. We must also be on guard that those who hold this view are not also found to hold other Pelagian teachings, no less unsound or even worse, and that their dreadful infec-

tion does not spread among unwary people, when we do not suppress or heal the evil that the care of brotherly love has discovered in some of them.

5. I commend our brother Justus to Your Most Faithful Holiness, so that you may not only defend him from slanderers but also be so good as to correct those whom he rightly holds suspect, lest they lose their souls and inject the Pelagian poison into them. Correct them with your pastoral care and with your fatherly gentleness or even with remedial severity, if there is need. Or, if you find them sound in the faith,[3] be so good as to remove this worry from the mind of this man. For both he and they are Latins, and they have come to those places from the Western Church, where we are too. Hence we ought especially to bring them to Your Reverence's attention, so that they may not seem to have chosen for themselves those lands, in order to hide unpunished among the Greeks, where, when they discuss these topics, they are less well understood and their error is thus not easily refuted. We are doing this, however, so that we may not be saddened by the loss of anyone but instead may rejoice, as far as possible, over the salvation of all.

---

3. See Ti 1:13.

Letter 5*

In this letter, whose date cannot be determined, Augustine wrote to Valentinian, the Catholic bishop of Baiana and primate of Numidia. Augustine tells Valentinian that he would have preferred a visit rather than a letter from him with questions (paragraph 1). He explains why the Lord's Prayer is recited immediately after baptism, even in the case of infants (paragraph 2). Then he answers Valentianian's question about Genesis 6:3, where he points out two errors in the text that Valentinian was using and explains the meaning of "spirit" in that verse (paragraph 3).

To his most blessed lord and venerable and loveable brother and fellow bishop, Valentinian, Augustine sends greetings in the Lord.

1. You promise a visit, and in place of it you send us questions to answer that, as you write, trouble your heart. Though I would prefer to have you here, I still respond somehow to you in your absence by writing, despite how busy I am, but I could have replied more easily in conversation if you were present.

2. Your first question is why the baptized immediately confess their debts in <the Lord's>[1] Prayer and ask that they be forgiven, since they were all forgiven in baptism. And though you resolved this same question for yourself on the basis of the harmful desires and illicit impulses of the heart, which easily sneak up on human weakness, you say that another question came to mind about infants who can neither think nor speak, as if anyone would command or force infants to be reborn, <like adults,>[2] if they did not have to be washed in baptism on account of original sin. Or do you say this as if adults do not respond with words from the Lord's Prayer on their behalf, as they do with words from the symbol of faith? Without that they cannot be baptized at all, and for this reason those who bring them to baptism reply on their behalf to the words when they are questioned. There is nothing, then, that ought to upset you in the case of infants with regard to the debts that the baptized ask to be forgiven immediately after the bath in which all past sins are forgiven. They do this because of those debts that overtake us due to the readiness of the human mind <to sin>.[3]

3. You likewise ask how we should interpret what God said: *My spirit will not remain in these men in this age* (Gn 6:3). Our own manuscripts, however, have it like this: *My spirit will not remain in these men for eternity*. Let the mistake of your book or books be corrected, and there will be no question over which to labor in asking why God said *in this age*, as if to signify that the punishment of

---

1. The Bibliothéque Augustinienne edition has added the words in brackets.
2. The BA edition has added the words in brackets.
3. The BA translation has added the words in brackets.

the present death suffices for wicked sinners. For he threatened eternal death, rather, when he said, *My spirit will not remain in these men for eternity.* But the ambiguity of the Greek word misled the translator, who translated it so as to say *in this age*, though it should at least have said *for this age* and not *in this age*. For the Greek expression, εἰς αἰῶνα, can be expressed in Latin as *for this age* or *for eternity.* The translator should consider the meaning of scripture in that passage so that he is not misled by an ambiguity. For, when you ask about which spirit he said this, whether about the spirit that gives life to the body or about the spirit that sanctifies the soul, there is no problem, since you hear God say *my spirit.* After all, he would say "their spirit" if he wanted us to understand the spirit by which the body is alive, since it belongs to human nature, and he could have correctly said, *My spirit will not remain in these men*, of the spirit that does not pertain to human nature and that could remain in them if they were not overcome by the pleasure of the flesh and did not abandon God and thus deserve to lose the Holy Spirit, who is the gift of God.[4] For, if you understand their spirit, by which they are human beings, in relation to their bodies, how could it remain in them since they were going to die at some point? But, if you understand it in relation to that part of them by which their body is living, how could it not remain in them since these are spirits that leave the body at death and necessarily exist wherever they are, whether they are happy or not? I think that I have sufficiently answered your questions. But I would not demand your physical presence if you had not promised it, and, since you did promise it, I demand it as a debt that you owe me.

---

4. See Rom 5:5.

Letter 6*

Between 416 and 421 Augustine wrote to Atticus, the bishop of Constantinople from 406 until 426, who succeeded John Chrysostom in that position. Augustine tells Atticus that the rumor of his death is not true, though he understands that it had excused Atticus from writing to him (paragraph 1). He tells Atticus of his joy at hearing that he had corrected some persons who held Pelagian errors (paragraph 2). He singles out the charge of some Pelagians that the Catholic, that is, Augustinian, teaching claims that marital concupiscence is the work of the devil (paragraph 3). These people fail to distinguish the good of marriage from the evil of concupiscence that was inflicted upon our nature by the sin of Adam (paragraph 4). As a result they do not draw a distinction between marital concupiscence, by which spouses procreate children, and the concupiscence of the flesh, against which even married people must fight to preserve chastity in marriage (paragraph 5). Augustine points out the great absurdity that arises for these Pelagians, since they are forced to locate in paradise the same sort of concupiscence of the flesh against which holy men and women must fight in this life (paragraph 6). Augustine insists that either the concupiscence of the flesh was not present in paradise before Adam's sin or, if it was present there, it was much different from the disorder and turbulent concupiscence that we now experience (paragraphs 7 and 8).

To Atticus, his most blessed lord, brother, and fellow priest, who deserves to be embraced with due reverence, Augustine sends greetings in the Lord.

1. Although I did not receive a letter from Your Holiness by means of our religious brother and fellow priest, Innocent, by whom I had presumed that I would receive it, after I knew from him why this had happened, I wrote these things as if I had received Your Reverence's letter and as if, safe and sound by the mercy of God and the help of your prayers, I were paying the debt of a reply. For, since rumor had spread about something else, as the brother I mentioned above reported to me, you believed him since he was speaking about a human being. After all, what is more believable than when it is reported that a mortal has died, which is eventually going to happen to everyone living in the flesh?[1] But, after he had heard from other more recent messengers that I was alive and had indicated this to Your Charity, he reported that you were very much gladdened and gave thanks to God, though it was still uncertain for you.

2. Hence, my lord, I ought not to doubt that you are happy to receive my letter, but by the law of love I demand with more confidence and eagerness the reply you owed and have passed over, though I have counted the letter of Your Beatitude sent to my brother, with whom I am of one heart, as if it had been sent to both

---

1. See Plotinus, *Ennead* I, 4, 7, line 24 in the Bréhier edition.

of us. To my joy I found in it that Your Holiness acted with a shepherd's care in order both to correct the error of some Pelagians and to guard against their clever arguments.

3. It is not surprising that they slander Catholics if they strive in that way to suppress what is said to refute their poisonous teachings. For what Catholic defends the correct faith against them in such a way that he would blame marriage, which the maker and creator of the world blessed? What Catholic would say that concupiscence in marriage is the work of the devil, since the human race would certainly have been propagated by this means even if no one had sinned, in order that this blessing, *Increase and multiply* (Gn 1:28), might be realized? This blessing did not, by the sin of the man in whom all sinned,[2] lose the effect of its goodness in the fecundity of nature, which is so evident and so wonderful and praiseworthy, as everyone can see. What Catholic does not praise the works of God in every creation of every soul and of all flesh and does not, in reflecting on them, burst forth in a hymn[3] to the creator who made and makes all things very good,[4] not only then before the sin but even now?

4. But with their misguided mind and their stubborn blindness they confuse with natural goods the evils that have befallen our nature as a result of sin. Consequently, in praising the creator of human beings, they deny that a savior is needed by infants, as if they had no sin, for that is their damnable teaching, and they think that they can defend their wicked error by praise for marriage, when they say that marriage too is condemned if what is born from marriage is condemned unless it is reborn. They do not see that the good of marriage, after all, which is a good that marriage did not lose even after the sin, is one thing, but that the original evil, which marriage did not produce and does not now produce, is quite another. Rather marriage finds it as something already produced and puts it to good use, when it does not do with it whatever it wants but only what is permitted. These people refuse to consider this because an error has invaded them, and they prefer to defend it rather than to avoid it.

5. Because of this error they do not distinguish concupiscence within marriage, that is, the concupiscence of marital chastity, the concupiscence aimed at the legitimate propagation of children, the concupiscence of the bond by which the two sexes are united in one society, from the concupiscence of the flesh that is inflamed indiscriminately for both licit and illicit acts and is reined in from forbidden acts by marital concupiscence, which makes good use of it, and is released only for those acts that are permitted. Against its impulses, which fight against the law of the mind,[5] every form of chastity fights—both that of

---

2. See Rom 5:12.
3. See Ps 119:171.
4. See Gn 1:31.
5. See Rom 7:23.

married people, in order that they may make good use of it, and that of the continent and of holy virgins, in order that they might be better and more glorious for not using it. Hence, not distinguishing this concupiscence of the flesh, in which there is only the desire for having intercourse, from marital concupiscence, in which there is the moral duty of generation, they shamelessly praise that over which the first human beings were ashamed when they covered with fig leaves those members[6] that before the sin were not anything to be ashamed of. For they were, indeed, naked and were not ashamed.[7] From this we can understand that this arousal over which they were ashamed was implanted in human nature along with death. For they had reason for being ashamed when they began to have the necessity of dying.[8] These people, therefore, laud with such great praises this concupiscence of the flesh, which must be prudently and wisely distinguished from marital concupiscence, that they suppose that, even if no one had sinned in paradise, children could not be procreated without it in the body of that life, just as now they are not procreated without it in the body of this death, from which the apostle longs to be set free though Jesus Christ.[9]

6. The upshot is that such a great absurdity follows upon this opinion of theirs, which stems from their thoughtless ignorance, that even they themselves cannot defend it, regardless of the amount of impudence with which they have hardened their hearts. For, if this concupiscence of the flesh, which we perceive has such a disordered arousal, existed in paradise before the sin, so that the reins of chastity had either to restrain it from all use or to put it to a good use by the good of marriage, though it was by itself evil, this concupiscence would either have been shamefully obeyed in that place of such great beatitude—if the man had intercourse with his wife as often as it was aroused, not out of any need to generate but in order to appease the passion of lust, even if his wife were already pregnant—or he would have had to fight against it by the strength of abstinence so that it would not drag him off to these shameful acts. Let them, therefore, choose whichever of these they want. For, if they submitted to the concupiscence of the flesh so that they would not have to fight against it, there was no genuine freedom in that place. But if they fought against it so that they might not submit to it, there was no peaceful happiness in that place. Either of these is opposed to the blessed beauty or beautiful blessedness of paradise.

7. Who would fail to see this? Who would contradict this perfectly evident truth except out of utterly impudent obstinacy? There remain, then, two alternatives: Either in that place there did not exist this concupiscence of the flesh, which we perceive is aroused by a turbulent and disordered desire against our

6. See Gn 3:7.
7. See Gn 2:25.
8. See Gn 3:19.
9. See Rom 7:24.

will, even when there is no need, though marital concupiscence existed there, which preserves the calm love of husband and wife and which, just as the choice of the mind orders the hands and the feet to their appropriate actions, likewise orders the sexual organs to the work of generation. In that way, offspring would be conceived in paradise in a marvelous way without the ardor of the flesh's lust, just as offspring would also be born in a marvelous way without the pains of childbirth. Or, if this concupiscence of the flesh existed there, it certainly was not the sort of burdensome and disagreeable concupiscence that those people who battle against it in the chastity of marriage, widowhood, or virginity now experience. For it intrudes where it is not needed and tempts the hearts of faithful and holy people with its untimely and even wicked desire. Even if we do not give in to these restless impulses of it by any sign of consent but rather fight against them, we would nonetheless, out of a holier desire, want them not to exist in us at all, if that were possible, just as eventually they will not exist. After all, this is the perfect good that the apostle indicated was still lacking to the saints in this life, when he said, *I am able to will the good, but I cannot bring it to perfection* (Rom 7:18). For he does not say "do good" but *bring it to perfection*, because a human being does good by not consenting to such desires, but he brings the good to perfection by not having them. *For*, he said, *I do not do the good that I will, but I do the evil that I do not will* (Rom 7:19). He was, of course, not doing evil by offering his members to the carrying out of evil desires. Rather, he said this about those movements of concupiscence: even though he did not consent to them or commit the sin to which they enticed him, he was still doing something evil in having those desires that he did not want to have. Then he adds, *But if I do what I do not will* (Rom 7:20), that is, though I do not consent to concupiscence—I still do not want to have concupiscence and yet I have concupiscence—*I myself no longer do it, but the sin that dwells in me* (Rom 7:20). The guilt of this sin is contracted by birth; it is removed by rebirth when all sins are forgiven. Some of its power and a certain harmful influence stemming from its infection remains, nonetheless, in the mortal and corruptible body, even after its guilt is removed, and the person who has been reborn fights against it, if he is making progress. For, even if he does not have complete continence but marital chastity, he will also fight against this concupiscence of the flesh in order not to commit adultery, in order not to commit fornication and to soil himself by any mortal and wicked acts of shame, and finally, in order not to use his wife without moderation. For, by mutual consent with her, he ought to abstain for a time from the act of sexual union in order to be free for prayer and then return to it *lest Satan tempt them on account of their lack of self-control*, which the apostle says to them *by way of indulgence, not by way of command* (1 Cor 7:5-6). Certain people who considered this insufficiently thought that marriage itself was conceded to them by way of indulgence, but that is not so. Otherwise—God forbid!—

marriage will be a sin. For where an indulgence is allowed it is of course recognized that a sin is forgiven. But it is by way of indulgence that the apostle permits spouses to have the sort of intercourse with each other to which they are not led by a concern to propagate children but to which they are dragged by incontinence for the satisfying of their passion. Otherwise they would commit sins deserving condemnation if he does not release them by this indulgence. Still, even if some married couples excel in virtue with such great marital chastity that the two sexes are united only for the sake of generation, and if, after baptism and rebirth, they live such lives, any offspring born from them by that concupiscence of the flesh, of which, though it is evil, they make good use through the good concupiscence of marriage, contracts original sin. For that which is only removed by rebirth is certainly found in the child that is born unless it is also reborn, just as the foreskin that is only removed by circumcision is found in the son of a circumcised father unless the son is himself circumcised.[10]

8. If this concupiscence of the flesh, then, existed in paradise in order that children might be generated to realize the blessing of marriage by the multiplication of human beings, it was certainly not the sort of concupiscence that exists now, the impulses of which indiscriminately chase after both what is licit and what is illicit. It would be carried off to many very shameful acts if it were allowed to go wherever it was inclined, and one would have to fight against it in order to preserve chastity. But it would have been the sort of concupiscence—if there were any there at all—by which the flesh would not have desires opposed to the spirit.[11] Rather it would, in a marvelous peace, not exceed the least sign of the will so that it would never be present except when it was needed, would never impose itself upon the thoughts of the mind with a disordered or illicit pleasure, would have nothing deserving reproach that would need to be restrained by the reins of temperance or eliminated by the labor of virtue, but would follow in ready and harmonious obedience the will of the one using it when it was needed. Now, therefore, since it is not like that and since it is necessary that chastity struggle in opposition to it, let these people admit that it was damaged by sin so that those who were first naked and not ashamed[12] became ashamed over its arousal, and let them not be surprised that the only son of the Virgin, who they cannot say was conceived by means of it, did not contract original sin. Pardon the fact that I have been a burden to your holy eyes and ears by the length of this letter—not to make you more learned but to refute their slanders before you.

---

10. See 1 Cor 7:18-19.
11. See Gal 5:17.
12. See Gn 2:25.

Letter 7*

Probably in 426 or 427, during the absence of Count Boniface from Africa, Augustine wrote to his deacon, Faustinus—undoubtedly the same man who is mentioned in Sermon 356,4 as having given up military life and entered the monastery of Hippo, where he was later baptized and ordained a deacon. In the present letter Augustine asks Faustinus to urge Novatus, the bishop of Sitifis in Mauretania Sitifensis, to help settle a financial issue concerning money that a widow may or may not owe to the Church. Augustine describes the situation (paragraph 1) and asks Novatus to investigate the matter in order that the Church might do what is right (paragraph 2).

A memorandum to the deacon Faustinus.

1. Although in the matter of the priest Heraclius you were sent to the Gauls in order to ask for a ship, if you have the opportunity, urge my brother and fellow bishop Novatus to be so good as to assist in the business of the Church. It is a question of the money that the widow of Bassus had sequestered until the first of July, after having requested a delay. For afterwards the tribune Felician wrote to the man who held the sequestered money that he should not give the Church the same money that Count Sebastian[1] had written should be given. It is the sort of case regarding which you ought to inform the bishop. Several years ago, when the domesticus,[2] Florentinus, was still alive, Count Boniface gave the Church a certain sum of money. The consignment was made to two men with whom the tribune Bassus had deposited it from his own funds, and he received from them the receipts issued in his name. One of these men, then, who was ready to hand over to the Church the part of the same money that he had in his possession demanded back the receipt that he had issued to Bassus. But the same Bassus had already died, and the receipts had remained with his wife. This man, nonetheless, made a payment to the Church of eighty gold coins, more or less, if I am not mistaken. The Church used them for her needs as if they came from her own resources. Then the banker[3] died, leaving heirs. Afterward, however, the widow of Bassus came to Hippo, and she received in coins the remaining money, which was the larger part of it, from the heirs of the same banker, and she returned to them the receipts for the deposit. But she said that she was prepared to give the Church the same gold coins and the receipt that remained in her possession from the man who had the other part of the money. For we said that the consignment

---

1. Sebastian, the son-in-law of Boniface, was acting count of Africa during Boniface's absence.
2. A domesticus was a member of a family, household, or retinue or an escort or bodyguard of some person.
3. A banker: *collectarius* was a money-changer or cashier.

255

was made to two different men. She said, therefore, that she wanted to give the Church the same coins that she received from the heirs of the one man and the receipt of the other. With regard to her husband's record, which he had sent to the count concerning this affair, she wanted it either to be restored to her or, if it could not be restored, to be voided. After this had been done, she began to refuse to turn over to the Church what she earlier said she was willing to turn over. Rather, she left it with the trustee[4] and asked for a delay until the first of July. Then she left Hippo for Sitifis, either in order to do something there, as she said, or to go on to Tipasa. But after a few days the tribune Felician wrote to the trustee that, according to the wishes of the woman, he should not turn over to the Church the coins that Count Sebastian demanded be returned to her after her husband's bill had been voided.

2. Hence, ask my brother Novatus to be so good as to investigate this case carefully, especially so that we do not seem to oppress the widow. If he ascertains that the same money belongs to her, he should make this known to Count Sebastian, especially because of the coins that the Church used from there, as if they were hers. For it is no problem if he has them restored to the woman so that the Church lays no claim to them. But if the bishop ascertains that the woman's case is unjust, he should act so that the trustee is ordered or permitted to hand over to the Church what was deposited with him, once the prohibition of the tribune Felician is removed. If, however, the woman is not at Sitifis, my brother Novatus should see to it that the tribune Felician replies concerning this matter and that the case is brought to the attention of Count Sebastian, who can determine regarding it what he sees is just.

---

4. A trustee: a *sequester* was an official who held property, the ownership of which was disputed.

Letter 8*

At an undetermined date Augustine wrote to Victor, an African bishop who is otherwise unknown. Augustine tells Victor of his sorrow over what the Jew Licinius has reported to him regarding the property that Victor bought from Licinius' mother, though she in fact had sold it to Licinius. Victor had allegedly evicted Licinius and told him to take his mother to court if he had any complaints. Augustine warns Victor that it seems that he has acted unjustly and tells him to bear in mind the words of Saint Paul, who urged that we give no offense to anyone (paragraph 1). Augustine explains how he had inquired further about whether Licinius had offended his mother, who in turn was seeking vindication. Licinius denied having done anything to his mother, though he admitted that his mother did complain about his wife and one of his wife's servants. Augustine goes on to suggest disciplinary measures against either Licinius or his wife, should such measures need to be taken (paragraph 2).

A memorandum of Augustine to his holy brother Victor.

1. Please consider how precious to me is Your Holiness's life and reputation. If they are true, the actions that the Jew Licentius deplored in my presence sadden me very much. He in fact proved to me by the tablets he brought that he had purchased some small fields from the people to whom his mother had sold them and that he gave a part of them to his wife as a dowry when he married her. But what he went on to say in his complaint is quite incredible, namely, that Your Holiness bought all his property from the same old woman, his mother, and drove him out, though he owned it with full right. And when he complained to you about what you yourself had done, you said to him, "I bought it. If your mother was wrong in selling it to me, take her to court. Do not ask anything of me since I owe you nothing." If he lied to me about this, please write back to me. But if through ignorance of the law you thought that you should answer him in that way, Your Charity should know that a person who has possession of property cannot legally be driven off of it and that she was not right in selling what her son possessed as his own, even if part of it belonged to her. For she ought first to have won her case against him and then to have sold what she had been able to obtain when he lost the case. The son, after all, had a real case. He certainly does not intend to take his own mother to court but the man who invaded his property, a situation in which I wish that Your Fraternity did not find himself. It is very odious and foreign to your way of life. If, then, he told me the truth, please restore his property to him and recover the price from his mother, if you paid her. But if she perhaps refuses to return to you the price you paid, this man must not, even in that case, be deprived of his property. For he must get it back because justice is on his side and the laws cry out in his favor. I beg you to bear in mind the

257

words of the apostle, *Give no offense to the Jews or the Greeks, nor to the Church of God* (1 Cor 10:32). But it is better that, after having been admonished by your most dear brother, you do what is just than that this case come before an episcopal court.

2. Of course, when I asked him if he had perhaps done an injustice to his mother and you wanted in this way to vindicate her without any desire to possess the man's property but were doing this instead to frighten him, he answered that his mother had complained of an injustice from his wife and her serving girl but that he himself had done her no injustice. Hence I beg Your Holiness that, if these are the facts, you either discipline him with a beating in the presence of his mother if you discover that he has been unjust to his mother, for he said that he would be willing to endure that, or discipline his wife with a beating if she is at fault. For she can also be disciplined with a beating from her husband in the presence of her mother-in-law in accord with the judgment of Your Reverence. Now with regard to the serving girl the case is simple, since his mother can more easily punish her. He says that he has not done this because he was unaware of the injustice she did to his mother. For he says that his mother complained about this only after the property was already sold.

Letter 9*

On 27 August of a year between 422 and 429, Augustine wrote to his friend Alypius, the bishop of Thagaste, who was at the time in Italy and was charged with hearing the case of a man who had carried off a professed nun and used her for his pleasure. After the man was discovered by clerics and allegedly beaten, he appealed to Pope Celestine against the clerics in order to obtain reparation. Augustine tells Alypius that he finds it hard to believe that the clerics involved would have refrained from inflicting bodily injury on the unnamed man whom they caught (paragraph 1). He discusses the difficulties involved either in letting sins, such as this man is accused of, go unpunished or in finding the proper punishment for them. He points out the ineffectiveness of excommunication in some cases and the inability to punish those who hold positions of honor, as does the man in question. Hence he wonders how the clerics in this case could have refrained from beating the man (paragraph 2). Augustine suggests to Alypius that they need first to establish a regular penalty for persons who commit crimes of this type and that clerics who do bodily harm to someone guilty of such a crime should not be penalized unless they go beyond the sort of penalties provided by civil law (paragraph 3). Augustine suggests that in the present case the pope would not have thought that the man deserved reparation if he had truthfully stated in his complaint what he had done. He tells Alypius that he simply does not know what to say if the man who has suppressed facts in his petition to the Holy See not merely goes unpunished but even receives reparation (paragraph 4).

A memorandum of Augustine to his holy brother Alypius.

1. I received the memorandum of Your Holiness on 26 August, and I have replied on the next day. I had already seen the priest Commodian, and I had not sent anything about the matter by means of him because I had not wanted to see him in order to do that. Rather, because I was worried that something might be done about the man, which reason could not justify, I wanted to know how those events about which he complained had really occurred. After this priest had given me his account, I saw that nothing should be done if the matter had come before your tribunal, except to make known to you what happened inasmuch as it pertains to the case of the same priest. For, regarding the violence inflicted, which was all Pope Celestine wanted to be punished, he could tell me nothing because, he answered, he knew nothing. Hence I had a single remaining worry about this matter: I found it hard to believe that those who found the man with that woman, a professed nun whom he had taken from her native town to make her the plaything of his debauchery, would have refrained from doing him bodily injury.

2. You know, after all, how this question tends to wear us down, that is, how these sins are left unpunished without harm to ecclesiastical discipline, or how

259

they ought to be punished by the Church when they cannot be punished by civil laws. What, then, is a bishop or what are other clerics going to do in the case of such crimes and not of just any sins of human beings? We must, first, ask this of those who think that no corporeal punishment at all should be imposed on anyone, especially on account of the sort of persons who do not have the least care about ecclesiastical excommunication at all, either because they are not Christians or Catholics or because they live such lives that they might as well not be. But if honors that anyone holds or has held in the world mean anything, we are not permitted to lessen them or to take them away in the case of such sins in order that we might hold in check the license for wrongdoing in those persons whom you cannot jail or beat. Yet if men who have a position of honor in the government or in the legal profession, which this fellow with whom we are dealing seems to have, wanted to dance in church, I do not see how those who hold in their hands the means for imposing the discipline of a beating could spare them. And it is much more serious to subject to one's lust someone vowed to holiness than to dare to dance within the walls of a church.

3. Those who want to deliver the correct judgment when these matters are brought to trial, then, ought first to investigate and determine what should be done with such people who in such cases as these are caught in the commission of their sinful actions. Otherwise, if we are moved by their complaints when they receive bodily punishment but are not moved by their actions when they do a most wicked injury to God and disturb by their restless wickedness the Church's reputation for goodness and holiness as well as her peace, or if we are moved by the wrongful actions of most wicked men, which they perpetrate in the church out of their unspeakable audacity, so that we punish the light penalties they suffer for the sake of discipline but judge that we should leave unpunished those serious crimes that they commit against discipline, or we are unable to find how to punish them, I certainly do not see what sort of account of our judgments we are going to give to our Lord.[1] We must therefore first seek, find, and establish a regular penalty for these restless and wicked persons. Thereafter we would only need to impose a penalty if it could be proved that any irregular or excessive punishment had been imposed upon them. Until that happens, I do not at all see what sentence should be pronounced against servants of God who, in defense of the house of their Lord, do to criminals something incomparably less than the civil laws provide for, in order that there might be something to fear on the part of those who have no fear that the bishop or clerics can bring the civil laws to bear against them.

4. But I certainly do not doubt that, if our deplorable son had set down in his statement what he himself had done, the venerable pope would by any means think that the plaintiff ought to receive reparation because he was beaten by

1. See Mt 12:36; Heb 13:17.

clerics, unless the man who did this to him exceeded the limits set by Christian moderation. I think, however, that in the tribunal of Your Holiness he cannot deny so obvious a matter, that is, the action of his about which he did not remain silent in his statement. Now, I do not know what to say if in ecclesiastical tribunals we do not preserve the justice that the civil laws have most wisely established so as to avoid having anyone brought to trial unjustly by means of an imperial rescript—I mean so that a man loses the favor he asked for and so that a person does not go unpunished if, in the petitions submitted to the emperor, he suppresses something that clearly pertains to his case. And I do not know what to say if the man who did this in the request he submitted to so holy a see is seen not only to escape punishment by the bishops but even to obtain reparation.

Letter 10*

In 428, or possibly as early as the fall of 423 or the winter of 423-424, Augustine wrote to Alypius, who was in Italy. Augustine tells Alypius of his desire to see him as soon as possible after his return to Africa. He mentions the books of Julian of Eclanum and of Caelestius that Alypius has sent him and wonders why Alypius did not tell him of Bishop Turbantius' reconciliation with Pope Celestine (paragraph 1).

Augustine then turns to the problem of the slave merchants who have created such a market in Africa that many free men, women, and children are captured and carried off to be sold (paragraph 2). He illustrates this with some stories about the capture of women and children and reminds Alypius of the laws that Emperor Honorius had passed to prevent the sale of free men and women (paragraph 3). Augustine tells Alypius that, if implemented, these laws are perhaps sufficient to stop the slave trade, but he wants him to get the emperor to decree that the slave merchants should not be punished by the most severe provisions of the law (paragraph 4). He insists that it is up to the authorities to work to prevent the enslavement of so many Africans, and he points out that enslavement of this sort is worse than being captured by barbarians (paragraph 5). Augustine adds more stories of such enslavements, which he knows from personal experience (paragraphs 6 and 7). From these incidents, which have occurred in Hippo, Alypius can infer the extent of the slave trade in Africa and the greed of the slave merchants that fuels it (paragraph 8). Finally, Augustine sends his greetings to Alypius and those with him (paragraph 9).

A memorandum: Augustine to his holy brother Alypius.

1. Since our holy brothers and fellow bishops are returning, though I have not seen them, I was nonetheless advised by letter that, if I wanted to write something to Your Holiness, I should send it to Carthage. Hence I have dictated this note by which I greet you, for I desire also to see Your Fraternity as soon as possible now that the hope for your return, which you indicated to me by letter, draws near. But I had already written back that the books of Julian[1] and Caelestius,[2] which you sent by means of our son, the deacon Commilito, arrived here with your memorandum and that I was highly surprised that you did not take care to report to me concerning the emendment of Turbantius, for whom

---

1. That is, either Julian of Eclanum's *To Turbantius* (*Ad Turbantium*), to which Augustine replied with his *Answer to Julian*, or his *To Florus* (*Ad Florum*), to which Augustine replied with his *Unfinished Work in Answer to Julian*.
2. Caelestius, Pelagius' supporter and ally, was condemned as early as 411 by the Council of Carthage. Augustine refuted his *Definitions* in *The Perfection of Human Righteousness*. It is not clear what books of his Alypius sent to Augustine.

Julian wrote the four books.[3] For I have heard from a man who I cannot say has lied that Turbantius condemned the same heresy with a quite humble confession and was taken back into the Catholic peace by Pope Celestine.[4] I rather suspect that you forgot this when you were writing to me. Therefore, though I had written these things, I nonetheless wanted to remind you now for fear that Your Holiness might perhaps receive this memorandum before the one that I wrote earlier. Meanwhile, I found among our papers a copy of the memorandum that you had made for yourself when you were first sent to the imperial court regarding the council,[5] and, after I read it through, I saw that you were unable to carry out many necessary tasks then, and, having removed certain items that were either taken care of then or do not seem very urgent, I thought that I should send it on in case they could be taken care of now.

2. But I also add something else. There is in Africa such a great multitude of men who are commonly called slave merchants[6] that they seem to drain this land to a large extent of its human population by transferring those whom they buy—almost all of them free men—to the provinces overseas. For scarcely a few are found to have been sold by their parents, and they do not buy these, as the laws of Rome allow, for work lasting twenty-five years, but they buy them precisely as slaves and sell them overseas as slaves. But only most rarely do they buy true slaves from their masters. Now from this multitude of merchants a multitude of trappers and raiders has grown so great that it is reported that they invade certain remote and rural sites, where the population is small, in shrieking mobs with the terrifying apparel of either soldiers or barbarians, and they sell to these merchants those whom they carry off by violence.

3. I pass over what rumor most recently reported to us, namely, that in a tiny village women and children were carried off to be sold after the men had been killed through such attacks. But it was not said where this happened, if it really did happen. When, however, I myself asked a certain girl from among those who, through our church, were set free from this wretched captivity how she was sold to the slave merchants, she said that she was seized from her parents' house. Then I asked whether she was the only one who had been there, and she answered that this happened when her parents and brothers were present. Her brother, who had come to take her back, was also there, and, because she was little, he explained how it had come about. He said that these raiders had broken

---

3. Turbantius was one of the bishops who, along with Julian, refused to accept Pope Zosimus' letter, known as the *Tractoria*, issued in the summer of 418, in which he condemned the teaching of Pelagius and Caelestius. Turbantius soon abandoned his errors and was reconciled with Rome.

4. Celestine became bishop of Rome in 422 and died in 432. See Letters 192 and 209 from Augustine to Celestine.

5. Alypius' first mission to Ravenna was in 419.

6. Augustine uses the word *mangones*, which is a slang term in Latin.

in at night and that the family hid themselves from them as best they could rather than venture to resist them, since they believed that they were barbarians. But if there were no slave merchants, those things would not happen. And I certainly do not think that rumor is silent about this evil in Africa, even where you are. It was incomparably less when Emperor Honorius gave a law to the prefect Hadrian forbidding such sales and prescribed that merchants of such wickedness were to be scourged with a leaden whip, have their possessions confiscated, and sent into perpetual exile. And he does not speak in that law of those who sell free persons who have been trapped and carried off, which is what these people do almost exclusively. Rather, he speaks generally of all those who transfer groups of slaves to overseas provinces in order to sell them. For that reason he ordered that those slaves be added to the treasury, which he certainly would not say of free persons.

4. I have appended this law to my memorandum, though it can also perhaps be found quite easily at Rome. For it is useful, and it could remedy this plague. But we began to use it simply for the purpose of setting human beings free, not for subjecting to such a punishment those merchants on account of whom such terrible crimes are perpetrated. For we are deterring those whom we can by such a law and not punishing them; on the contrary, we have been afraid that others might perhaps drag those men, as despicable and damnable as they are, off to the punishment due to them according to this law, once they have been taken by us. Hence I am writing these lines to Your Beatitude precisely in order that it may be decided by the most pious and Christian rulers that, when people are set free from these men through the Church, they do not face the risk of the condemnation that was determined by this law, especially scourging with a leaden whip, from which men readily die. But it is perhaps necessary that this law be publicly promulgated in order to stop them. Otherwise, if we cease out of fear of these punishments, wretched free persons may be deported into perpetual servitude. For, if we do nothing for them, who could easily be found who, if he has some position of authority on the coast, would not prefer to make a profit from these terribly cruel sailings rather than, out of Christian or human pity, to have one of those wretches disembark from a ship or to refuse to allow one of them to board a ship?

5. It is up to the authorities or administrative services, which have charge of how this law or any other passed on this matter can be implemented, to see to it that Africa is no longer being emptied of its native inhabitants and that, as if in an endless river, so many human beings in groups and crowds of both sexes do not lose their freedom in a worse manner than by being captured by barbarians. For there are many who are bought back from the barbarians, but those deported to the overseas provinces do not find the help of being redeemed. Moreover, the barbarians are resisted when the Roman army is managed well and successfully, so that Romans are not held as captives of barbarians. But in defense of Roman

freedom—I do not mean our common freedom but our personal freedom—who resists these merchants not of some sort of animals but of human beings, not of some sort of barbarians but of Roman provincials? These merchants are spread out so far and wide that the persons who have been seized with violence or caught by ambush are led everywhere and from everywhere into the hands of those who promise a payment of money.

6. On the contrary, one cannot stress enough how many have drifted into this wicked traffic out of an amazing blindness due to greed and out of I know not what infectious disease. Who can believe that a woman was found, even here in Hippo with us, who, under the pretext of buying wood, used to trap, imprison, beat, and sell women from Giddaba? Who would believe that a tenant of our church, a man quite well off, sold his wife and the mother of his children, though he was not offended by any failing on her part but driven only by the heat of this plague? A certain young man of about twenty, an accountant and clever secretary, was lured from our monastery and sold, and he was scarcely able to be set free by means of the Church.

7. If I should want to enumerate only such crimes as we have experienced, I could not by any means do so. Take this one example from which you can conjecture all of them that are being perpetrated throughout Africa and on all its coasts. Almost four months before I wrote this, people from different regions and especially from Numidia gathered up by Galatian merchants—for these men alone or these men principally are involved in this traffic—were brought here to be transported from the shore of Hippo. One of the faithful who knew our practice in such almsgiving was present and reported this to the Church. Immediately, while I was absent, almost one hundred and twenty human beings were set free, in part from the ship on which they had been loaded, in part from the place where they were hidden while waiting to be loaded, and among them scarcely five or six were found who had been sold by their parents. Hardly anyone, however, could refrain from tears at hearing of the various conditions under which the rest fell into the hands of the Galatian trappers and raiders.

8. Now it is up to Your Wisdom to imagine the size of the deportation of wretched souls that rages elsewhere on the coast, if the Galatians' greed is so ablaze, if their cruelty is so daring in Hippo Regius, where by God's mercy some sort of diligence on the part of the Church stands guard to set free wretched human beings from such captivity and where sellers of such merchandise are certainly punished far less than by the severity of this law, but still at least by the loss of the money they were paid. In charity, I beg that I may not have written this to you in vain. For the Galatians do not lack patrons by means of whom they try to get back from us those persons whom the Lord set free through the Church, even after they have been returned to their people who were searching for them and who have come to us with letters from bishops for this purpose. But as we are dictating these lines, they have begun to trouble some believers, our children,

among whom certain of these persons remained at our recommendation—for the Church is not able to feed all whom she sets free—and they have not ceased entirely from this request for their return, though a letter has arrived from an authority whom they could have feared.

9. I greet in turn in the charity of Christ, in accord with their merits, all those who graciously greeted us by means of the letter of Your Reverence. My fellow servants who are with me greet Your Holiness along with me.

Letter 11*

In 420 Consentius, the recipient of Letters 120 and 205 from Augustine and the sender of Letters 119 and 12*, also wrote Augustine the present letter about the spread of the Priscillianists in Spain.[1] Augustine also wrote for Consentius *Against Lying*, which touches upon some of the issues addressed in the present letter. Consentius tells Augustine that Patroclus, the bishop of Arles, has directed him to write a book against the Priscillianists. He explains how he had been instructed to deal with these heretics by means of guile and then turns to an account of a certain Fronto's confrontation with them (paragraph 1). Then, using Fronto's own words, Consentius narrates how certain Priscillianist books were seized from the baggage of Severus by the barbarians and came into the hands of various bishops, who were eventually exposed by the courageous and nearly foolhardy behavior of Fronto. Fronto himself was saved from being stoned only by several miraculous events by which the perjury of the Priscillianists was revealed and in the course of which his worst opponent met with sudden death (paragraphs 2 to 23).

Then Consentius tells Augustine of the council at Béziers, to which Patroclus of Arles has summoned the bishops of Spain, and of his arrival in the Balearic Isles (paragraph 24). He says that the Priscillianists have appealed to the precedent set by Augustine in dealing with the Donatist clergy, who were accepted back into the Catholic unity in the same rank they held in their schismatic group (paragraph 25). Hence Consentius asks Augustine to write to Patroclus to explain the reasons why the Priscillianists are treated differently than the Donatists (paragraph 26). Finally, Consentius informs Augustine that he is sending him the book he mentioned earlier that he has written against the Priscillianists (paragraph 27).

A memorandum: Consentius to my lord, holy Father Augustine.

1. My most blessed lord, a brother of Your Holiness, Bishop Patroclus, has compelled me by his intense love to write certain perhaps inept and absurd ideas against the Priscillianists, who were ravaging even the Gauls. For fear that I might perhaps inflict upon Your Paternity a greater weariness if you read them, I had decided to keep them with me. But it turns out that a certain servant of Christ by the name of Fronto,[2] whom the Holy Spirit has inspired with most ardent flames of zeal for the faith, arrived unexpectedly. When I questioned him about

---

1. On Priscillian and the Priscillianists, see the introductions to Paul Orosius' *Memorandum to Augustine* and Augustine's *To Orosius in Refutation of the Priscillianists and Origenists.* For an excellent assessment of the life and teaching of Priscillian, see Henry Chadwick, *Priscillian of Avila: The Occult and the Charismatic in the Early Church* (Oxford: Clarendon Press, 1976). The Priscillianists seem to have held dualist views similar to the Manichees though it is difficult to know what they held since they were accused of almost every error and perversion.

2. For Fronto, see *Against Lying* 3-4.

what he had done regarding the orders he received, he reported to me many things not only to rejoice over but also to be amazed at. I had ordered him the previous year to make war, while relying upon an utterly innocent ruse, against the above-mentioned Priscillianists, who swarm over Spain to such an extent that the barbarians seem to have done nothing of such magnitude in comparison to them. I had also taught him and certain other persons the trick by which he ought to attack them, sending to him the books that I was recently compelled to write at the command of my aforementioned lord, your brother, especially this third book, the one in which, after I learned everything more fully, the reason why I wrote in the guise of a heretic is noted in the text of the very brief preface. My venerable brother Fronto, therefore, arrived here in excellent time, while unfavorable winds detained Brother Leonas[3] here, and he reported to me very many things, from among which I relate a few for your information.

2. "In the city of Tarragona," he said, "in which I set up a monastery for myself, I received a sealed packet that you sent me by the hands of Bishop Agapius. In it I found the letter, memoranda, and books that you sent, and, soon after having absorbed every argument and instruction, I hurried off to that famous heretic Severa, whose name you had clearly made known to me, and, having approached her by the trick that the text of your preface explained, I asked for the names of the heretics. She told me among other things that a certain priest, Severus, renowned for his wealth and power as well as for his writings, the leader of this teaching, had in vain cast upon his deceased mother the odium of his treachery. For, when in the previous year the same Severus, thinking that the barbarians had withdrawn, tried after his mother's death to reach the village in which he lived, our Lord Jesus Christ, who sees all secrets and governs all events, willed that his baggage be seized by the barbarians in order that such a great crime might be revealed. Since they took it all as booty, they brought three huge volumes that contained all kinds of sacrileges to the neighboring city, named Lerida, believing that the volumes were good and that they might be bought by someone. When they learned that they were filled with abominations, they left them with Sagittius, the bishop of that city. But he went through them all, and since he was a man proven evil in the sight of God, he was given the opportunity to be revealed as such also in the sight of human beings. For, since in his madness he took pleasure in these sweet poisons and since the affair had become public and could no longer be covered over by dissembling, he deceitfully cut from those books sections that contained shameful and sacrilegious knowledge of magic incantations. Then, having reviewed everything by himself, he sent one volume, from which he had excised whatever seemed dangerous, to Titian of Tarragona, that is, to the metropolitan bishop, along with letters in which he stated that three volumes were captured in the baggage of the

---

3. Leonas is mentioned in *Against Lying* 1, 1.

priest Severus and were turned over to him by the enemy, and that among them this volume displeased him most, but that he put the others in the archives of the church.

3. "Bishop Titian handed over the book he received to Syagrius, the bishop of Huesca, because in his church Severus had assumed the title of priest by a lie, and Titian advised him to examine the faith of his priest by a careful investigation. But Bishop Syagrius, a man quite holy and Catholic but too credulous and unwisely kind, believed Severus, who covered up his sacrilege by arguments, lies, and perjury so that he also convinced the others that Severus, judging harmless those books that he had inherited from his mother, had wanted to take them with him to his own village in order that, when his mind was unoccupied, he might read them there or even test their character. Since these claims, then, were believed by all, that little woman, Severa, who disclosed all the secrets of her crimes to me as if I were a heretic, also betrayed the priest Severus, saying that for a price he had received from Bishop Sagittius the books that he had pretended belonged to his mother, though they had been fraudulently mutilated.

4. "After I learned all this, then, and was reassured by indications, signs, proofs, and witnesses, I brought the matter to the rigor of a church inquest and made an accusation first against Severa herself, who had betrayed everyone, and soon after against the priest Severus. But Severa, confused by the unexpected novelty of the situation, at first did not dare to deny whatever she had remembered that she told me. Afterward, however, when in opposition to me Severus relied on the power of an illustrious and prominent man, his relative, Count Asterius, he brought it about that the woman I mentioned had recourse to the help of a very powerful woman, his niece, the daughter of Count Asterius, and, after being received into his headquarters, which were surrounded by numerous soldiers, she denied all her confessions, while using perjury for her defense.

5. "After all had withdrawn, when Severus and his supporters realized that I, a man of no importance because of the lowliness of my person and a beggar because of my lack of resources, had been completely stripped of every proof and was attacking the power of so great a faction with bare words, they wanted to stop me from bringing accusations against them even by the fear of death, with which they threatened me. They said, 'Figure out for yourself the risk that awaits you if the priest proves himself innocent!' And I immediately said, 'What more do you want, if I am unable to prove what I intend to prove, than that I be expelled from every church for my whole life, like a pagan?' Then the heretics were thrown into confusion and said, 'Do you see, O holy and venerable bishops and you people of every age and sex, that a man has emerged, lacking in resources, rich in lies, armed with audacity, lacking in innocence? Watch out that you do not set a dangerous example for all slanderous men! For if in the case of this one man, who was not afraid to stain with the black mark of a false charge so holy and so noble a man, an inconsiderate pardon from your tribunal does not

give others a lesson in fear, the impunity of this man will inevitably arouse throngs of slanderous accusers against each of you.'

6. "When the people of Tarragona, who were aroused against me by such cries of the heretics, began to rage in violent actions aimed at my destruction, I cried out and said, 'Is it enough for you that, if my accusation is proven false and the faith of Severus is proven correct, you stone me to death?' 'It is enough,' they said, 'but this provision must be confirmed by the records of the present proceedings.' In that way it came about that I entrusted the peril of my lifeblood, and Severus the peril of his honor, to these declarations recorded in the acts of the church. In these, he testified, under every sort of oath, that he neither received, nor had, nor saw his mother's books after they were carried off by the barbarians.

7. "The result was that letters were sent to the bishops of Lerida and Huesca to the effect that they should be so good as to bring the books with them, since the case demanded this—Sagittius the two volumes that he had long ago claimed in a letter sent to Titian, the metropolitan bishop, that he retained, and Syagrius the one volume that he had publicly received from the same bishop, Titian. But at the same time, having composed a list of false charges, Severus sent a letter to his relative, the illustrious man Count Asterius, and to all his other friends and relatives, very powerful men. In it he pretended that I was a most harmful and deceitful imposter and had attacked with intolerable charges the count himself, his house, and his daughter, and heaped upon them injuries and violence. The illustrious man Count Asterius (to whom was entrusted the charge of a great army and the conduct of an important war) immediately came to Tarragona, and along with him a multitude of men raging against me, who was a single dead flea.[4] But the whole affair had a contrary outcome for Severus and was quite different from what he believed.

8. "For, though the perfectly obvious truth of our side was being crushed by the very great influence of all, especially the priests, yet such great strength came to the aid of my weakness from our Lord Jesus Christ that even the count himself was frightened, as innocent and as Catholic as he was. For, when he came to Tarragona, he learned that I alone was being attacked by the most odious accusations of his relative, his daughter, and all his friends and servants. Since he is a righteous man who fears the Lord and does not readily believe such reports, he did not want to punish indiscriminately and with great brutality the injuries done to him in particular or to his people, and he ordered that I, whom he knew to be a Christian, though a poor man, be summoned to his headquarters without injury. But, taking up the confidence that the help of our Lord Jesus Christ had given me, I answered that I could not go to his house, which I knew was filled with gangs of heretics, for fear that I might perhaps fall into the ambushes of enemies

---

4. See 1 Sm 24:14.

who were threatening to kill me in public. But if there were some aspect of that case or its terms that could not be entrusted to messengers or to a letter, he ought, if he would agree to that, to come to the church in order that I might there learn what it was.

9. "But he came without delay to the church at the crack of dawn and immediately, in the tribunal where the bishops sit, he himself, along with the others, sought to bring into the open the complaints against me. And first, all of them spoke at length with Bishops Titian and Agapius, and they gained great favor with them in opposition to me. They claimed that I was a most deceitful and slanderous accuser who deceived an incautious and simple little woman with great guile and forced her to tell a false story about a priest and that now, on account of an utterly inane cloud of suspicion, which even she who was said to be the betrayer stated was false, the whole house filled with illustrious persons was struck by an accusation from me, while the count was made the object of insults from me and the count's daughter had her reputation blackened.

10. "By these words and others of the sort they aroused against me such great hatred on the part of all that not only the people but even certain priests threatened me with death. I was summoned at that point to the tribunal alone, to be rebuked by the bishops, put to shame by the clerics, torn apart by the heretics, blamed by the count, spat upon by the soldiers, and even stoned by the people. After I had been brought in, Bishop Agapius terrified me at once by the fearsomeness of words such as these: 'Where,' he asked, 'are the letters of Consentius and the memoranda that you found in the packet that I brought you?' To this I replied firmly that everything was at my house. But he said, 'Bring everything here immediately and hand it over to me, unless you prefer to incur a sentence of condemnation pronounced now!' At this, confidently ridiculing his utterly absurd threats, I asked why he was commanding that everything be revealed to him. Then he said, 'In order that we may read everything and learn what it is that has suddenly incited you to persecute utterly innocent human beings.' In reply I myself said, 'You brought everything to me, as you claim. How can it be that you do not know what you brought?' Then he said, 'Consentius handed me under a seal everything that was to be brought to you. Was it right that a disloyal curiosity would move me to break the seal?' I asked him, 'Why, then, do you now want so badly to know what he who sent it did not want you to know? For, surely, if he had chosen you as a suitable messenger, he ought not to have handed over to you under seal what you now finally ask for out of concern. Why, then, do you blame me if I am now afraid to disclose it to you, since he gave a splendid testimony concerning your trustworthiness when he sent it by means of you under seal?'

11. "When I said this, the bishop was aroused against me with such a ferocious spirit that he angrily leapt from his throne in the sight of all and wanted to strike me dead with his own hands. But who would dare to believe it? With even

the count rebuking him, the insanity of the bishop was quieted, quelled by the power of the Lord Jesus Christ. The count himself, however, asked with wisdom and moderation why I was attacking his house and his relative, a priest, with such hatred. I said to him, 'Do you, O noble and illustrious man, think that it is hatred because I want to purify your house, because I want those whom the snake Severus has injected with a deadly venom to be set free from the dangers of eternal death by the infusion of an antidote of most merciful strictness?' While he looked at the ground in silence and modestly held his head with his hand, the count listened to me not only patiently but even willingly as I pursued these and other such topics. Finally he replied that I should even be given the greatest thanks in return for such a benefit, at least if my claim were true. Then I said, 'Let Severus and the others now prove that I spoke some word, even in passing, that injured your reputation in particular, and yet, if you were not relying upon a most solid profession of the Catholic faith, terror inspired by your power would never have shut the unbridled mouth of Fronto.' Then the count said, 'I thank you for being so gracious as to testify to my faith. But with regard to the faith of Severus and the others, although they are linked to me by some blood relationship, it is certain that it cannot be opposed to my faith.'

12. "With this statement, then, the count rose and entered his headquarters, while everything was interrupted, and he regarded the confidence with which the Lord had inspired me with such great admiration that he immediately sent to me—something that no one could have believed—the following orders. He said, 'Forgive, I beg you, O servant of Christ, if we have perhaps harmed you in any way, and with the power of your prayers follow me as I hurry, as you see, with the army into battle!' But Severus and the others were thrown into confusion by the unexpected fairness of the count and quieted down for a little while at least on that day. After a few days, however, they stirred up against me such great hatred on the part of all that almost none of the people in the city could be found to have so pious a mind and holy an intention as not to judge me worthy of death. As a result, my heart was so crushed by despair that it had no solid hope and gave forth only feeble sighs. But the Lord, who does not scorn contrite and humble hearts,[5] showed me a greater gift of his help the more he saw that I was attacked with greater intensity. For there was a very powerful servant by whose judgment not only the whole family of the aforementioned count but also his daughter, whom he raised, was guided—a man with great physical strength, with a very cruel mind, and with most arrogant power. Often he laid ambushes for me in vain since, out of concern for my life, I did not leave the church. At last, having turned to undisguised fury, he merited to experience very clear punishment from our defender.

---

5. See Ps 51:19.

13. "For he burst with weapons into the midst of the mobs of the rebellious and, stretching his hand out toward me, he said, 'Give me this dog. I will quiet his barking right now with the death he deserves.' Then the people, and even those who were threatening to stone me with great rebelliousness, drove that most bloodthirsty and furious man from the church with their pious shouts. On the same day he left for his suburban home and enjoyed a pleasant banquet, but in the morning my vindicator struck him with the pain of such a mortal blow that only after six days could he be brought to the city as dead. After this event, some of the faithful, terrified by the power manifested in this sign, ceased for a little while from their attack upon me, but my enemies and the whole house of the count were provoked to a greater fury of hatred and demanded punishment for me as a murderer who had slain that man with savage verbal attacks. But a few without any faith emerged who said that his death was a matter of chance.

14. "While these events were taking place at Tarragona, at Lerida Bishop Sagittius was being forced by a letter of Bishop Titian to return, or rather to present, the volumes that he had claimed were in his house. For in that way it was brought about by a marvelous act of providence that, since Severus had immediately sent a letter to Sagittius, undoubtedly a secret one, in which he explained what had happened, its bearer strove with all speed to arrive earlier at Severus's town, which was at a rather long journey's distance, in order to compel Ursitio, a certain monk and friend of Severus, to bring out the volumes that Sagittius was asking for from the places where Severus hid them and to deliver them secretly to Sagittius. But Sagittius remembered that he had secretly received gifts from Severus and had returned the volumes to him, and since he was being burned by the inner fires of a bad conscience and was amazed that he had received no letter from Severus on this matter, he believed that Syagrius, the bishop of Huesca, who he knew had likewise returned his volume to Severus, had done this with a similar greedy conscience. Sagittius, then, writes a secret letter to Syagrius in which he says that he has no doubt that Syagrius too was being forced by a similar letter of the metropolitan bishop to return the one volume. For this reason he had, by means of a certain deacon named Paulinus, long since sent the two volumes that he had at his house to Syagrius, to whom the inquest concerning his priest had been entrusted, but, since Paulinus had not found Bishop Syagrius in his town, he handed them over to the priest Severus. He now beseeches him urgently that, since this event was utterly unknown to anyone, for fear that some suspicion might perhaps arise, he would be so good as to open the hiding places of the priest Severus and bring secretly with him the volumes he had brought forth in order that he might be able to prove in court that he had not handed the volumes over to Severus.

15. "While this letter is being carried to Syagrius, the bishop of Huesca, Ursitio, that servant of Severus, secretly carried the books to Sagittius. After having received them, Sagittius was filled with a joy as great as the sadness by

which he was long afflicted, and, carrying in his heart the intention of perjuring himself, he set out for Tarragona. But since Syagrius had received both Bishop Titian's letter of convocation and the secret letter of Sagittius, he saw that he, who had out of thoughtless simplicity returned to Severus the volume he had received, was involved in an accusation bringing very great suspicion. After he suffered some period of anxiety, he decided to go there instead in order that he himself, having the proof of the lie he had been told, might extract both the priest Severus and his fellow bishop Sagittius from the chain of so great a suspicion, when suddenly that same night he was terrified by a marvelous vision of our Lord Jesus Christ. He saw himself standing before the tribunal of the dreadful judge in sorrow and receiving the sentence for the great crime that was on his conscience. Frightened, he immediately got up and was stricken with such consternation of mind that he not only made public the letter of Sagittius and compelled the notorious monk Ursitio, who had been the bearer of the books, to confess everything before an ecclesiastical tribunal, but he also undertook a very long, very difficult, and very dangerous journey on foot and followed in the footsteps of Sagittius, who was making his way to Tarragona.

16. "But when Sagittius, who by the marvelous providence of the Lord had left much earlier, had taken his seat in the court with the other bishops, he said, 'Look, O most blessed brothers, here are the volumes that Your Holiness has commanded to be produced.' At this I—who, as I said before, knew their secrets through their betrayal by that heretic, Severa—began to prove that Sagittius had in the recent past certainly received from Severus in secret the volumes that had long before been sold. For I said that I knew the gift he had received and when and by whom he sold to Severus these wicked weapons for destroying the souls of many. Then Sagittius, well versed, of course, in the law and educated in the liberal arts, rose up against me with a great outcry and demanded that, unless I immediately proved my accusations, I should die by stoning. But in the sight of all the people, with the gospels and everything holy as his witnesses, he perjured himself not once but many times, saying that the volumes had remained hidden in the archives of his church since that time and that Severus had never seen them. Severus, in his turn, bound himself by similar perjuries. All those also whom I produced as witnesses or accusers, stating the same lie, shouted that I was a sacrilegious enemy of the venerable priests.

17. "In the first place Severa herself denied all her denunciations and accused me, while perjuring herself, of devising an unheard-of lie. When the unbearable shouting of the whole people threatened me with immediate punishment, I demanded that judgment be postponed until the next day—the only remedy that my distraught and confused mind could find. For I promised that Christ, the source of imperishable truth, would make public on the morrow, by the ways that he would chose, the obvious perjuries of Sagittius, Severus, and all. It seemed reasonable even to the heretics that they should permit the punishment

of my stoning to be postponed for the short time I demanded. On the same day in the afternoon Bishop Syagrius arrived, and because I knew that he was the principal supporter of his priest, Severus, and had secretly returned the volume to him, I attacked him in a similar manner. After I learned that he had made such a long and arduous journey on foot, I wondered what it was that compelled a rich man, weighed down by age and impeded by bodily weakness, to undertake the difficulty of so great a task. I immediately ran to the lodging where he had stopped, and, after a greeting, I said, 'Do you want yourself and Sagittius to drink my blood together by the same lie, denying that you secretly returned the volumes to Severus in order that I, though innocent, might perish because I cannot prove the accusations that I would certainly not have made if I did not know them with full clarity?'

18. "Then he asked, 'Who, my son, was able to reveal to you what was done in complete secrecy?' I was astonished that the man who I believed had come to confirm the perjuries of them all had immediately uttered a statement of confession, and I told him in reply of the whole series of my informants from the very beginning. And after I said that Sagittius and Severus had denied this by a great invocation of everything holy, indignant at such wicked perjury he was driven to cry out, 'My child, bring as quickly as possible the letters of Sagittius in which he admitted having handed over the books to Severus; bring also the proceedings by which he was proven guilty of recently receiving the same books from the hands of the monk Ursitio.' And without disguising the fact that he was reluctant to bring everything into the open but was compelled by the fear of the Lord, he recounted for me in simple words the whole course of his surprising and terrifying vision.

19. "Then I said, 'I beg you, venerable father, who have been snatched from the company of the wicked by so great a grace of Christ, that, after handing over these papers to me now, you be silent about them for a short while until we discover whether their consciences may force Sagittius or Severus to show some reverence at least tomorrow to the altars of Christ.' The next day came and, with all the people present in the court, I saw that the aforementioned sacks of lies were breathing forth similar or even greater perjuries. Then I said, 'Why, Sagittius, why do you boast over the title of bishop that is not yours? Are you not afraid of slaying your own soul by such great perjuries? Did you not recently send a letter of this sort to Syagrius? Did you not receive the books by the hands of the monk Ursitio?'

20. "Hearing this, he not only denied everything and bound himself by repeated perjuries, but also stirred up the people to destroy me, who had made up so many and such incredible and unheard-of charges, until, when I produced the letter, he was proven guilty and fled from the courtroom and from his disgrace. When that happened, since Bishop Titian was pressed by great outcries from the people for his condemnation, he said that only many bishops could pass sentence

upon the status of a bishop. But I pursued Sagittius, who was fleeing with a certain part of the people and was already beyond the walls of the city, and when I confronted him concerning the return of the pages that he had stolen from the books, he swore that he had received from the barbarians volumes that had long before been unbound and were in pieces, and that there was no doubt that all the things that we said were missing from those books had perished in the hands of the barbarians. But afterwards, stricken with fear, he was forced to return everything that was missing, and when I demanded that it be read out in the hearing of the people, such unheard-of crimes emerged from that reading that some ears could not endure the virulence of that poison.

21. "It is well known that a council was held on this matter but that by the unbelievable influence on the part of all involved the truth was suppressed. In fact it was cried up in such a way that the sacrilegious were restored to communion and both the books and the proceedings were destroyed by fire so that we could never take up the case again. But since I stood before the bishops in freedom and spoke out most strongly against their venal judgment, one of the seven bishops, that notorious Agapius, carried out in act the slaughter with which he threatened me. For, after he seized me and beat me with blows and punches and was scarcely prevented by the other bishops, who detested such great insanity, he said, 'Let this fellow get out of here now if he prevails who boasts that he brought down by his statements the chief functionary of the count's household and who is now destroying me by similar verbal attacks.'

22. "But I rejoiced over the injury I received and said, 'Let Christ hear these words and be their judge!' Now an intense fear of sin has sealed our lips lest we repeat what happened next. Who, after all, would dare to fathom fearlessly the great abyss of the Lord's judgments?[6] In fact we saw that the aforementioned bishop was seized about a week later by a sudden disease of the throat and did not give up his spirit before he asked pardon of me, most unhappy man that I am, for what he did and what he said. But could we state without serious sin that a bishop who was considered Catholic was struck with such a blow by the Lord?

23. "During the same time, as the hatred of all for me grew stronger, I was driven to the point that I undertook the effort of a long journey and fled to the help of the holy and most blessed Patroclus, the bishop of Arles, whose renowned constancy in the pursuit of this heresy is highly praised. I in fact obtained from him without difficulty that all, both the accused and the judges who turned aside the weight of justice by an unjust hearing, should come together for a council, though we do not know whether it is still going to be held in the town of Béziers, as was announced. Meanwhile, during this short period of time, he granted me a most welcome escort, and I headed for this island[7] for the

---

6. See Ps 36:6.
7. That is, the Balearic Isles.

sole purpose of enjoying the sight of you and recounting to you these events in your presence, in order perhaps to be instructed by you on some point, after I had again undertaken the labor of a very dangerous sea voyage."

24. In almost precisely these words the account of the holy and venerable man Fronto came to an end. I have brought it to the ears of Your Beatitude just as I very recently received it from his lips. Now, then, though there is no doubt as to the truth of this history, in bringing this question to the heavenly senate of Your Beatitude, I first of all call your attention to this point, namely, that, even if it was not spread about by any rumor, not even an uncertain one, it is nonetheless credible and very certain that the Spanish bishops will never come to the council that your holy and most blessed brother Patroclus convoked, who was moved not by the force of his power but by that of his piety. But the same holy and most blessed brother of yours and the other bishops of Gaul, illustrious and outstanding men, who do not tolerate that so great a defilement pervade the Church of our Lord Jesus Christ and who are inflamed, as I am sure, with the fire of a greater zeal, will perhaps report these events to the ears even of our illustrious emperor, and they will bring it about that, since the cancer of this teaching has by its secret creeping already been spread throughout the whole world, it may be cauterized by a uniform sentence through all the provinces.

25. But I have clearly found that there are some who protect the most obscene and sacrilegious Priscillianists by the example of Your Beatitude. For they say, "The African bishops did not remove the Donatists who returned to them from the rank of the priesthood, and indeed the illustrious and famous teacher Augustine, or rather the grace of the Holy Spirit which speaks through his mouth,[8] believed that, though there is among us such great relentlessness that we remove from the priesthood priests proven guilty of the crime of holding this teaching and impose upon them a uniform severity of judgment, the sanction ought to be that, for none of them among whom these sacrileges have been discovered, will the doors of the Church be opened except through their doing penance."[9]

26. Hence, by an opportune suggestion, I believe, stemming from the confidence I have from my familiarity with you and your love, if you graciously permit this, I venture to advise you that Your Holy and Venerable Paternity should order that a letter be sent to your most blessed brother, Bishop Patroclus, who, as I have discovered, desires to be visited by your writings. That letter should explain the difference among provinces, persons, and teachings and should inform us as to why different sentences ought to be pronounced. For there is a big difference, as I see it in my stupidity, between Spain, which harbors a

8. See Mt 10:20.
9. See Letters 128 and 129. Augustine argued that, for the sake of the unity of the Church, Donatist clergy ought to be accepted into the Catholic unity in the rank they held among the Donatists, though this provision was a mitigation of the previously imposed penalties.

hidden incest, and Africa, which publicly commits fornication. So too, there is a great difference between the Spaniards, who tremble in fear when caught in sacrilege, and the Africans, who even boast stubbornly in their schism. In the same way the Priscillianists, who are truly worthy of every execration and of a different abomination, undoubtedly differ from the Donatists who, by the character of their crime, are cruel and violent.

27. But if you place little value on my inept and foolish little suggestion, I beg that you graciously pardon my rather audacious love. Encouraged by so fair a success, I of course thought that I should send to Your Paternity the book of which I made mention in the beginning. If Your Paternity orders that it be handed over to young men who are very astute and carefully selected and instructs them as is necessary, I think that the many battalions of Priscillianists that are in hiding, especially in this city, will be publicly revealed. May you be mindful of me and prosper forever, my holy and most blessed lord.

Letter 12*

In 419 at the earliest, Consentius, the author of the previous letter, wrote this letter to Augustine, in which he tells Augustine about himself and his love of leisure and distrust of learning.[1] He informs Augustine that he had received a copy of *The Confessions* approximately twelve years previously but has read very little of it (paragraph 1). He explains that his distaste for reading has caused him to read only the canonical scriptures but that he has nonetheless found that he is eager to enter into theological discussions (paragraph 2). Hence he tells Augustine of the motives that led him to write against the priest Leontius (paragraph 3). He says that he desires to know the truth as a matter of simple faith, while avoiding all the labor of study and learning (paragraph 4). He tells Augustine of his fear of learning and distaste for reading, which have led him to take up writing (paragraph 5). Furthermore, since he has no hope of visiting Augustine personally, writing is his only option for presenting his thoughts to him (paragraph 6). Consentius admits that Augustine's letter to him, perhaps Letter 120, led him to interrupt very briefly the leisure that he loves like a mistress (paragraph 7). He describes how Augustine's letter had gotten him to take up reading and how he has returned to the leisure he loves (paragraph 8).

Consentius tells Augustine of his finding an unnamed kindred soul who loved leisure as much as he did, but who was more productive (paragraph 9). Together they congratulated themselves on avoiding the vainglory associated with the sort of learning that a Christian does not need (paragraph 10). He recalls the example of Origen, who was led into error by his pursuit of learning and who lost his soul as a result (paragraph 11). Though Augustine is now considered free from all error, Origen, Consentius observes, was condemned only long after his death (paragraph 12). Consentius admits that he had turned to reading the works he had received but was recalled by the Lord to the leisure he loved. Furthermore, at the urging of Bishop Severus he undertook a work against the Jews, from whose attacks the Church was suffering (paragraph 13). He tells Augustine that the insistence of the courier has forced him to break off his long and rambling letter (paragraph 14). He says that he will send Augustine two works out of the many he has written, namely, that against the Jews and a letter to Bishop Patroclus (paragraph 15). Finally, he mentions that the *Tractoria* of Pope Zosimus came into his hands the previous year and that he has written some things against the errors of Pelagius (paragraph 16).

A memorandum: Consentius to Augustine, my holy lord and venerable father who is eternally worthy of my respect.

1. I obtained around twelve years ago the books of *The Confessions*[2] and very many others, out of a reprehensible desire to have them rather than out of a good

---

1. For more on Consentius, see Letter 11*, as well as Letters 119, 120, and 205.
2. That is, about 407. Augustine wrote *The Confessions* between 397 and 401.

and praiseworthy love of learning. Even now I possess them almost as if still under seal, overwhelmed as I am by an incredible lethargy. Having only recently undertaken to read them, I found in them certain ideas perfectly expressed in the investigation of which I had sweated and labored. And in recognizing many forms of my own thoughts as a portrait can reveal them, I begin to realize that, for learning other things that I also desire to know, it is not that the teacher is not there for me but that I am not there for the teacher.[3] Finally, to admit it in the presence of the Lord, almost four years ago, that is, before I thought of seeking to meet Your Holiness, I had read no more than two or three pages from the first book of *The Confessions*, but, just as Your Paternity has the custom of comparing the minds of all foolish people to squinting eyes,[4] I was repelled by the painful brightness of your thoughts, and, because I found there nothing soft and gentle that might soothe the wounds to my eyes, I immediately returned to the darkness of my ignorance, which was very comfortable for me, and I avoided not only those books but also the others "more cautiously than the blood of a viper."[5]

2. In fact I have so great and so deadly a distaste that, apart from the canonical books, which their reputation made venerable for me, my crazy stomach felt nauseated at the letters of all the commentators. Lactantius[6] alone I found pleasant on account of his plain and elegant style. In my most ardent love for idleness, nonetheless, I cast him aside, once I had read him, along with all the rest, and since my soul was weighed down by my incalculable distaste for reading, as if by the disease of lethargy, over the course of so many years I scarcely made my way through the canonical scriptures once or twice in a very desultory manner. And yet, though laziness thoroughly possessed the whole of me in both mind and body, if any question on topics relating to God arose among the servants of Christ in my presence, as often happens, I was one of those whom the words of the apostle described, since I was willing to be a teacher of the law but did not understand either what I said or what I maintained.[7] I tried to defend with hollow words, however, whatever I thought more correct.

3. Hence it also came about that I was aroused against the priest Leontius, of holy memory, by a love not of learning but of natural justice, and that I fought most vigorously against him on the question that was decided by the judgment of Your Holiness, on which he seemed to me not to think correctly. And soon, fired with rivalry in his regard, admiring the reputation of Your Holiness and burning with the love of knowing the truth, I wrote those pages in which I rejected many ideas and praised a few. And yet, I think, all these events have taken place by

---

3. See Cicero, *In Defense of Cornelius Plancius* (*Pro Cn. Plancio*) 36, 89.
4. See Letter 119, 2; *Soliloquies* I, 6, 12; *Confessions* VII, 16, 22; *Order* I, 10, 29.
5. Horace, *Odes* (*Carmina*) I, 8, 9-10.
6. Lactantius was born in 240 and died in 320; he was the author of, among other things, *The Divine Instructions* (*Divinae institutiones*).
7. See 1 Tm 1:7.

God's judgment either that I might write or that I might write in a blameworthy manner.

4. Such a thought, in fact, now pushes me to write in order that, with the solitude of the Balearic Islands placed before my eyes, in which it is most rare to find I do not say a learned but even a believing Christian, I desire—not out of a love of learning, which I utterly rejected, recognizing that it involves so much toil, but out of a love for the Catholic faith, which it is deadly not to know—to come to a simple knowledge of the truth without any desire to read or even to evaluate any works. And I could perhaps have accomplished this if I myself had either heard or found persons who had heard some of these questions debated by men of wisdom. I would at least perhaps have accepted even the slight labor involved in reading if someone had given me books that might resolve precisely the knotty problems that especially bound my thoughts. For I refused to undertake the certain labor of research on account of the uncertain hope of discovery.

5. After I had utterly rejected the writings of all the wise men, therefore, I was pondering in my heart great and arduous questions, and since it was not possible to find anyone even now on these islands—I will not say someone who might teach important subjects and shed light on obscure ideas but even someone who understands minor questions and considers them clearly—my mind was corrupted by so perverse a plague of diseases that my excessive fear of reading gave birth to an excessive boldness in writing. Thus it happened that, in mistakenly looking out for myself, I preferred to write two volumes deserving ridicule rather than to study the admirable works of many others. I decided, then, to set forth all my thoughts in writing as if in a discussion between two opponents in order that, once it was captured in writing, the most insane quarrel raging in my heart might be set before your eyes and calmed by the mercy of your instruction. But this could be done only by writing.

6. For I admit that, if I had believed that I could in any way enjoy the sight of Your Paternity with the eyes of the flesh, I would certainly never have labored over writing such lengthy bits of nonsense. But since I had come to these islands with the intention or desire of ingloriously passing the whole time of my life here in the leisure and laziness that I even now desire in a hardly lazy way, the interior languor of our fevers could not be revealed to you, my physician, unless the role of words were put into writing. But if in those writings of mine there was found nothing at all that was pleasing or nothing that was displeasing, modesty would never have permitted me to rush to your presence. For I am by nature so weak and fearful that I would blush more, if one can believe this, over praises than over reproaches.

7. But by the plan and judgment of Christ it has come about that Your Paternity has addressed to me a truly wonderful letter by such messengers.[8] For,

---

8. This is possibly Letter 120 which Augustine sent to Consentius in 411 in answer to Consentius' Letter 119.

unless Maximian and Caprarius, deacons respectful of and devoted to my lord, had pressed me with strong goads of love, our laziness, though enticed by the pious and sweet counsels of your writings, would never have preferred even for a short time my lukewarm desire for learning to my most ardent love of leisure. For that young man in the play of Terence,[9] angry at the prostitute who rejected him as a lover, could not, though offended, keep away from his beloved even for a short time, although he was being forced by insults. In fact, he thought that he did something memorable with the full strength of his courage, if for only three days he went without the prostitute who had offended him. How much more would I—in whose marrow a greater passion for my leisure is perhaps burning, especially since I was never offended but was always warmly welcomed by her—have been unwilling to go without the pleasure of the solitude prepared for me even for a few days unless the Lord, the charioteer who drives a chariot[10] better than ten thousand,[11] turned by his hidden reins, as they say, the mouths of our minds![12]

8. I came to you, therefore; rather, though I resisted, I was pulled by the Lord's bit.[13] By many conversations you laid bare my thoughts; by many arguments you treated the wounds of my heart. You saw that my soul was full of illusions,[14] and you wanted to cut away the phantasies of my presumption like gangrene, using, as well as you could, the keenest knives of argument, the flaming cauterization of admonition, and the soothing salve of exhortation. But when, in forcing me to a love of reading, you frequently asked whether I had read the books that you yourself had given me to read, like sick people who are forced by physicians to take food they find distasteful, I was compelled by shame to taste finally some few passages from your letters.

9. The harm from my fasting had already begun to displease me when it suddenly came about that I was bound by a very strong affection of the mind for a certain holy and venerable man. Involved in friendship with him, when I weighed with my mind all the emotions of his heart, I recognized and strongly loved my own defect in him. In fact I congratulated myself at having found someone as a rival of the highest authority and merit who sighed with a love of the same leisure. But my conscience was caressed by empty joys insofar as, comparing myself, a bad tree, with that fruitful one,[15] I rejoiced because I had found in him something like my barrenness. For I was boasting over the similarity of the leaves, not seeing the great fruits of the virtues by which that good

9. See Terence, *The Eunuch* (*Eunuchus*) 222-224.
10. See Lactantius, *Divine Instructions* (*Divinae institutiones*) VII, 3.
11. See Ps 68:18.
12. See Ovid, *Letters of Heroines* (*Epistulae Heroidum*) IV, 46.
13. See Ps 32:9.
14. See Ps 38:8.
15. See Mt 7:17.

tree was bent over. Resting upon that man with all the force of my weakness, I shoved away all the medicines that you used, and I spit out all the potions that you gave me to drink. For what seemed most attractive to me, what seemed imbued with a tempting sweetness beyond all else, was that I should always hear my desire being praised by the lips of that most holy friend and that the words of that venerable man might utter what my accursed heart kept pondering.

10. By such conversation we were scratching each other's itch in that we maintained that nothing is more useless, nothing is more dangerous, than the desire for knowledge. We said that nothing was as useless as that a desire for such vainglory should attract a Christian man so that, corrupted by the vices of the Pharisees, he would arrogantly long *to be called Rabbi by human beings* (Mt 23:7). And though he himself has perhaps been blinded by the light of intelligence, he nonetheless tries to attract all the others, who will undoubtedly fall into the pit,[16] especially since scripture declares that there are very profound questions that ought not to be investigated at all and that one who studies snakes will be bitten by a serpent.[17]

11. But what is more dangerous than that, though one could attain life without so great a detour through useless leaning, a person would undertake the meandering of a long and arduous journey from which no one as yet has emerged unscathed, because he has been aroused by the unhealthy goads of an illicit curiosity? What else, after all, did Origen,[18] the greatest of all the commentators, obtain by virtue of his untiring labor but that he should pass over, as a result of the vice of his long investigation, the salvation through the Word which is near at hand and dwells in our heart and on our lips,[19] and should meet with the same misfortune as those who were knowledgeable with respect to grace, who withdrew further from it the more zealously and laboriously they pursued wisdom? Finally, if the desire for learning had not driven this same man to these illicit studies in which he fell, he could certainly have merited the glory of martyrdom, but because he fell into the pit of senseless learning[20] when he wandered off too far, it inevitably came about that the old man refused the reward of martyrdom that he desired when he was unlearned and an infant.[21] What teacher of the law, then, clung to the pursuits of learning more vigorously, more learnedly, more attentively, more prudently, and more cautiously than Origen, or who,

---

16. See Mt 15:14.
17. See Eccl 10:8.
18. Origen, perhaps the greatest of the Eastern theologians, was born in Alexandria c. 185 and died in Tyre c. 254. Toward the end of the fourth century various views of Origen were found suspect or even heretical, and still later some of the positions attributed to him were condemned. Consentius' view that Origen was not saved is extreme.
19. See Jn 1:14; Rom 10:8.
20. See Eccl 10:8.
21. See Eusebius, *Ecclesiastical History* VI,2.

supposing that vain curiosity might find salvation by its laborious research, will by wisdom escape the death into which Origen unwisely rushed?

12. Let us recall in order the other commentators, however great, however Catholic they are. Yet it is difficult not to notice some stains of error in the body of their works, as beautiful as they may be. For, even though we said that Bishop Augustine writes works beyond reproach, we still do not know what judgment posterity will pronounce on his books. After all, no one criticized in their life-time all the authors of heretical perversity and especially Origen, who there is no doubt was condemned after two hundred or more years.[22] In the clutches of such arguments our inactivity held us bound, and it suggested the salve of such words for the fires of our love.

13. In the meanwhile I was reading, though unwillingly, the works I had received and, like that young man I mentioned before from the comedy, embracing my beloved in my heart, but in my madness I left, wandering now here and now there, the path of reading that I had taken up. And while I was passing through fields full of the fruits of my holy father and my mind was blinded in its madness, it yearned for the ardor of idleness alone until, stricken by the great force of my love, I turned my rapid steps to my ease and hurried by a very swift course to embrace leisure more vigorously, insofar as I was thinking of undertaking the labor of a long journey and seeking it even in the East. This is in fact the advice that my rival gave me, as fond of me as he is. But since we felt that the strong hand of the Lord was resisting our desires and efforts, I was somehow or other rescued from the proposed journey I had taken up and was brought back to myself with the resolution in mind to go through only the canon-ical books without wearing myself out, but to give up my writing, if possible, even of letters to friends. I kept to this resolution diligently for a short time and got through the canon in such a way that the love for leisure that I was cultivating was not impaired. But just as it helps very much to separate ourselves a little from the things that we love most in order that we might long for them more ardently when the strength of our desire has been renewed, so I too interrupted the pleasure of my leisure by devoting very brief and rare moments to reading. At the same time it happened that certain marvelous events took place among us by the command of the Lord. When the blessed prelate, the brother of Your Paternity, Bishop Severus,[23] along with the others who were present, reported

---

22. Origen was not officially condemned by a council of the Church until much later. See Augustine's *To Orosius in Refutation of the Origenists and Priscillianists* for some of the errors of which Origen was accused during the first Origenist controversy in the late fourth century.

23. Severus was bishop of Minorca early in the fifth century. He wrote a letter on the conversion of the Jews on his island after the relics of Saint Stephan were brought back from Jerusalem by Paul Orosius. Consentius seems to want to take credit for the letter, at least in part.

them to me, he attacked my proposal with the full strength of love and borrowed my words alone in order to write a letter containing the sequence of events. From this there developed a greater transgression of the rule that I had set for myself, and I decided that the slowness of our memory would be helped by a slow and leisurely but fresh reading of the canon in order that I might produce some weapons against the Jews for our governor, since we were being pressed by their attacks, with the provision, nonetheless, that my name absolutely not be mentioned in the work.

14. When I was dictating this letter and thinking of disclosing to you all the misguidedness of our will, the fluctuation of our thoughts, the attacks of our sins, our share of mishaps, the sequence of our life, our laziness in reading, and our rashness in writing, the courier suddenly demanded with strong insistence that I cut off everything immediately. Hence, breaking the very long thread of our discourse because silence has been imposed, I tie together everything with the knot of a few words, stating that I wanted to declare war upon my laziness,[24] but, in rashly taking up arms against my very lazy mistress, the only thing that I accomplished was that, like Hercules stripped of his strength, I subjected myself more deeply and more shamefully to my Omphala.[25] And finally, as if softened by a blow of a sandal,[26] I bowed my head to her seductive floggings in order that, like a stubborn slave, I might serve the more miserably and shamefully, the more fear subjects the conquered to the proud victors.

15. Some strange habit of my insanity has, however, driven me to write many works, and, if it were possible, I would have wanted all of them to come under the scrutiny of Your Paternity. But now I have kept the others here and sent you twelve chapters against the Jews and just one letter that I recently sent to your blessed brother, Bishop Patroclus.[27] When Your Paternity recognizes in it his own thoughts and words, let him extend to his son, who is following his father with smaller steps,[28] the loving right hand of kindness and favor, and let him graciously carry on the strong shoulders of his prayers my feeble infancy lest I fall. If I had the chance to have a messenger who could assume a trustworthiness for saying and discussing everything with you, I would especially have wanted to send to you, even unfinished, the works that I am venturing to write against the questions raised by Pelagius.

16. For last year there came to us the letter from Zosimus of holy memory, the bishop of the church of Rome, in which, after an examination of the questions of

---

24. See Horace, *Satires* (*Sermones*) I, 5, 8.
25. See Terence, *The Eunuch* (*Eunuchus*) 1027. Omphala was the queen of Lydia to whom Hercules made himself subject.
26. See Terence, *The Eunuch* (*Eunuchus*) 1028.
27. Patroclus was the bishop of Arles from 412 to 426.
28. See Virgil, *The Aeneid* II, 732-733.

Pelagius and Caelestius, we are shown how to avoid their deadly venom.[29] After I had read these, though I was encumbered by many worldly problems, I was nonetheless set ablaze by our usual passion for writing, and I labored to hammer out a fourth book, while still maintaining unwaveringly our rule of leisure, though we have at home as if under seal nearly everything that has been written against Pelagius. We also added a most powerful argument, upon which our laziness rests most of all. That is, we persuaded ourselves quite absurdly that we ought not to read all those things before we ourselves write something. In that way I have an incredible fear that the tortuous impulse of my mind may be led astray by the perversity of my judgment. But if one can believe authors who, like fathers, embrace with the greatest tenderness whatever they have begotten, however twisted and deformed, in my own eyes I seem to be fathering an Achilles, though in the eyes of others I am bringing forth a Thersites.[30] May you keep me in mind and prosper in Christ, my holy lord and most blessed father.

---

29. Zosimus was pope from March 417 to December 418; Consentius refers to his letter, called the *Tractoria*, issued in the summer of 418, in which he finally condemned the doctrine of Pelagius and Caelestius. The letter is now extant only in fragments, most of them found in the writings of Augustine.
30. See Ovid, *Letters from Pontus* (*Epistulae ex Ponto*) III, 9, 9-10; Juvenal, *Satires* (*Saturae*) VIII, 269-271. In the *Iliad* Thersites was a paradigm of ugliness while Achilles was a model of handsomeness.

Letter 13*

At an indeterminate date Augustine wrote to Restitutus, the same priest who is mentioned at the end of Letter 18*. Augustine offers Restitutus counsel on what to do about an unnamed priest who has been accused of misbehavior with a nun when he was a deacon. Augustine reports that he has questioned the man, and he recounts the man's version of the incident to Restitutus (paragraphs 1 and 2). Since there is no evidence against the priest except the words of the nun herself, Augustine refuses to condemn him. He notes the danger for clerics in going out alone. And, finally, he asks Restitutus to urge the people for whom the priest was ordained to continue to love him, as they had begun to do (paragraph 3).

A memorandum: Augustine to the priest Restitutus.

1. Although your letter deeply disturbed me concerning the wiles of the devil by which he either drives the servants of God into sin or ruins their reputation to the scandal of the Church, I nonetheless investigated, to the extent I could as a man, the mind of the man, dealing with him not once but often and terrifying him with God's judgment so that he would confess to me if by chance he had had intercourse or committed some impurity with the woman who accuses him. But if what he says is true, any great and holy man could have met with that temptation. He says that a woman came to him where he had gone to sleep by himself and that she lay down at his side and that he did not want to denounce her since she said nothing to him of any shameful desire but spoke only about her troubles and difficulties. In a temptation of that sort he thought that he had nothing to do but to prevent her by all means from drawing close to him, and, if she refused to comply, he would resist any impure embrace and scandalous conversation.

2. He says that he did this. He was sleeping on a terrace apart from all those who were residing in the house where he had been received as guest. He was present there on account of the demands of his office, and he was prevented by reason of nightfall from being able to return from there to his own home. When he had awakened and was shocked at her coming to him, as he says, a woman whom he believed had not yet fallen but who he saw could fall, he took care that she would not fall on his account and that he would not by an inconsiderate outcry ruin the reputation of a nun who was perhaps not yet lost. He allowed her to remain at his side and to murmur some complaints or other about her parents, while he held himself back from her and said nothing in reply to her but that she should get up and go away. She refused for a somewhat longer time. Then it rained, and in that way he was freed from her company when he came down from the terrace, went out of the house, and situated himself before the door under the awning. There the woman did not dare to approach lest she be discovered by one

287

of her own people as he was going out or be noticed opening the door and, if she did not return, be suspected by those who noticed that she had gone out.

3. This much the man admitted to me, and I judge that he should not be condemned for this unless perhaps he be proved guilty of a lie. The words of that woman should not be listened to and accepted against him because, fallen as she is, she is undoubtedly looking for a man to attach herself to, and there need to be some other proofs by which any scandalous sin on his part would be disclosed. But these things would not have happened so easily to clerics if they did not go out alone because of their own or the Church's needs. But since we scarcely get the priests, especially in the country, to avoid going out alone, how much less can we get clerics of a lower rank to avoid this! If, then, the people for whom he was ordained are in no way upset by this rumor against him and have not believed anything shameful about him, and if there is no proof of scandal from other evidence, as I said, let him remain in his state. But if other things are revealed about which we can pronounce some judgment, I would like to know them. If, however, the church for which he was ordained a priest is disturbed over this matter, because it is said to have occurred when he was still a deacon, read this letter to them and explain it to them, as the Lord gives you the ability, in order that they may love, as they began to, their priest, who met with the sort of temptation that any holy man could have met with. And let their love toward him not grow cold in order that the devil, from whom these wiles and snares usually stem, may be defeated by their peaceful behavior. If, however, you see that it is necessary that I send a letter to them, take care to let me know it.

Letter 14*

In October 419 Augustine wrote to Dorotheus, a Catholic layman and landowner in the neighborhood of Thagaste in Numidia. Augustine tells Dorotheus that his reputation as a Christian and as the head of a Christian family is well known (paragraph 1). Augustine informs him that he has a complaint about one of Dorotheus' men but that he will not disclose the man's name or his crime until he has Dorotheus' promise not to punish him more severely than is proper and fitting to punish someone because of a bishop's complaint (paragraph 2). Letter 15* reveals the name of the man who has been complained about and provides details about the nature of the complaint.

To his excellent lord and rightly distinguished and honorable son, Dorotheus, Augustine sends greetings in the Lord.

1. I know how much you love Christ, and all of us who know you know that your whole house is his family and, as the apostle says, *a household church* (Rom 16:5), and how you want the possessions of Christ to bear fruit and to grow in your possessions, my excellent lord and rightly distinguished and honorable son.

2. I had reason to complain about one of your men, though I have not dared to make known to you by this letter either his name or his sacrilegious crime lest perhaps you become more seriously angry and punish him more severely than is proper or necessary because of a bishop's complaint. And so I have revealed by a memorandum: to these brothers from whom Your Excellency is receiving this letter what the issue was. And I asked that they first obtain the most trustworthy promise of Your Reverence that you will not punish him more than I indicated in the same memorandum and that, when they have your promise, they should give it to you to read. If you are unwilling to make the promise, however, they should reveal nothing. But I beg you by Christ rather to make the promise so that we can confidently bring to you whatever our pastoral care demands so that you may correct it if we cannot.

Letter 15*

In October 419 Augustine wrote to certain unnamed clerics in Thagaste. He explains that a memorandum from Alypius, the bishop of Thagaste, who we know from other sources was at the time on a mission in Italy, had arrived with the ship used for the mail (paragraph 1). Augustine quotes from the memorandum, in which Alypius indicates the progress he has made in obtaining pardon for some Carthaginians and explains that he is still awaiting the arrival of an important personage in order to bring his business to completion (paragraph 2). The rest of the letter concerns the misconduct of Cresconius, about whom, without mentioning his name, Augustine had written to Dorotheus in Letter 14*. From the present letter we find out that Cresconius, a married man and a supervisor of Dorotheus' estate, had raped a nun who came to the estate to work with the wool (paragraph 3). Augustine here explains how he believes that Cresconius, who has been excommunicated, should be further punished by being removed from his position as supervisor, although he hopes that Dorotheus will not punish him with excessive severity (paragraph 4).

A memorandum: Augustine to the holy brothers whose names my letter contains.

1. After our letter to be sent to Your Benevolence was already finished, a memorandum came from Brother Alypius that he addressed to Thagaste, since the same ship used for the mail was driven into our harbor. I have taken care that Your Holiness knows what we learned from that memorandum, inserting the words of the same memorandum into this letter of mine.

2. A memorandum of Alypius to his priests.

Our son Severian has left us. We were still waiting for the reply of the highly placed man and his arrival, because it was announced by those who stated that he had most certainly left Gaul that he would be here by the Ides of October. And so, may the prayers of Your Charity assist us in order that with the help of the Lord we may accomplish something before winter, so that, by the Lord's aid and in accord with both your desire and mine, we may return to you before winter. Much has already been granted as a result of our letter, to be sure. For on the day we dictated this a silentiary departed with the pardon sent to the people of Carthage. It remained, therefore, for us to deal with the people who took refuge in the church of Carthage for the same reason.

3. These are the extracts from the memorandum sent to Thagaste that I thought were necessary to copy and send to you. In addition, I ask that you graciously give the other letters that I sent to those to whom they were addressed and to give those letters your backing in interceding before them, each as he can. For, if you all want to do everything at the same time, it will be difficult for you to accomplish what you want, because it is extremely rare that you are all free at a

single time. I wrote to the honorable and pious man, our son Dorotheus,[1] that he should not be angry at his man, who brutally violated a nun who came from another village to do woolworking, so that he punishes him more severely than is proper on account of our complaint. For it is sufficient that he should remove him from the supervision of the place where he put him so that he may not tempt others to imitate himself if he goes completely unpunished. He in fact is already doing penance, but this is precisely because, after he was proven guilty and was obliged because of his conviction to make a confession of what he had done, he was immediately forbidden communion. For, if he had willingly confessed and had revealed out of fear of God's judgment what was not known and what no one had accused him of, who would have been so misguidedly severe as to seek a further correction?

4. But now, just as he would lose the honor of his rank if he were a cleric, so this man also ought to lose the honor of his position as procurator, in which his impunity is inflated with pride, and for this reason we must take care that he not have any imitators. This man, however, is Cresconius, the procurator of Spanish Defile,[2] who has a wife, a factor that adds to the seriousness. But do not reveal either the action or its author unless you have first obtained the promise of Dorotheus, with God as his witness, that he will not punish him further, and do not specify the manner of punishment before he has promised that he will not do anything with greater severity than what he shall have found in this memorandum. For he, given the faith and piety that he has in Christ, although he could be very upset. . . .[3] Surely, if he is willing to punish more leniently than I had asked, without any consideration of corporeal punishment, I do not forbid it, but he should not be more severe. Let him promise this first, then, and after he has promised, without going out of your way to explain it, make him read the part of this memorandum that pertains to the issue.

---

1. The addressee of Letter 14*.
2. Saltus Hispaniensis was in the diocese of Hippo, undoubtedly the same place mentioned in Letter 35.
3. The sentence is incomplete in the Latin text.

Letter 16*

Shortly before or after December 419 Augustine wrote to Aurelius, the bishop of Carthage and his long-standing friend. Augustine sends Aurelius two sermons he has written and asks him for any news he may have concerning Alypius and those who are with him, who are at the imperial court in Italy (paragraph 1). Augustine mentions that he has seen a memorandum from Alypius but has heard from more recent messengers of a concession granted to Largus, though he does not know whether it is something distinct from what Alypius' memorandum contained (paragraph 2). He hopes for further news from Aurelius, mentions the action that Pope Boniface has taken against the Pelagians, and urges Aurelius to send his circular letter to the primate of Numidia (paragraph 3).

To Bishop Aurelius, his most blessed lord, holy brother, and fellow priest worthy of reverence with due love, Augustine sends greetings in the Lord.

1. Since no reliable occasion has presented itself, I have sent by means of our . . .[1] two sermons, one on the birth of the Lord, the other on the Epiphany, which I thought I could furtively take from all the work I must do. I ask that you graciously accept the homage of our greeting and continue to pray for us. Of course you do this even if we do not ask or encourage you to do it, most blessed lord and holy bishop worthy of reverence with due love. I ask that we may know by means of this courier what Your Holiness might perhaps have learned concerning the brothers whose return from the imperial court we await.

2. But because the same ship touched our shoreline, we have learned from a memorandum of Brother Alypius, which he sent to Thagaste, that a silentiary has already been sent with the pardon for Carthage, and he said that he had obtained this by letter. For that most illustrious man has not yet returned from Gaul, and Alypius indicated that only this point of business still awaited his presence, namely, that those who had taken refuge in the church should also be relieved of fear. But I believe that Your Reverence could have already learned something certain about these people as well. For more recent messengers were present here who reported to us, by means of a certain bishop of Numidia named Renatus, that Brother Alypius sent a copy of the concession that they said was already granted to our son Largus. But I do not know whether it was what he reported in his memorandum to Thagaste that was sent by means of the silentiary or something else that he obtained for those who are in the church, but I think that the bishop I mentioned could have already arrived in Carthage.

---

1. The name of the courier is not given.

3. And so we look forward to learning something certain about this, by means of the young man whom we have sent with this letter, from the reply of Your Beatitude. But since he himself has reported this to us, I do not doubt that Your Holiness had already heard from the old man, the bishop of Mauritania Caesariensis, Priscus, what the venerable Pope Boniface has done at Rome regarding the Pelagians and of the salutary severity he used. I do not know, however, why the encyclical of Your Beatitude has not arrived in parts of our Numidia, that is, Proconsular Numidia. I know that it was sent when I was still present in Carthage, unless it was perhaps thought that it should not be sent to the elderly Valentine. I suggest that Your Reverence investigate this and that you correct this if it was an oversight. For the letter ought also to be delivered to the primate of Numidia, who should send it on to the brothers who belong to the same council.

Letter 17*

The present letter is from Augustine to Boniface, who had two careers in Africa, first as military tribune between 423 and 427 and then as count of Africa between 429 and 432. In this letter, which probably dates from the earlier period, Augustine tells Boniface of some persons who were on their way to him (namely, Boniface) but whom a violent storm drove to Hippo instead; they barely managed to escape with their lives after losing all their possessions (paragraph 1). Augustine assures Boniface of his own good health and tells him that his good reputation gives glory to God (paragraph 2).

To his excellent lord and rightly distinguished and most beloved son, Boniface, Augustine sends greetings in the Lord.

1. The chance to greet Your Charity was given me, which I know is most gratifying to you, when the people who had to hasten on to you were driven to our shore. Observing in their case, then, the mercy that one human being owes another and their love for you, we welcomed these men who were nearly shipwrecked, and we supplied them with what they needed as best we could. They were severely tossed about and put in danger by the violence of the sky and the sea, and they barely escaped death, having lost all their possessions.

2. And so, my excellent lord and rightly distinguished and most beloved son, we report to Your Sincerity that by God's mercy we are in good health and that we hear and always desire to hear nothing but good about you. For your most excellent reputation gives glory to him in whom you place your hope, whom you fear, worship, and love, and whose eternal peace you seek, even in actions of war, provided you keep the faith and love righteousness in all things.

Letter 18*

Sometime during his episcopate Augustine wrote to the people of Memblibanum, a town in Numidia whose location cannot be further identified. Augustine tells the people that he cannot give them Gitta as their priest, as they had requested. In fact their request occasioned the discovery that he should not even have been a deacon on account of his acts of impurity with a woman (paragraph 1). Augustine therefore urges the people to look for a man whom he can ordain as their priest and promises to provide someone if they cannot find one (paragraph 2). After all, just as farmers do not cease from planting because some seeds do not sprout, neither should we give up on clerics because some of them do not turn out well. Hence Augustine urges the addressees of his letter to keep their eyes on eternal life rather than on the scandals of this life (paragraph 3).

Bishop Augustine sends greetings in the Lord to the church that is at Memblibanum.

1. It was quite quickly evident, as I told those of you who were with me at Unapompei, that you ought not to ask for Gitta as priest, since I was very concerned about his manner of life. But God was bringing about by means of you something you did not know. For, at the occasion which you provided, this same man was also removed from the clergy of the church of Unapompei, where he was a deacon, because, being the sort of man he was shown to be, he ought not even to have been a deacon. For, if some of those things that the woman said of him are true, the situation has been taken care of, but if she committed perjury and the only thing that is true in his regard is what he himself admitted, he still cannot be a cleric, because all Christians—and clerics even more so—ought to refrain not only from illicit intercourse but also from illicit kisses, from illicit embraces, and from all impurity.

2. Since this man was, according to his own admission, found not to be pure in these matters, we necessarily had to remove him from the rank of the priesthood. May the Lord console you, for we are very sad because of your sadness. May he, therefore, console all of you by the mercy of him who has gathered you together and rescued you from the dominion of the devil, because he will not abandon you if you do not abandon him. Look for someone, therefore, who might be ordained a priest for you, or, if you do not find someone, we will provide one in the name of the Lord and by his help.

3. After all, are people slow to plant seeds because not all seeds begin to grow, but ants carry some off, while the birds gather others, and still others perish for different reasons?[1] Or are they slow to plant fruit trees because not all take hold

---

1. See Mt 13:24-27.

or come to bear fruit, but the saplings of some dry up, the animals gnaw at others, and still others perish for different reasons? So we do not cease to work in the Church, which is like the field of a great landowner, but it is up to God to give the increase,[2] because, even if all do not make progress and persevere up to the end, the Lord nonetheless, as the apostle says, *knows those who are his* (2 Tm 2:19). He foretold the coming of all these scandals that cause us sadness. He warned that we should not give up, and he promised to us who persevere with his help a reward so that we may live there with him for eternity where there cannot be such trials and such scandals, because there will be no sadness there but only joy and the certain security of everlasting joys, blessed immortality, and happiness without end. Place your hope, then, in him, my sons and brothers, and let your love not grow cold, in order that you may be found to be persons of proven virtue on the last day. For on account of that day you became Christians through the grace of him who redeemed you by his blood.[3] With this letter I have sent you the priest Restitutus. I found it difficult to console him, since he was suffering from a greater sadness. But may the Lord also console you by him, just as he was consoled by me.

---

2. See 1 Cor 3:6.
3. See Rv 5:9.

Letter 19*

In the summer of 416 Augustine wrote to Jerome of Bethlehem. He tells Jerome of the different ways in which he has received news of him and informs him of various writings of his that he is sending to him (paragraph 1). He says that he has heard of the positive influence that Jerome's work against the Pelagians has had at the imperial court. He mentions his own work and expresses his hope that Pelagius may still give up his error and accept the truth (paragraph 2). Augustine explains how he came into possession of Pelagius' work, *Nature*, and how he replied to it in his own *Nature and Grace*, both of which he has sent to Jerome (paragraph 3). Finally, he alludes to another letter that he wrote in reply to Pelagius and also several letters to Eastern clerics (paragraph 4).

To Jerome, his lord, who is rightly honorable in the heart of Christ, his holy brother and fellow priest, Augustine sends greetings in the Lord.

1. By means of our son, my fellow citizen, the deacon Palatinus,[1] I received the letter of Your Holiness along with another letter that you kindly sent by means of the holy priest Lazarus.[2] But I had already received news of you, both earlier from our son, the priest Orosius,[3] from whom I learned many things, and a few days ago from another letter of yours sent by means of the priest Innocent.[4] By means of him I had already replied not only to Your Charity but also to others whose letters he brought me and to certain persons who had not written to me by means of him. And I asked him to carry to Your Holiness the necessary copies of my writings that I produced for him at the same time. In them I was not silent about what I thought should be said concerning the wicked error of certain persons by which the Church is upset to no small degree.

2. I certainly heard that the books you recently published against this same plague[5] have already arrived at the imperial court and that, as they have become known, the multitude of misguided people who were impudently defending such ideas has already begun to decrease, since Pelagius himself does not dare to defend such ideas openly but defends himself on the grounds that he does not hold them. For he arranged that his recent and brief defense of himself against

---

1. Palatinus was a deacon in Hippo.
2. Lazarus was one of the Gallic bishops who accused Pelagius at the Council of Diospolis; see *The Deeds of Pelagius* 1, 2.
3. Paul Orosius, a Spanish priest, had in 414 come to Augustine in Hippo, and Augustine sent him on in 415 to Jerome in Bethlehem, where Orosius was actively opposed to Pelagius. Early in 416 he returned to Augustine. Orosius is best known for his *Seven Books of Histories against the Pagans*.
4. For Innocent as courier, see Letters 202 and 6*.
5. That is, Jerome's *Dialogues against the Pelagians* (*Dialogi contra Pelagianos*).

the opinions which the Gauls, as he writes, raised as objections[6] should also come into my hands. He denies that many of these opinions—and the serious ones—are his own, but he changes the sense of some of them by a dark shrewdness. It is therefore not insignificant that, thanks to the mercy of God, he himself does not dare now to defend openly those views that we feared were believed by the weak. For this reason I would not give up hope, since he is a human being, that he will at some point confess in sincere repentance that he has been involved in an impious error, my lord and holy brother who are rightly honorable in the heart of Christ.

3. Now, then, I have found the opportunity to use the servant of God, Luke, as a courier,[7] whom the deacon Palatinus has informed me is very well known to him, and he has promised that he will return as soon as possible and has assured me concerning him that we ought not to hesitate to hand over to him any letter to carry. By means of him I sent you the book of the same Pelagius that was given me by the servants of God, Timasius and James,[8] whom the Lord delivered from that error by my efforts. They were, however, most devoted disciples of his. I also sent the book by which I replied to it. For they had insistently asked this of me, and I had foreseen that this would be useful and salutary for them. Of course I wrote to them, not to Pelagius, but I was replying to his work and words without as yet mentioning his name, since I desired that he be corrected as a friend, something that I still desire, and I do not doubt that Your Holiness desires it as well.

4. Finally, I have now also written for him something that, unless I am mistaken, he will receive with bitterness, but perhaps later it will profit him toward salvation. I have as well written a long letter concerning him to Bishops Eulogius and John[9] and briefly to the priest Passerion.[10] I ordered that all these be brought to Your Sincerity. But whatever opportunity next comes along for me, I will take care, with the help of the Lord, to send copies of all the same letters signed by my hand to Your Fraternity in order that you may know and write back to me not only whether they were all delivered to you but whether they arrived whole and without error.

---

6. See Letter 179, 7. The Gauls in question are the bishops, Hero and Lazarus, who had rather feebly attacked Pelagius at the Council of Diospolis.

7. On Luke as courier, see Letter 179, 1.

8. Timasius and James, who were once disciples of Pelagius but were instructed by Augustine and brought around to the correct doctrine on grace, gave Augustine a copy of Pelagius' work, *Nature*, which Augustine responded to in *Nature and Grace*. See Letter 168 from Timasius and James to Augustine.

9. Eulogius of Caesarea and John of Jerusalem were both present at the Council of Diospolis. See Letter 179 to John of Jerusalem. For Eulogius, see *Answer to Julian* I, 5, 19 and 7, 32.

10. For Passerion, see Orosius, *Defense against the Pelagians* (*Liber apologeticus contra Pelagianos*) 6 and 7.

Letter 20*

In the fall of 422 or the winter of 422-423, Augustine wrote to Fabiola, a Roman laywoman, to whom he had written Letter 267. The present letter throws further light on Augustine's problems with Antoninus of Fussala, the young bishop about whom Augustine had written Letter 209 to Pope Boniface. Augustine thanks Fabiola for her response and asks her forgiveness for bothering her with his troubles by this letter (paragraph 1). He also thanks Fabiola for welcoming Antoninus and narrates the early life of the young man, his entrance into the monastery, and his ordination to the priesthood (paragraph 2). He explains how Antoninus came to be made bishop of Fussala when the man whom Augustine had originally wanted backed out at the last moment (paragraph 3). He tells how Antoninus, who was in his early twenties and quite inexperienced, began to use his episcopal power so that he was feared rather than loved (paragraph 4). Antoninus ordained to the priesthood a renegade monk and made another monk his deacon, both men like himself (paragraph 5). With these men and a few others Antoninus robbed and plundered the people of Fussala, even helpless widows (paragraph 6). The lists of their crimes are so long that there is not a sufficient number of judges to hear the cases (paragraph 7). Augustine explains the penalties imposed upon Antoninus, namely, that he was removed from Fussala and assigned to another parish in his diocese and that he was excommunicated until he made restitution for the properties he had stolen (paragraph 8).

Antoninus tried to appeal these decisions but did so too late. He then asked to have, along with the other communities assigned to him, the estate of Thogonoetus, which was very close to Fussala (paragraph 9). The mistress of the estate and her workers all protested having Antoninus present in their community (paragraph 10). When Antoninus saw that he was not going to get what he wanted, he set sail to lodge a complaint with Pope Boniface, though he did not disclose that he had been excommunicated at least briefly (paragraph 11). Boniface appointed judges to hear the case, and the bishops gathered in Tegulata, where Antoninus demanded that the church of Fussala be returned to him (paragraph 12). The priests and people of Fussala, however, made it clear by letter that they would never accept him back. Antoninus challenged the authenticity of the letter but agreed to accept Thogonoetus instead, if the people of Fussala did not want him back (paragraph 13). The people of Thogonoetus, however, were equally opposed to having him there (paragraph 14).

A delegation was sent to Fussala to ascertain the true attitude of the people, though Augustine himself did not go there because of the hostility of the people toward him (paragraph 15). The people of Fussala showed that they were even more strongly opposed to having Antoninus back than their letter had expressed (paragraph 16). Meanwhile Augustine received a letter from the mistress of Thogonoetus in which she denied that she had said that she was willing to accept Antoninus (paragraph 17). When the bishops returned to Tegulata to continue hearing the case, Augustine produced that letter from the mistress of Thogonoetus, and Antoninus gave another interpretation of the events (paragraph 18). Augustine, however, produced still another letter from the mistress of the estate that contradicted Antoninus's version of events (paragraph 19).

Because of further complaints from Antoninus it was decided to question the people of Fussala once again. Augustine meanwhile interceded with the primate of Numidia to restore the people of Thogonoetus to communion (paragraph 21). When questioned, the people of Thogonoetus complained of everything that they had suffered from Antoninus, though they did not want what they said to be recorded for fear of reprisals (paragraph 22). Meanwhile a message from the people of Fussala arrived in which they expressed similar concerns about being questioned again. The people of Fussala were questioned again, however, and records were kept, which the bishops brought back to Tegulata (paragraph 23). Antoninus was summoned to hear the decision of the bishops, including the primate. When told that he should be content with the communities assigned to him, he expressed his desire to go off alone and live as a servant of God, though he would not commit his plans to writing (paragraph 24). Once again, Antoninus insisted on being bishop in Fussala, at which point Augustine urged the primate to draw up proceedings that could be sent to the Apostolic See (paragraph 25).

Hence Augustine tells Fabiola that the bishops sent a letter and a copy of the proceedings to the Apostolic See, and he prays that all this disturbance may not result in the loss of the souls of those in Fussala who have recently been converted from Donatism (paragraph 26). Augustine counsels Fabiola on how she should provide for the needs of Antoninus's soul as well as those of his body and prays that Antoninus will be content to be a good bishop over the communities assigned to him (paragraph 27). He urges her to counsel Antoninus to seek the things of God rather than worldly power in the Church (paragraph 28).

Augustine adds that Antoninus, who became a bishop with only the clothes on his back, has managed to acquire property in his own name by various dishonest means (paragraphs 29 and 30). He used one property to make restitution to a man whose house he had plundered in order to build his own house in Fussala, and Augustine laments the fact that he still demands that house for himself (paragraph 31). He tells Fabiola of his concern for Antoninus, who is seeking not merely property for himself but also the people whom Christ has redeemed (paragraph 32). Hence Augustine begs Fabiola for her help with the whole problem so that Antoninus does not do further harm to himself (paragraph 33).

To his most devout lady and most revered and excellent daughter, Fabiola, Augustine sends greetings in the Lord.

1. I was overjoyed at the reply of Your Holiness, which came by means of my lord and brother. . . .[1] Would that I were repaying the word of greeting without annoying you. But now, first of all, tormented as I have been by my affliction, I have made myself unwelcome and troublesome to your holy repose, but tolerate

---

1. The name of the courier is missing.

me patiently. By progressing in that way, may you persevere in the grace of Christ up to the end.[2] I know that a letter from me is never a burden but rather a joy for you. Pardon this letter, for it has many things over which you will grieve; share my pains with me by mutual love in Christ; and add your prayers to the Lord our God that he may console us.

2. I have heard of the pious goodness with which you welcomed my beloved son and fellow bishop, Antoninus, and of the Christian kindness with which you eased his destitute travels. Learn, then, what I mean to Antoninus, what I owe to him, and what I ask of you. As a child he came to Hippo with his mother and stepfather; they were so poor that they lacked what they needed for daily sustenance. At length, when they had taken refuge in the church and I had discovered that the father of Antoninus was still alive and that his mother was united to another man after having been separated from her husband, I convinced both of them to lead lives of continence. And so all of them, he with the boy in a monastery and she in a home for the poor whom the Church supports, began in this way to live under our care by the mercy of God. Finally, as time went on—not to dwell on many events—he died, she grew old, and the boy grew up. Among his comrades he performed the office of lector and soon began to be viewed as a man of such qualities that Brother Urbanus (who at that time was a priest among us and superior of the monastery but is now bishop of the church of Sicca) wanted him, in my absence, to become a priest in a certain large estate situated in our diocese. For I had, when departing, given orders that he should find someone whom the neighboring bishop might ordain for that place without waiting for my return. This of course could not have been done if he had refused. Nonetheless, when I learned of this afterwards, I began to consider him as fit for such an office—not because I had come to know him as I ought to have but on account of the testimony of his superior.

3. Meanwhile, because I was not capable of governing, as the need demanded, a diocese that was so spread out, since many people not only in the city but also in the countryside had come over from the sect of Donatus, I decided, after having consulted with the brothers, that in a certain town called Fussala, which is subject to the see of Hippo, someone should be ordained as bishop, to whom the care of the region would fall. I sent a request to the bishop of the primatial see. He agreed to come. At the last moment the priest whom I thought I had ready disappeared. What ought I to have done at that point, if I were to do the right thing, but postpone such an important action? But I was afraid that, if the holy primate,[3] who had with great difficulty come to us from a distance, went back from us without accomplishing anything, the spirits of all those who needed the ordination to take place would be crushed and that there

---

2. See Mt 10:22; 24:13.
3. That is, Silvanus of Summa.

would be some people whom the enemies of the Church would begin to lead astray by mocking the failure of our action. Hence I believed it useful to present for ordination the man who was there, because I had heard that he also knew the Punic language. And when I presented him, they trusted me. After all, they did not ask for him on their own, but, as one of my men who was acceptable to me, they did not dare to reject him.

4. I introduced to such a great burden, then, a youth not much more than twenty years old, who had not been proven in any tasks of the clerical ranks and who was unknown to me in those respects that ought to have been known about him beforehand. You see, of course, my great mistake; look at what ensued. Not having merited anything by previous service, the soul of the young man was seized with awe and suddenly swept away by the honor of the episcopacy. Then, seeing that the clergy and people were subject to him, as the affair itself reveals, he was puffed up with the arrogance of power, and, teaching nothing verbally but compelling people to everything by his power, he was happy to be feared when he saw that he was not loved.

5. To carry out this role, he sought men of his own kind. There was in our monastery a certain former secretary who, much to my distress, did not turn out well. Subjected to a beating by the superior of the monastery because he was found conversing alone with certain nuns at an inappropriate hour, he was considered a scoundrel. He abandoned the monastery, and, as soon as this fellow presented himself to the bishop under discussion, he was ordained a priest by him, without consulting me and without my knowledge. For I heard that the deed was done before I could have believed it possible, even if I had been informed by someone whom I ought to have believed. But I wish that you would believe the great sorrow that filled my heart, because I feared the destruction of that church which he would one day bring about, for I cannot describe it. When I found the opportunity, because the same bishop himself presented to me serious complaints about the sort of person that his priest was, I tried to have him excommunicated and returned to his native land, from which he had been given to me. And it happened—but I do not know how, and again without my having been consulted—that Antoninus restored him to his communion and friendship. He also created another deacon, following the correct procedure, who was given to him from our monastery, but he was not seen as troublesome until he was a deacon.

6. Anyone whom it would not disgust to read the records can easily learn what evils that town and the surrounding region suffered because of these two clerics, the priest and the deacon, and because of the defender of the church[4] and a

---

4. The defenders of the church (*defensores ecclesiae*) were advocates who, by a decree of the Emperor Honorius in 407, were given the task of being legal representatives of the Church and of defending its interests. See S. Lancel, "L'affaire de Antoninus de Fusala," in *Les lettres de saint Augustin découvertes par Johannes Divjak* (Paris: Études augustiniennes, 1983), p. 277.

certain other man, a former soldier or deserter, to whom he gave orders as friends, and because of those men from the same town whom he made into guards for night watches and whom he used when there was need of a slightly larger number. These records were compiled before the bishops in the church of Hippo, where I myself presided, after many people with lists of grievances had complained. Anyone will find in them the pitiful complaints of men and women and—what is worse—of widows, whom neither their name, which holy scripture especially recommends to our defense,[5] nor even their elderly age could protect to some extent from the robberies, plunderings, and unspeakable injustices that those people committed. Whoever fell into their hands lost money, furniture, clothing, cattle, harvests, timber, and even building stones. The homes of some were occupied; those of others were torn down in order that what the construction of new buildings demanded might be carried off from there. At times they made purchases but did not pay the price. The fields of some were invaded and were returned after the harvests had been seized over the course of several years, but some of them were retained and occupied up to the time of the episcopal judgment.

7. Besides the facts that are recorded in the judicial proceedings we have come to know many things from a different source, and on the lands of those who suffered them they are spread about not by the groans of grumbling people but by the outcries of screaming mobs, and they are piled up waiting to be proved, if judges would hold court where the small number of them would not be exhausted or where even those who do hold court might be sufficient to hear all the cases. For hardly anyone would endure the review of these cases that we have heard about from the ecclesiastical proceedings. Of these a very small number were settled somehow or other, but many were set aside or postponed in part because of the absence of those who committed the acts. It would, however, take a long time to say how the appearance of those clerics, that is, of the priest and the deacon, was kept from and is still kept from the episcopal tribunal. Yet we do have the words of the bishop [i.e., Antoninus] in which he himself admitted that they were warned by him to come because they were with him and that they had wanted to come.

8. We, however, commanded the restitution of what they plundered, but we left to the bishop the full and complete possession of his episcopacy. But, so that those evils might not remain unpunished and be left either for him to continue or for others to imitate, we imposed punishment to this extent: that the bishop would indeed sit on one of his seats—in order that he might not be said to have been transferred contrary to the canons into another see—but that he would no longer preside over the people of Fussala against their will. I think that this kind of punishment should even have been considered a benefit for him insofar as he

5. See 1 Tm 5:3.

would not be living with those whose most bitter hatred his very presence would most dangerously exacerbate. We of course judged that he should be deprived of communion until he had first restored what he had taken. He himself embraced this sentence of ours to the point that he did not appeal and within a few days paid with borrowed gold coins for the goods he had stolen in order that he might no longer be denied communion. And many of our brothers and sons had, along with us, taken pity on him because he was acquitted, and quite probably justly, of four grave and capital charges of adultery. It was not the people of Fussala but other people whom he harmed, who on some grounds had raised these charges against him and had caused them to be raised against him. And so these brothers and sons of ours were delighted with fraternal joy that such a judgment had been rendered concerning him.

9. He also asked by a petition that the holy primate of the primatial see in Numidia[6] graciously postpone until the council the desire of the people of Fussala by which they most ardently demanded that a bishop be ordained for them, and he postponed it. When it had been convened and all who were present decided to implement our decisions, he did not appeal against them. And if he had done so, he would certainly have done so too late, since he had not appealed against our decisions several months before. Then our superior, the primate, sent bishops to Fussala in whose presence the faithful would choose by votes who would be ordained bishop for them and would be sent to them for ordination, and that was done. But when the day of ordination dawned, then the idea of appealing entered his mind. Yet he remained quiet after the holy primate had given him an explanation, and, because he was appealing such a long time after judgment had been passed concerning him, he understood that he was appealing in vain, and he agreed that eight communities, which for some reasons had not come to the church of Fussala to vote for the ordination of a bishop, should be assigned to him. But, in order to sow discord once again,[7] he obtained by his insistence that it be added to the letter of the holy primate that one community should also be given to him from those which had come to Fussala to ask for a bishop, namely, the estate of Thogonoetus, where he might have a seat to which his others would be subject.

10. This estate, however, was so close to the town that it seemed that he was seeking nothing in it but occasions for quarrels by which to disturb the peace of the church. Then, since the same tenant farmers had already had experience of him from nearby and had borne those evils with the others, they wrote to the mistress of the property that, if she permitted this to take place, they would immediately move away, and they likewise wrote to me that I should intervene

---

6. That is, Aurelius of Macomades.
7. See Prv 6:19.

on their behalf in order that this would not take place. On their account she and I wrote to the primate.

11. When Antoninus saw that he was not going to be granted this, then, he thought that he should set sail, carrying a letter of recommendation from the same superior, the primate, not one that he had received at that time, but one that he had received before, when that grave man had naively believed that he had absolutely no guilt and had wanted to set sail in order to obtain the release of persons whom the vicar of Africa held prisoner. At that time he had not clearly come to know from the church records the woes of the people of Fussala and their righteous sorrow. Antoninus, therefore, gave a formal complaint to the venerable Pope Boniface in which he stated falsely that he had remained in communion from the time that judgment had been pronounced concerning him—for, as I mentioned above, he had been excommunicated until he returned the goods that he had taken from the people of Fussala. On this account he had paid the gold coins after only a few days, of course, but still after some days, so that he might be restored to communion. He also passed over in silence the whole sequence of events that was necessary in order to understand the case, and he obtained from the pope a letter that was clearly very tentative.

12. For Pope Boniface of venerable memory assigned judges to learn whether the explanation he gave was supported by the facts, whether he had faithfully reported the sequence of events, and whether the facts were such as he had set them forth in the text of his complaint. Only then would the church of Fussala be returned to him as to someone having no sins for which it would justly have been taken from him. Those who were able to come assembled in a certain place in Numidia, that is, in the church of Tegulata. Other bishops were also present there whom Antoninus had not asked for and who had other reasons for coming, and though the number of bishops that he had demanded had not appeared, he nonetheless said that they were enough for him. We were also present, that is, Brother Alypius and I, alerted by the letter of the primate, not in order that we might pronounce judgment on him again—after all, what could be worse than that?—but in order that we might give an account of our judgment, if the situation demanded. All this was to be referred to the Apostolic See. After the complaint that Antoninus brought was read out, the primate of Numidia, the elderly Aurelius,[8] explained the reason why he had ordained a bishop for the people of Fussala.[9] In his explanation it became clear what Antoninus had omitted in order to obtain from Rome such a letter and that he had not faithfully reported the sequence of events.

13. Then Bishop Antoninus asked that the priest whom the people of Fussala had sent be brought in. When he entered, the letter of the priests and of the people

---

8. That is, Aurelius of Macomades.
9. That is, Antoninus' successor.

of Fussala was read out. When he saw that it was full of pitiful complaints
against him, on account of which they were refusing by every means to accept as
bishop a man from whom they had been justly and rightly freed, he refused to
believe that the letter was sent by them and asked the holy primate that, with
some bishops from the number of those who had been granted him, he himself
would deign to visit those places and explore the attitudes of the priest and the
people under the following condition. If the people of Fussala raised a protest
about taking him back, he would accept the community of Thogonoetus added to
those eight communities that he had already had before, and the holy primate
would also ask me to give him a confirmation by entering into the records the
promise concerning those five communities that I had already made him apart
from the proceedings so that he would not act with hostility toward the people of
Fussala.

14. After I had done this without any difficulty, we parted as if in peace,
except for the fact that I saw that the locality of Thogonoetus was resisting him
no less than the people of Fussala and that the mistress of the property would not
agree to this, something that the venerable primate Aurelius also saw. Finally,
the primate promised in the proceedings, as he had been asked, that he would
come to Fussala, but no one promised Thogonoetus to Antoninus in those
proceedings. The declaration of the same bishop, Antoninus, was to the effect
that the bishops should recognize from the response of the people of Fussala
what ought to be done.

15. After some days, as had been decided, they came to Fussala; there were
present with the primate two bishops whom Antoninus asked for from those who
had been in the city,[10] and those were also granted him whom he was able to find
closer to the same town. Another three also accompanied the primate out of
respect, as is usually done. I myself was absent, because I do not dare to face the
people of Fussala. They were already at peace after having received a bishop in
accord with our judgment, and, now that they were again in turmoil on account
of the restlessness of this man, I myself have also become odious to them. They
no longer complain in hushed murmurs but shout out in clear cries and wailing
that I have brought a great disaster upon them, and Antoninus himself in his utter
ingratitude suspects nothing of me but that I am his enemy. Brother Alypius,
who had returned to his own town, was also absent.

16. And so, under the eyes of six bishops, that community, having assembled
quickly and in large numbers, was questioned and was found to have the same
disposition as when it had sent a letter to the church of Tegulata by a priest, and in
fact it was more vehement and bitter. It is not necessary to write what Antoninus
did in advance out of a desire to terrify them. He himself will perhaps admit it if
he is constrained, though these people who hand you our letter can also reliably

---

10. That is, Tegulata; see the following paragraph.

make it known to Your Reverence. After the crowd had been questioned and had expressed well enough in a single day what they thought of him, they most insistently demanded the presence of their own bishop, because he was not present either when the first interrogation was held. And so, after an interval of one day, with their bishop now present, they gave many answers in their own defense and against Antoninus and did much shouting, and everything was written down.

17. Then the primate wrote to me so that I would meet him at some place where all of us together might see what should be done. When I was traveling to that place, I received en route a letter of the illustrious lady who owns the estate of Thogonoetus. She informed me that her steward had written her that the holy primate said to him that he had heard from Bishop Antoninus that she had agreed to his being at Thogonoetus. "I know nothing about that," she said. "Rather, when he came to me, he himself asked that I not agree." I carried with me this letter from the pious woman since I saw that it was very necessary, although I had already learned that he acted in this way, but I did not see by what certain proof he could be shown to be guilty if he denied it in the absence of that honorable woman.

18. After we had assembled, then, at a certain place ten miles away from Fussala, to which I did not want to go, we all began to deal with him as each was able, in order that a Catholic bishop would not devise further trouble and ruin for Catholic Christians. And when it was a matter of the estate of Thogonoetus, I brought out the letter of the mistress of the property. After it was read, when all the brothers and our fellow bishops who were present began to be horrified and to reproach him gravely, he replied that he had not spoken in that way but that, when she first said that she would not grant him that place, he had said, not in the tone of a petitioner but in that of someone indignant, "If you do not want to, do not grant it, nor do I want it." From this we turned to other terms by which we were trying to bring it about, if possible, that he would accept two other places instead of that estate and that he would in the future be troublesome to no one from those communities that had already begun to belong to the bishop of Fussala. But this could not be done since they all rejected him most emphatically.

19. We were also in a certain place from among the eight that had been assigned to him and where he presided without any dispute. For the manager of that estate had asked that we meet, and we dealt with Antoninus on many issues, but in vain. There, in any case, I received another letter from the mistress of the estate of Thogonoetus, because I had written in reply to her what Antoninus had answered, and I had asked that she indicate by letter the order in which events had taken place. She wrote, however, that Antoninus had informed her by means of her son-in-law that he would ask her to do him the favor of not agreeing to his being at Thogonoetus nor to his being in its parish[11] if he was going to have his

---

11. The Latin word is *diocesi*, which in the context seems to have the meaning not of "diocese" but of "parish."

see as bishop anywhere else but in Fussala. And afterwards she confirmed from her own lips that he had asked this of her. She wrote with perfect clarity that not merely her son-in-law but also the bishop of the place where they were at that time were witnesses to this.

20. When this letter was read out in the presence of the brothers, Antoninus was so disturbed that he replied with nothing but abuse for me. And since the primate had said to me that he had complained that their bishop was present on the day when the people of Fussala were questioned for the second time, it was decided that the people be consulted a third time with that bishop absent, separating the tenant farmers of each area with the supervisors or procurators, but without the managers. But to get to Fussala it was necessary to pass through Thogonoetus, and I asked repeatedly that the primate restore its people to communion, because he had excommunicated them when they produced a serious disturbance in his presence against Bishop Antoninus. And I deeply feared that they might utterly perish because of their peasant despair. For between the two bishops they had been abandoned in such a way that I knew that they had begun to apostatize in some instances. For this reason I feared that this wound to my heart would increase, and I hastened to heal it as fast as I could.

21. Since we arrived there in the evening, we saw them gathered in the church on the next day. But when the venerable primate began to speak to them about Antoninus in the Punic tongue, they made known their will with great shouts, and when he asked them how the man had injured them to whom they were opposed with such great stubbornness, they began to say individually what they had suffered. When they were ordered to do this by name for the records, they replied that they were afraid that he would come to know them and would pursue and destroy them individually. But when they were ordered even more insistently to do what was said, all of them suddenly abandoned us and departed with very angry protests so that not even a single nun remained. Who could say how much we were all upset with the fear that, in the judgment of Christ, their loss would be tied around our neck as an object heavier than that millstone turned by an ass, of which the gospel speaks?[12] They were scarcely called back when the primate promised that he would do nothing that they would not want with regard to giving them a bishop.

22. And so, when we had left the church after celebrating the divine rites, we found that two inhabitants of Fussala had been sent with a dispatch in which they said that the rumor had reached them that we wanted to question them separately, although their will had already been made indisputably clear so often regarding whom they considered their bishop and that they were not individually going to say anything other than what they were all able to say together. But if this were being done in order that their enemy might know whom he ought to

---

12. See Mt 18:6; Mk 9:42.

pursue once their names were taken down, we should understand that they would be handing themselves over to death by this provision, and that it certainly ought to have been enough that we killed their souls by giving them to Antoninus without handing over their bodies so that they might die again at the hands of Antoninus. In the same dispatch they also set down that, if it seemed good to us, we should order their case to be heard again after the documents containing the charges against Antoninus that they had submitted at Hippo Regius were returned to them, as well as other things that it would take too long to mention. But because someone could say that the dispatch did not reflect the will of the people but was sent by one or by two or surely by only a very few, we decided that we should not change our plan of going to them.

23. Then the primate arrived at noon in Fussala with those who were required; their bishop and I remained in the same place.[13] But on the following day, when the primate questioned the people for the third time, we met him at a certain place through which he was going to pass on his way from there, and we spent the whole day there while he was situated in Fussala. After this, the bishops came from there to us along with the holy primate, carrying the written record of the groans and cries of the poor people, in which they did not think that even I was to be spared. For they also shouted about me things that I deserved to hear because I was the author of such a great disaster for them, since I had given them a man for whom they had not asked and who afflicted them with such great evils.

24. Then a letter was sent to the same Bishop Antoninus, and he met us in a certain town called Gilva, where the needs of the church required the primate to go. For Antoninus had left us with the proviso that he would meet us wherever he had been told to go by letter. When he had heard even from the very bishops, whom among others he had asked for as judges, what they had seen and heard in person, and after all of them tried to persuade him, as each was able to do, that he ought to do nothing else if he considered himself a bishop but to govern in peace the communities that had accepted him without any scandal to the Church and without any disturbance, he replied that they did not want to have him either and that he had the firm resolve to sit as bishop in some very remote place, at a distance from the crowds, away from hatred, and as a servant of God. He desired, if we were willing, to prove this even by witnesses to whom he said that he had told this before he saw us. Since I was unwilling to believe readily so favorable a disposition of mind in his regard, I said to him that, if he were sincerely thinking and saying such things, he should not hesitate to offer that sacrifice of mercy to our God whereby he would make his church secure by removing the fear that it had of him and by expressing this will of his in the episcopal records. And after he had said that he would state nothing for the records, we said that he should at least express it in his own writing. And after he answered that he would not do

---

13. That is, in Thogonoetus.

this either, he heard what he deserved, namely, that he was not sincerely thinking of being a servant of God, when he took pleasure in leaving in such an upheaval of fear the church of him whose servant he was going to be.

25. But then, when he saw that he was pressed by the words of the bishops to which he had not been able to reply, he blurted out at long last what he was hiding in his heart, and he said with a frightening countenance and voice that he could in no way be persuaded not to try somehow or other to return to the church of Fussala. After hearing that, I began to insist with the holy primate that, in accord with the records of the church of Tegulata, he should set something down in the ecclesiastical records that could be referred to the Apostolic See. He said, "I am not saying anything for the record," and in much agitation he got up and left, and, immediately returning in a distraught mood of body and soul, he announced that he would go to the Apostolic See, as if we were going to send to some other see whatever we accomplished with him in the records.

26. It remained, then, for the Apostolic See to be informed by sending a letter and the proceedings to it. We took care to do this with as much speed as possible. See what a long tale we have become for the Jews and the Gentiles,[14] for heretics and also for any who are our enemies within. May this be without the loss of those who have been set free from heresy and are already aspiring for some light of unity, for whom we are making the name Catholic something odious, if their weakness is not at least consoled to the point that they do not have as bishop the man whom they shout with righteous sorrow that they cannot have.

27. I thought, however, that I should write this to Your Excellency so that you might know how you ought to advise him if he comes to see you. You will, of course, do much better to give the poor fellow counsel for eternal life than sustenance for the present life. For he lacks much more dangerously the former alms, for want of which the heart dies[15] even if the flesh is unharmed. May he stop desiring to lord it over the members of Christ gathered together by the blood that others have shed. For, from the time he began to be bishop there, he suffered no losses or wounds from the Donatists—neither he himself nor any of his priests and clerics nor anyone placed under his authority. But in order that he might find such peace there, it is horrifying to state what sufferings our people have endured there. Let the communities that God wanted him to receive without scandal satisfy him, for governing even one of them with piety and care earns a great reward in God's eyes. But this man does not bear this in mind, for he desires to rejoice, with blasphemy to the name of Christ and with the dying groans of wretched human beings, over the number of his communities, not seeking to gain many persons for God but to boast of having many. Otherwise he

14. See Acts 19:17.
15. See Prv 10:21.

would not desire with such a great effort to make his own those people he sees are already Christ's.

28. Let him hear this from you, I beg, and do not keep from him whatever the Lord gives you to say to the man over whose soundness of heart I desire to rejoice. After all, you have in relation to him such an age that you can properly show him the affection of a mother. For, unless he is living under God's very great anger, he does not disdain in you the advice of his own mother. I know that you have risen with Christ so that *you seek the things that are above, not those on earth* (Col 3:1); do not, then, be afraid to give the advice of a believer to a bishop who is seeking the things of earth. You are in fact seeking God in this world; he is seeking this world in the Church.

29. For (this is something that you perhaps would not believe if someone else told it to you) he has not hesitated to buy farms in his own name, not in the Church's—he, a man who became a bishop right from the monastery, who had nothing but the clothing he wore that day. You perhaps ask with what he bought them. I do not want to say from those robberies that the people of Fussala complain that they suffered. The things that were stolen in that way were immediately consumed. But for his own sustenance and that of those who were with him I gave him an estate belonging to the church of Hippo, which was located in the same territory of Fussala. He rented it out, and, after having received the rent for five full years, he found the sum by which he could buy it. But, as for the complaint that the seller lodged about him before the emperor in a petition and the risks of a trial that he faced or how the defender of the church of Fussala, with whom the seller complained that he was held in a private jail so that he would sell his property to the bishop at the lowest price, just barely escaped the penalty of public condemnation through our efforts because he had already admitted that he did this under orders of the bishop, though this bishop said that he had commanded him to be held in custody, not in order to force him to sell him this farm but on account of another wrong—if I wanted to recount all this, when will there be an end to this letter?

30. He also bought another small property, it too in his own name, but with what I do not know. But in this affair also it was said in a complaint from the partner in our court that he dealt with him, with whom he owned a half of the undivided property, in such a fashion that he took all the harvest and stripped the tiles from the house they owned in common. We heard the case; proof was given us; we ordered restitution. This partner also produced a letter of his brother, and it was read out in our court. He wrote that he was forced by the bishop to sell his part of the property and had not received the price that he ought to have had. But because it was not proven to us that it was really his brother's letter, we somehow ended the debate among those present and reserved action for the man who was absent.

31. But Antoninus gave that property to another man whose house he had torn down, and he carried off to his own building all the materials out of which the

man's house had been built. I myself made intercession with this man so that he would not charge the bishop in our court by a formal petition and complaint. And the case was settled between them by private arbitration in such a way that, for his share, he would receive from Antoninus that farm, by which he might make up for his losses. And this miserable monk who had become a bishop still said to the people of Fussala,"Give me back my house, which I have built in your town"—the house that he was thought to have built not for himself, of course, but for the church. And would that he had built it by good means and from just offerings, not from robberies! For it is said that there is almost nothing in the fabric of that house that one cannot show was stolen from someone else and point with one's finger at the place from which it was stolen.

32. But there is another aspect to this affair. I wanted to pour out my groans before Your Sincerity because a young man raised by us in the monastery—who, when we accepted him, abandoned nothing that was his own either to distribute it to the poor or to contribute it to our community—now prides himself over farms and a house as if they were his own, and he wants not only to make them his own but also the flock of Christ, insofar as he wants to belong to the number of those who *seek their own interests, not those of Jesus Christ* (Phil 2:21), and he who would heal this wound of my heart sees how great a wound it is.

33. I beseech you by Christ and by his mercy and judgment to help me in this affair both for his sake and for the sake of the Church. After all, I wanted you to be informed, perhaps with more words than moderation, not in order that you might hate him but rather that you would look after him in a true and spiritual fashion, to the extent that the Lord chooses to give you the ability, by not allowing him to do harm to himself. For whom will he harm more grievously than himself if he tries to disturb and destroy a church that he ought to want to gain for Christ, not for himself? I believe that he will obey Your Holy Benevolence and will not raise up his pride against you if the fountain of mercy hears my weeping for him, which is so frequent and so abundant.

Letter 21*

After 411, perhaps around 420, Augustine wrote to the people of Suppa, who had requested to have Donantius, a citizen of Suppa, as their deacon. In Letter 26* Augustine wrote to Honoratus, the bishop of Suppa, and mentions Donantius by name. Augustine reprimands them for writing to him rather than to their own bishop, Honoratus, and tells them that the man they want is not the sort of person from whom they can obtain sound discipline.

To the people of Suppa, my most beloved lords and sons, whose letter I have received, Augustine sends greetings in the Lord.

1. Since I know that by the mercy of God you have as bishop my venerable brother and fellow bishop, Honoratus,[1] you ought not to have sent a letter to me without his advice and directive. But since you made him a request that he could not have granted, knowing as he does the discipline of the Church, you wanted for this reason to write to me, circumventing his authority. Let this very brief reply, then, be sufficient for Your Charity. The man whom you ask for is not the sort of man through whom you might obtain, as you wrote, the sound practice of our discipline. The other thoughts I had concerning him I thought that I should write rather to my holy brother, your bishop. But if you want to have him as a fellow citizen, I do not forbid this; in fact, I recommend it, provided that you know that he cannot be a deacon.

---

1. Honoratus was bishop of Thiava, a town near Thagaste.

Letter 22*

In March of 420 Augustine wrote to Alypius, the bishop of Thagaste, and Peregrinus, the bishop of Thaenae in Byzacena, who were at the time in Italy on Church business. Augustine first lends his support to the complaint of the council of Numidian bishops about the difficulty of finding clerics to ordain because of the civic duties imposed upon them by the laws (paragraph 1). Augustine turns to the decline of the social classes, which is due to the lack of officials to defend them from heavy taxes (paragraph 2). He explains his own lack of power against the wicked (paragraph 3) and expresses his desire to have a defender for the people of Hippo (paragraph 4).

The rest of the letter deals with a matter of ecclesiastical discipline in the church of Caesarea: After the death of Bishop Deuterius, some of the people of Caesarea wanted Honorius, who was bishop of Cartenna, transferred to their city. Though such a move was forbidden by Church law, the people were able to appeal to a precedent set by Honorius' father. Augustine informs his brother bishops of Honorius' installation as acting bishop (paragraph 5). He tells them of a letter he received from the bishops of Numidia removing Honorius until the question had been settled by the Apostolic See (paragraph 6). He says that, when this letter was read to them, the people of Caesarea rebelled, that Honorius is presently with him in Hippo, and that they should present the case to Pope Boniface (paragraph 7). Augustine explains the precedent set by Honorius' father, to which the people were appealing contrary to Church law (paragraph 8). He also informs them of the letter, supposedly from fifteen bishops of the province, removing Honorius (paragraph 9). He tells them of his concern for the safety of the people who wrote to him in opposition to Honorius' appointment (paragraph 10). Furthermore, Honorius' supporters had written to him and had claimed that the letter from fifteen bishops removing him from the see of Caesarea was not authentic. Hence Augustine asks the help of Alypius and Peregrinus in settling the matter (paragraph 11).

A memorandum: Augustine sends greetings in the Lord to his brothers, Alypius and Peregrinus.

1. The day before the Nones of March[1] a council of Numidian bishops was held in Numidia at Mazacos, where I could not be present for other reasons and also because of the cold that Your Holiness knows that I endure with great difficulty. So great was the complaint there about the lack of clerics, on account of the law that forces them to be involved in civic duties at their own expense, that the brothers who had gathered there were compelled to send envoys to the imperial court. When one of these, our brother and fellow bishop Peter, was arranging to set sail from our shores, he asked that I write to Your Charity. If he finds you in

---

1. That is, on 6 March 420.

314

such a position that you can by the mercy of God help in some way this cause, which must not be viewed as worthless, the Lord will have assisted their labor to no small degree.

2. For this is what troubles the thoughts of us all quite seriously since, during the time when the idols were worshiped, there was no lack of people who had immunities to carry out the ministries of those sacrileges and to multiply them uselessly. We, however, are caught in such difficulties that there are not found or there are scarcely found the kind of men from which clerics might be ordained, especially in the cities where there are either men of rank or plebians, and Your Holiness knows that among us one cannot distinguish the members of these groups, though one could take care of the needs of all if we could determine the number of men for each part that it would be permissible to ordain from the whole. But little attention is paid at this time to the reasons why the classes are disappearing, because, of course, defenders are lacking who might protect them from the dishonesty of persons of power by whom they are being crushed and who would be able to uphold the laws that have been issued in their defense against those by whom they are held in contempt. These defenders need to be men supported by suitable dignity and chosen by their fellow citizens, with whom they would have had a good reputation, so that in them may be found both honesty and authority. When these men are lacking to the cities or to the territories belonging to the same cities, we groan in vain in defense of these wretches whom we cannot help.

3. For we are held in contempt by the dishonest, because they know that we, bound as we are by our ecclesiastical profession, cannot do anything as a result of which they might be put in danger or be punished. After all, if we want to repel their violence by the arm of the Church, they complain about us to the authorities who send them that we are impeding necessary public services. And they are readily believed and say without any fear whatever they want, knowing that we are not permitted, even in justifying ourselves, to expose their actions to those who could punish them once they were found out. But if we take the initiative and complain about them, we seem to have taken up the role of accusers. The result of this is that we are able somehow or other to be a comfort or protection to very few who take refuge in the church. But the others, far more numerous, who are caught outside the church are plundered, either themselves or their property, while we groan and are unable to help.

4. For this reason our people of Hippo by all means want to have a defender, and I want this most of all. But we are uncertain whether it is permissible to obtain a military man. If it is permissible, however, we all want our son Ursus, the son-in-law of Glycerius, but if it is permissible to have only a private person, we think that one of our sons, that is, either Eusebius or Eleusinus, could fulfill this role, although in the curials of the cities there could also be found men who are suitable in terms of their morals and resourcefulness, if a position of honor

were given them in which they could have sufficient authority. I have written this to Your Reverence in order that, if the Lord gives you the opportunity, you will not hesitate to plead this cause as well.

5. There is something else: to the great scandal of the Church, the people of Caesarea are demanding that Bishop Honorius of the Province of Mauretania Caesarienis, whom you, Brother Alypius, know well, be himself made bishop there after the death of our brother, Deuterius of holy memory. Certain religious have written from there to us about the great evil that would be caused if this should happen. Meanwhile, after the bishops had assembled in that city on account of this necessity, so that the people might choose whom they wanted to be ordained, they were compelled by injuries, even serious ones, from the turbulent mob to install Honorius there to act in place of the local bishop until the Apostolic See and the head of the church of Carthage might be consulted so that this would be done if these others agreed. But they could by no means agree to this in contravention of the Council of Nicaea and the other councils of bishops.[2]

6. Meanwhile we wrote to the bishops that we had not sent on the response that the Apostolic See had given to our report because the metropolitan bishop had not yet been established there, and as a result of this situation we tried to dissuade them as much as we could from doing with Honorius what the rebellious mob is seeking, and we received a reply from a very few, but very good ones. For fifteen bishops wrote to us, though only one signed his name. At the top, however, it has the name of the bishop of the primatial see, but we know that he was absent. They thought, though, that they should add his name because he had written that some of them should assemble in the city of Castellum in order to reply to us quickly. They also wrote to the same bishop, Honorius, that he should either depart from Caesarea or the clergy would not be in communion with him, and that he should realize that one should not be in communion with him. And they addressed an appropriate letter to the people themselves, at the same time admonishing the clerics that they should ask for a bishop of the sort that could be ordained for them without violating ecclesiastical discipline.

7. But the people, and especially the poor, were incited to a horrible rebellion when the letter had begun to be read to them. Although this action was taken in his absence—for, after he received our letter, he immediately left there and came to us and was in Hippo with us when I dictated this, promising that he would do nothing but what we wanted—he nonetheless said that he would not have been released by them if he had not promised that he would return if the fathers responded to their envoys according to their will. But with regard to his ambition, it is not necessary to mention all the things that are bruited about, because they perhaps cannot be proved. Your Holiness should mention these things to

---

2. Canon 15 of the Council of Nicaea forbade the transfer of clerics from one city to another.

Pope Boniface,[3] although with the help of the Lord there is no need to fear that in such a case it is necessary to take a cautious approach with regard to such a man. The defenders of Honorius want to plead his case by examples of neglect of discipline, gathering them from wherever they can, where such events have occurred, as if we ought for this reason to add them together rather than stop them and guard against their being repeated in the future, especially when a man has been established in the Apostolic See with whom intrigue has no place. And because they are making illicit demands leading to the ruin of ecclesiastical discipline, they are of course trying to plead this argument; in fact, they lay the foundation, as it were, of their case on the fact that this same Honorius was ordained in the community that belongs to the church of Cartenna.

8. But it came about in this way that the predecessor of our brother Rusticus, who at that time presided there, ordered him to occupy the see there as bishop, and this was done by the will of him who then had it in his power to prevent it. But before this Honorius his father presided over that church, and from there he had been transferred to Caesarea and had ordained his son in place of himself. For this reason they now think that it is permissible to do regarding the son what they did regarding the father and because Bishop Rusticus demanded that the same community[4] be returned to him. But, as you know, he demanded several parishes—not, however, the mother church in which Honorius had been made bishop. But they have a letter of Brother Rusticus that he is said to have given to the same parishes so that they would know that from then on they belonged to Cartenna, as if Honorius had been confirmed in a better position. But Brother Rusticus wrote back to us that false rumors had been spread about, and he denies that the letter that they have is his. And yet, even if it were, we would of course need to correct even more the will of Rusticus, who wants to change what was done under his predecessor rather than to permit what no one can fail to know is done illicitly.

9. There was produced, however, in the name of the people of Caesarea—we do not know whether they themselves wrote it—a letter to the primate of the same province, because they wanted to send to the imperial court in a case of public concern the same Bishop Honorius in order to promote their case by means of him. And they asked that the primate give Honorius a letter of recommendation, adding that, if he refused to give it, they would force him to set sail without it. But the primate did not give it, and Honorius told us that he did not want to set sail in that matter of public interest, but that in a matter of private interest he deeply wanted to pay the expenses of a legal case to Felix or to that old man called Quietus who had publicly presented to us a list of charges against him. But we were acting in such a way that, if it were possible, this case might be

---

3. Boniface became pope in 418 and reigned until 422.
4. *Diocesim*. See Letter 20*, 19 and note 11.

brought to an end before us, if only Honorius would send the people of Caesarea a letter of the sort that we would want him to send in order that they might choose a bishop for themselves.

10. I am, however, especially worried about those people who sent a letter to us from there, lest perhaps he set sail and create some problems for them from the imperial court. For, when it was known at Caesarea that they wrote to me, a large rebellious mob shouted out against them and said that the bishop had declared them heretics and had drawn up a record of what was done concerning them. And when they had wanted to be given a copy, he did not give them one, and they heard that he had taken it with him. But when we questioned him, he said that he had not drawn up any record concerning them. I am nonetheless very worried because they asked me by letter that I take care of this matter lest the Catholic people meet with some danger.

11. Of course, those who favor him wrote to him at Hippo, as he reported to us, that the letter bearing the names of fifteen bishops that was sent to us from there concerning his removal from the church of Cartenna was false. And it really troubles us that we find no signature of the primate, whose name stands at the beginning, and that there is only one signature and that it is uncertain whose it is. And for this reason it is most difficult for this case to be able to be settled here, for the temper of the people and the urgency of the matter demand rather that it be brought to an end by the judgment of the Apostolic See. We are not upset over this matter, because we are certain of the judgment which that see can render, but, as I said, the danger to the people upsets me—that Catholics should not suffer some penalties like heretics. May the Lord prevent this by his mercy either through Your Charity or—what is most preferable—through the insistence and most merciful and most just vigilance of the Apostolic See.

Letter 23*

In January of 420 Augustine wrote to Renatus, a monk in Caesarea in Mauretania Caesariensis. During Augustine's stay in Caesarea in 418, Renatus showed Augustine a letter of Optatus, a Spanish bishop, for whom Augustine wrote Letter 190. Renatus also sent Augustine two books by Vincent Victor, a recent convert from Rogatism, a schismatic branch of Donatism, on the same question, namely concerning the origin of the soul. With the present letter Augustine sent to Renatus the first book of *The Nature and Origin of the Soul*, which he dedicated to Renatus. Augustine expresses his doubts about the authenticity of the letter of the bishops of Caesarea that was mentioned in Letter 22*, 11 and asks Renatus for proof of its authenticity (paragraph 1). He informs Renatus that Bishop Honorius, whose transfer to the see of Caesarea was the topic of Letter 22*, 5-11, is present with him and that he is willing to do whatever is required for the peace of the Church (paragraph 2).

To Renatus, his rightly most dear lord and brother worthy of being praised and honored in Christ, Augustine sends greetings in the Lord.

1. An excellent opportunity has arisen to send Your Holiness the book I had promised by means of the man through whom you sent me the books of our son Victor, so that I might reply to them. I ask, however, that you not be slow to inform us of what happened to those men after the departure from here of the servant of God, our son Marcellinus, since I found out that their bearers will return more quickly. But we have doubts about the letter of the brothers that he brought to us, because we did not recognize the signature of the holy primate, and we heard that he was not present in that gathering of fifteen bishops, although we are not certain whether the rest were present there and replied in person. For this reason we ask that you assure us with some proofs about which there can be no doubt, my rightly most dear lord and brother worthy of being praised and honored in Christ.

2. Bishop Honorius is present here with us, promising that he will do nothing other than what we want for the peace of the Church and for ecclesiastical discipline. May the Lord grant that he is speaking the truth. For, just as we cannot accept the bad things that are said of him, so that we already think that he should be condemned, since this too is foreign to ecclesiastical discipline, neither do we readily believe him unless he confirms by action what he says. . . .[1]

---

1. The text of the letter is incomplete.

Letter 23A*

In December 419 Augustine wrote this letter, which lacks a salutation and a beginning, to Possidius, the bishop of Calama. Augustine tells Possidius that he has heard from Alypius, the bishop of Thagaste, who was at the time in Italy on ecclesiastical business, only what he read in the memorandum to the people of Thagaste (paragraph 1). He mentions the arrival of the priest Josias (paragraph 2). He lists for Possidius the numerous works he has written over the past three months and complains of interruptions (paragraph 3). He tells Possidius that he wants some matter concerning Donatian to be taken care of, mentions something he has written and published for the Spanish bishops, and tells him of several other things he has done or wants done (paragraph 4). He says that he is keeping the deacon who brought the message from Rome with him until the question is settled about the new bishop of Caesarea (see Letters 22*,5-11; 23*) (paragraph 5). So too, Bishop Priscus, now restored to communion, is staying in Hippo until the question of the succession in Caesarea is settled (paragraph 6).

1. I have not found out anything certain concerning Brother Alypius except what I read in his memorandum, which was sent to Thagaste by means of the son of Severian Longus,[1] who was driven ashore at our coastline. For in that way it happened that I read what he was carrying, though I was very surprised that he carried no message for me. In the memorandum I read, then, that they were awaiting the arrival of the important count because of the people who had taken refuge in the church. For, on behalf of the people of Carthage, about whom we had been especially concerned because of what they had done, he said that a silentiary was sent on the day that he had written with the pardon for them that they were able to obtain by letter, even though they were not present. For those who come from Carthage tell us that they do not know whether he has arrived but that they have only heard that the pardon was sent to Largus[2] and that they are at Rome where they were sent.[3]

2. There has also arrived a certain Josias, a priest of the diocese of Rusicca, who reported to us that on the day he departed from there they met a patrician who was now nearby. But after that he left us. . . .[4]

3. I do not know which of our works we were dictating when you left. Hence I mention everything I have dictated since we left Carthage. I wrote to Optatus, the Spanish bishop, again on the question of the origin of the soul.[5] I wrote to Gaudentius, the Donatist bishop of Thamugadi, who more or less replied to the

---

1. See Letter 15*, in which Augustine quotes part of this memorandum.
2. Largus was the proconsul of Africa.
3. There is a lacuna at this point.
4. There is another lacuna here and at the beginning of the next paragraph.
5. See Letter 190, which Augustine wrote to Optatus on the question of the origin of the soul.

replies I sent him earlier.[6] I dictated something against the Arians, in reply to what our Dionysius from Vicus Juliani sent me,[7] and three sermons to be sent to Carthage. When in the midst of these I was preparing to return to the books on *The City of God*, I suddenly received a letter from the holy Renatus from Caesarea,[8] who sent me two books of some Victor or other, who was a former disciple of that Vincent to whom I had replied in the past and who has become a Catholic from being a Donatist, in fact from being a Rogatist. And he wanted to write about the soul, reprimanding our hesitation, because I did not dare to state definitively whether it came by propagation or was infused as entirely new in each person who is born, and he himself declared that the soul is not derived from propagation but is given to us. In his two books he said very many incorrect and absurd ideas and ones opposed to the Catholic faith. And because our friend whom I mentioned above earnestly asked me to refute those ideas, since some of them would mislead many people because of their charming style, I wrote one book on this for the same very dear friend of ours, and I want to write to Victor himself, since it is very important. And, to finish as well what remains of the Gospel of John, I have already begun to dictate some popular and not very long homilies to be sent to Carthage on the condition that, if the same primate of ours wishes that the rest be sent to him,[9] he should say so and not delay in publishing them when he says so. I have already dictated six; for I have devoted the nights of Saturday and Sunday exclusively to them. And so, since I arrived, that is, from the third day of the Ides of September up to the Calends of December,[10] I have dictated approximately six thousand lines.

4. But as for what Your Holiness wrote to me about the honorable Donatian,[11] who is very dear to us, I deeply desire that it take place. May the Lord grant that it does. For the brothers themselves have added to the same question something or other that they previously did not say, to which we ought to reply. I would have inserted it into that work if it had not already been published for our dearest brothers, the Spanish bishops, and for this reason I thought it should be dictated

---

6. After Augustine wrote the first book of *Answer to Gaudentius*, the Donatist bishop of Thamugadi replied by a letter to Augustine, to which Augustine in turn replied in the second book of *Answer to Gaudentius*.

7. The document sent to Augustine was most probably *An Arian Sermon*, in response to which Augustine wrote *Answer to an Arian Sermon*.

8. As we know from Letter 23*, Renatus, a monk in Caesarea, sent Augustine some writings of Vincent Victor, a convert from Rogatism, which was a splinter group that had broken off from the Donatists. Augustine wrote *The Nature and Origin of the Soul*, dedicating the first book to Renatus, the second to the priest, Peter, and the last two to Vincent Victor.

9. As we know from Letter 23*, Augustine refers to his *Homilies on the Gospel of John*, which he was writing for Aurelius, the bishop of Carthage and primate of Africa.

10. That is, from September 2 to December 1.

11. See Letter 196, which Augustine wrote to Asselicus, a bishop in Byzacena, who had written to his primate, Donatian, a letter about some Judaizing Christians, which Donatian fowarded to Augustine.

in another work. But I find it annoying that the things that people from one side or another unexpectedly call upon us to dictate interfere with the projects that we have under way and that they neither cease nor can be put off. As soon as I read the memorandum of Your Charity, I immediately ordered that the ecclesiastical proceedings in the case of Brother Maurentius[12] be copied in order that they could be sent to you. After you have received them, I ask that you be so good as to carry out without delay what you have decided. But what they wrote to us by means of the priest Numedius I either do not recall or did not receive. We had sent to Your Reverence, if I am not mistaken, a copy of the letter of Pope Boniface[13] in which he replied to our report; I want to know whether you received it. We ought, however, to write together to our brothers in Caesarea.

5. The deacon who brought the same letter is here with us since he arrived from Rome. I was keeping him here until we know who will be ordained for the people of Caesarea in place of Brother Deuterius[14]—for that is very important—and until someone writes us in order that we may know how we ought to write. We have, of course, heard about the well-known case of Bishop Honorius,[15] who intensely ambitions the same see and—something at which you will be surprised—that the hearts of many are said to be inclined toward him. But the bishops refused to agree and, in order to avoid the influence of those applying pressure, they answered that they had first to consult us or even Pope Boniface. Rumor has brought this to us. Meanwhile, the Church, as is evident, is troubled by disturbances.

6. Bishop Priscus[16] is also here; he first arrived in Carthage from Rome and it was there that he first began to be in communion in Africa. From there he chose to stop with us on his way to you, and, after he arrived, he decided to remain until we know what has been done there about the ordination of a new bishop, because his is the most important issue about which we also ought to write.

---

12. Maurentius was bishop of Thubursicu Numidarum. After being accused of misconduct by certain elders, he was tried by seven bishops, including Augustine and Possidius.
13. Boniface became pope in 418 and reigned until 422.
14. Deuterius was bishop of Caesarea in Caesarian Mauretania. After his death the people were divided in their choice of a new bishop.
15. Honorius was bishop of Cartenna, whom many in Caesarea wanted as their new bishop, though such a transfer was contrary to Church law.
16. See Letter 16*, where Augustine speaks of Priscus of Quiza. When deprived of ecclesiastical communion outside of his diocese, he went to Rome where the pope removed the sanction. When he arrived in Carthage, Aurelius entered into communion with him.

Letter 24*

Sometime during his episcopacy Augustine wrote to Eustochius, a Catholic layman and legal consultant, about various juridical matters relative to cases that had come before Augustine. Augustine tells Eustochius that, in following the apostle's command that legal cases between Christians should be settled in the Church, he needs to hear various cases. He explains that he wants juridical advice relative to the enslavement of children born of different sorts of marriage and to parents' rights to sell their children into slavery or to sell their children's labor for a number of years (paragraph 1). He asks similar questions about stewards and the children of stewards, noting that he finds it extremely harsh that a man's freedom and that of his children should be put in jeopardy by his taking the position of steward, since the position of a steward is generally regarded as a benefit (paragraph 2).

To his excellent lord and rightly honorable and most desired son Eustochius, Augustine sends greetings in the Lord.

1. Since you ought faithfully to give true replies to all who consult you, how much more ought you to do so to us, who are ministers of Christ! For by your faith in him you are a believer in order to obtain the inheritance of which the gospel is the testament, <my excellent lord and rightly honorable and most desired son>.[1] The apostle has commanded that, if Christians have with one another cases concerning worldly affairs that need adjudication, they should be heard in the Church, not in the courts.[2] For this reason we have to endure the sort of petitions on the part of litigants in which we have to learn the laws of this world, especially concerning the temporal condition of persons. In accord with the teaching of the apostle we can command slaves to be subject to their lords,[3] but we cannot impose the yoke of slavery upon free persons. I therefore ask you, whose love is most sincere, that you would graciously instruct me as to what directive we should follow regarding those who are born of a free woman and a slave. For I know that those born from a female slave and a free man are slaves. Also, what about those whose fathers sell their work for a definite number of years? I ask whether, if the fathers who sold this labor have died, they should be forced to fill out the same number of years or whether they are set free by the death of those who sold them or rather in some sense rented them out, because they begin to be, as it is said, legally independent. I also ask whether free fathers can sell their children into perpetual slavery and whether mothers can sell at least

---

1. I have translated the conjectured text from the BA edition.
2. See 1 Cor 6:1-6.
3. See Ti 2:9.

the work of their children. I likewise ask whether, if a tenant farmer sells a son, since it is permissible that a son be sold by his father, the buyer has more right to the one who was sold than the master of the estate from which the tenant farmer originates, and whether it is permissible for the owner of the estate to reduce to slaves his tenant farmers and the children of his tenant farmers.

2. Also, what has been clearly established concerning these stewards by right or by law? For it seems very harsh to me to attack the condition of a free person and the advantage it entails. After all, free men are often asked to be stewards, and they think that they gain an advantage if they do what they are asked to do. And they really do gain an advantage to the point that the one who asks them thanks them if he manages to get what he asked. If a free man became a slave as a result of this advantage, he would in no way do anything of the sort if he knew about this, nor would anyone dare to ask this of someone who knew about it. I am nonetheless troubled by certain rulings that were presented to us when we were handling a case of this sort concerning the children of a certain man who it will perhaps be proved had been a steward. But I do not want to force the man who makes this claim to prove it unless I first know what directive I should follow if he does prove it. Hence I sent these rulings to Your Excellency for consideration. I think that two of these speak clearly, but I either do not understand the other two or they do not at all pertain to the question under consideration. I beg you to help me as you used to help me when I was present, though I am now not physically present.

Letter 25*

In the latter part of September 419, Augustine wrote to a group of clerics of the church of Carthage. He tells them that he has arrived back in Hippo safely and has celebrated the feast of an unnamed martyr who is almost certainly Saint Cyprian. He asks Brother Comes to arrange for the hospitality that the priest Mascelio is requesting.

To our most dear lords and most sincere brothers and fellow priests Deogratias and Theodore, and to the deacons Titian, Quintian, Quodvultdeus, and Carissimus, and to his brother Comes,[1] Augustine sends greetings in the Lord.

We announce that by God's mercy we have arrived home safe and sound and that we have celebrated the solemnity of the most blessed martyr with the people of God, who were complaining greatly concerning my absence. We trust that this news is most welcome to you. I recommend, however, the bearer of this letter, our brother, the priest Mascelio. I believe that Your Holiness recalls him. Through me he also asks of you, Brother Comes, that you arrange for the hospitality that he requests to be offered him without any difficulty.

---

1. Deogratias later became bishop of Carthage. Quodvultdeus became a priest and later bishop of Carthage. Deogratias, Theodore, Titian, and Comes are also mentioned in the salutation of Letter 173A. Carissimus is mentioned in Letter 174.

Letter 26*

Shortly before writing Letter 21*, Augustine wrote to Honoratus, bishop of Thiava, regarding Donantius of Suppa, about whom he had written in Letter 21* to the people of Suppa. Augustine gives Honoratus the background on Donantius: He had sought ordination as a deacon from Xanthippus of Thagura, though he belonged to Augustine's church. When Xanthippus discovered this, he sent him back to Augustine, who made him porter at a chapel, though the priests there threw him out for misconduct (paragraph 1). Now the people of Suppa have asked for Donantius as their deacon. Augustine counsels Honoratus, who he is confident will observe the legislation of the Church, not to allow Donantius to be anything more than a lector (paragraph 2).

To his most blessed lord and rightly venerable holy brother and fellow bishop, Honoratus, Augustine sends greetings in the Lord.

1. A certain Donantius of Suppa, whose father was situated in Hippo and was deriving his livelihood from the alms of the church, had begun to live in our monastery. He was unable to last there. While the primate Xanthippus[1] of blessed memory did not know his situation, Donantius fraudulently attempted to be ordained a deacon contrary to the episcopal statutes of the councils.[2] But when that venerable primate whom I mentioned learned of this by my letter, he immediately removed him from his post and returned him to me. But so that he would not give others a harmful example by being in charge of them, I managed to arrange that he would be the porter at Saint Theogenes, since he did not have the means to live. Nor was he able to carry out his function there in a worthy manner, so that in my absence he was thrown out by the priests.

2. Now, my most blessed lord and rightly venerable holy brother, his fellow citizens are asking me for him as a deacon—a man who for so many years was in union with the Church as a member of the laity. Hence, since they do not know what they are asking for, I advise Your Holiness—confident as I am of your moderation and vigilance, which are gifts of the Lord, since you are not going to permit him to make a mockery of the episcopal councils to the destruction of the discipline by which the servants of God need to be governed—that, if he wants to dwell in his own city, which I do not forbid, you order that nothing more be given him except perhaps the office of lector, which is often granted even to laymen, where necessary, as we know. For, if I thought that he ought to be something more, I would certainly not begrudge him my assistance or rather that of the

---

1. Xanthippus was the primate of Numidia and bishop of Thagura, who died before 411.
2. The Council of Sardica in 343 and the Council of Carthage in 345-348 both forbade making someone from elsewhere a cleric without the consent of his own bishop.

Church of God. I do not, however, want to say anything about his morals, since for the present issue what I thought that I should say is sufficient. If only by the mercy of God he would live so that there would be no complaint about him! It is enough for him that, while serving God in a lowly position, he attain what God has promised. Otherwise, if he aims higher as it were, he might bring upon both himself and those by whom he is trying to attain this the anger of God, by attempting to violate what has been established for preserving discipline in a way conducive to salvation.

Letter 27*

Letter 27* is the only letter among those discovered by Johannes Divjak that was not written by or to Augustine. Soon after Aurelius' consecration as bishop of Carthage in 393, Jerome wrote him this letter of congratulations. He thanks Aurelius for the letter informing him of his elevation to the episcopacy and recalls their meeting in Rome when, under Pope Damasus, Aurelius had as a deacon accompanied Cyrus, who was then bishop of Carthage (paragraph 1). Jerome comments on the works of his that Aurelius claimed to have, belittling some of them and disowning another. He also tells him of some works that he is sending along with the courier (paragraph 2). Furthermore, Jerome tells Aurelius that Africa is so rich in men who have commented on the scriptures that he hardly needs works from Jerome. But if he does want them, Jerome asks him to send men to copy his writings because there are not enough Latin copyists in Jerusalem to do this (paragraph 3).

Jerome to my truly holy lord and most blessed Bishop Aurelius.

1. You who surpass me in merit also surpass me in rank. As I was hiding and bewailing my sins a single word of Your Grace announced to me that you were in good health, that you are most kindly disposed toward me, and that you have become the pontiff of the church of Carthage. Where the beginnings of our relationship are so favorable and the sowing of love so abundant, we believe in Christ our God that a most lavish crop will spring up in order that our hunger, which has lasted so long, may be assuaged by a harvest beyond belief. You remind me, and I recall, that you were sent as envoy to Rome along with the holy bishop of pious memory, Cyrus, the bishop of the church of Carthage.[1] And one day when I asked my holy and venerable bishop, Damasus,[2] who you were—for your countenance, though silent, gave promise of your keen mind—he answered that you were the archdeacon of the church of Carthage, a position that your life and his testimony about you merited. But that I did not attain a greater familiarity with you and did not gradually enter into friendship in conversing with you was the result of my reserve. For I did not want to seem impudently to seek out someone I did not know and impose myself on the company of a man who had given me no opportunity for conversing with him. But let us not speak about past losses, and let us prove by future acts of kindness that what happened in the past was a mistake, not a lack of respect.

---

1. Cyrus preceded Genethlius, who preceded Aurelius as bishop of Carthage. Cyrus and Aurelius came to Rome between 382 and 384.
2. Damasus was pope from 366 to 384.

2. You write that you have certain small works of our lowly self, that is, a few homilies on Jeremiah and two on the Song of Songs. When I was a youth, at the request of a certain brother, I played around in exercises of that sort,[3] apart from the two homilies on the Song of Songs that I translated at Rome on the advice of Blessed Damasus. And so, whether we have written any more mature works suited to our present age is something you must judge. You add that you also have my short commentaries on Matthew, but I am utterly unaware that I have published this work, unless out of the brotherly love with which you love me you think that whatever you see to be noteworthy is mine.[4] But now Brother Felicissimus has journeyed to Africa on account of certain family obligations, which he can report to you when he arrives. He set out on a fast horse, and there was no opportunity to carry more baggage. And so I have sent you some small works, namely, commentaries on Psalm Ten and on Hebrew questions on Genesis,[5] which I want you to read as a friend, not as a judge.

3. Otherwise, since in your province such great rivers have flowed forth upon the holy scriptures—Tertullian, Cyprian, Lactantius[6]—it would be ridiculous to want to drink from me, since I am a creek that is almost dry. But because we read in the Old Testament that not only gold and silver and precious stones but also the skins and hides of goats were offered in the tabernacle of God in accord with the resources of those making the offering,[7] we too make bold to offer the sweat of our penance like certain hides, as we said, of goats. These are a few works out of many. But, because with the help of your prayers we have composed some not unimportant works on the holy scriptures, if you wish and find it handy, do what other brothers of yours, holy bishops from Gaul and from Italy, have done, that is, send someone you trust who can spend a full year here, where I will give him exemplars to copy, and who can carry back to you everything we have written. There is a dearth of Latin copyists in Jerusalem. For the two holy brothers whom I myself have as secretaries can scarcely keep up with what we dictate. My holy brother Paulinus, my holy brother Eusebius, and all who are with our humble self greet you. I ask that you greet with my respect the saints who are with you. I recommend Brother Felicissimus, and I beg that I may receive your writings by means of him. May Christ our God enlighten you as you are mindful of me, and may the Almighty protect you, my truly holy lord and most blessed father.

---

3. Jerome refers to translations of Origen's works, *Homilies on Jeremiah* and *Homilies on the Song of Songs*. His remarks reflect his changed attitude toward Origen, whom he had once admired greatly.

4. These commentaries on Matthew were the work of Fortunatus of Aquilea.

5. The commentary on Psalm Ten may be one of those edited in CCL 78. *Hebrew Questions on Genesis* was written in 391 and is edited in CCL 72.

6. Tertullian (born c. 155/160; died c. 220), Cyprian (born c. 200; died 258), and Lactantius (born 240; died 320) were the three greatest African Christian authors prior to Augustine.

7. See Ex 35:5-7.

Letter 28*

Probably in 418 Augustine wrote to Novatus, the bishop of Sitifis in Mauretania Sitifensis, to whom he had also written Letter 84. Augustine thanks Novatus for his long letter, in which he informed him of the conversion of nearly all the Donatists in Zabi, apart from a few exceptions (paragraph 1). Augustine encourages Novatus to follow the example of other churches and to have the proceedings of the Council of Carthage, which in principle ended the Donatist schism, be read to the people annually in church (paragraph 2). He does not want these records to be read, however, in the same way that the scriptures are read (paragraph 3). Certain Donatists apparently misled the vicar of Africa with respect to something that the letter does not clearly delineate, and Augustine discusses measures to be taken in regard to this (paragraph 4). Augustine mentions an episode concerning a certain Victorinus, a citizen of Hippo, who had sought sanctuary in the church and was removed by the tribune, Peregrinus, on the basis of a falsified order from the count, who is not named (paragraphs 5 and 6). Finally, Augustine commends to Novatus the servant of Victorinus and his mission and mentions Bishop Rogatus, who had been mutilated, most likely by the violent branch of the Donatists called Circumcellions, after his conversion to Catholicism (paragraph 7).

To my most blessed lord, venerable brother and priest, Novatus, and to the other brothers, Augustine, along with the brothers who are with me, sends greetings in the Lord.

1. Although Your Charity sent me a very long letter concerning the case of the people of Zabi, yet it was not burdensome for me, because I deeply desired to know the whole story, and for this reason I completely accepted your explanation. I thank the Lord our God, therefore, because, after the first part of your letter, in which you reported everything, caused me to give up any hope of their communion with us and their salvation, I was filled with sudden and unexpected joy when you announced both that all their basilicas were handed over to the Catholic Church and that the whole multitude of them were converted with the greatest speed to the peace and unity of Christ. The only exceptions were a small number of officials whom an intervention of the judge made more recalcitrant and alienated, as it were, from the constraints of the laws. For they deceived him, acting against their own salvation, by whatever ruse they could. And yet, once they had received his more recent letter, of which you chose to send me a copy, I believe that they too could have been converted, since their excuse had been removed.

2. If this has taken place or is about to take place, I beg you not to neglect to inform us at whatever opportunity you have. Although I know that you will take care of this on your own in the spirit of the Lord with more zeal than I, I certainly

advise that, through their awareness of the proceedings of the conference and any other documents that are useful in this affair, they learn the great evil from which they have been set free by such an insistent action. In that way they may be retained in the Catholic peace not only by fear of temporal penalties but also by fear of eternal fire and by love of the truth. For, if I am not mistaken, I recall that I had at some point written that the same proceedings should be solemnly read in the church every year during the days of Lent, when the people who are fasting have time to hear them, just as our church of Carthage and some other churches diligently do, which I wish could be done throughout Africa. We have also written a single book, commenting on the proceedings themselves,[1] and, when the same proceedings came to an end, it was read in our presence and heard by the people with the greatest joy. If you do not have it, you ought to.

3. But these texts are not read out before us from the lector's place, as the canonical scriptures are, because it is not proper. Rather, the lectors read them in such a way that they do not take off their cloaks and sit down when they want, where those who want to sit down can be easily heard by the people who are seated, as if they were being read privately at home. But this is done in the church, because it holds a large number and both sexes are not forbidden to hear them, until the hour comes at which the sacred readings are heard and the sacraments are celebrated in the customary manner.

4. I believe, however, that the vicar has also sent a letter to Your Holiness concerning his interlocutory judgment, just as he has also promised to send it to us. If he did so, you have undoubtedly replied. And I am surprised that Your Charity has not taken care to share with us his letter to you—except for this later one—or your reply, which you could have sent now, since you send so many things that you seem to overlook nothing. Or, if it did not arrive in your hands or he did not send it, though he sent it to us, I am much more surprised. But I do not know what we should do, whether we should write back to him after having come to know of the affair from your letter or we should rather not stir up anything about this affair in his mind. After all, by this second letter of his he instilled an appropriate amount of fright and recalled to a fear of the implementation of the laws even those to whom he had given a guarantee, so to speak, that they would not be disturbed. Hence he will not hereafter readily believe heretics if their deceitfulness has now been proven to him. The events themselves will inform him sufficiently, though I was also not silent about this matter in the letter that I wrote to him when I received the letter of his of which I sent a copy to you. But since I had not sent to Your Charity a copy of my reply that I sent to him, I have added it now to this letter. If, nonetheless, a favorable opportunity arises, with the help of the Lord a letter will be sent to him under our common name, that is, mine and Brother Alypius's.

---

1. Augustine probably refers to his *Summary of the Conference with the Donatists*.

5. That man Victorinus is presently in the church, about whom I had previously written to Your Holiness so that you might handle the business concerning his means of subsistence, which you graciously agreed to handle. He has a legal conflict with his mother- and father-in-law, because of which he took refuge in the church. I was also not silent about this matter in the letter addressed to the pious count. The tribune Peregrinus, however, said that he had received the memorandum of the count when the church was seriously disturbed because that Victorinus had supposedly been ordered to be removed from the church. This, of course, took place in my absence. But, when I arrived, the tribune I mentioned read me the memorandum itself because I did not believe it was authentic. And for that reason I wrote in order that the same tribune would know by the count's reply that he ought not to disturb the church by lies of this sort. Even if he himself did not fabricate them, still, if he readily believes them, you see what problems we could suffer.

6. But I could not do more than I did. For I could not have sent the memorandum that the tribune only read to me. He did not, however, give it to me or deposit it in the municipal archives. Hence, if I was silent, the Christian man and pious count ought to blame me more, but I do not want something to be said to him on this subject now lest perhaps this tribune deny the whole thing, when he sees that the count is angry at him, and we would be forced to find him guilty, which is not expedient. But if perhaps the count questions him on his own accord about this matter, please agree to read to him what I wrote to you on this point. I do not want anything more.

7. I recommend to Your Holiness the servant of our son Victorinus, whom I mentioned before, in order that you may be so good as to help him to do that for which he was sent. I gratefully welcome the secretary about whose sending Your Reverence wrote. We heard about Olympius as soon as he arrived; now I have also received his letter. But I do not know whether I shall go to see the count. For a certain one of the brothers from Carthage has come who said that he is planning to go still further on account of the case of Bishop Rogatus, whose tongue and hand the heretics cut off. For an agent in the special branch,[2] who had set out along with the aforementioned bishop and by the emperor's order before Olympius arrived, was seriously beaten there by these wicked men. But we await a letter from Carthage that will inform us about all these matters in a more certain fashion.

---

2. Henry Chadwick comments on *agentes in rebus* in his translation of *Confessions* 8, 6, 15, that they "were an inspectorate of the imperial bureaucracy, sometimes used as intelligence gatherers and secret police, but mainly responsible to the Master of the Offices . . . for the operation of the *cursus publicus* or governmental communications system" (Oxford: Oxford University Press, 1991). Here *agens in rebus* is translated as "agent in the special branch."

Letter 29*

At an undetermined date during his episcopacy Augustine wrote to Paulinus, the deacon who had been the secretary to Ambrose of Milan (died 397). He brought accusations against the Pelagian Coelestius at Carthage in 411, and probably soon after that he wrote the first biography of Ambrose. It is not clear where Paulinus was when he received this letter. Augustine wrote it in response to Paulinus's request that Augustine write in his own language the lives of the martyrs. He tells Paulinus that he does not see how he can improve on the accounts others have produced before him or on the judicial records (paragraph 1). The accounts of the deaths of the martyrs that Ambrose composed in his old age included details that were not otherwise available from the records (paragraph 2). Hence Augustine again pleads that he does not know what to do and asks Paulinus to reply with his suggestions (paragraph 3).

To his rightly most beloved lord and most sincere son and fellow deacon, Paulinus, Augustine sends greetings in the Lord.

1. I do not yet see, though I desire to do so very much, how I may carry out your wishes concerning the publication of the acts of the martyrs in our own language. For I have read what you were so gracious as to send, and I found certain accounts narrated in the language of others, while certain others, which gave me great pleasure, were expressed only in the judicial proceedings. Hence, if I want to recount afterwards those events which others have recounted ahead of us, I will seem like an untimely teacher or a useless worker. But if I want to recall in my own language those events that are contained only in the judicial proceedings, I fear that I will not only not add to the feeling of genuineness that they produced for me when I read only the proceedings....[1]

2. After all, certain accounts that in his old age Ambrose of venerable memory had composed about the martyrs delighted me so that I was moved to do something of the sort when I spoke with Your Charity.[2] I held him before me as a model compared to the others whose accounts I had read on this topic. But in his old age Ambrose recounted especially those events that could not be known from the public records. And for that reason his work seems not only not superfluous but also highly necessary, like the account composed by someone or other, in which one can read about the most blessed martyr Cyprian that he was in his garden when he was marched off to his martyrdom and that, when he was being held at Vicus Saturni and a large number of the brethren kept watch at the

---

1. The Bibliothéque Augustinienne editors suggest that there is a lacuna here in the text.
2. These works of Ambrose are not extant, though traces of them may survive in various hagiographies dating from later centuries.

gates, he ordered that the young girls be protected, and anything else of this sort that cannot be found in the judicial proceedings.[3]

3. But what am I to do, since I do not have any way of knowing what one should know about the martyrs apart from the public records, except for the works I had read of those who have preceded me in this undertaking? If, however, I want to recount in my own words only what I read in the public records, I will be trying to make the account less vivid rather than more vivid. I ask that you consider this idea and write back with brotherly confidence what you think.

---

3. See Sermon 309 in which Augustine mentions some of these details concerning the arrest and martyrdom of Cyprian.

Index of Scripture

(prepared by Michael Dolan)

The numbers after the scriptural reference refer to the section of the work

Old Testament

Genesis

1:28	6*, 3
6:3	5*, 3

Leviticus

19:18	233

Deuteronomy

6:4	238, 3, 18
6:5	233; 258, 4
32:39	219, 2

2 Samuel

21:17	228, 10

Tobit

12:7	237, 4; 237, 8

Judith

16:15	227

Job

7:1	217, 4, 14

Psalms

4:3	3*, 1
6:2	216, 4
7:8.3	250, 3
11:6	258, 3
18:2	218, 2
19:10	266, 1
22:21	243, 4
24:7	237, 8

25:17	220, 10
36:10	237, 8
37:5-6	218, 2
37:23	217, 1, 3; 217, 2, 5; 218, 3
41:5	216, 5
41:9	263, 4
42:5	270
49:7	218, 2
51:10	266, 2; 266, 3
59:11	214, 4
68:10	217, 4, 12
78:39	238, 2, 15
86:11	217, 4, 15
94:8	214, 7
94:17	216, 5; 248, 2
96:1	237, 8
98:1	237, 8
100:3	231, 6
101:1	2*, 10
104:4	238, 2, 15
112:7	270
116:16	237, 5
118:19	237, 8
119:4	215, 6
119:125	214, 7
119:158	248, 1
127:1	216, 5
143:2	216, 4
146:7	237, 5
149:1	237, 8

Proverbs

4:26	215, 7
4:26-27	215, 5
4:27	215, 7; 218, 2
8:35 LXX	217, 2, 5; 217, 6, 23; 218, 3
9:8 LXX	220, 12
9:12 LXX	264, 2
18:18	228, 12

335

1 John

2:15-17	220, 6; 220, 9
3:8	211, 4
3:15	211, 14
3:16	228, 3
4:8.16	219, 2

4:18	218, 2

Revelation

3:19	247, 2
14:13	217, 6, 22
22:12	214, 1

General Index

(prepared by Kathleen Strattan)

The first number in the Index is the Letter number.
The number after the colon is a paragraph number.